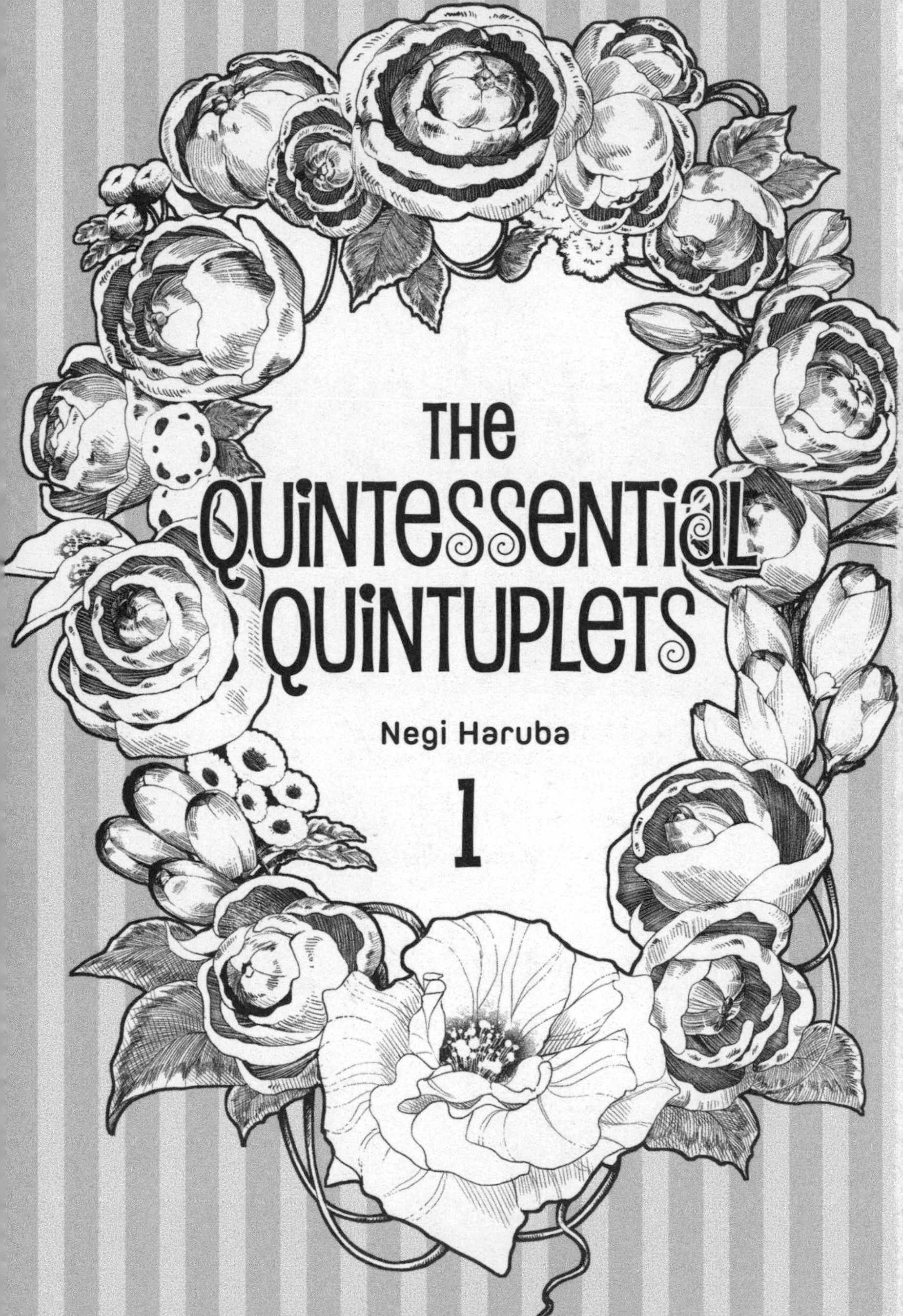

THE QUINTESSENTIAL QUINTUPLETS

Negi Haruba

1

CONTENTS

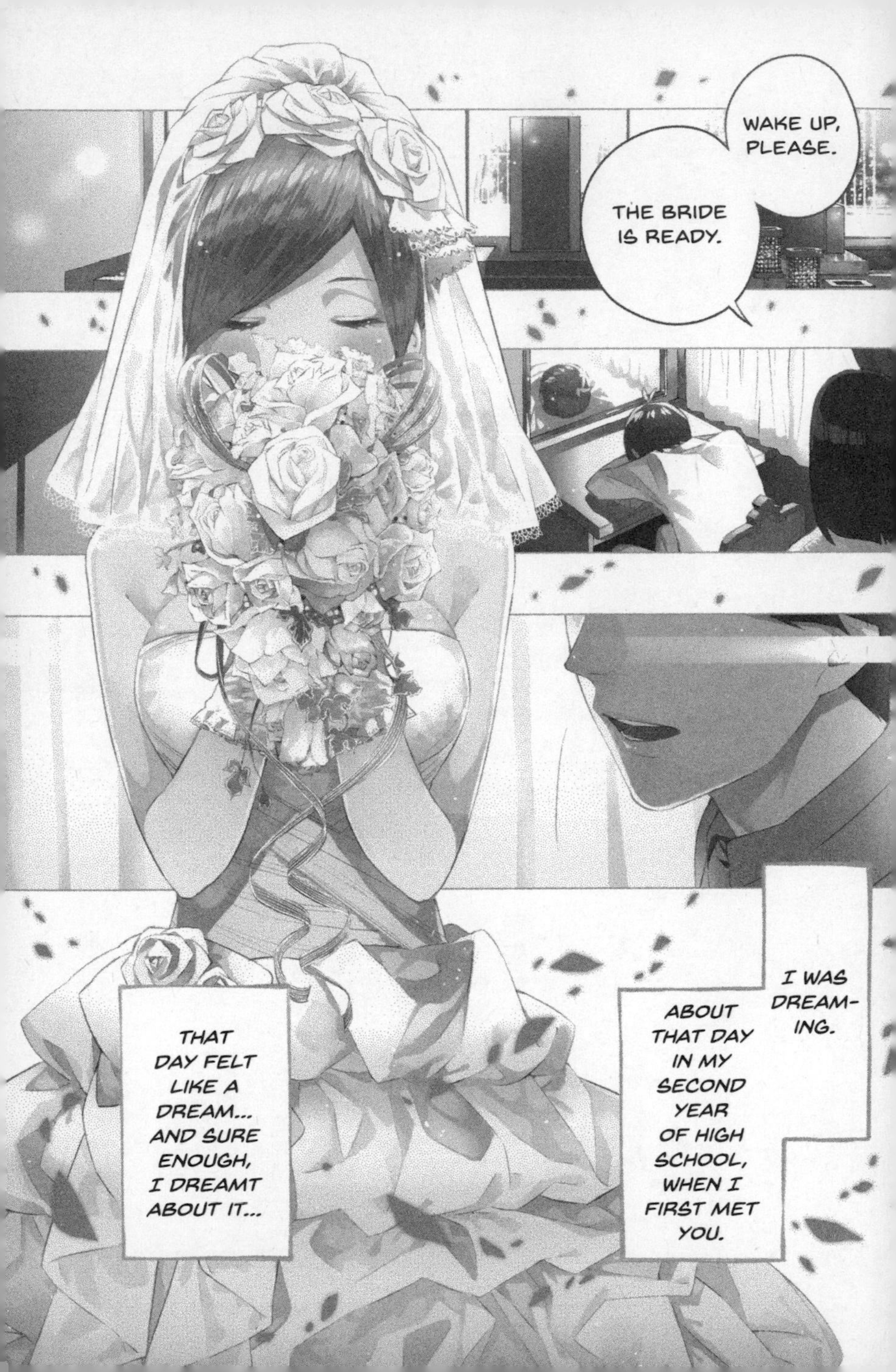
WAKE UP, PLEASE.
THE BRIDE IS READY.
I WAS DREAMING.
ABOUT THAT DAY IN MY SECOND YEAR OF HIGH SCHOOL, WHEN I FIRST MET YOU.
THAT DAY FELT LIKE A DREAM... AND SURE ENOUGH, I DREAMT ABOUT IT...

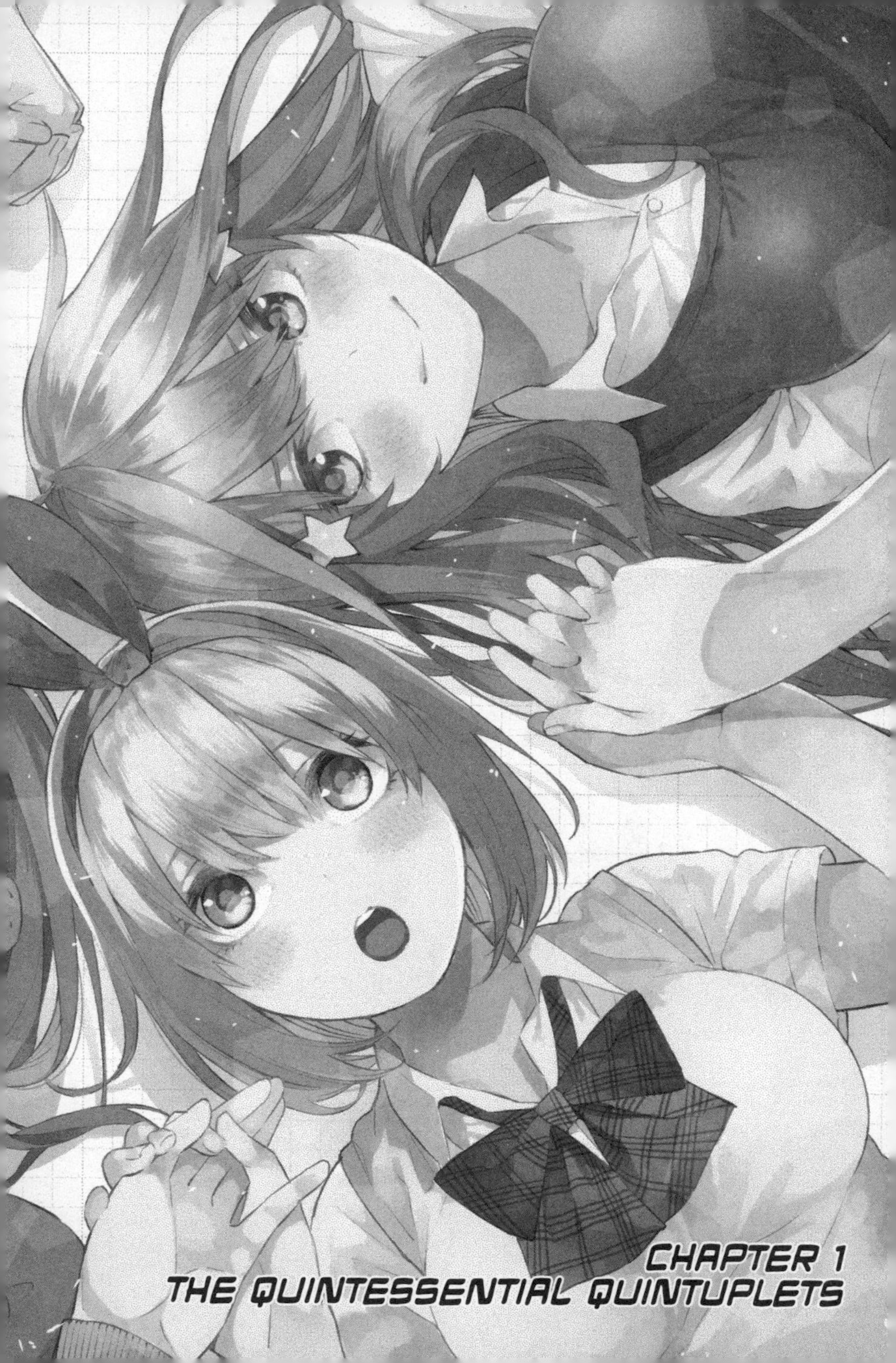

CHAPTER 1
THE QUINTESSENTIAL QUINTUPLETS

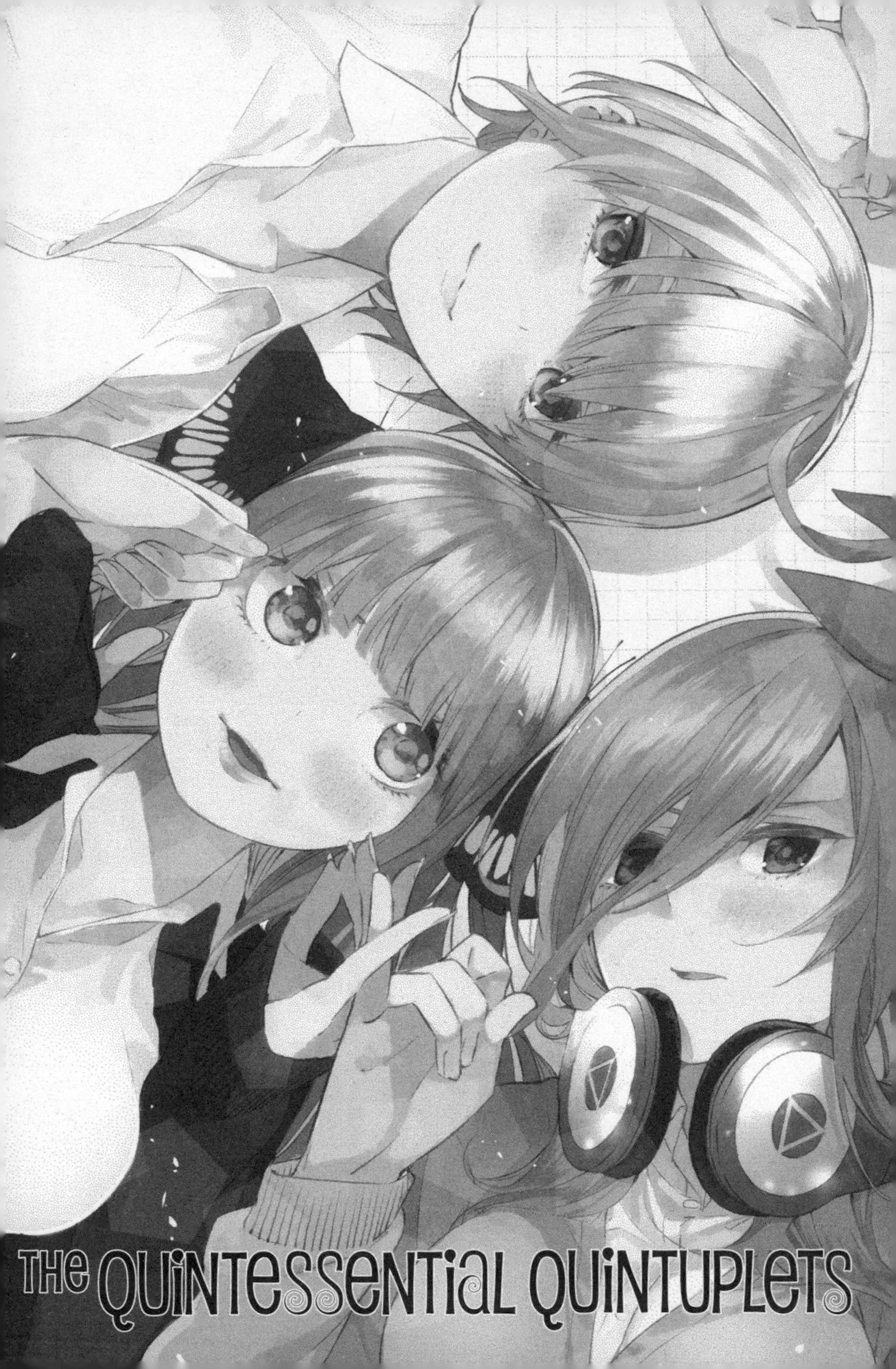
THE QUINTESSENTIAL QUINTUPLETS

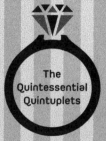
The
Quintessential
Quintuplets

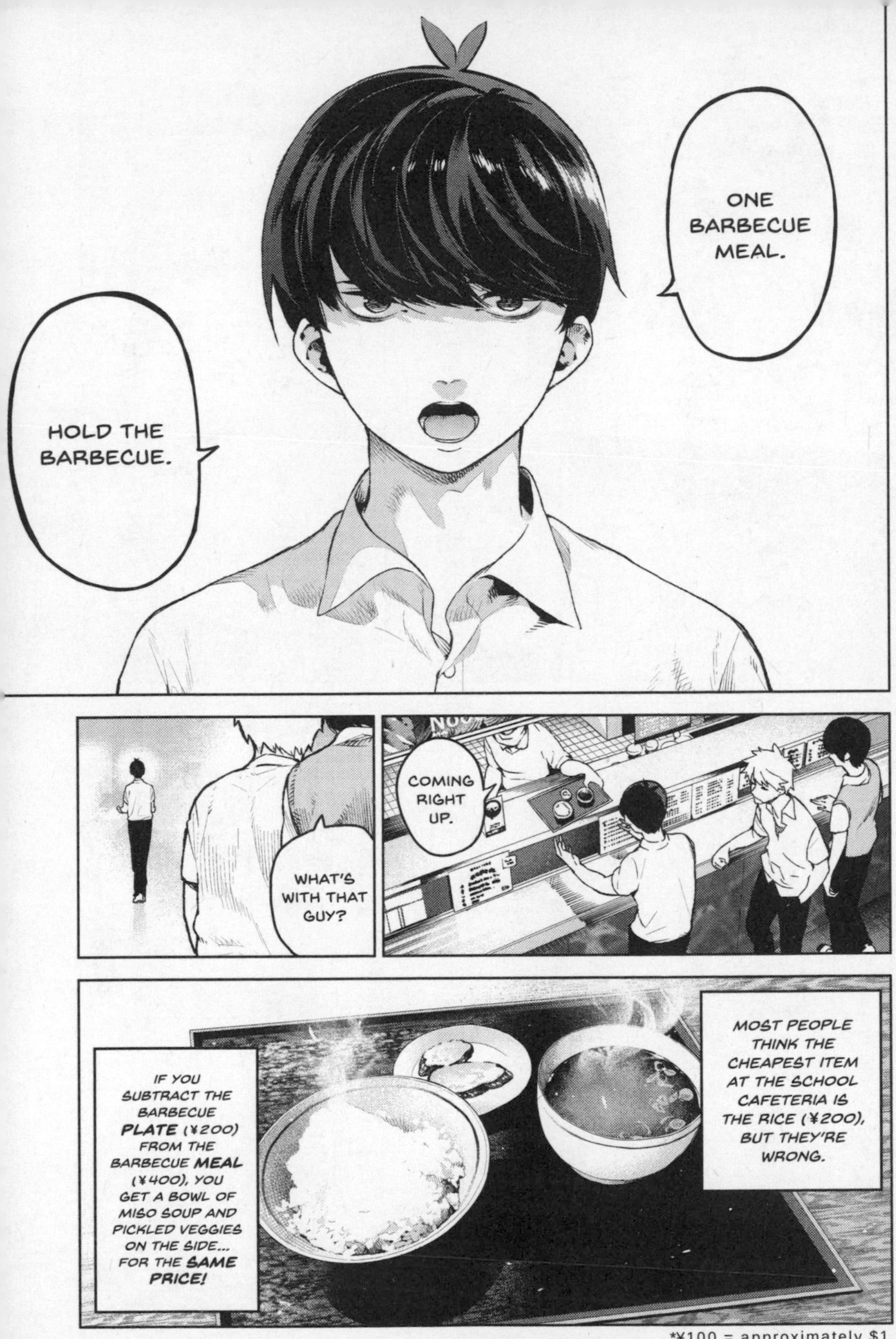
ONE BARBECUE MEAL.
HOLD THE BARBECUE.
COMING RIGHT UP.
WHAT'S WITH THAT GUY?
MOST PEOPLE THINK THE CHEAPEST ITEM AT THE SCHOOL CAFETERIA IS THE RICE (¥200), BUT THEY'RE WRONG.
IF YOU SUBTRACT THE BARBECUE **PLATE** (¥200) FROM THE BARBECUE **MEAL** (¥400), YOU GET A BOWL OF MISO SOUP AND PICKLED VEGGIES ON THE SIDE... FOR THE **SAME PRICE!**

*¥100 = approximately $1.

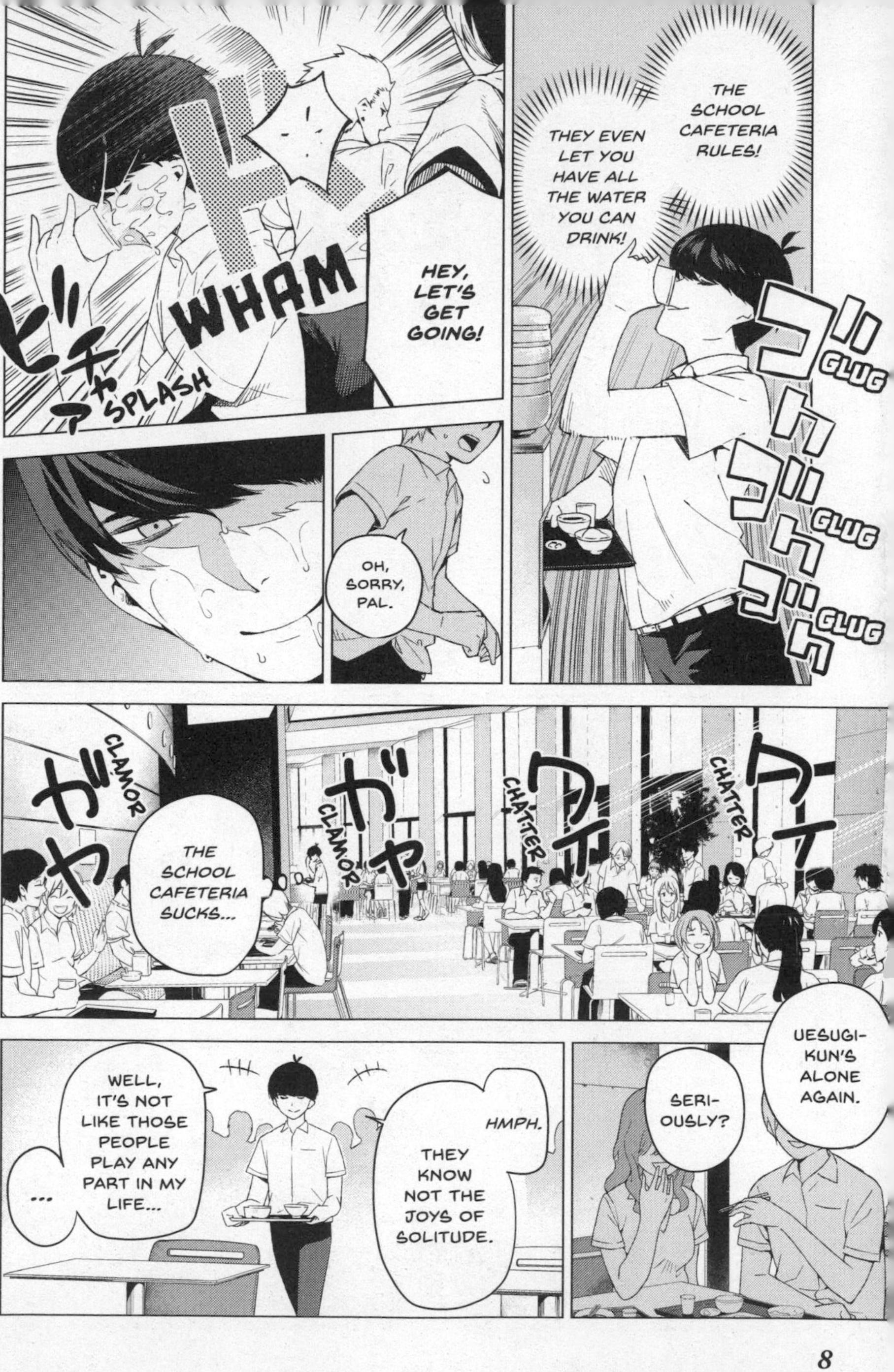
THE SCHOOL CAFETERIA RULES!
THEY EVEN LET YOU HAVE ALL THE WATER YOU CAN DRINK!
GLUG
GLUG
GLUG
WHAM
SPLASH
HEY, LET'S GET GOING!
OH, SORRY, PAL.
CHATTER
CHATTER
CLAMOR
CLAMOR
THE SCHOOL CAFETERIA SUCKS...
UESUGI-KUN'S ALONE AGAIN.
SERI-OUSLY?
HMPH.
THEY KNOW NOT THE JOYS OF SOLITUDE.
WELL, IT'S NOT LIKE THOSE PEOPLE PLAY ANY PART IN MY LIFE...
...

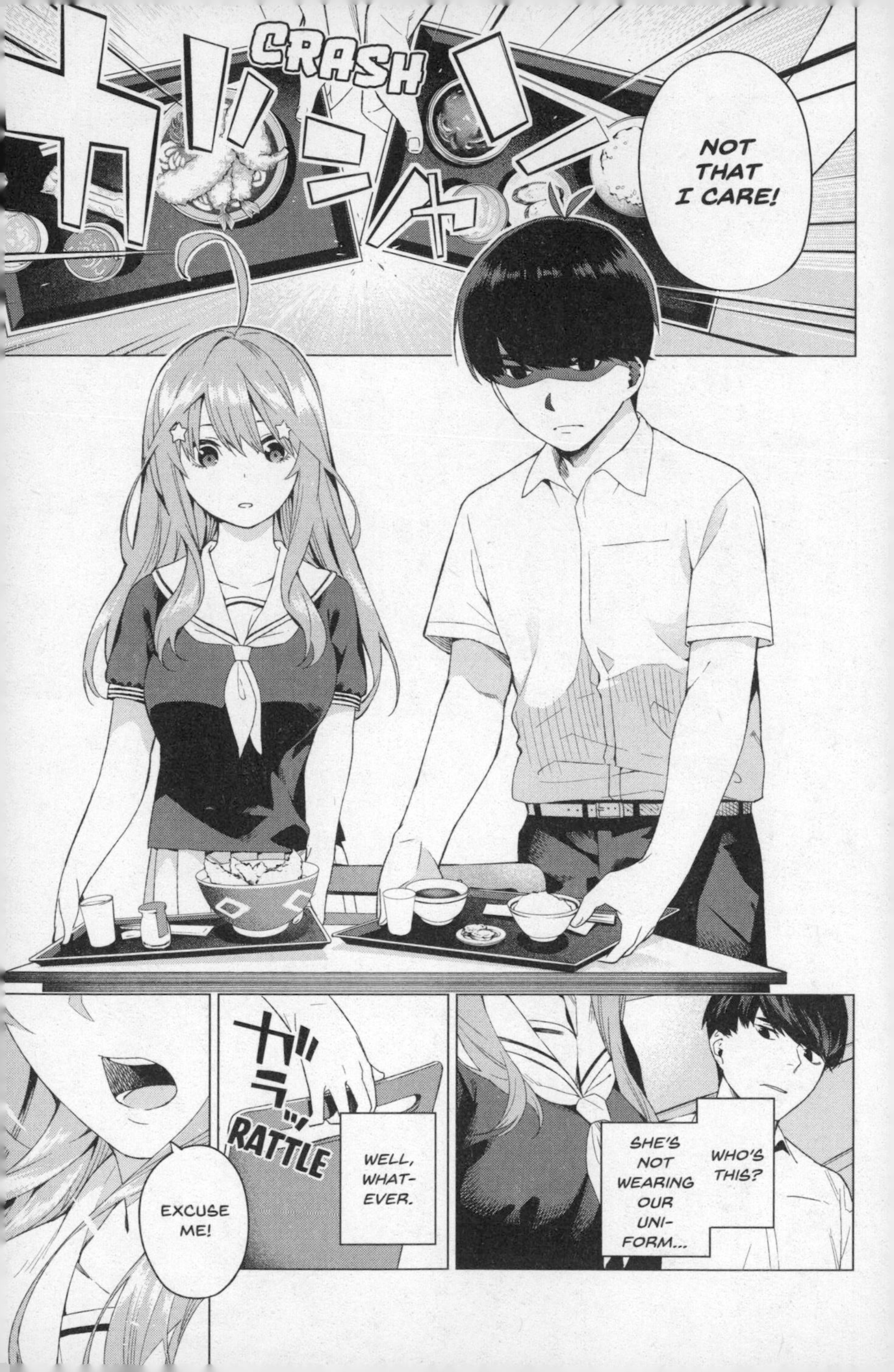
CRASH
NOT THAT I CARE!
WHO'S THIS?
SHE'S NOT WEARING OUR UNIFORM...
RATTLE
WELL, WHATEVER.
EXCUSE ME!

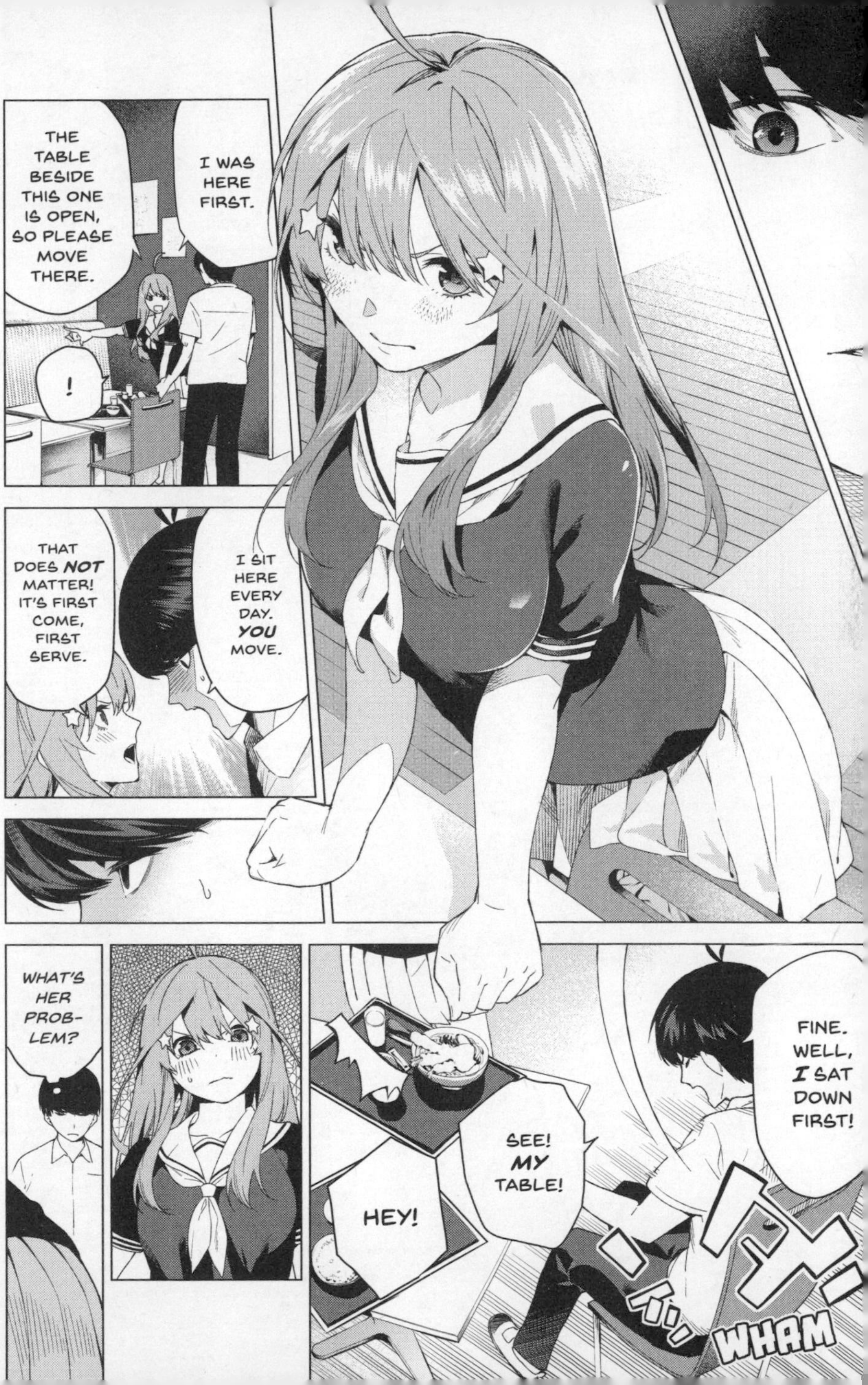
I WAS HERE FIRST.
THE TABLE BESIDE THIS ONE IS OPEN, SO PLEASE MOVE THERE.
!
I SIT HERE EVERY DAY. YOU MOVE.
THAT DOES NOT MATTER! IT'S FIRST COME, FIRST SERVE.
FINE. WELL, I SAT DOWN FIRST!
SEE! MY TABLE!
HEY!
WHAM
WHAT'S HER PROBLEM?

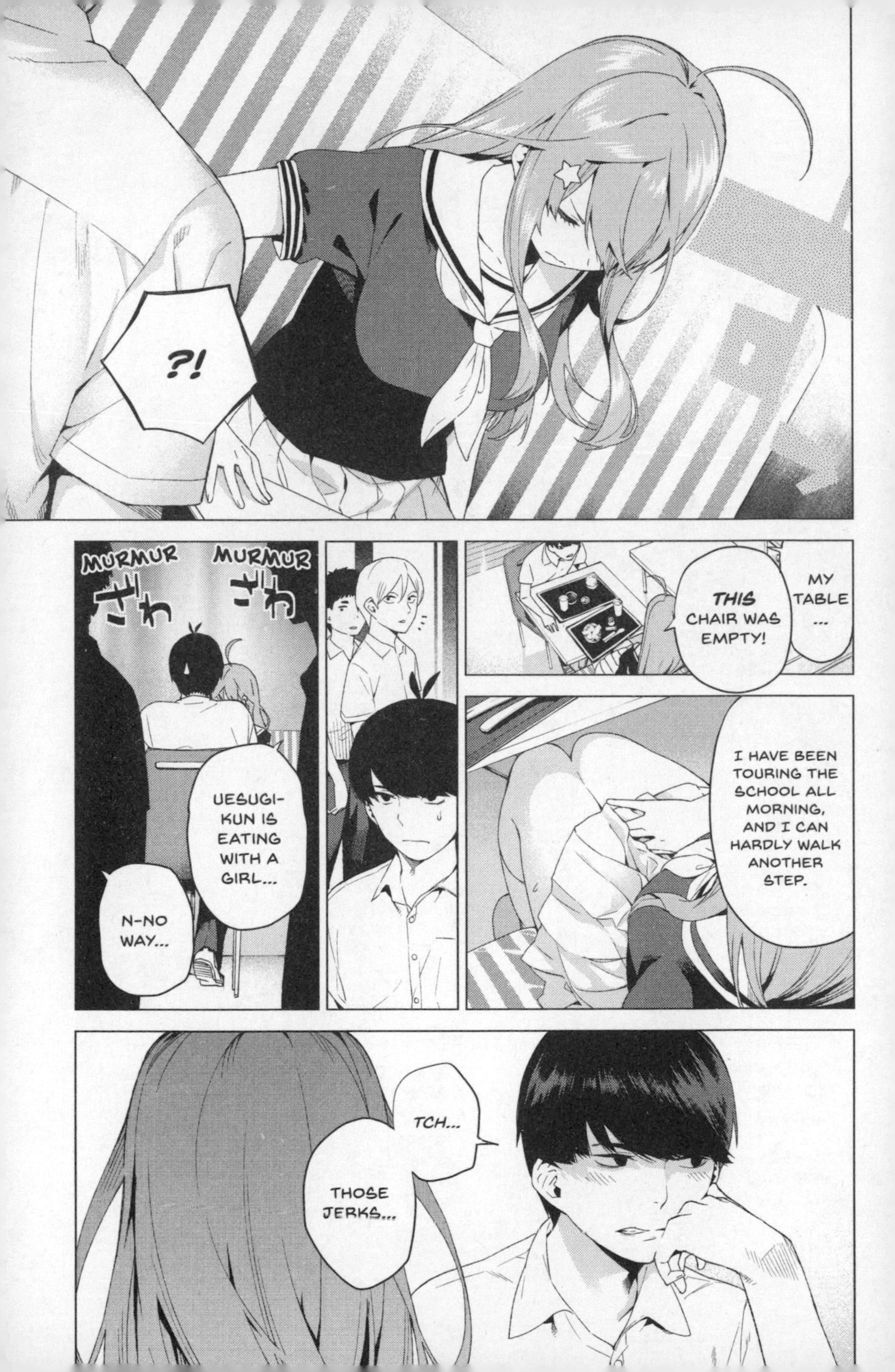
?!
MY TABLE ...
THIS CHAIR WAS EMPTY!
I HAVE BEEN TOURING THE SCHOOL ALL MORNING, AND I CAN HARDLY WALK ANOTHER STEP.
MURMUR ざわ
MURMUR ざわ
UESUGI-KUN IS EATING WITH A GIRL...
N-NO WAY...
TCH...
THOSE JERKS...

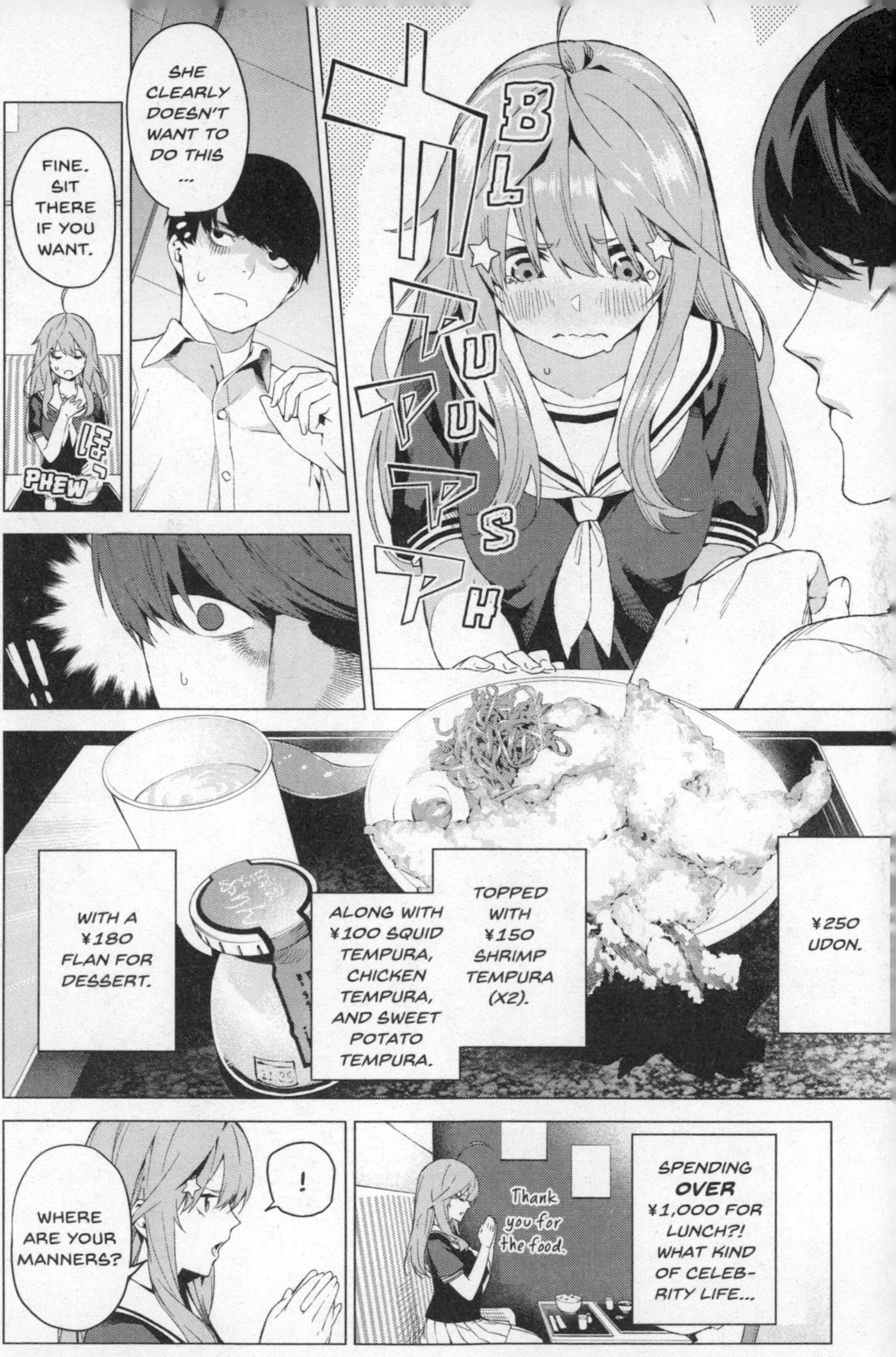
BLUUSH
SHE CLEARLY DOESN'T WANT TO DO THIS ...
FINE. SIT THERE IF YOU WANT.
PHEW
!!
¥250 UDON.
TOPPED WITH ¥150 SHRIMP TEMPURA (X2).
ALONG WITH ¥100 SQUID TEMPURA, CHICKEN TEMPURA, AND SWEET POTATO TEMPURA.
WITH A ¥180 FLAN FOR DESSERT.
SPENDING OVER ¥1,000 FOR LUNCH?! WHAT KIND OF CELEB-RITY LIFE...
Thank you for the food.
!
WHERE ARE YOUR MANNERS?

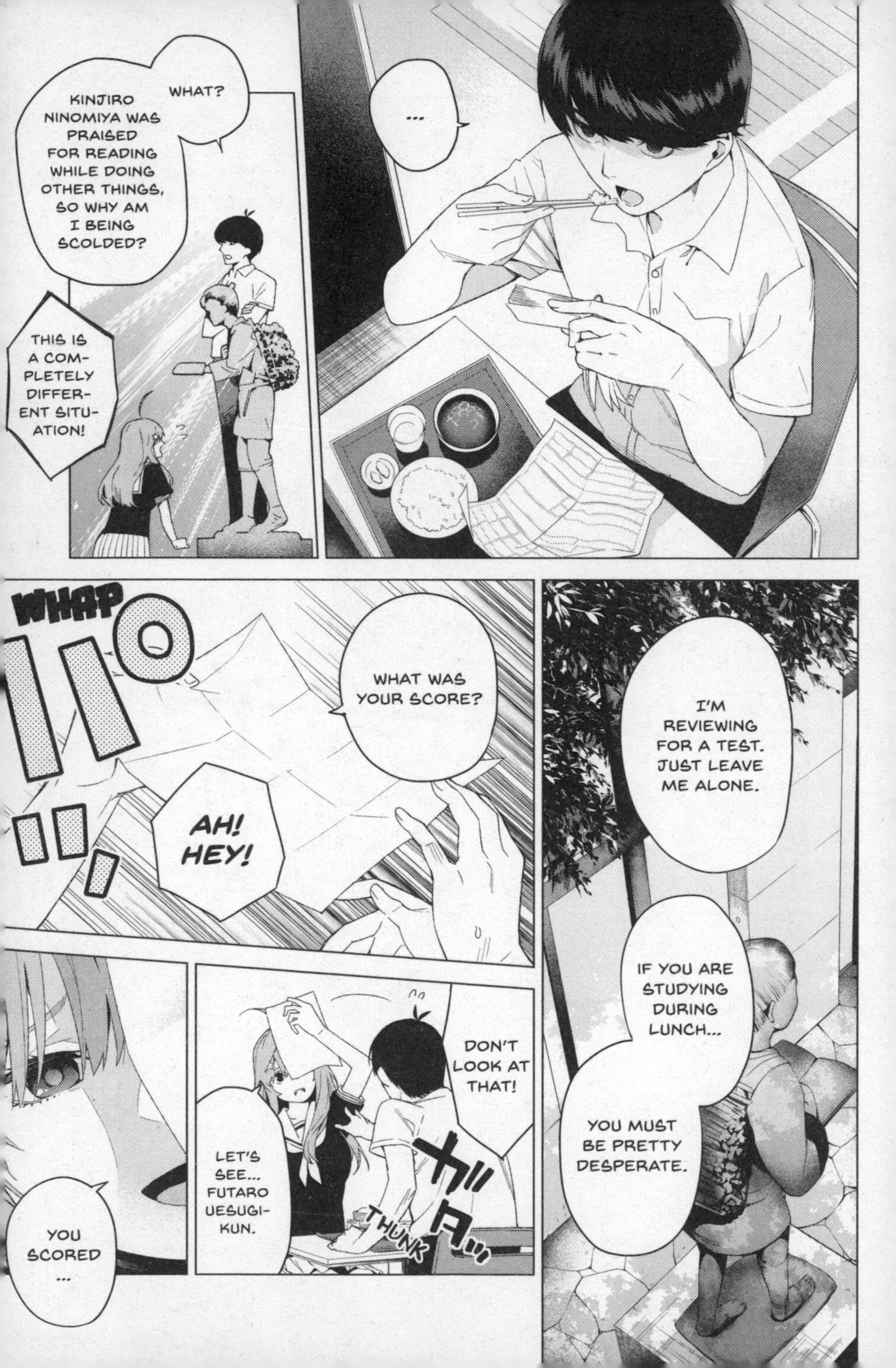
...
WHAT?
KINJIRO NINOMIYA WAS PRAISED FOR READING WHILE DOING OTHER THINGS, SO WHY AM I BEING SCOLDED?
THIS IS A COM-PLETELY DIFFER-ENT SITU-ATION!
I'M REVIEWING FOR A TEST. JUST LEAVE ME ALONE.
IF YOU ARE STUDYING DURING LUNCH...
YOU MUST BE PRETTY DESPERATE.
WHAT WAS YOUR SCORE?
WHAP
AH! HEY!
DON'T LOOK AT THAT!
LET'S SEE... FUTARO UESUGI-KUN.
THUNK
YOU SCORED ...

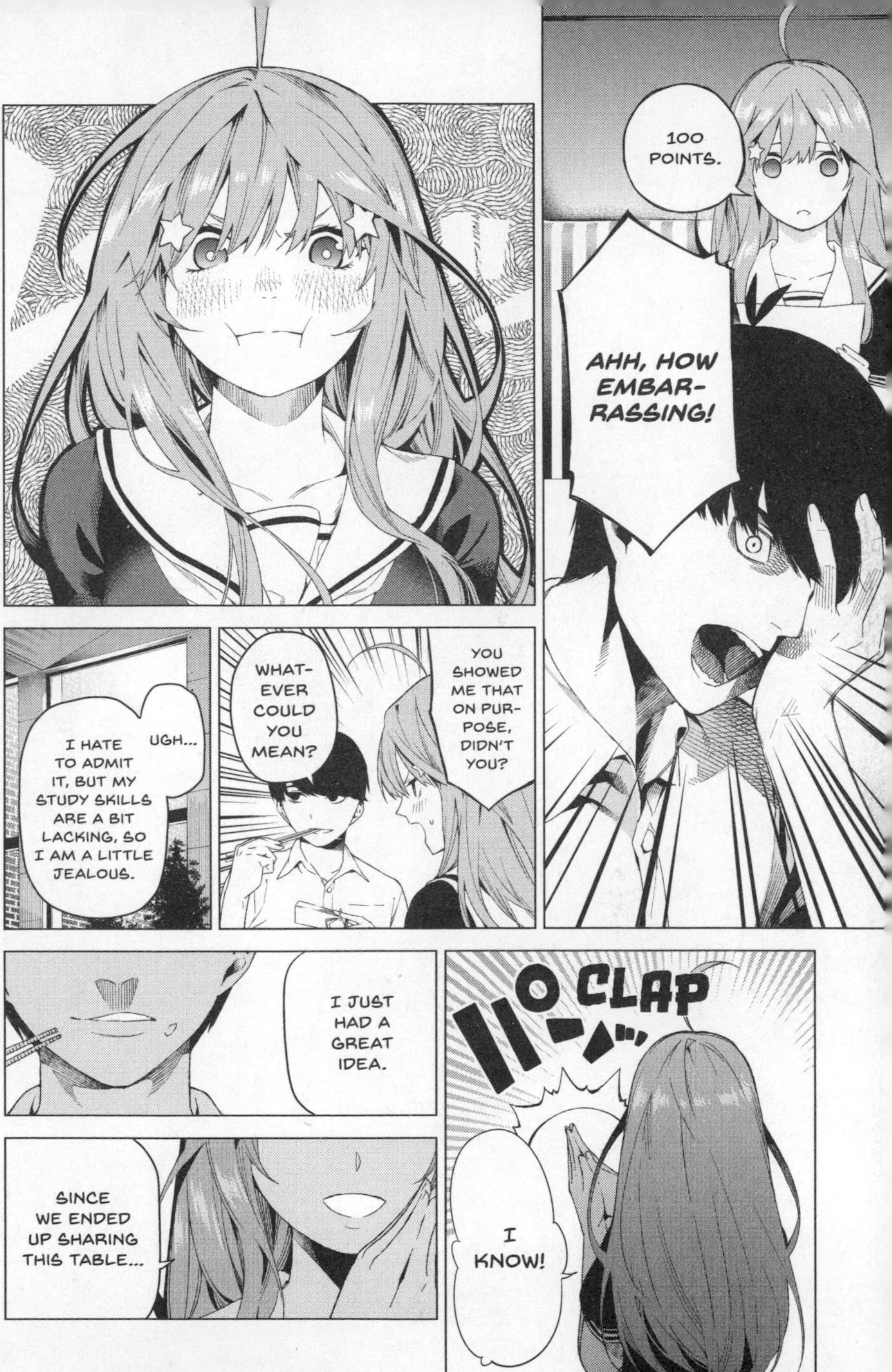
100 POINTS.
AHH, HOW EMBARRASSING!
YOU SHOWED ME THAT ON PURPOSE, DIDN'T YOU?
WHATEVER COULD YOU MEAN?
UGH...
I HATE TO ADMIT IT, BUT MY STUDY SKILLS ARE A BIT LACKING, SO I AM A LITTLE JEALOUS.
CLAP
I KNOW!
I JUST HAD A GREAT IDEA.
SINCE WE ENDED UP SHARING THIS TABLE...

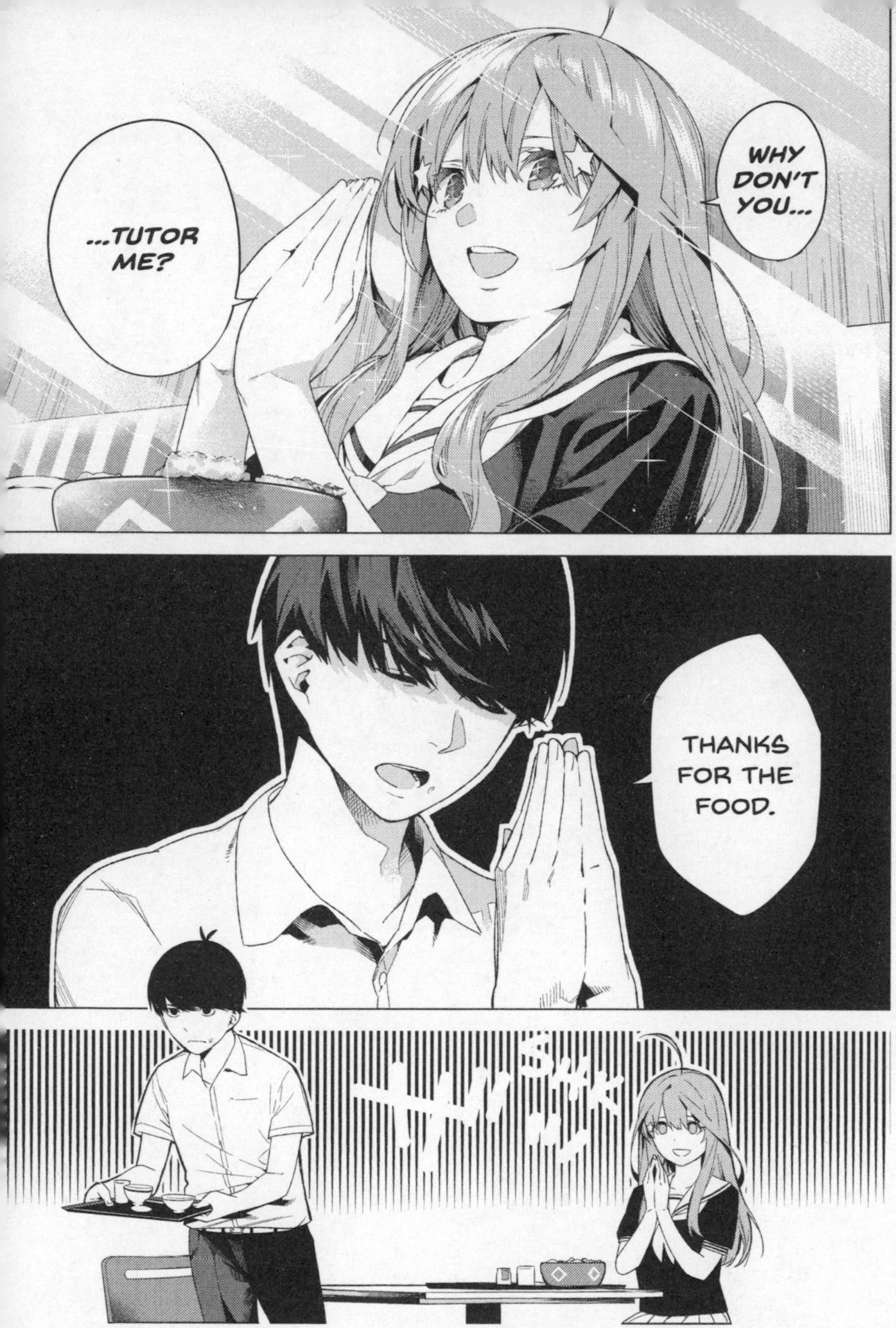
WHY DON'T YOU...
...TUTOR ME?
THANKS FOR THE FOOD.

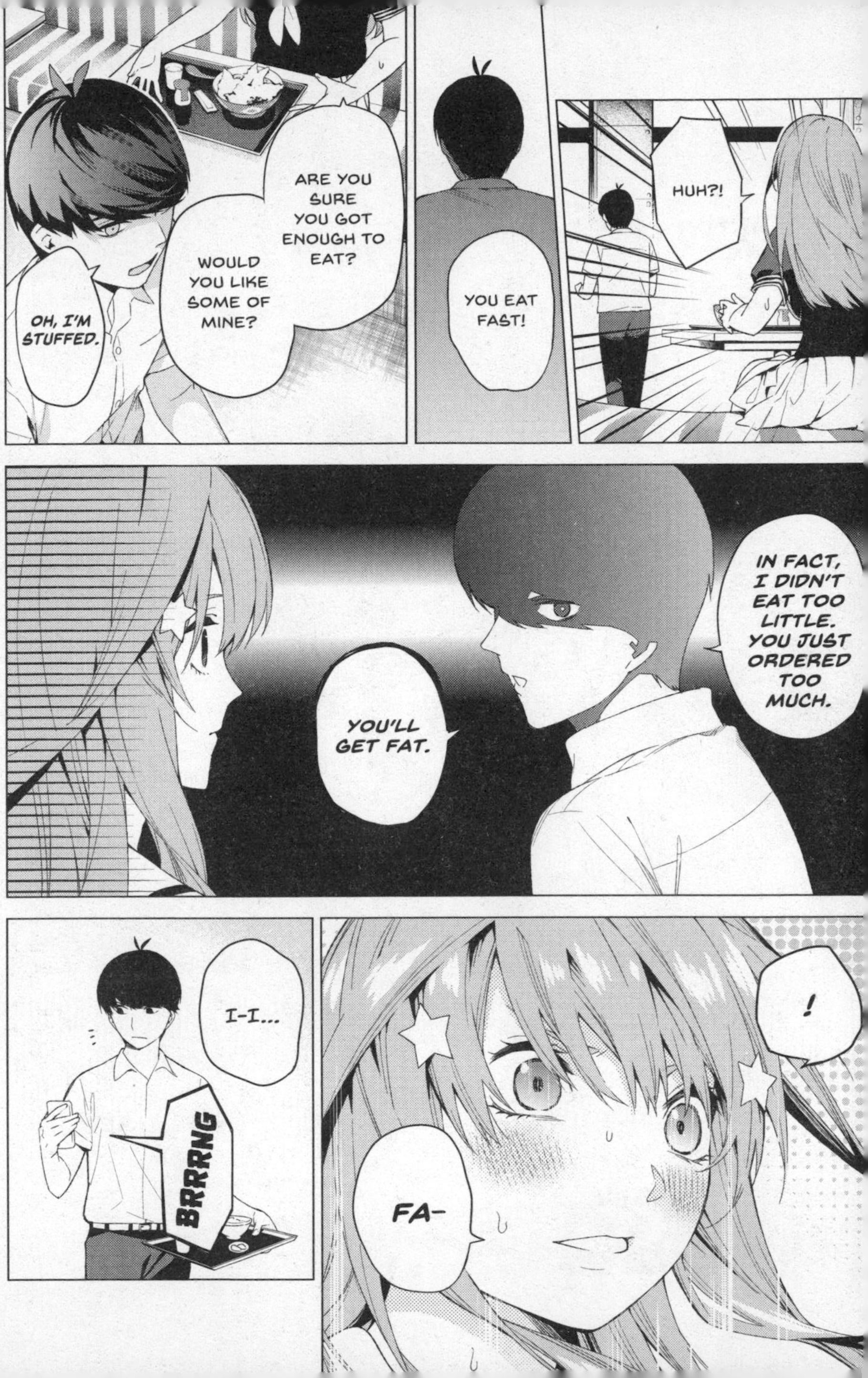
HUH?!
YOU EAT FAST!
ARE YOU SURE YOU GOT ENOUGH TO EAT?
WOULD YOU LIKE SOME OF MINE?
OH, I'M STUFFED.
IN FACT, I DIDN'T EAT TOO LITTLE. YOU JUST ORDERED TOO MUCH.
YOU'LL GET FAT.
!
FA-
I-I...
BRRRNG

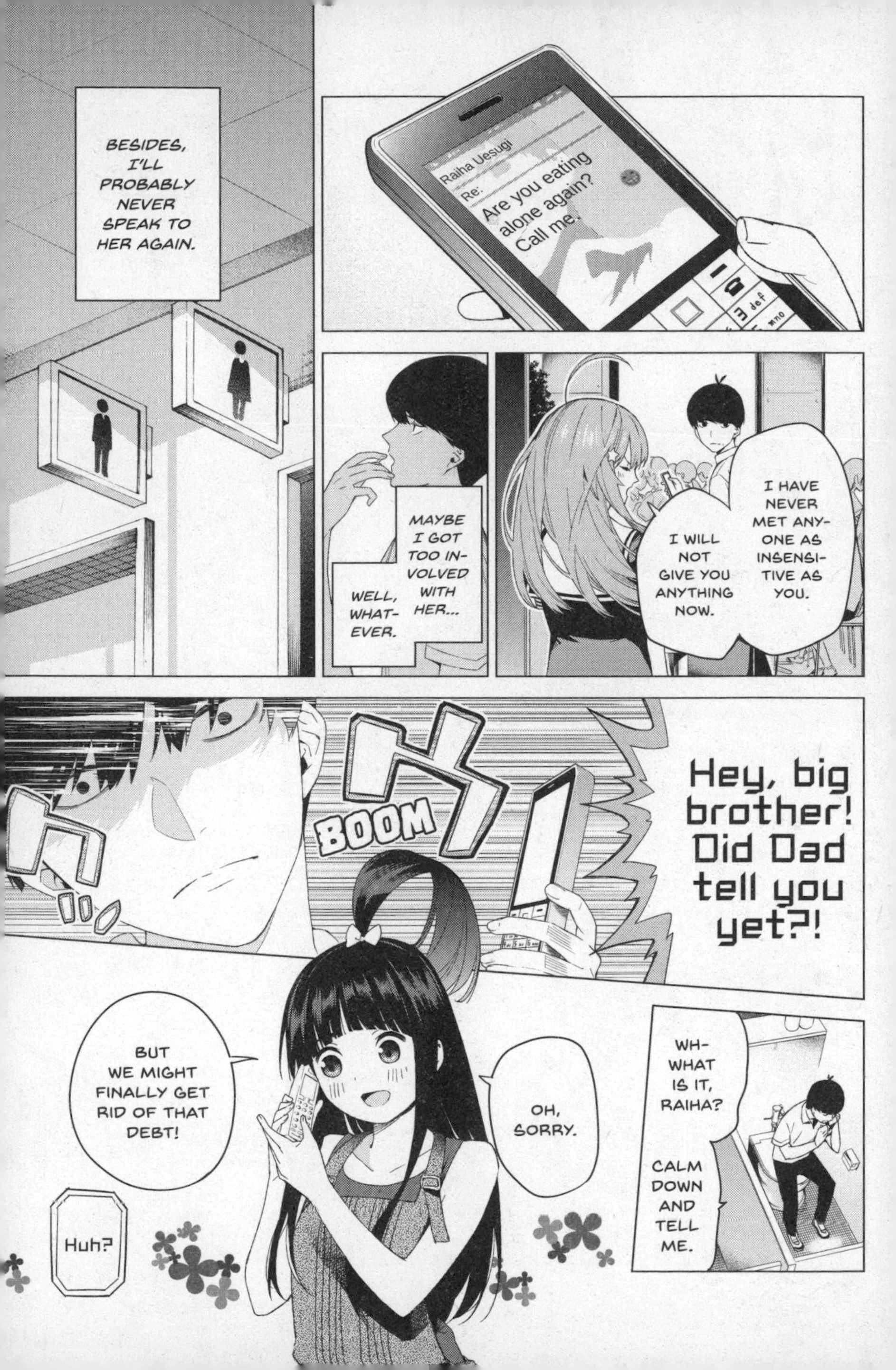
Raiha Uesugi
Re:
Are you eating alone again? Call me.
I HAVE NEVER MET ANYONE AS INSENSITIVE AS YOU.
I WILL NOT GIVE YOU ANYTHING NOW.
MAYBE I GOT TOO INVOLVED WITH HER...
WELL, WHATEVER.
BESIDES, I'LL PROBABLY NEVER SPEAK TO HER AGAIN.
Hey, big brother! Did Dad tell you yet?!
BOOM
WH-WHAT IS IT, RAIHA?
CALM DOWN AND TELL ME.
OH, SORRY.
BUT WE MIGHT FINALLY GET RID OF THAT DEBT!
Huh?

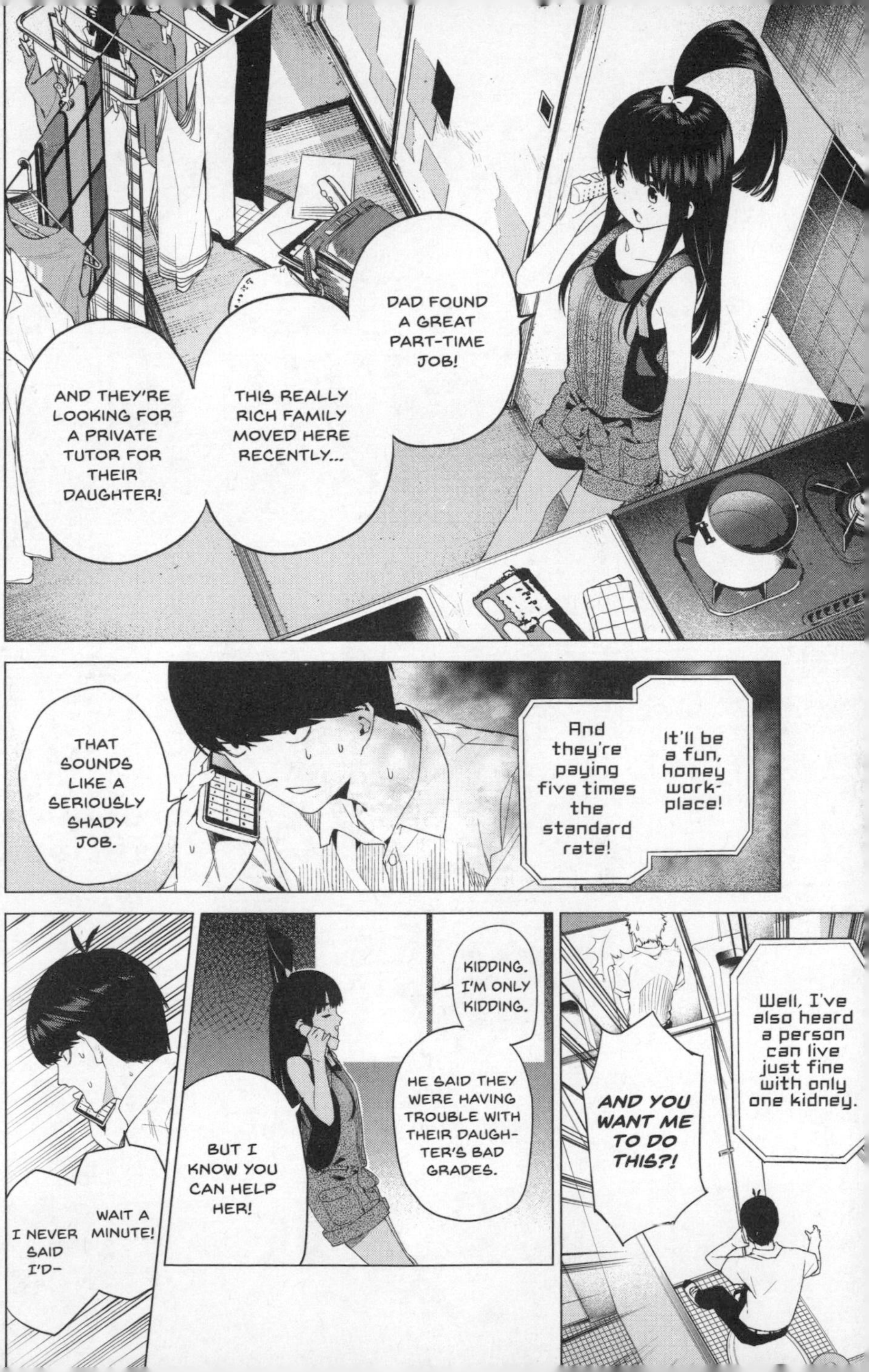
DAD FOUND A GREAT PART-TIME JOB!
THIS REALLY RICH FAMILY MOVED HERE RECENTLY...
AND THEY'RE LOOKING FOR A PRIVATE TUTOR FOR THEIR DAUGHTER!
It'll be a fun, homey work-place!
And they're paying five times the standard rate!
THAT SOUNDS LIKE A SERIOUSLY SHADY JOB.
Well, I've also heard a person can live just fine with only one kidney.
AND YOU WANT ME TO DO THIS?!
KIDDING. I'M ONLY KIDDING.
HE SAID THEY WERE HAVING TROUBLE WITH THEIR DAUGH-TER'S BAD GRADES.
BUT I KNOW YOU CAN HELP HER!
WAIT A MINUTE!
I NEVER SAID I'D–

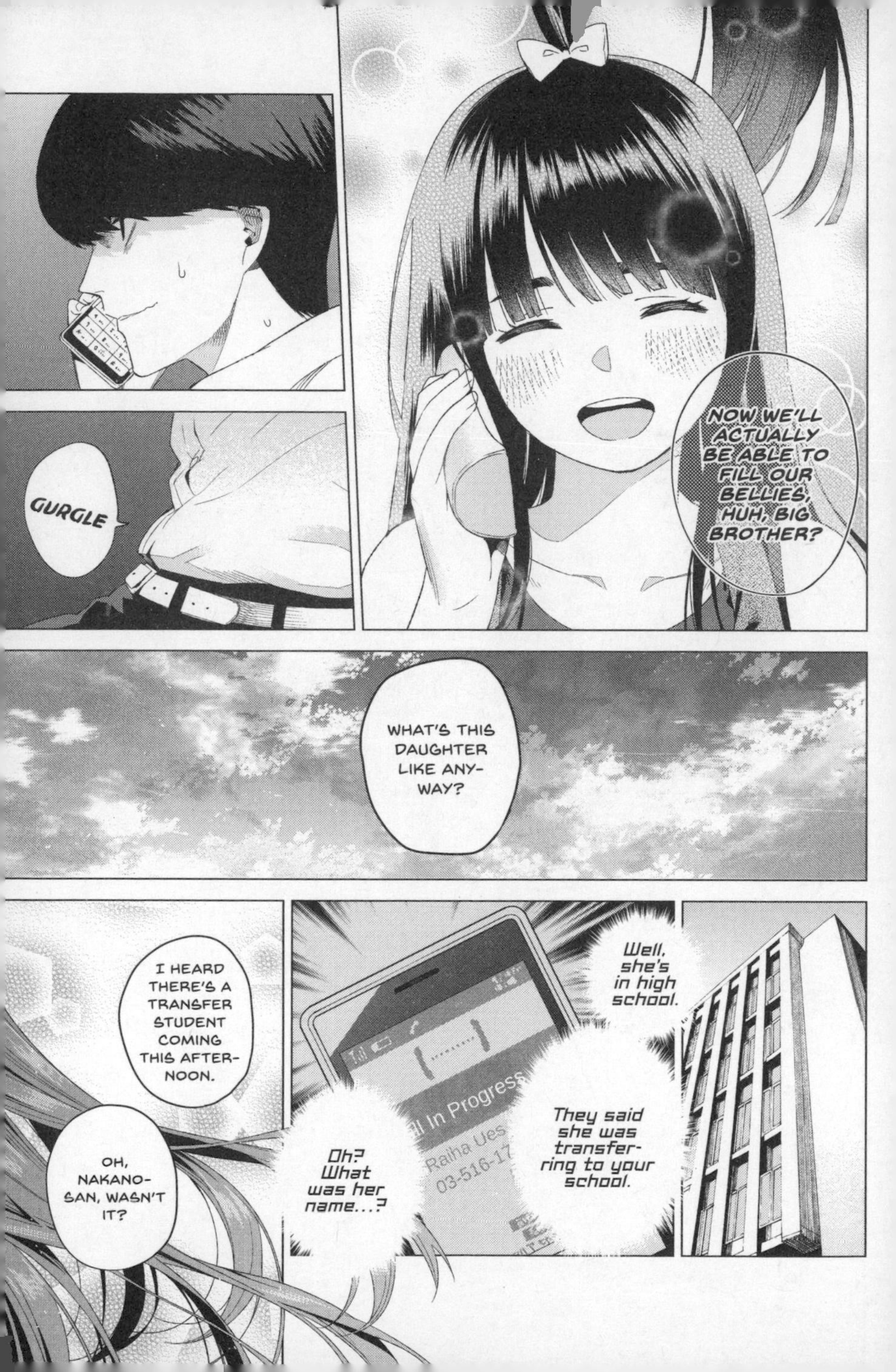
NOW WE'LL ACTUALLY BE ABLE TO FILL OUR BELLIES, HUH, BIG BROTHER?
GURGLE
WHAT'S THIS DAUGHTER LIKE ANY-WAY?
Well, she's in high school.
They said she was transfer-ring to your school.
Oh? What was her name...?
I HEARD THERE'S A TRANSFER STUDENT COMING THIS AFTER-NOON.
OH, NAKANO-SAN, WASN'T IT?

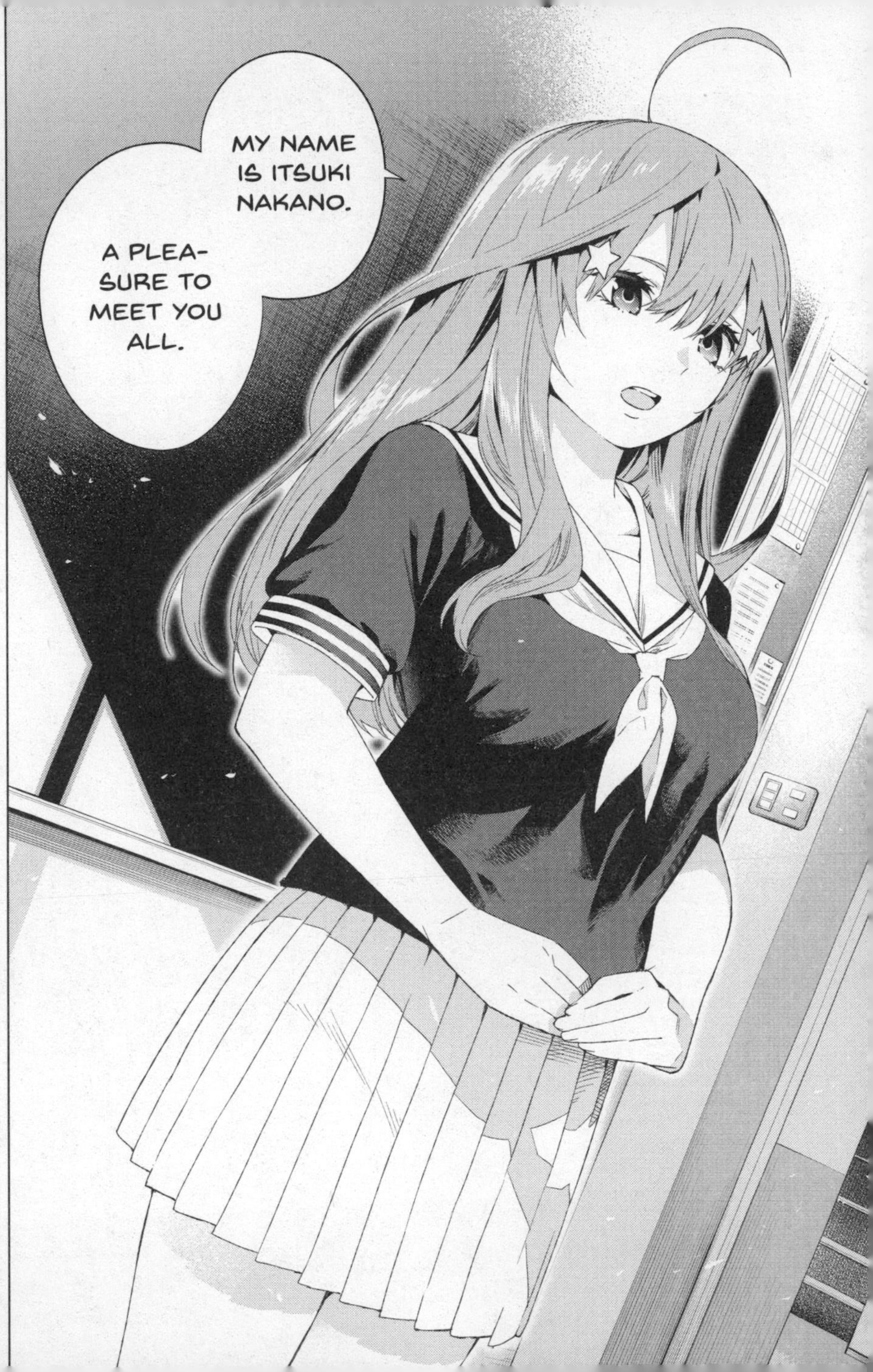
MY NAME IS ITSUKI NAKANO.
A PLEA-SURE TO MEET YOU ALL.

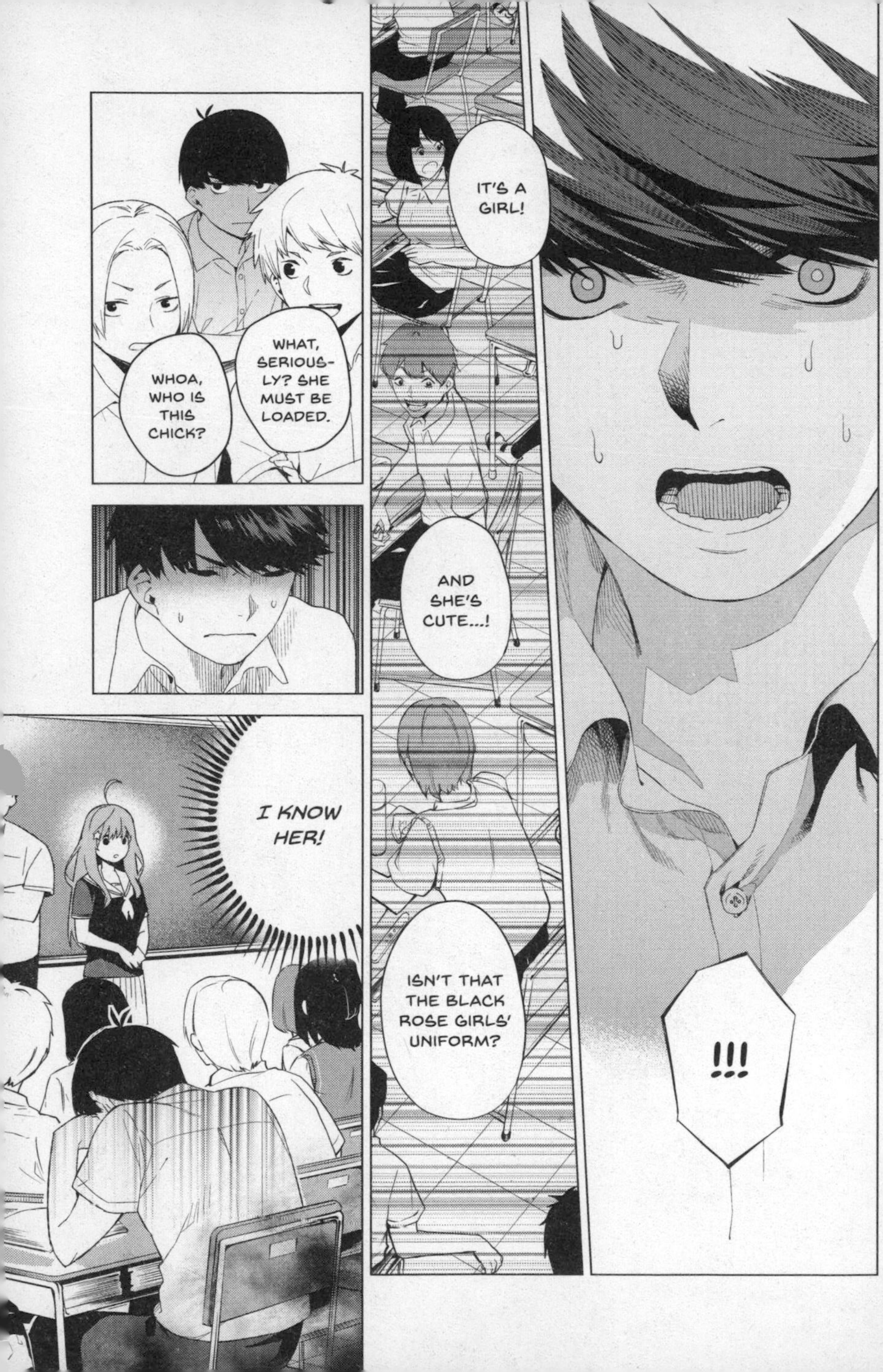
!!!
IT'S A GIRL!
AND SHE'S CUTE...!
ISN'T THAT THE BLACK ROSE GIRLS' UNIFORM?
WHAT, SERIOUSLY? SHE MUST BE LOADED.
WHOA, WHO IS THIS CHICK?
I KNOW HER!

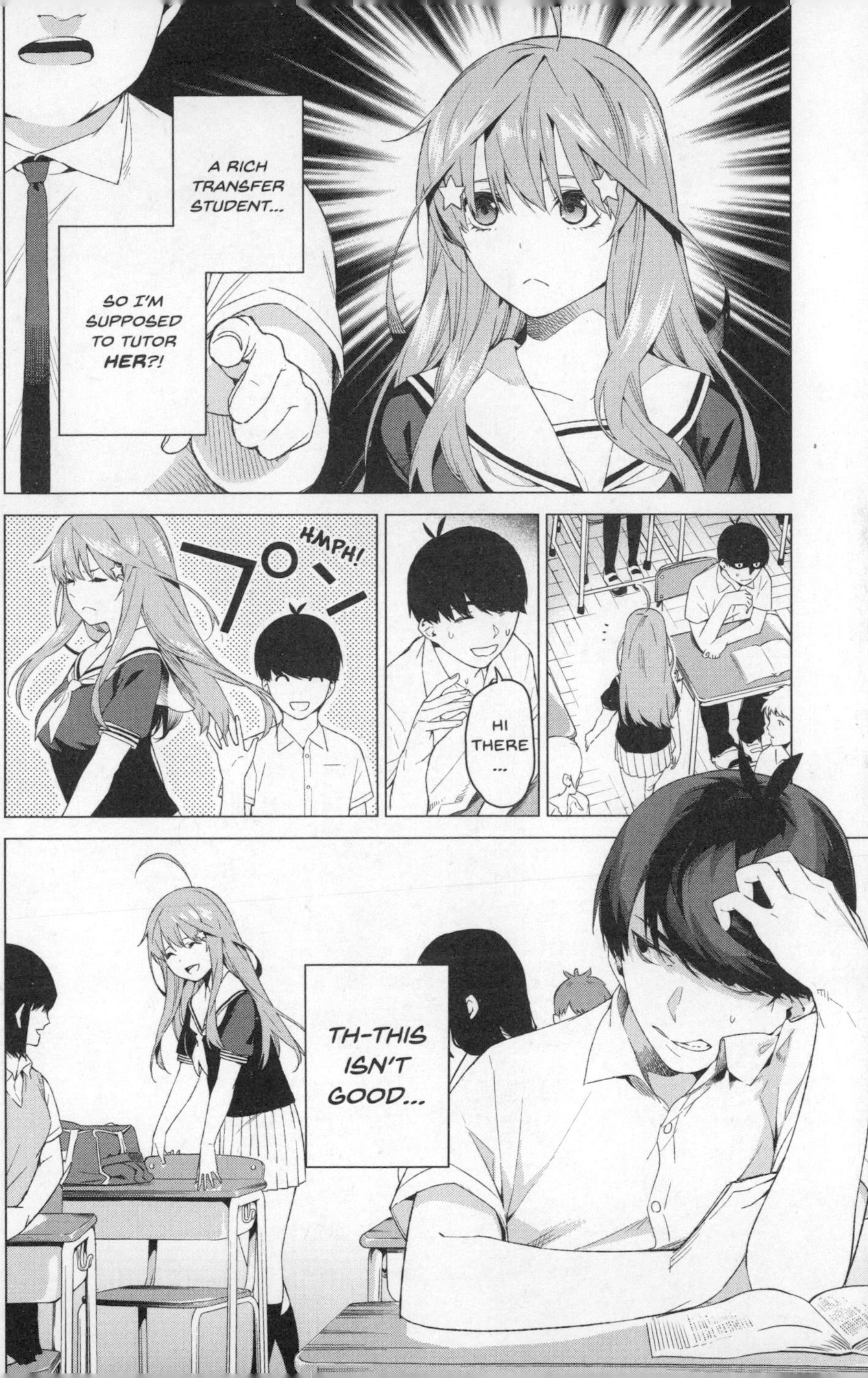
A RICH TRANSFER STUDENT...
SO I'M SUPPOSED TO TUTOR HER?!
HI THERE ...
HMPH!
TH-THIS ISN'T GOOD...

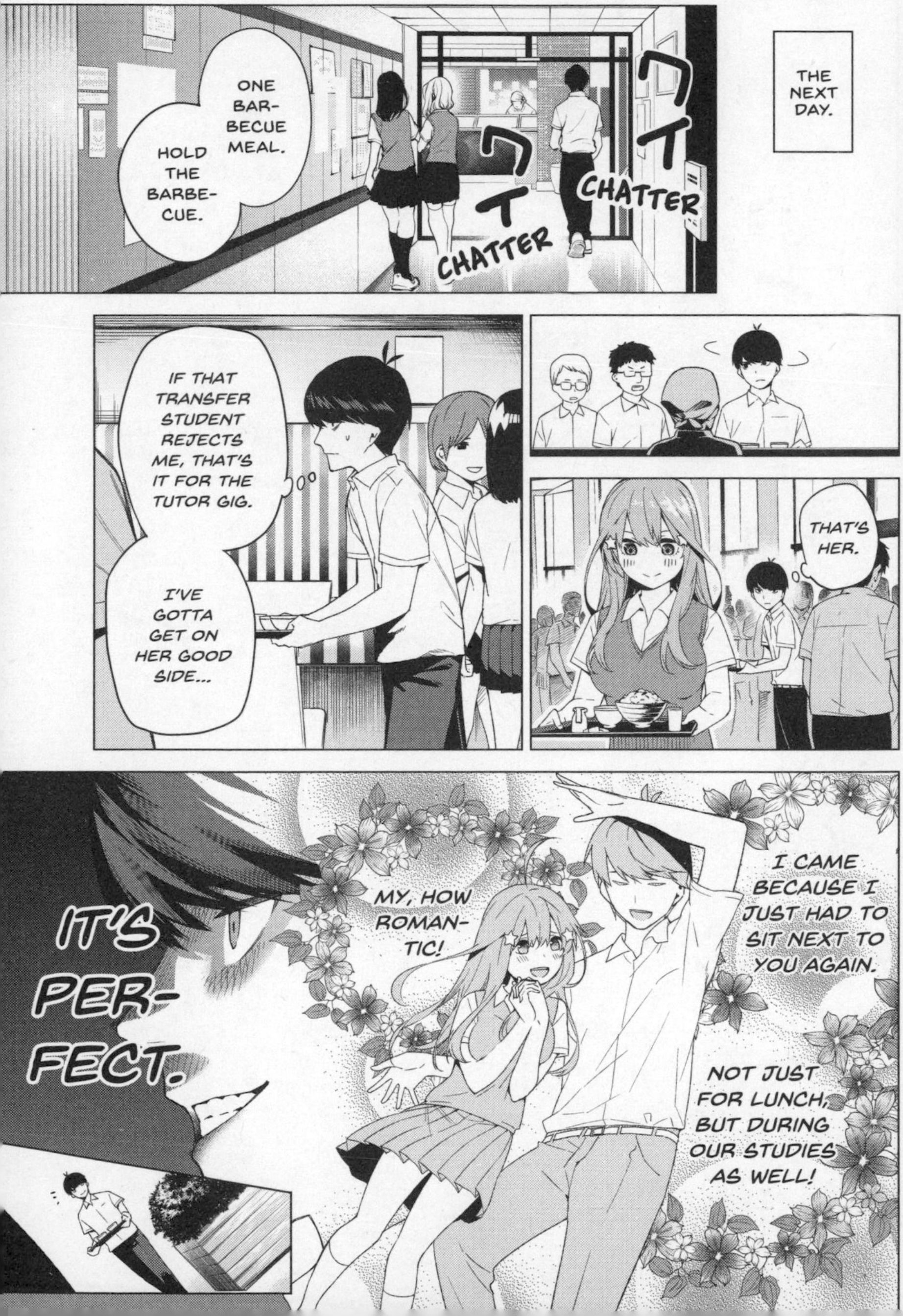
THE NEXT DAY.
ワイ
CHATTER
ワイ
CHATTER
ONE BARBECUE MEAL.
HOLD THE BARBECUE.
THAT'S HER.
IF THAT TRANSFER STUDENT REJECTS ME, THAT'S IT FOR THE TUTOR GIG.
I'VE GOTTA GET ON HER GOOD SIDE...
I CAME BECAUSE I JUST HAD TO SIT NEXT TO YOU AGAIN.
MY, HOW ROMANTIC!
NOT JUST FOR LUNCH, BUT DURING OUR STUDIES AS WELL!
IT'S PERFECT.

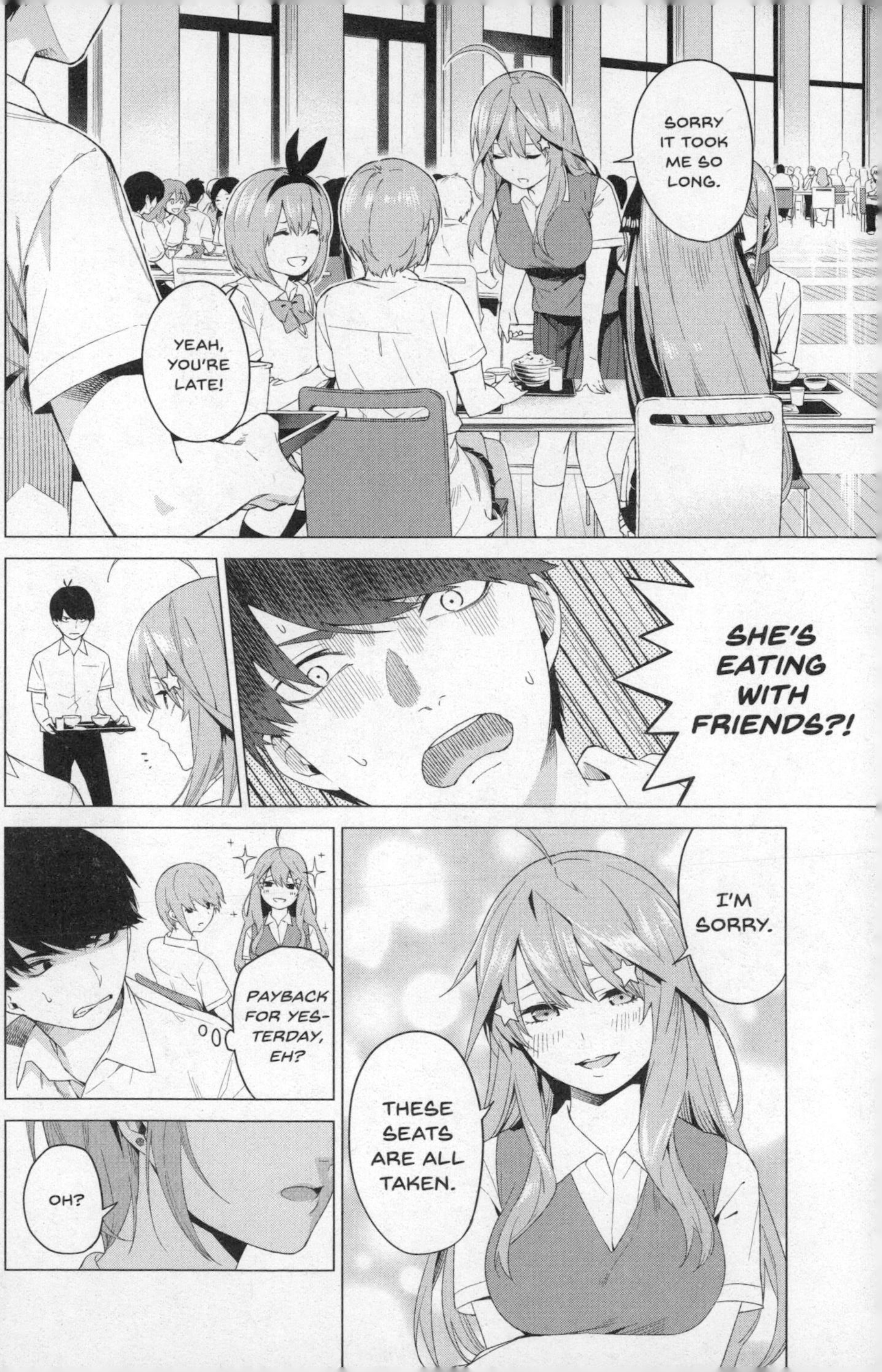
SORRY IT TOOK ME SO LONG.
YEAH, YOU'RE LATE!
SHE'S EATING WITH FRIENDS?!
I'M SORRY.
THESE SEATS ARE ALL TAKEN.
PAYBACK FOR YES-TERDAY, EH?
OH?

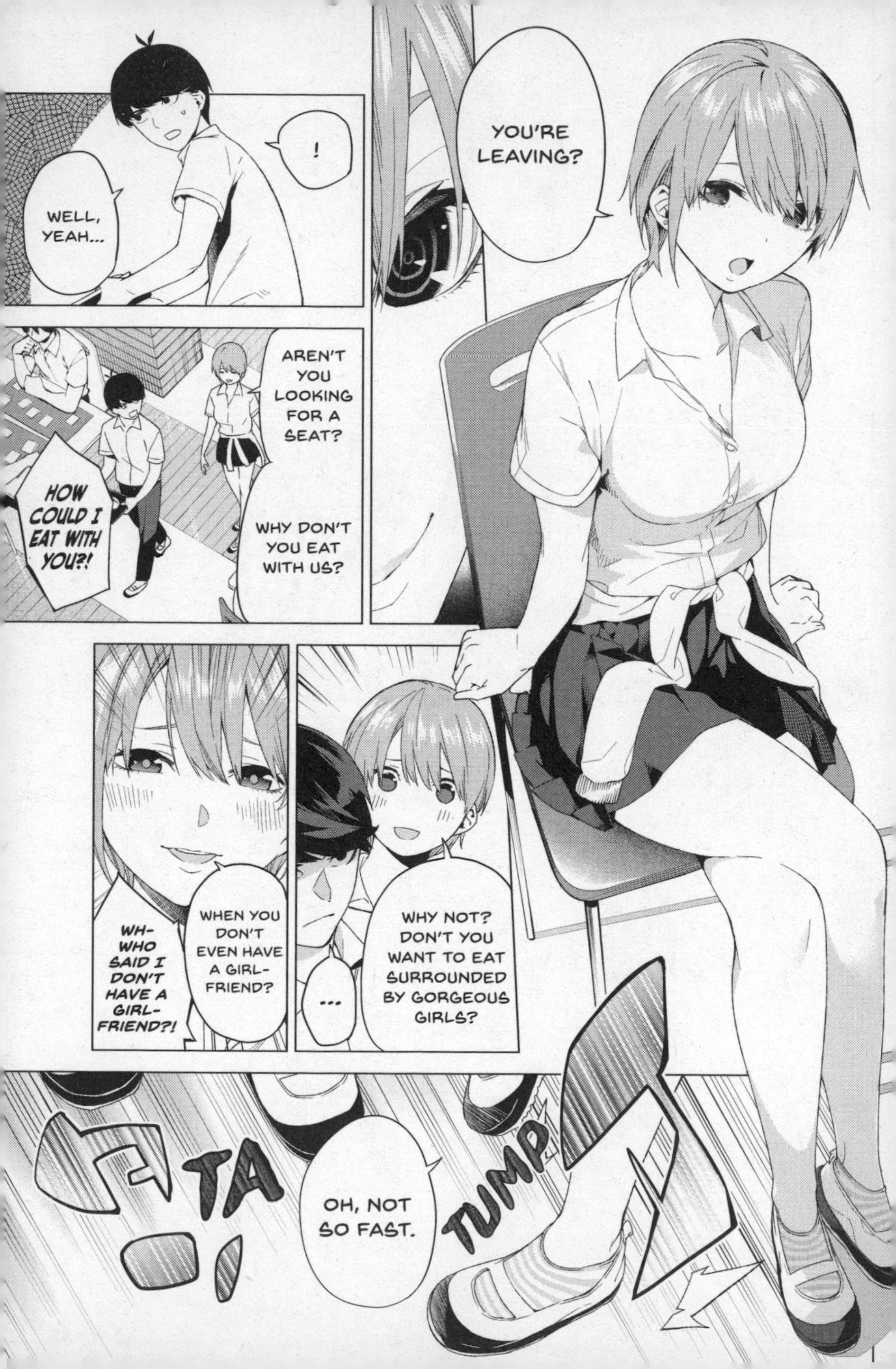
YOU'RE LEAVING?
!
WELL, YEAH...
AREN'T YOU LOOKING FOR A SEAT?
WHY DON'T YOU EAT WITH US?
HOW COULD I EAT WITH YOU?!
WHY NOT? DON'T YOU WANT TO EAT SURROUNDED BY GORGEOUS GIRLS?
...
WHEN YOU DON'T EVEN HAVE A GIRL-FRIEND?
WH-WHO SAID I DON'T HAVE A GIRL-FRIEND?!
TUMP
OH, NOT SO FAST.
TA

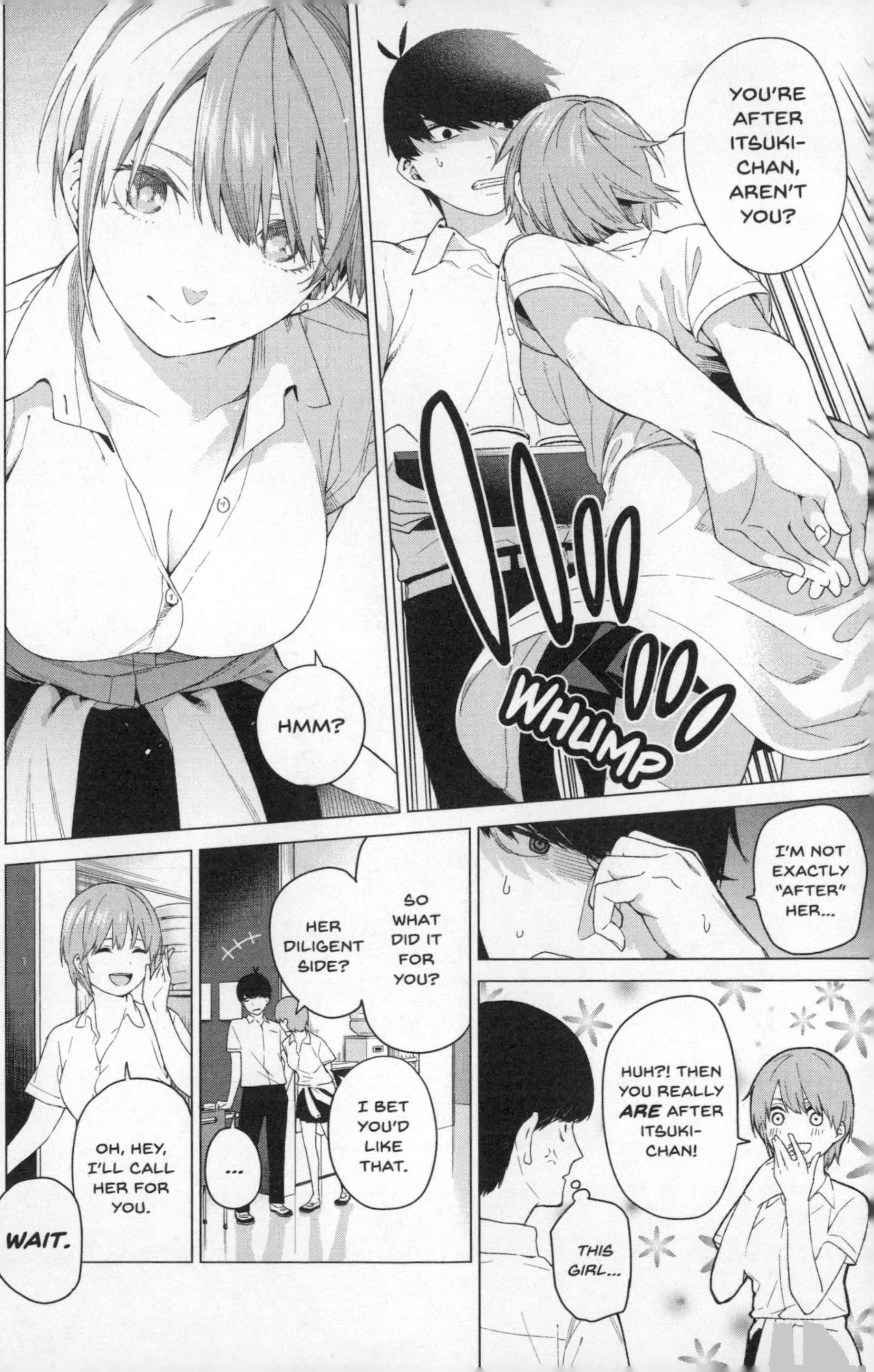
YOU'RE AFTER ITSUKI-CHAN, AREN'T YOU?
WHUMP
HMM?
I'M NOT EXACTLY "AFTER" HER...
HUH?! THEN YOU REALLY ***ARE*** AFTER ITSUKI-CHAN!
THIS GIRL...
SO WHAT DID IT FOR YOU?
HER DILIGENT SIDE?
I BET YOU'D LIKE THAT.
...
OH, HEY, I'LL CALL HER FOR YOU.
WAIT.

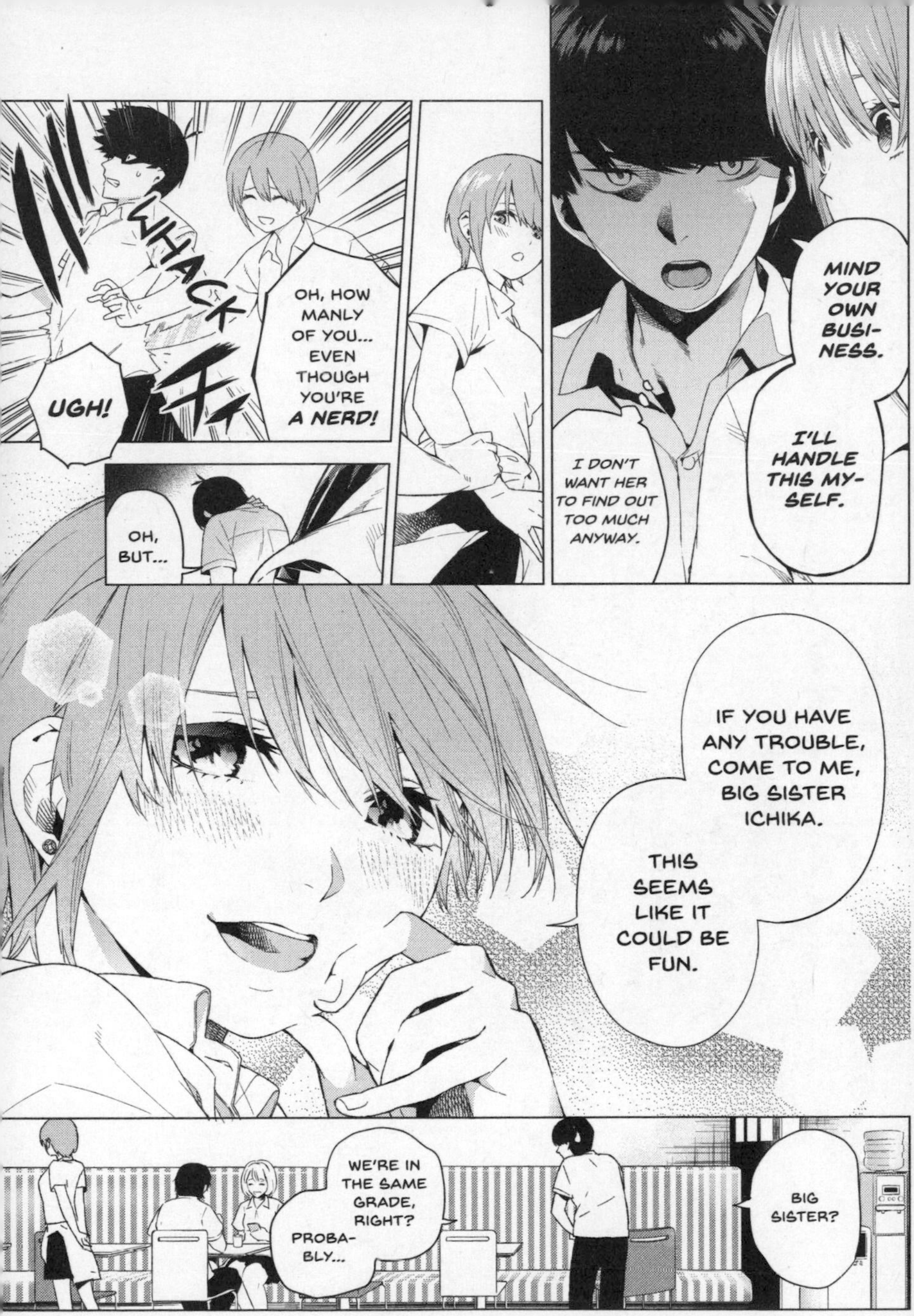
MIND YOUR OWN BUSINESS.
I'LL HANDLE THIS MYSELF.
I DON'T WANT HER TO FIND OUT TOO MUCH ANYWAY.
OH, HOW MANLY OF YOU... EVEN THOUGH YOU'RE A NERD!
WHACK
UGH!
OH, BUT...
IF YOU HAVE ANY TROUBLE, COME TO ME, BIG SISTER ICHIKA.
THIS SEEMS LIKE IT COULD BE FUN.
BIG SISTER?
WE'RE IN THE SAME GRADE, RIGHT?
PROBABLY...

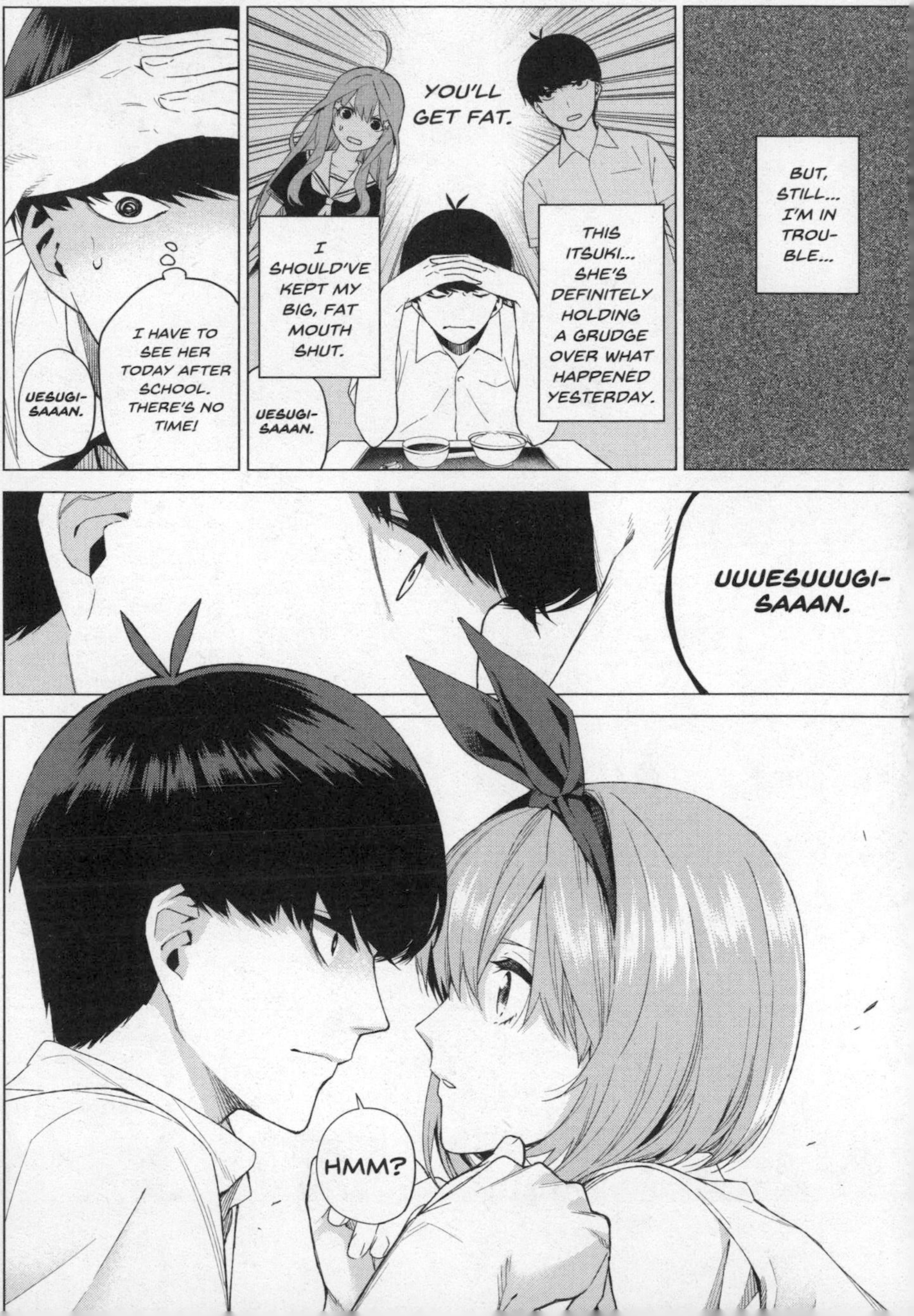
BUT, STILL... I'M IN TROUBLE...
THIS ITSUKI... SHE'S DEFINITELY HOLDING A GRUDGE OVER WHAT HAPPENED YESTERDAY.
YOU'LL GET FAT.
I SHOULD'VE KEPT MY BIG, FAT MOUTH SHUT.
UESUGI-SAAAN.
I HAVE TO SEE HER TODAY AFTER SCHOOL. THERE'S NO TIME!
UESUGI-SAAAN.
UUUESUUUGI-SAAAN.
HMM?

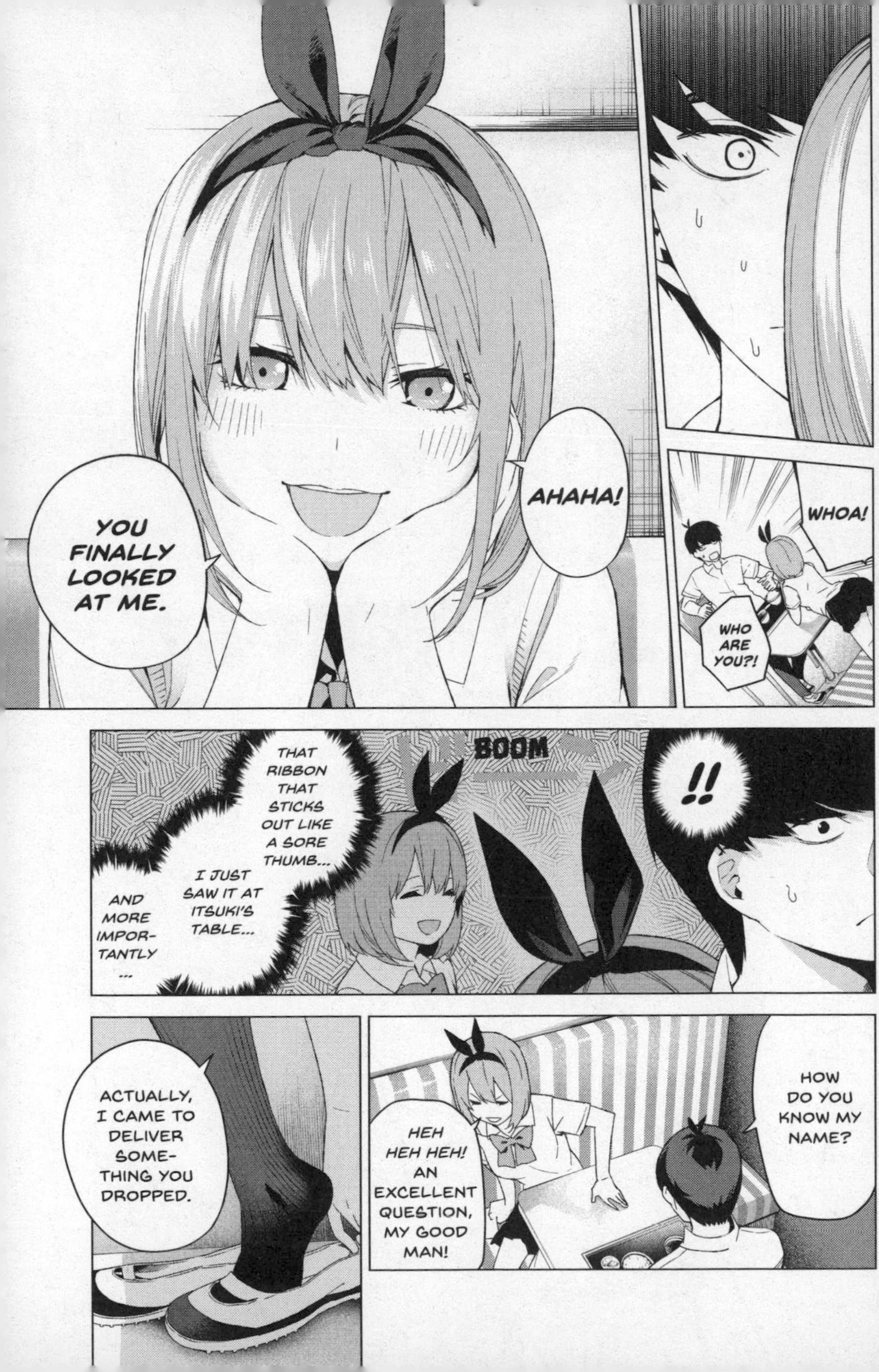
WHOA!
WHO ARE YOU?!
AHAHA!
YOU FINALLY LOOKED AT ME.
!!
BOOM
THAT RIBBON THAT STICKS OUT LIKE A SORE THUMB...
I JUST SAW IT AT ITSUKI'S TABLE...
AND MORE IMPOR-TANTLY ...
HOW DO YOU KNOW MY NAME?
HEH HEH HEH! AN EXCELLENT QUESTION, MY GOOD MAN!
ACTUALLY, I CAME TO DELIVER SOME-THING YOU DROPPED.

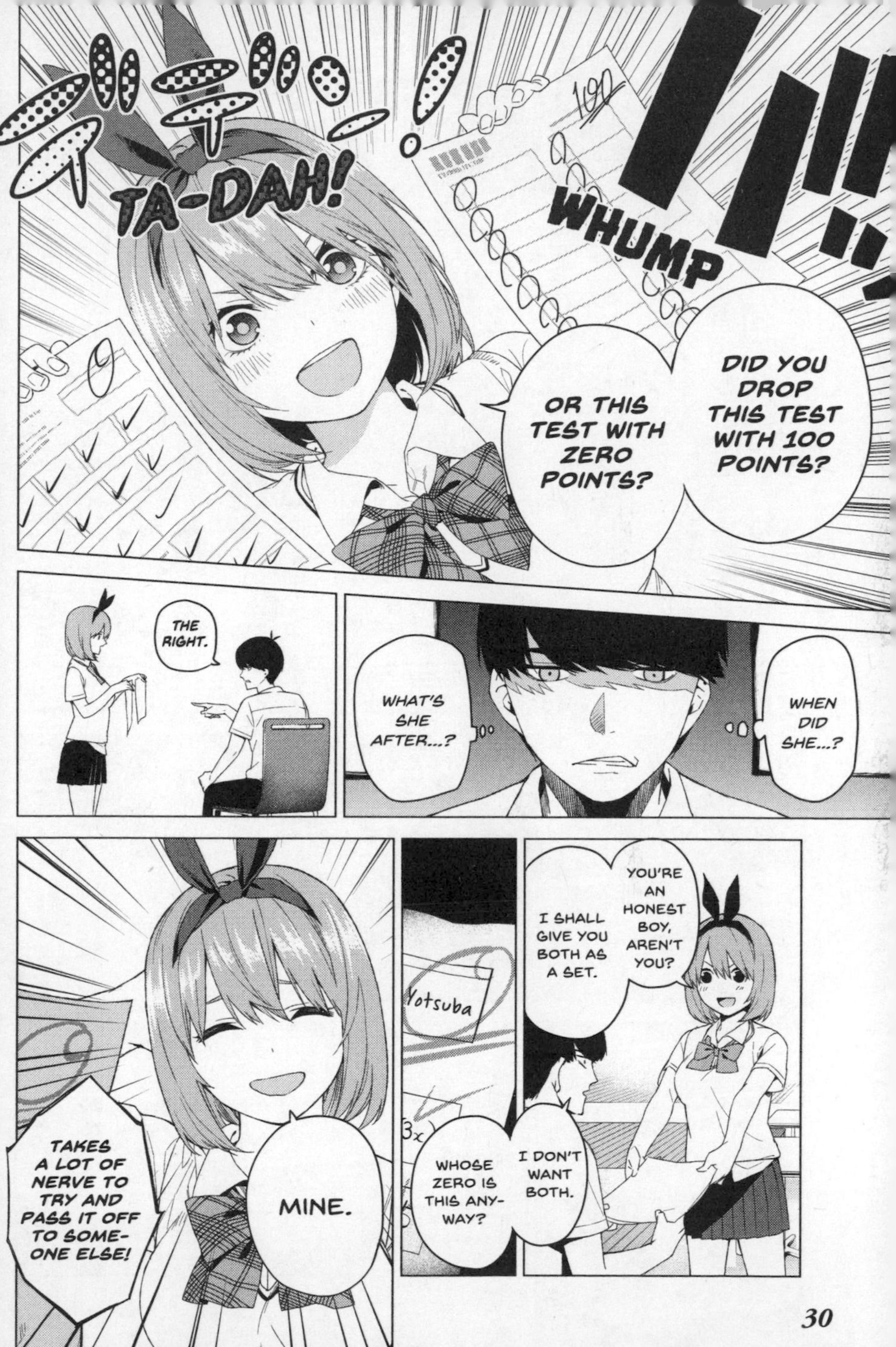
TA-DAH!
WHUMP
DID YOU DROP THIS TEST WITH 100 POINTS?
OR THIS TEST WITH ZERO POINTS?
WHEN DID SHE...?
WHAT'S SHE AFTER...?
THE RIGHT.
YOU'RE AN HONEST BOY, AREN'T YOU?
I SHALL GIVE YOU BOTH AS A SET.
Yotsuba
I DON'T WANT BOTH.
WHOSE ZERO IS THIS ANYWAY?
MINE.
TAKES A LOT OF NERVE TO TRY AND PASS IT OFF TO SOME-ONE ELSE!

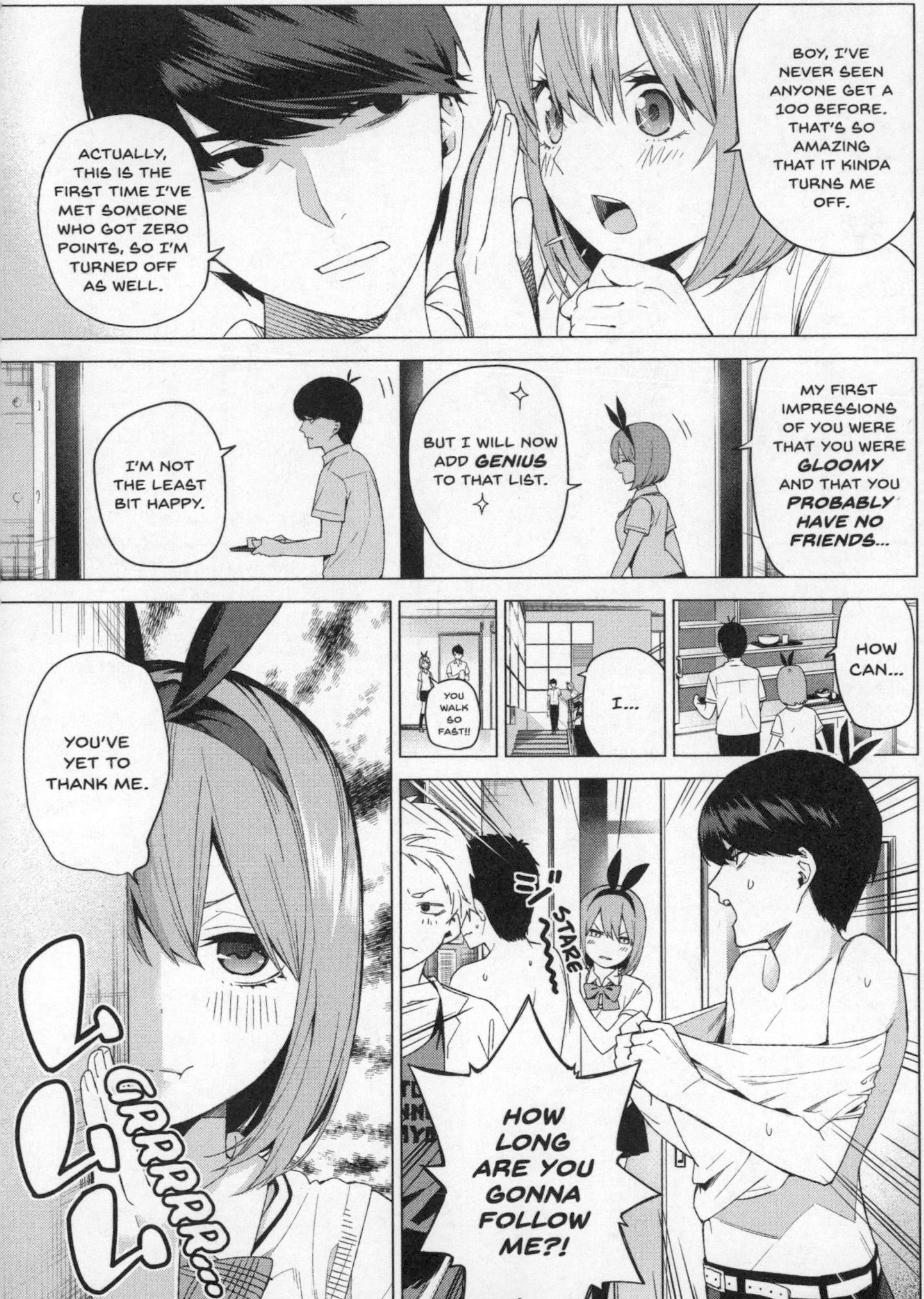
BOY, I'VE NEVER SEEN ANYONE GET A 100 BEFORE. THAT'S SO AMAZING THAT IT KINDA TURNS ME OFF.
ACTUALLY, THIS IS THE FIRST TIME I'VE MET SOMEONE WHO GOT ZERO POINTS, SO I'M TURNED OFF AS WELL.
MY FIRST IMPRESSIONS OF YOU WERE THAT YOU WERE GLOOMY AND THAT YOU PROBABLY HAVE NO FRIENDS...
BUT I WILL NOW ADD GENIUS TO THAT LIST.
I'M NOT THE LEAST BIT HAPPY.
HOW CAN...
I...
YOU WALK SO FAST!!
STARE
HOW LONG ARE YOU GONNA FOLLOW ME?!
YOU'VE YET TO THANK ME.
GRRRR...

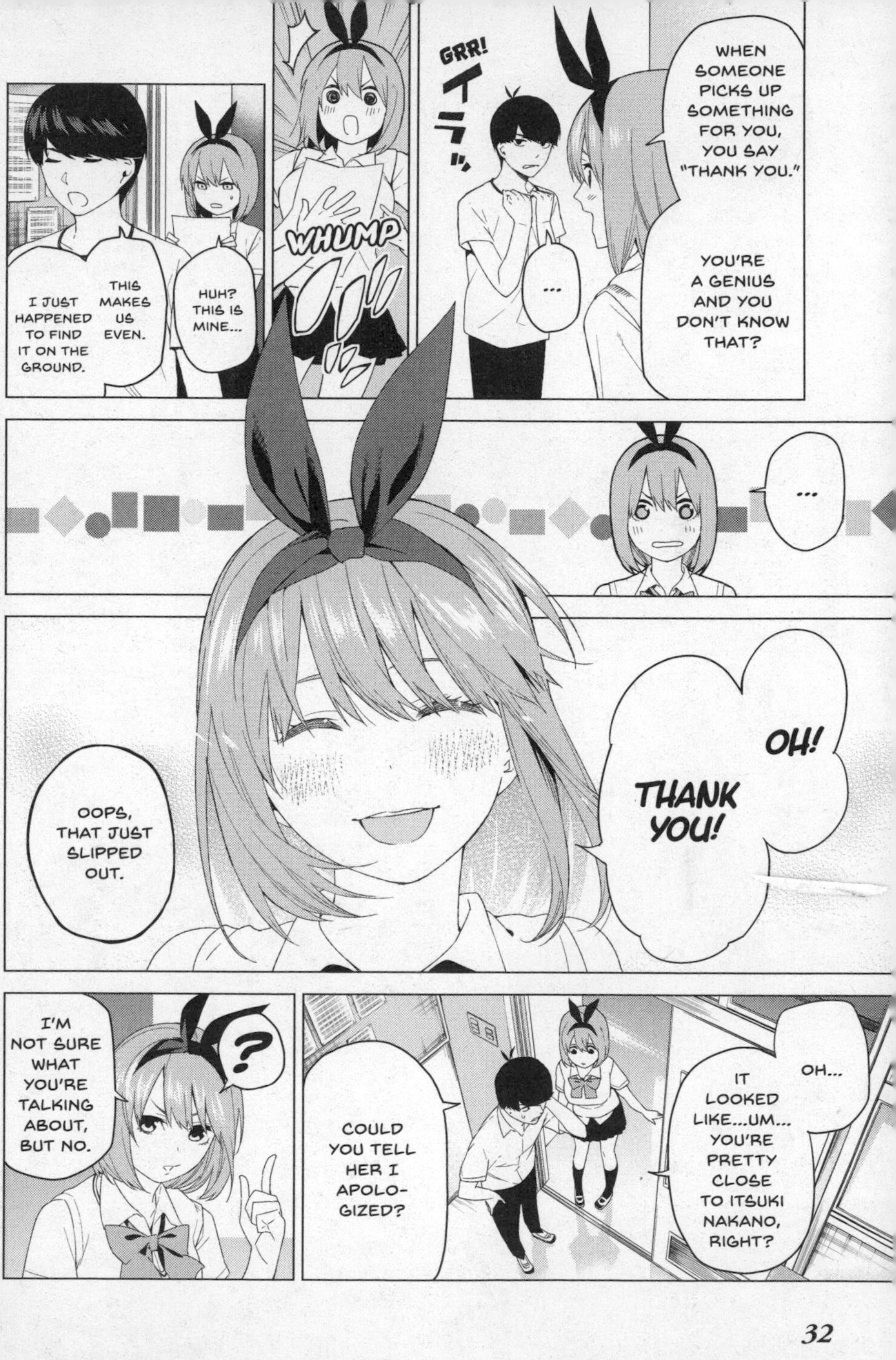
WHEN SOMEONE PICKS UP SOMETHING FOR YOU, YOU SAY "THANK YOU."
GRR!
YOU'RE A GENIUS AND YOU DON'T KNOW THAT?
...
WHUMP
HUH? THIS IS MINE...
THIS MAKES US EVEN.
I JUST HAPPENED TO FIND IT ON THE GROUND.
...
OH! THANK YOU!
OOPS, THAT JUST SLIPPED OUT.
OH...
IT LOOKED LIKE...UM... YOU'RE PRETTY CLOSE TO ITSUKI NAKANO, RIGHT?
COULD YOU TELL HER I APOLOGIZED?
?
I'M NOT SURE WHAT YOU'RE TALKING ABOUT, BUT NO.

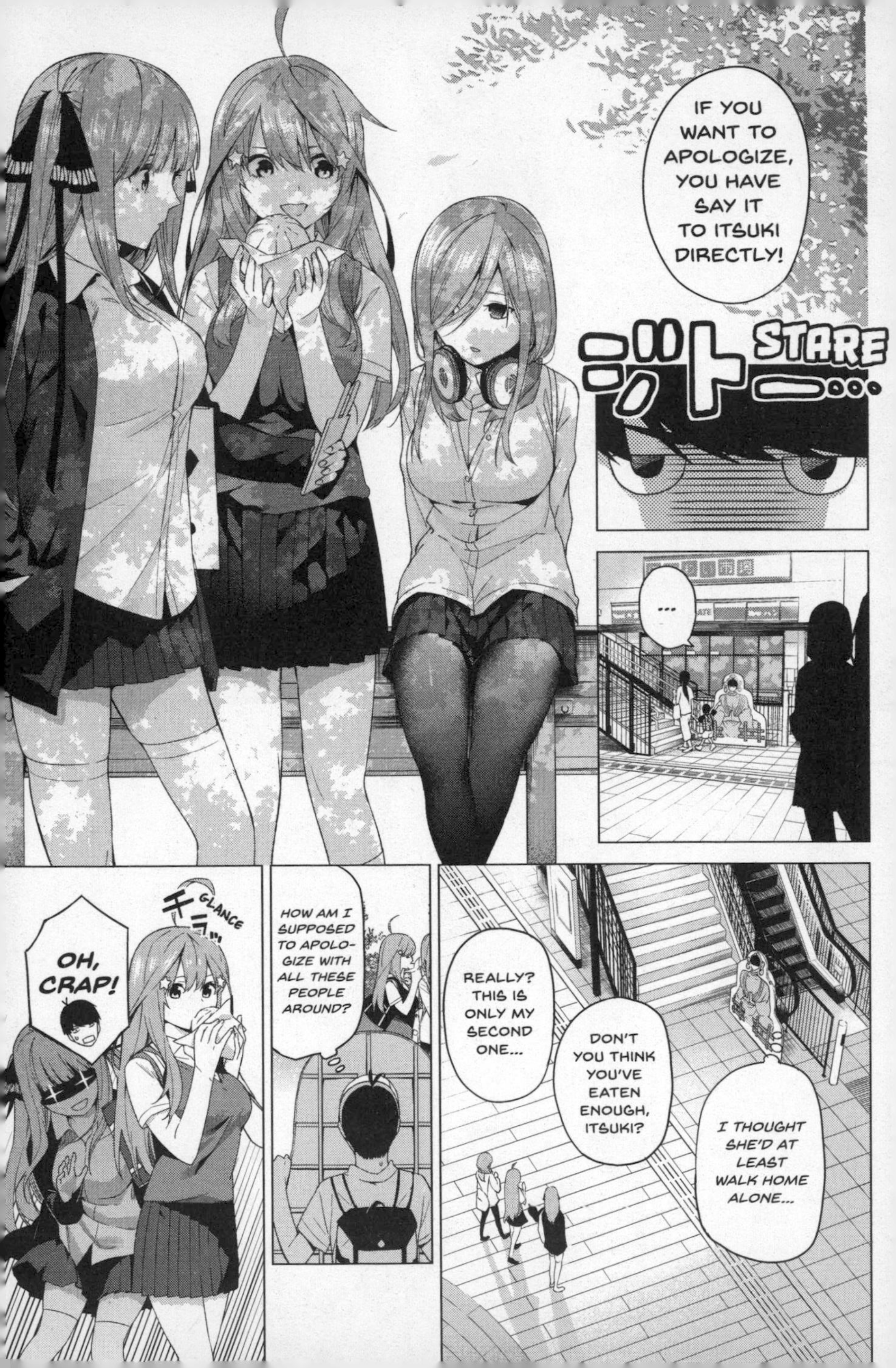
IF YOU WANT TO APOLOGIZE, YOU HAVE SAY IT TO ITSUKI DIRECTLY!
STARE
...
I THOUGHT SHE'D AT LEAST WALK HOME ALONE...
DON'T YOU THINK YOU'VE EATEN ENOUGH, ITSUKI?
REALLY? THIS IS ONLY MY SECOND ONE...
HOW AM I SUPPOSED TO APOLOGIZE WITH ALL THESE PEOPLE AROUND?
GLANCE
OH, CRAP!

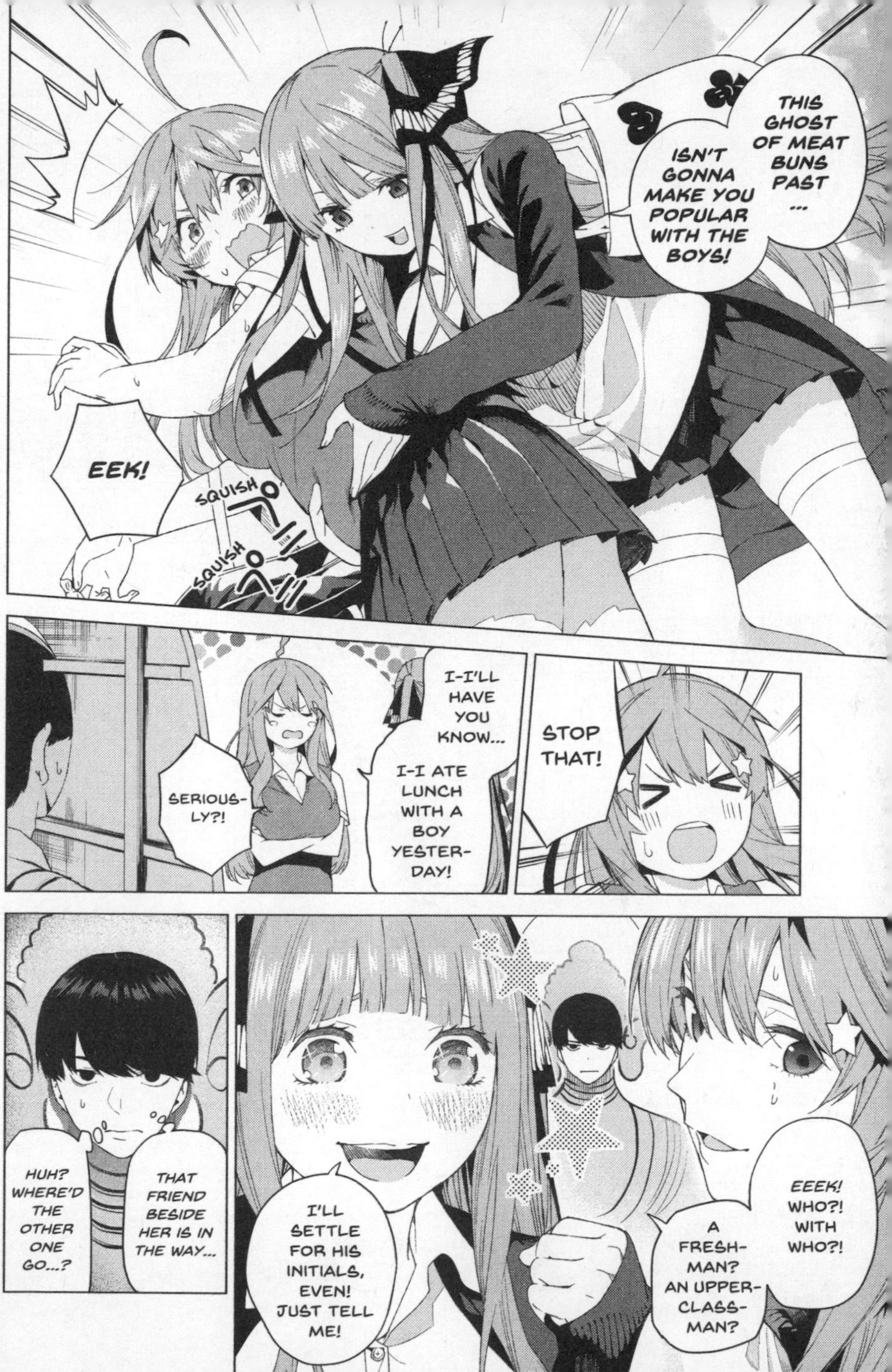

THIS GHOST OF MEAT BUNS PAST ...
ISN'T GONNA MAKE YOU POPULAR WITH THE BOYS!
EEK!
SQUISH
SQUISH
STOP THAT!
I-I'LL HAVE YOU KNOW...
I-I ATE LUNCH WITH A BOY YESTERDAY!
SERIOUSLY?!
EEEK! WHO?! WITH WHO?!
A FRESHMAN? AN UPPERCLASSMAN?
I'LL SETTLE FOR HIS INITIALS, EVEN! JUST TELL ME!
THAT FRIEND BESIDE HER IS IN THE WAY...
HUH? WHERE'D THE OTHER ONE GO...?

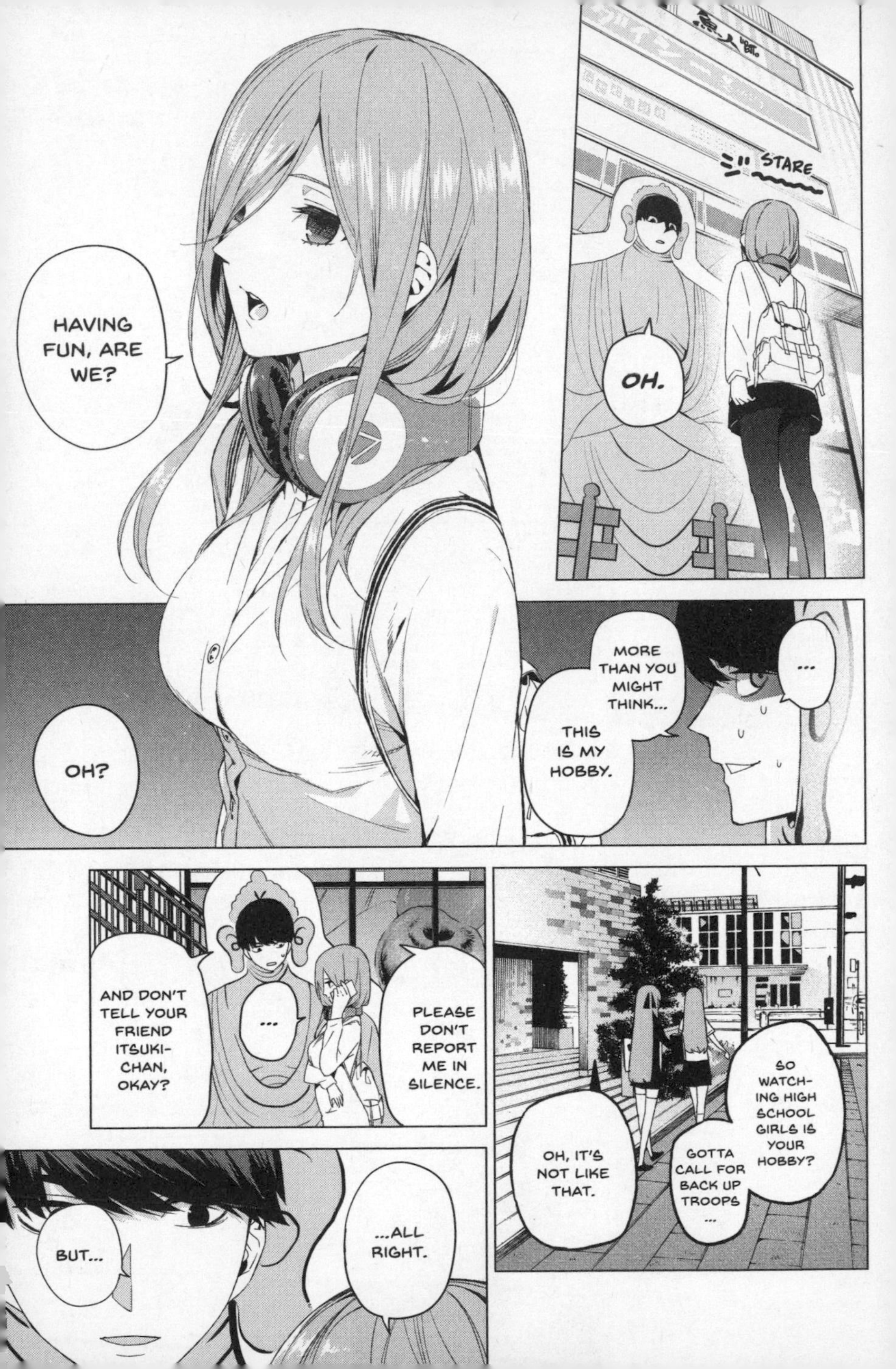
STARE
OH.
HAVING FUN, ARE WE?
...
MORE THAN YOU MIGHT THINK...
THIS IS MY HOBBY.
OH?
SO WATCHING HIGH SCHOOL GIRLS IS YOUR HOBBY?
GOTTA CALL FOR BACK UP TROOPS...
OH, IT'S NOT LIKE THAT.
PLEASE DON'T REPORT ME IN SILENCE.
...
AND DON'T TELL YOUR FRIEND ITSUKI-CHAN, OKAY?
...ALL RIGHT.
BUT...

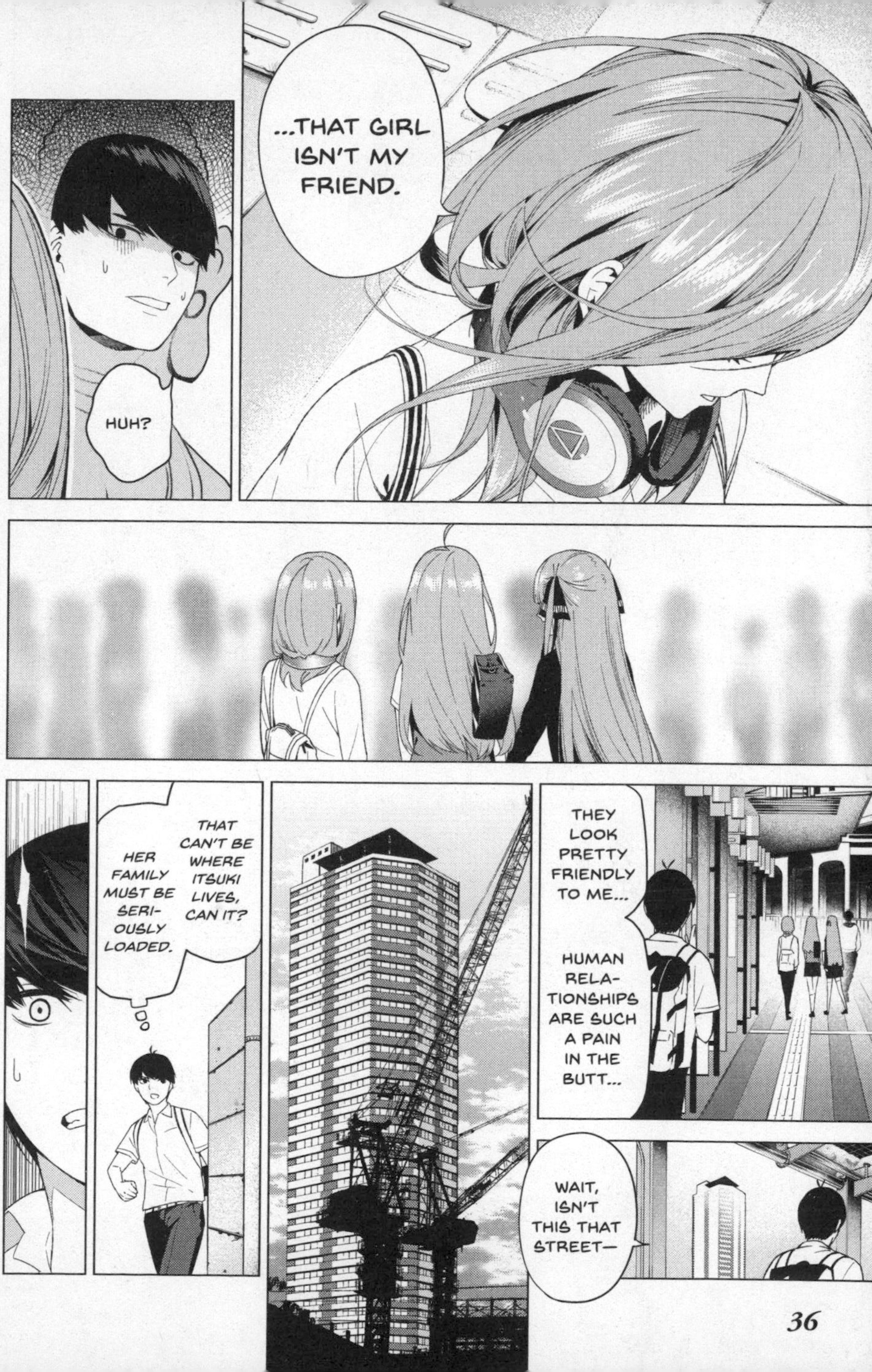
...THAT GIRL ISN'T MY FRIEND.
HUH?
THEY LOOK PRETTY FRIENDLY TO ME...
HUMAN RELATIONSHIPS ARE SUCH A PAIN IN THE BUTT...
WAIT, ISN'T THIS THAT STREET—
THAT CAN'T BE WHERE ITSUKI LIVES, CAN IT?
HER FAMILY MUST BE SERIOUSLY LOADED.

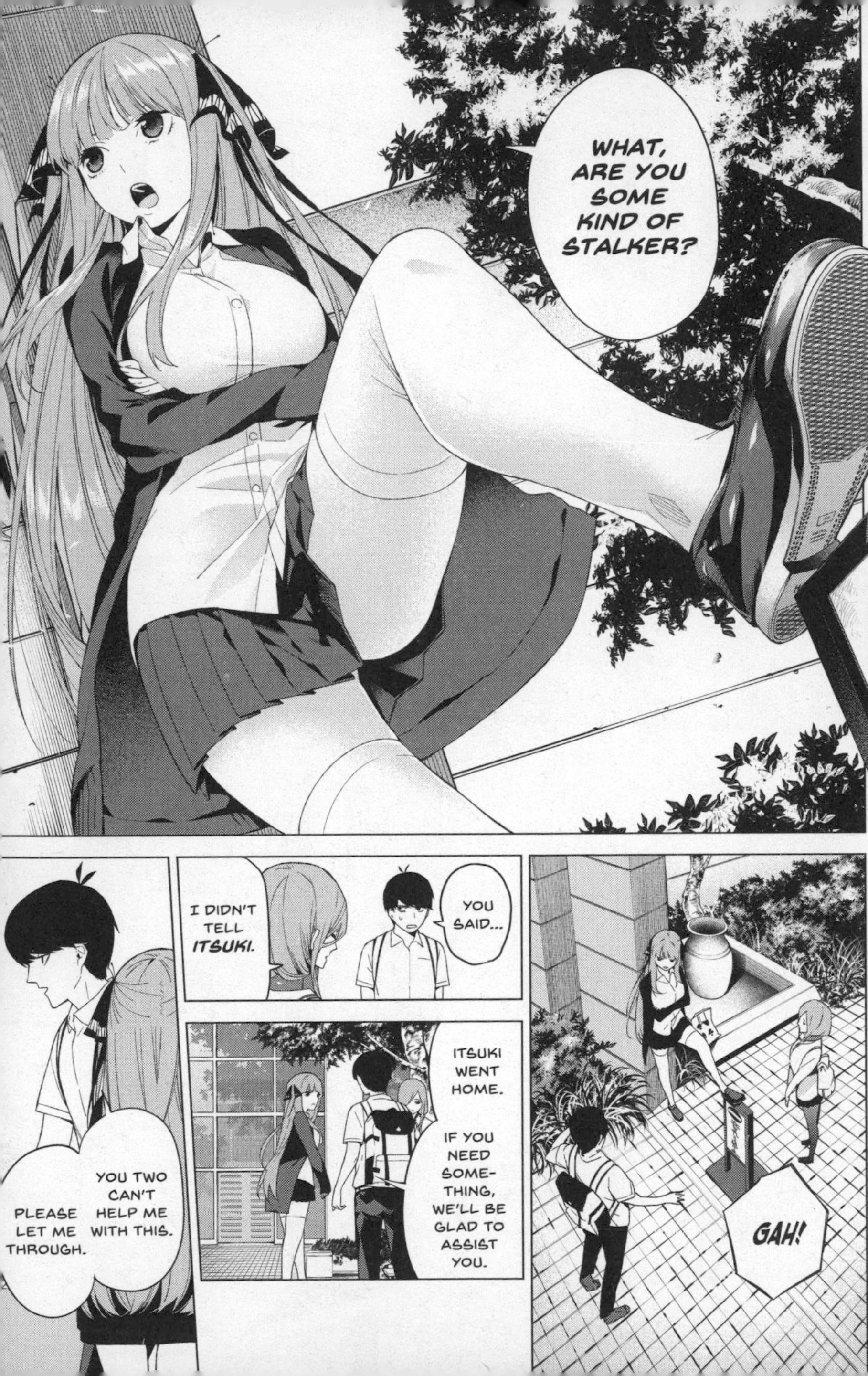
WHAT, ARE YOU SOME KIND OF STALKER?
GAH!
YOU SAID...
I DIDN'T TELL ITSUKI.
ITSUKI WENT HOME.
IF YOU NEED SOME-THING, WE'LL BE GLAD TO ASSIST YOU.
YOU TWO CAN'T HELP ME WITH THIS.
PLEASE LET ME THROUGH.

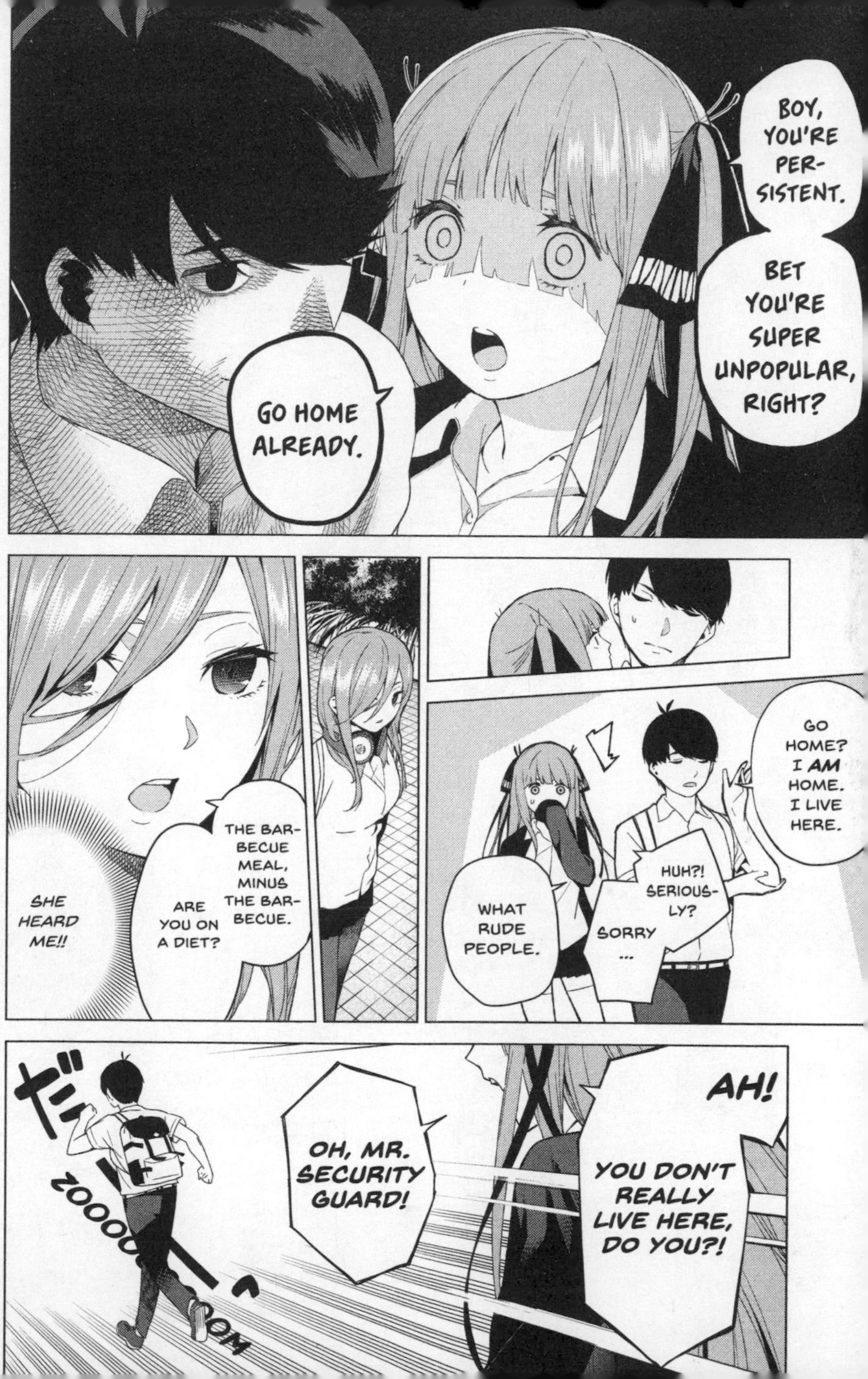
BOY, YOU'RE PER-SISTENT.
BET YOU'RE SUPER UNPOPULAR, RIGHT?
GO HOME ALREADY.
GO HOME? I *AM* HOME. I LIVE HERE.
HUH?! SERIOUS-LY?
SORRY ...
WHAT RUDE PEOPLE.
THE BAR-BECUE MEAL, MINUS THE BAR-BECUE.
ARE YOU ON A DIET?
SHE HEARD ME!!
AH!
YOU DON'T REALLY LIVE HERE, DO YOU?!
OH, MR. SECURITY GUARD!

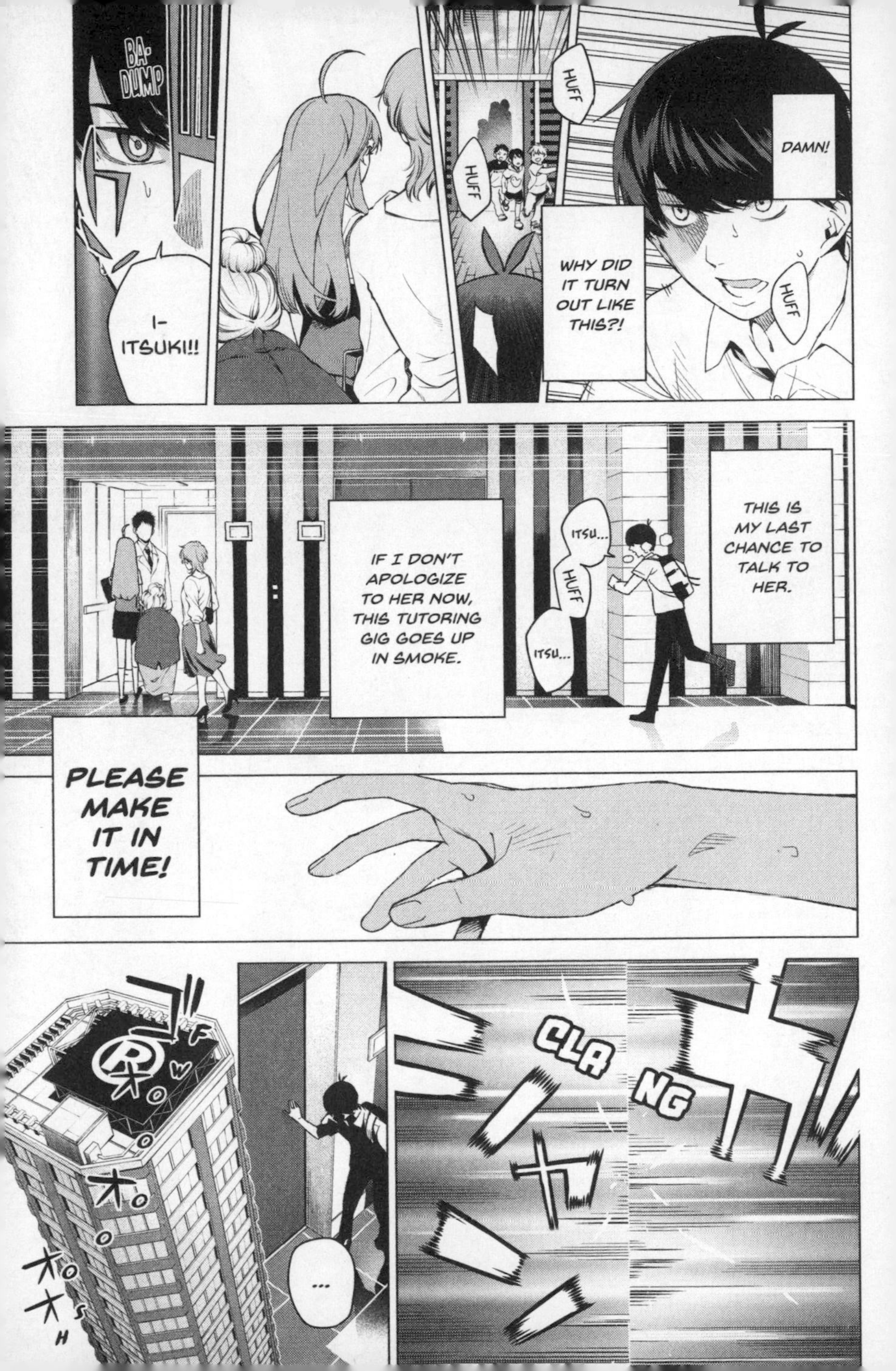
DAMN!
HUFF
HUFF
HUFF
WHY DID IT TURN OUT LIKE THIS?!
BA-DUMP
I- ITSUKI!!
THIS IS MY LAST CHANCE TO TALK TO HER.
ITSU...
HUFF
ITSU...
IF I DON'T APOLOGIZE TO HER NOW, THIS TUTORING GIG GOES UP IN SMOKE.
PLEASE MAKE IT IN TIME!
CLANG
...
WOOOOOSH

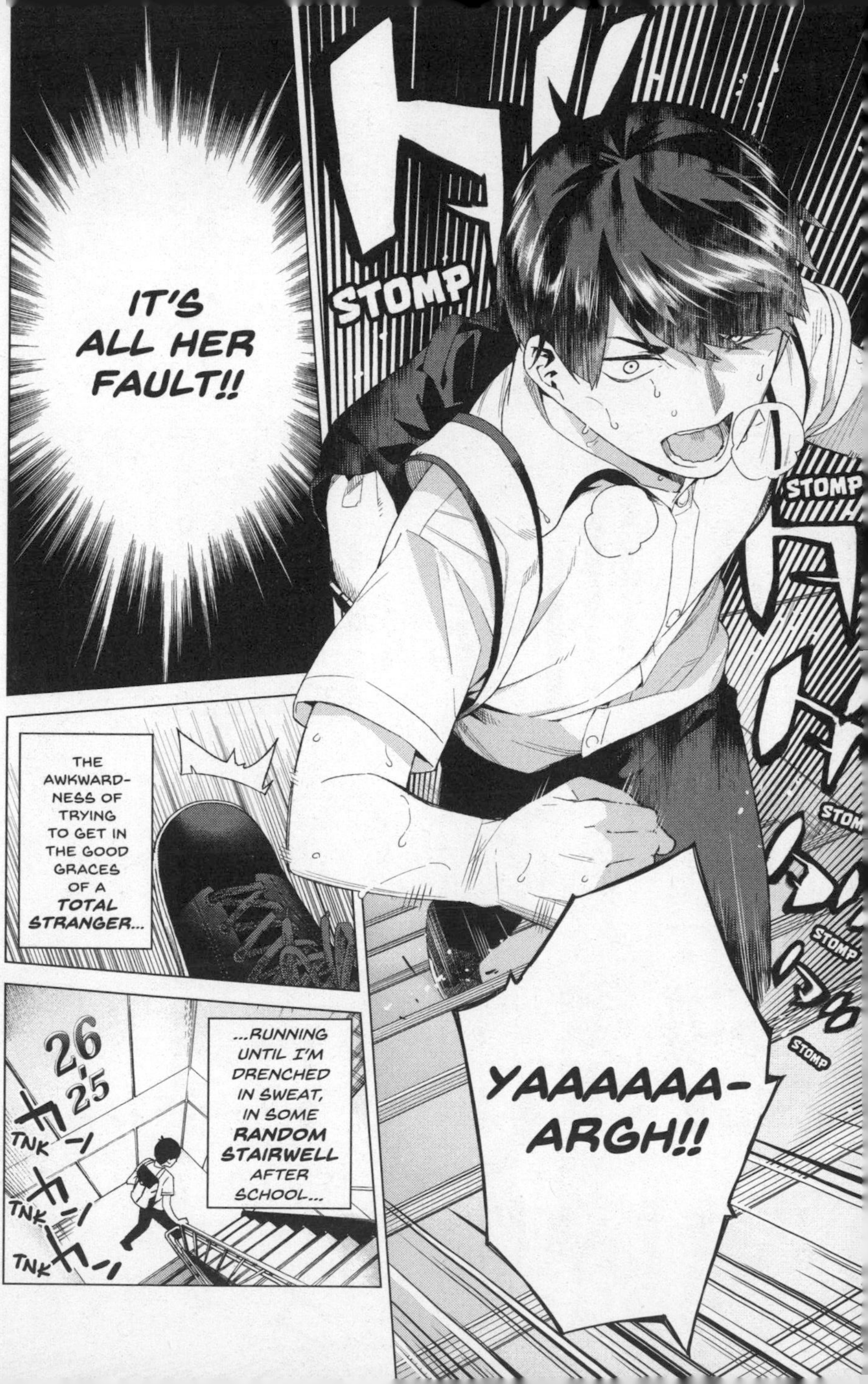
STOMP
STOMP
STOMP
STOMP
STOMP
YAAAAAA-ARGH!!
IT'S ALL HER FAULT!!
THE AWKWARD-NESS OF TRYING TO GET IN THE GOOD GRACES OF A TOTAL STRANGER...
...RUNNING UNTIL I'M DRENCHED IN SWEAT, IN SOME RANDOM STAIRWELL AFTER SCHOOL...
26
25
TNK
TNK
TNK

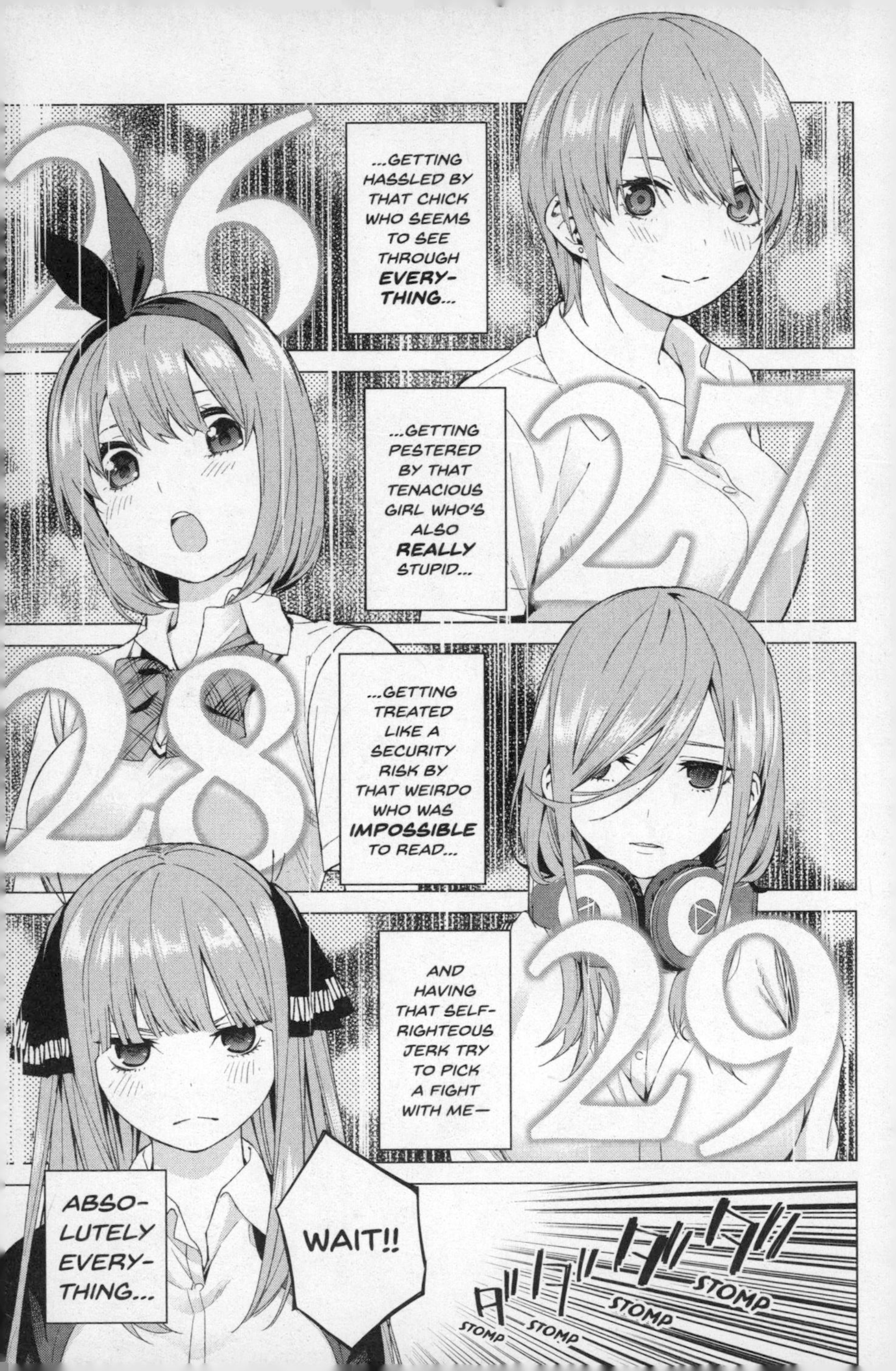

...GETTING HASSLED BY THAT CHICK WHO SEEMS TO SEE THROUGH **EVERYTHING**...
...GETTING PESTERED BY THAT TENACIOUS GIRL WHO'S ALSO **REALLY** STUPID...
...GETTING TREATED LIKE A SECURITY RISK BY THAT WEIRDO WHO WAS **IMPOSSIBLE** TO READ...
AND HAVING THAT SELF-RIGHTEOUS JERK TRY TO PICK A FIGHT WITH ME—
STOMP
STOMP
STOMP
STOMP
WAIT!!
ABSOLUTELY EVERYTHING...

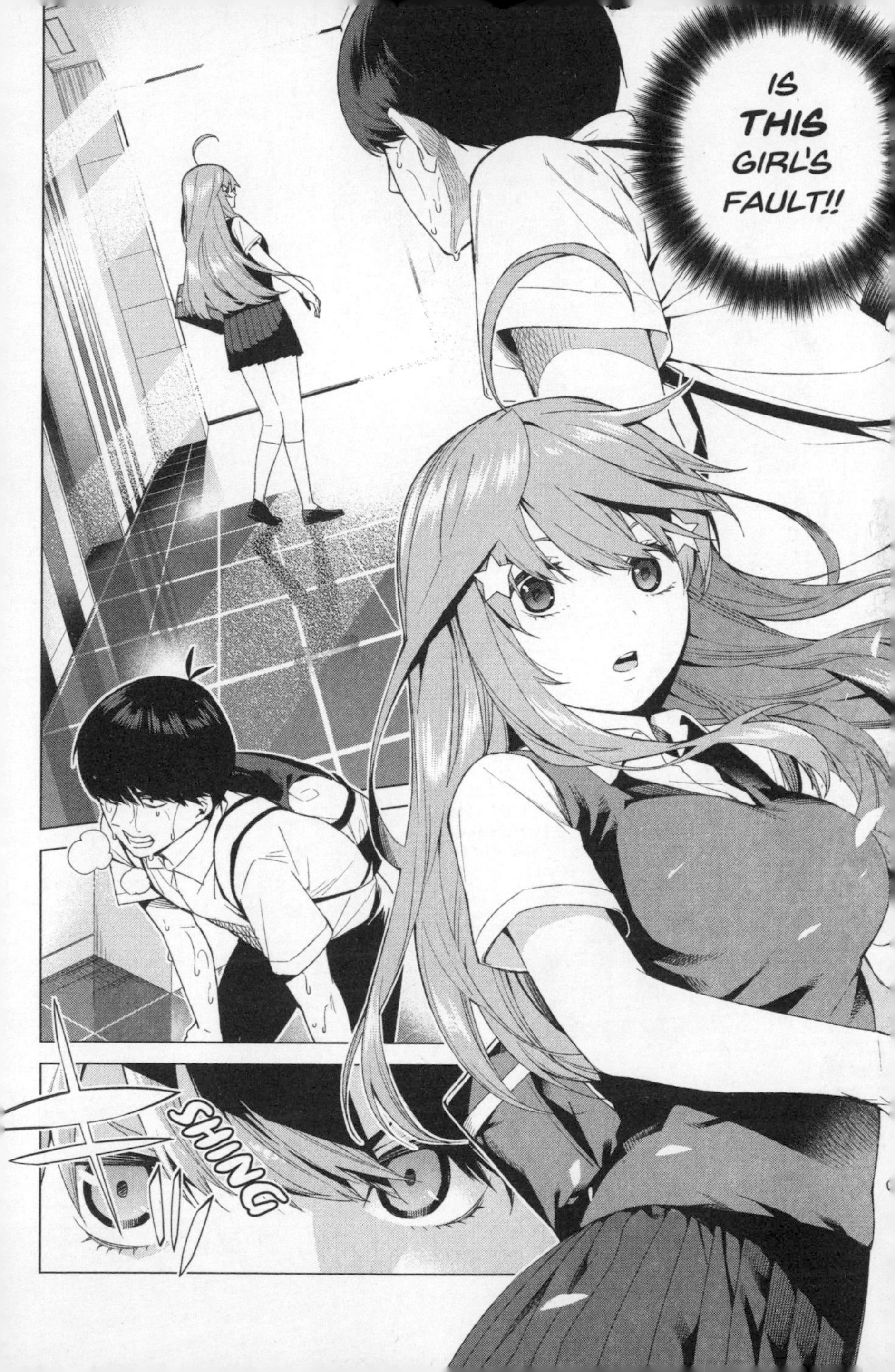
IS THIS GIRL'S FAULT!!
SHING

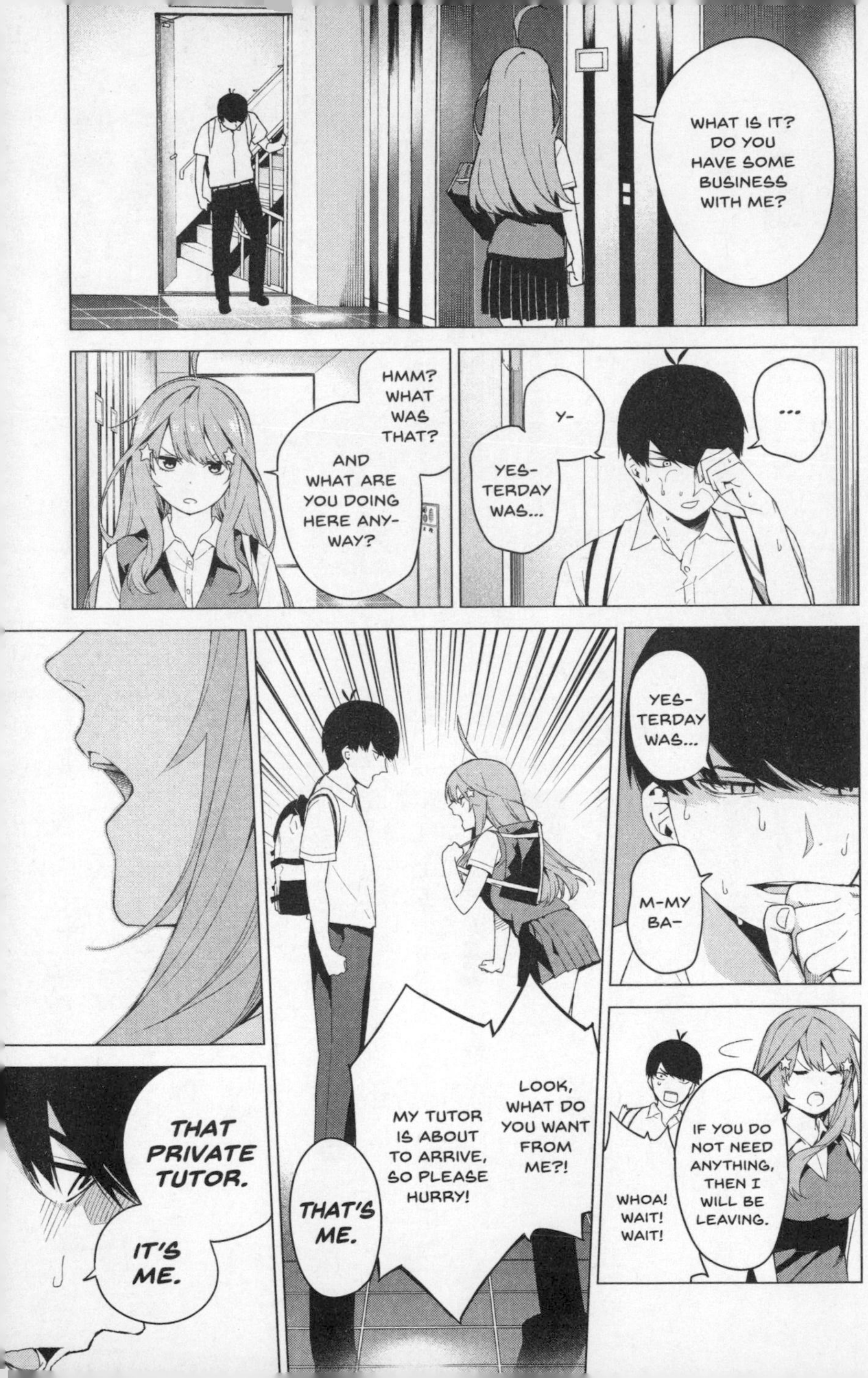
WHAT IS IT? DO YOU HAVE SOME BUSINESS WITH ME?
...
Y-
YES-TERDAY WAS...
HMM? WHAT WAS THAT?
AND WHAT ARE YOU DOING HERE ANY-WAY?
YES-TERDAY WAS...
M-MY BA-
IF YOU DO NOT NEED ANYTHING, THEN I WILL BE LEAVING.
WHOA! WAIT! WAIT!
LOOK, WHAT DO YOU WANT FROM ME?!
MY TUTOR IS ABOUT TO ARRIVE, SO PLEASE HURRY!
THAT'S ME.
THAT PRIVATE TUTOR.
IT'S ME.

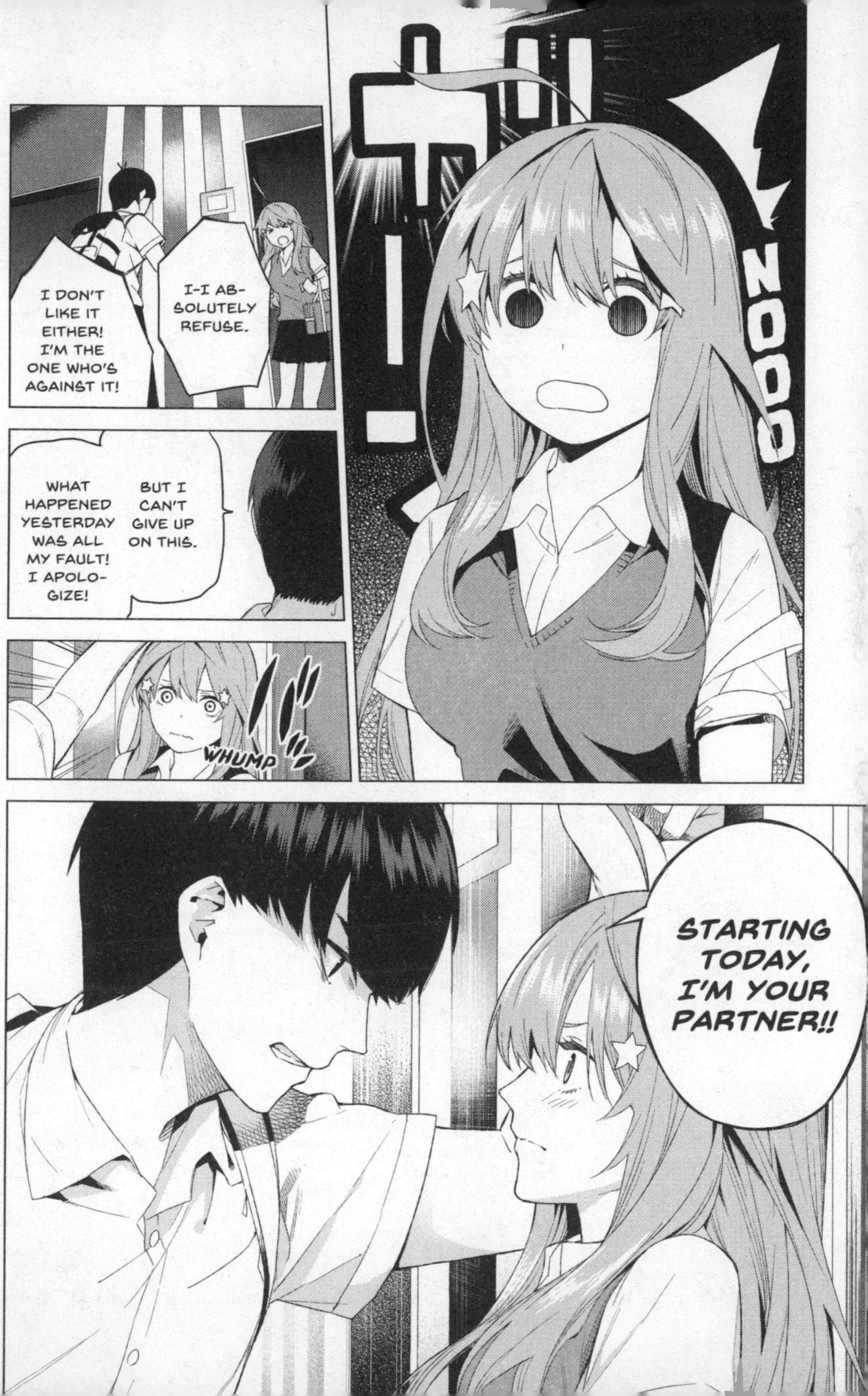
NOOO
I-I AB-SOLUTELY REFUSE.
I DON'T LIKE IT EITHER! I'M THE ONE WHO'S AGAINST IT!
BUT I CAN'T GIVE UP ON THIS.
WHAT HAPPENED YESTERDAY WAS ALL MY FAULT! I APOLOGIZE!
WHUMP
STARTING TODAY, I'M YOUR PARTNER!!

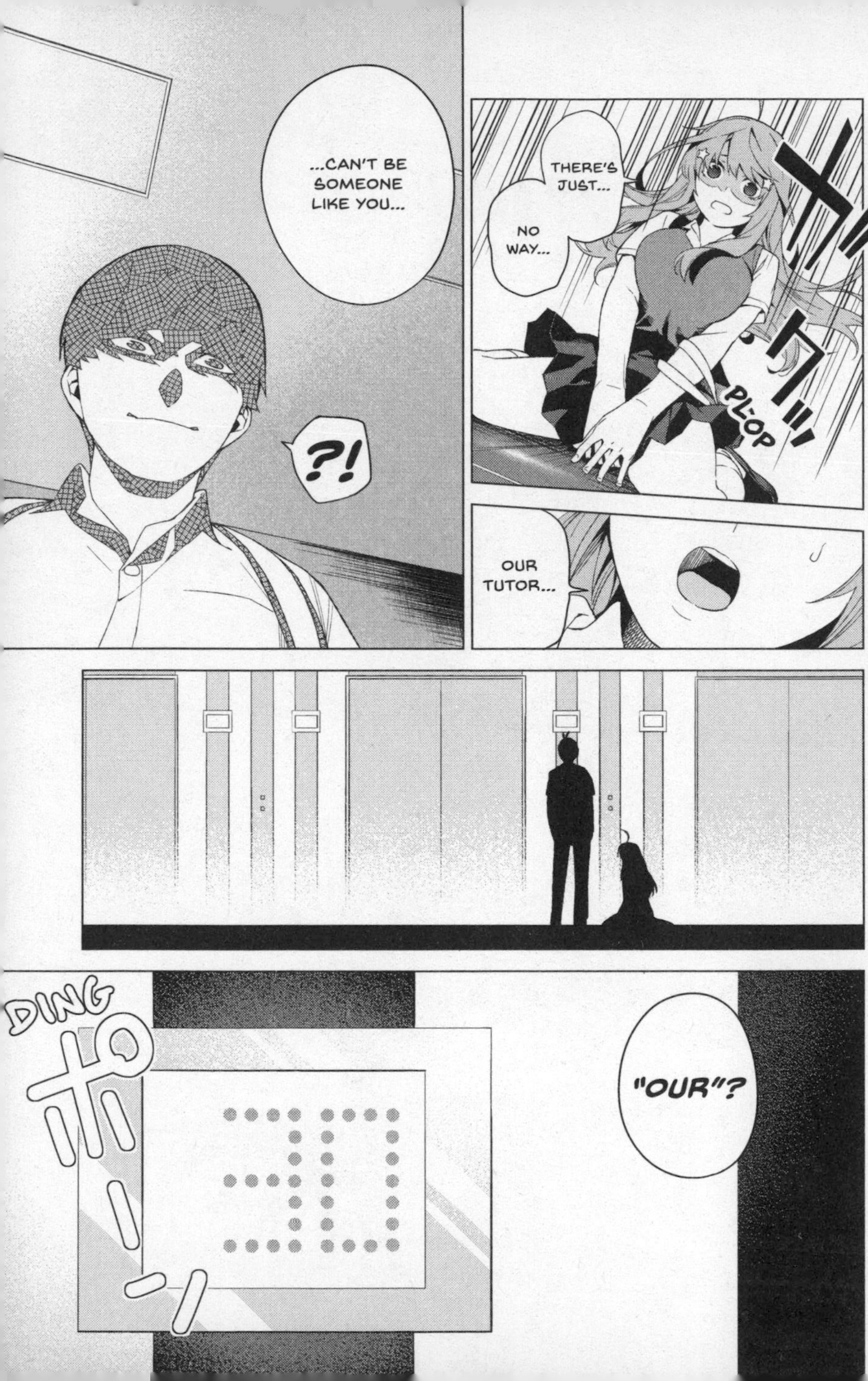
THERE'S JUST...
NO WAY...
PL-OP
OUR TUTOR...
...CAN'T BE SOMEONE LIKE YOU...
?!
"OUR"?
DING

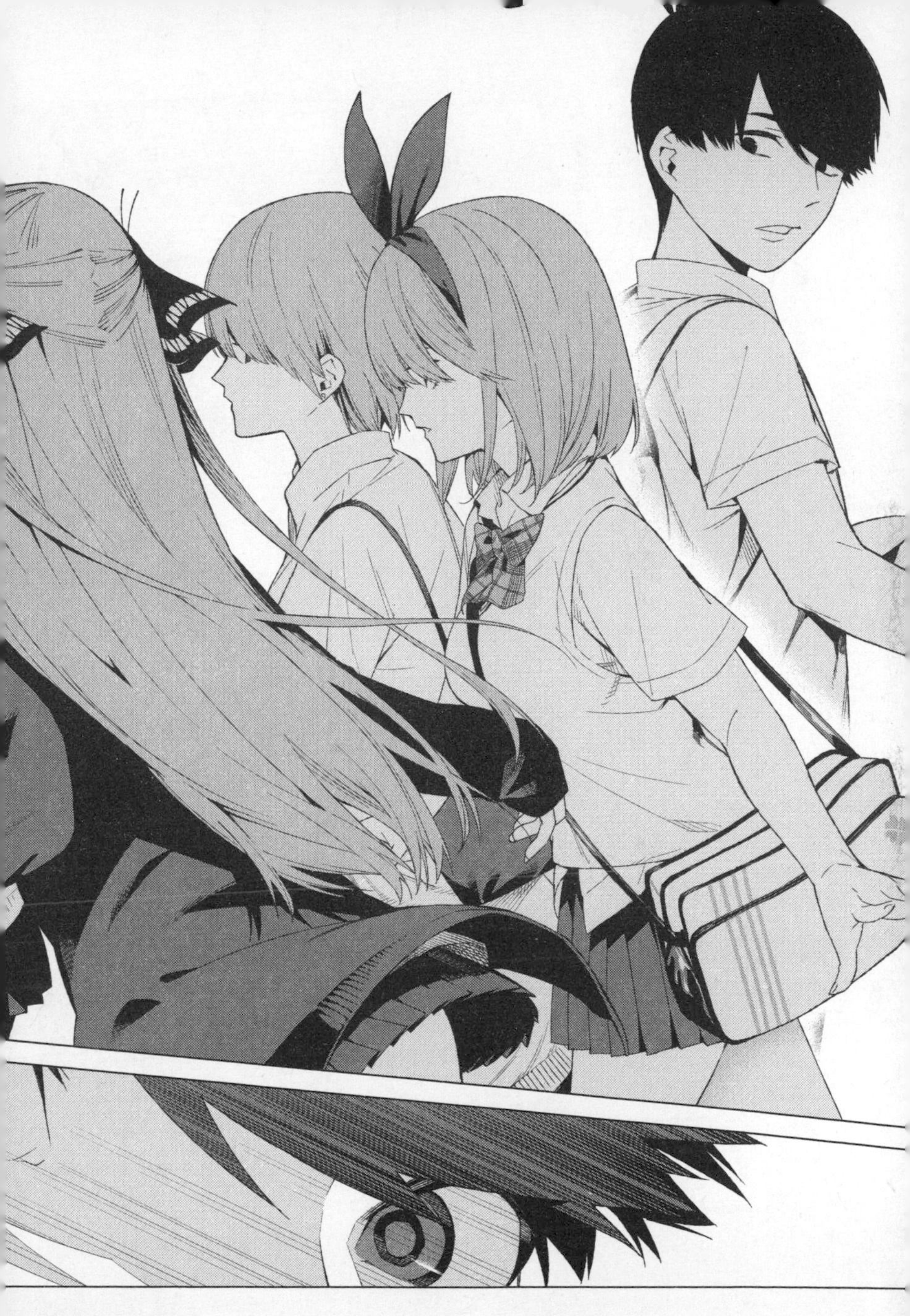

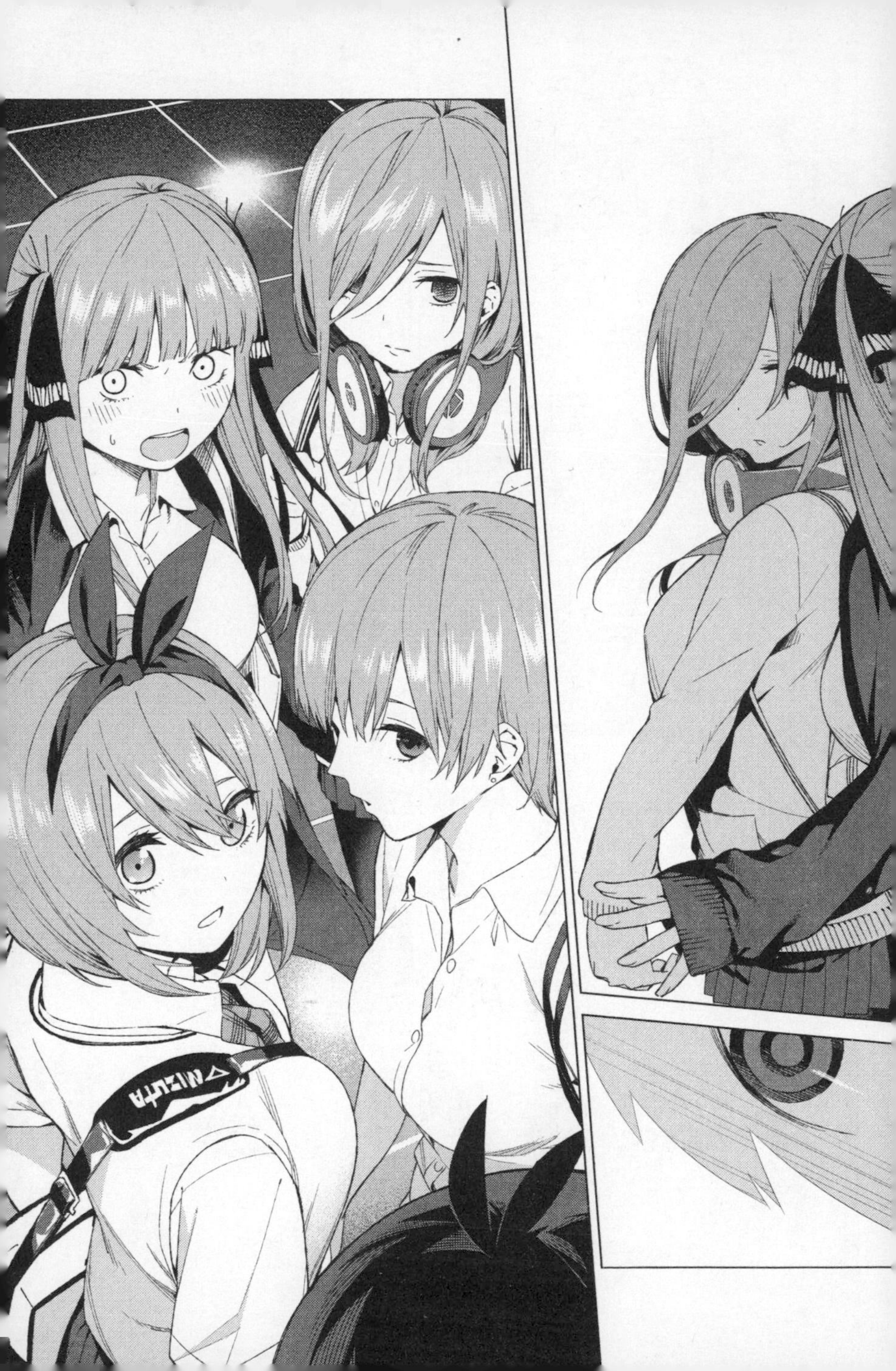

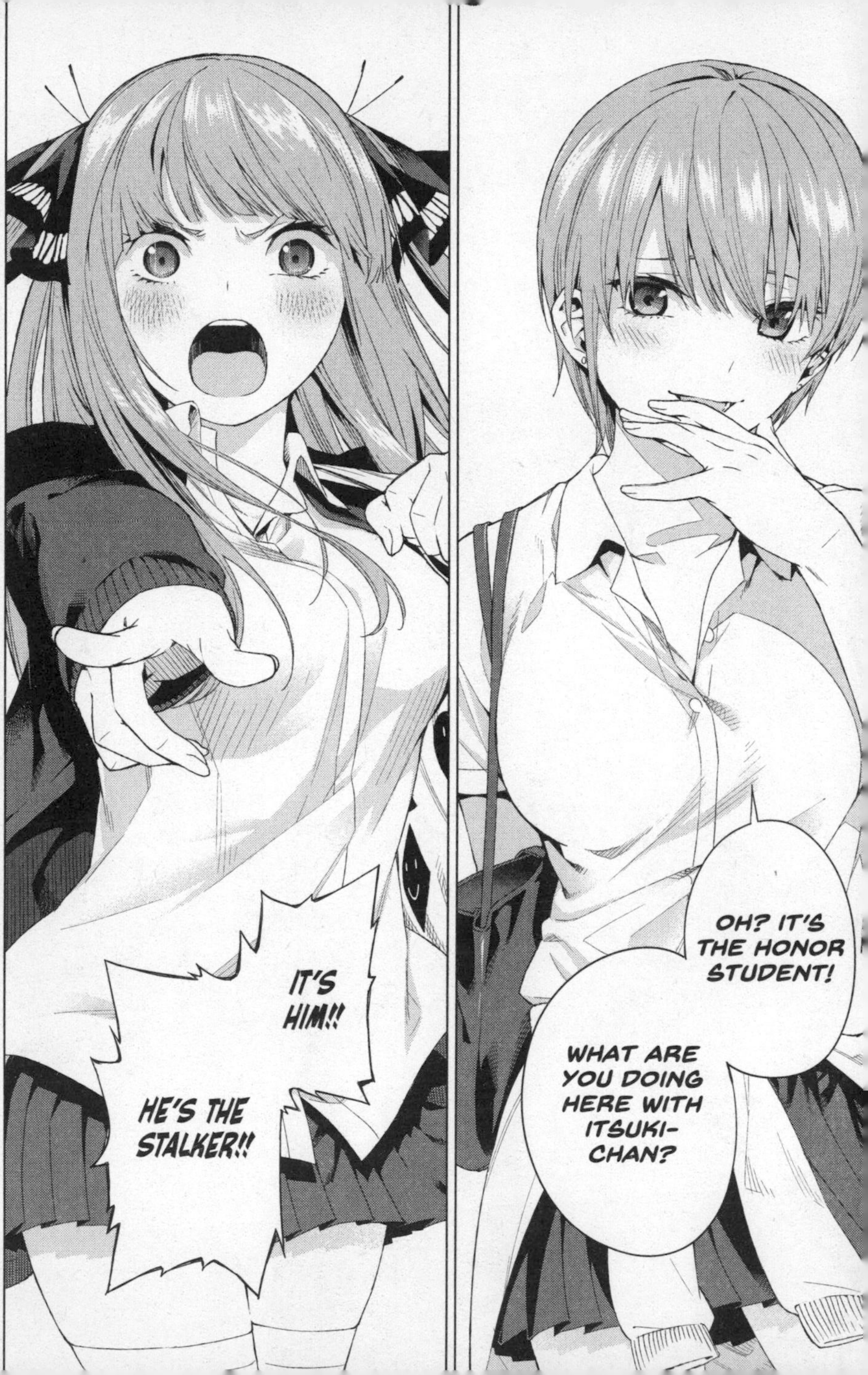
OH? IT'S THE HONOR STUDENT!
WHAT ARE YOU DOING HERE WITH ITSUKI-CHAN?
IT'S HIM!!
HE'S THE STALKER!!

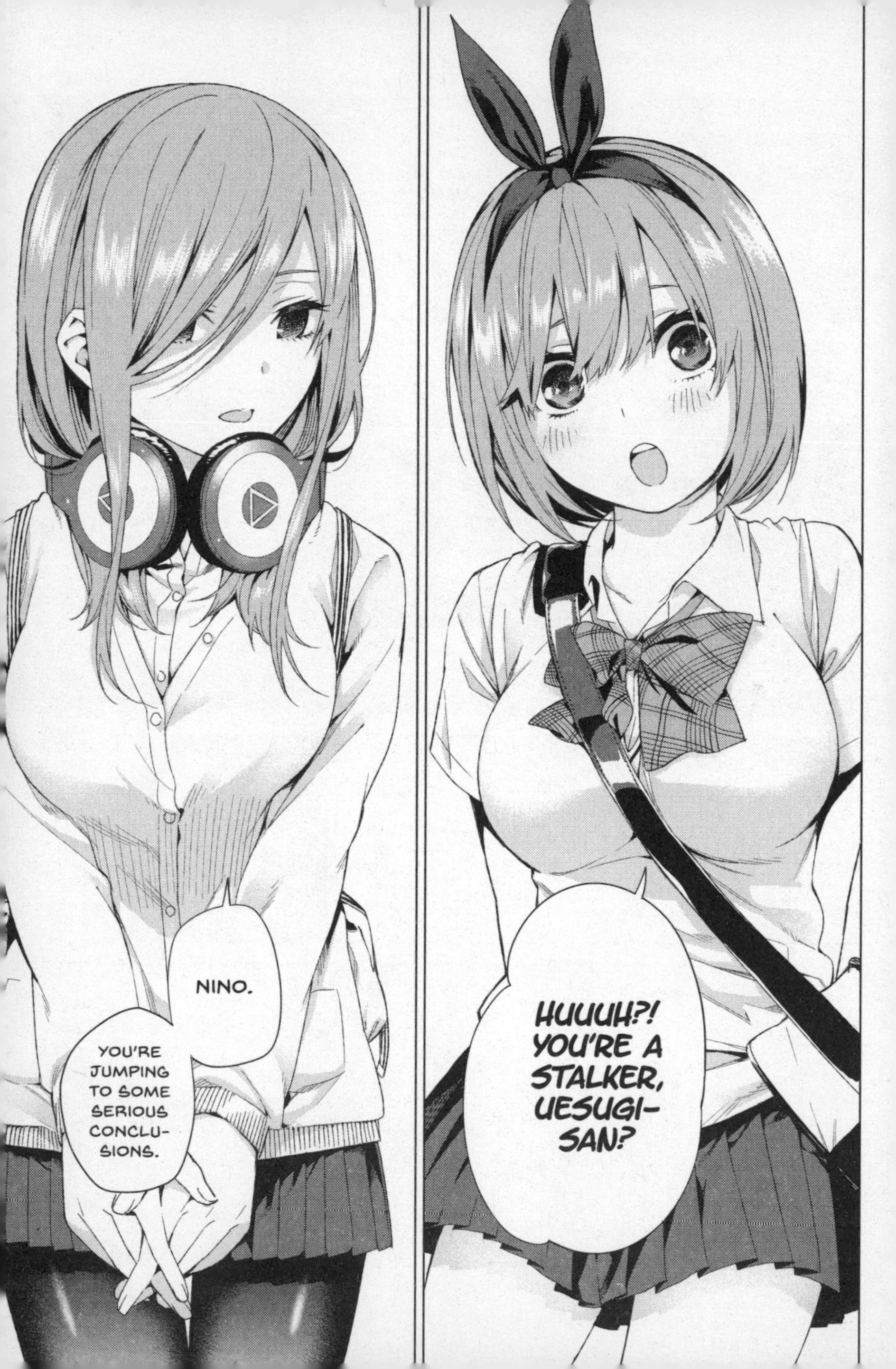
HUUUH?! YOU'RE A STALKER, UESUGI-SAN?
NINO.
YOU'RE JUMPING TO SOME SERIOUS CONCLUSIONS.

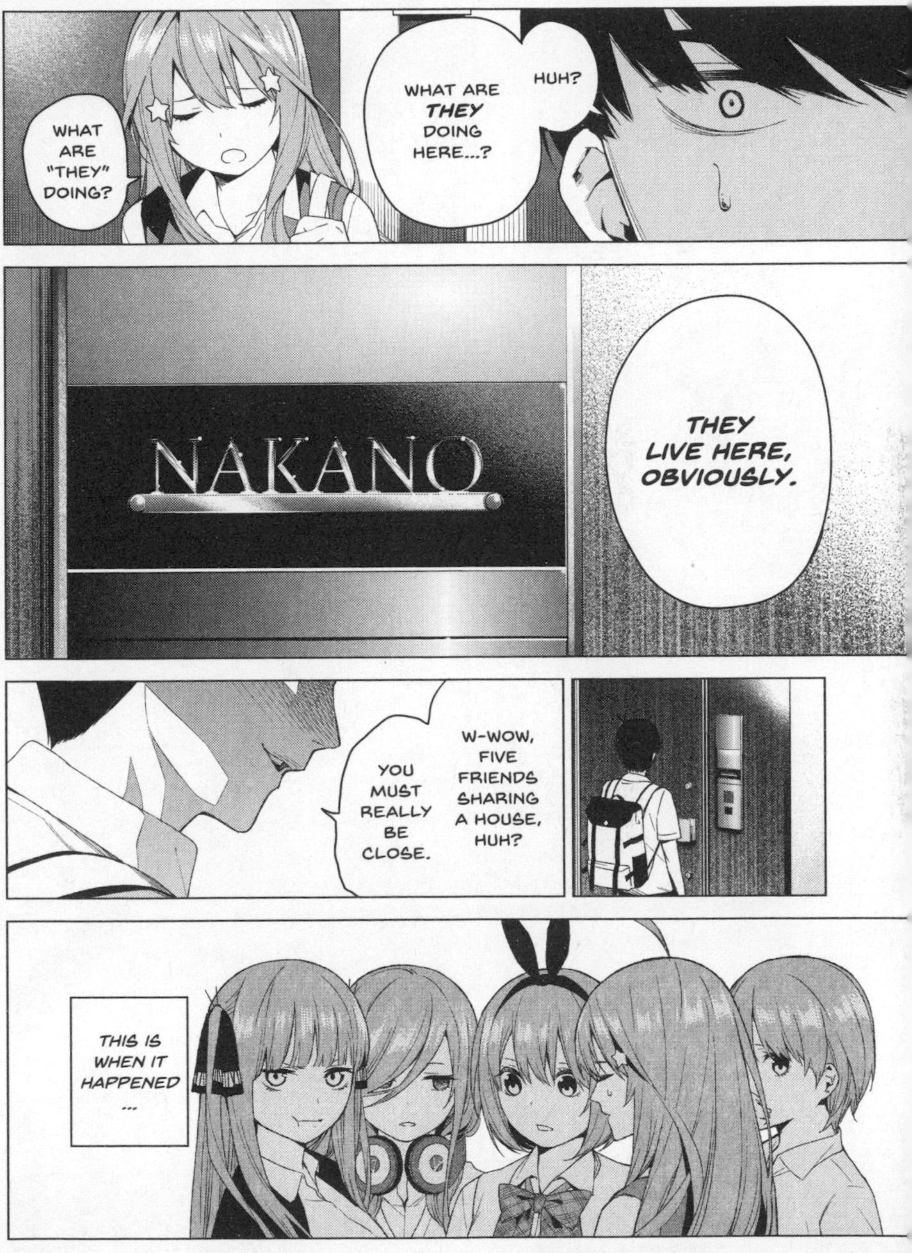
HUH?
WHAT ARE THEY DOING HERE...?
WHAT ARE "THEY" DOING?
THEY LIVE HERE, OBVIOUSLY.
NAKANO
W-WOW, FIVE FRIENDS SHARING A HOUSE, HUH?
YOU MUST REALLY BE CLOSE.
THIS IS WHEN IT HAPPENED ...

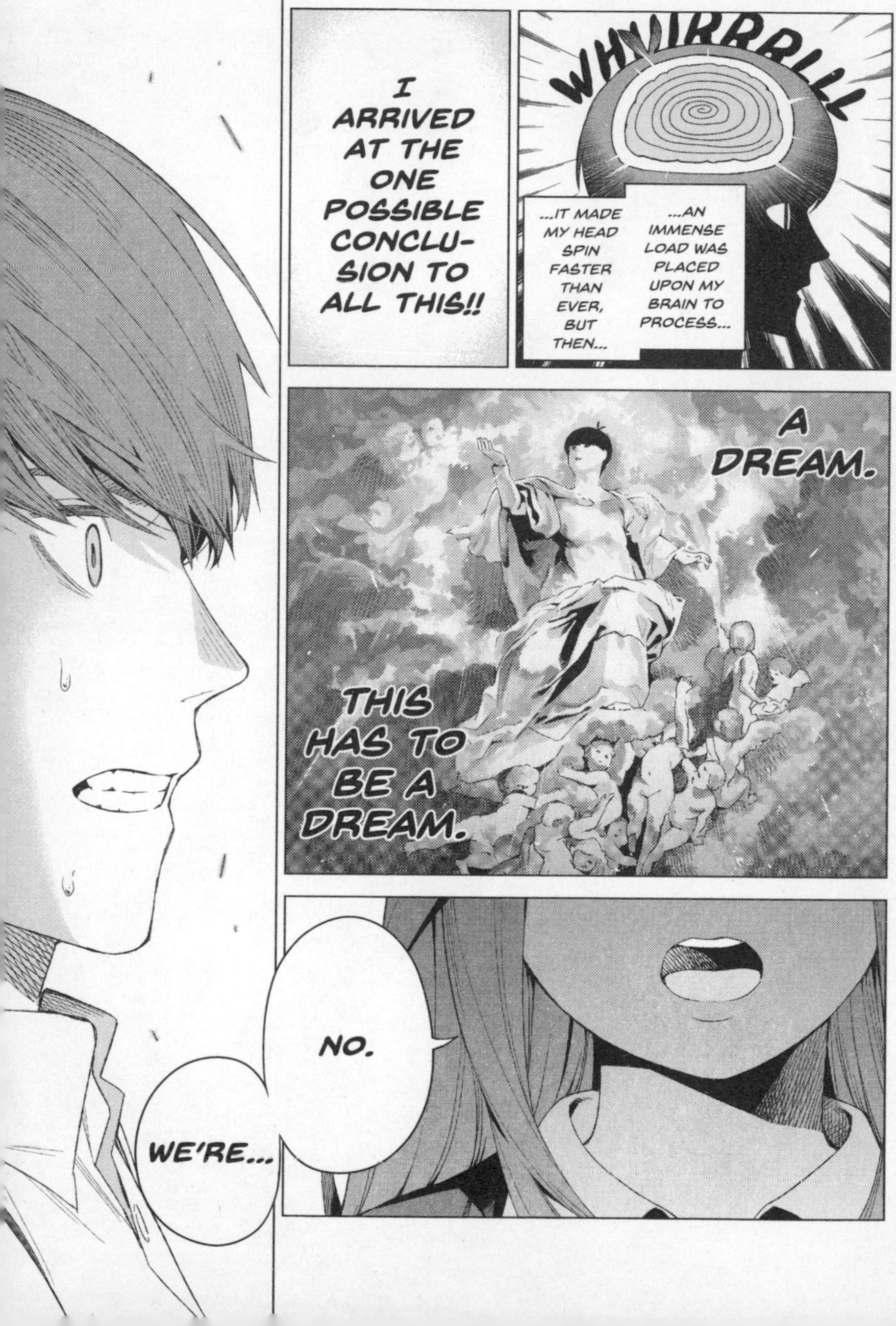
WHIRRRLLL
...AN IMMENSE LOAD WAS PLACED UPON MY BRAIN TO PROCESS...
...IT MADE MY HEAD SPIN FASTER THAN EVER, BUT THEN...
I ARRIVED AT THE ONE POSSIBLE CONCLUSION TO ALL THIS!!
A DREAM.
THIS HAS TO BE A DREAM.
NO.
WE'RE...

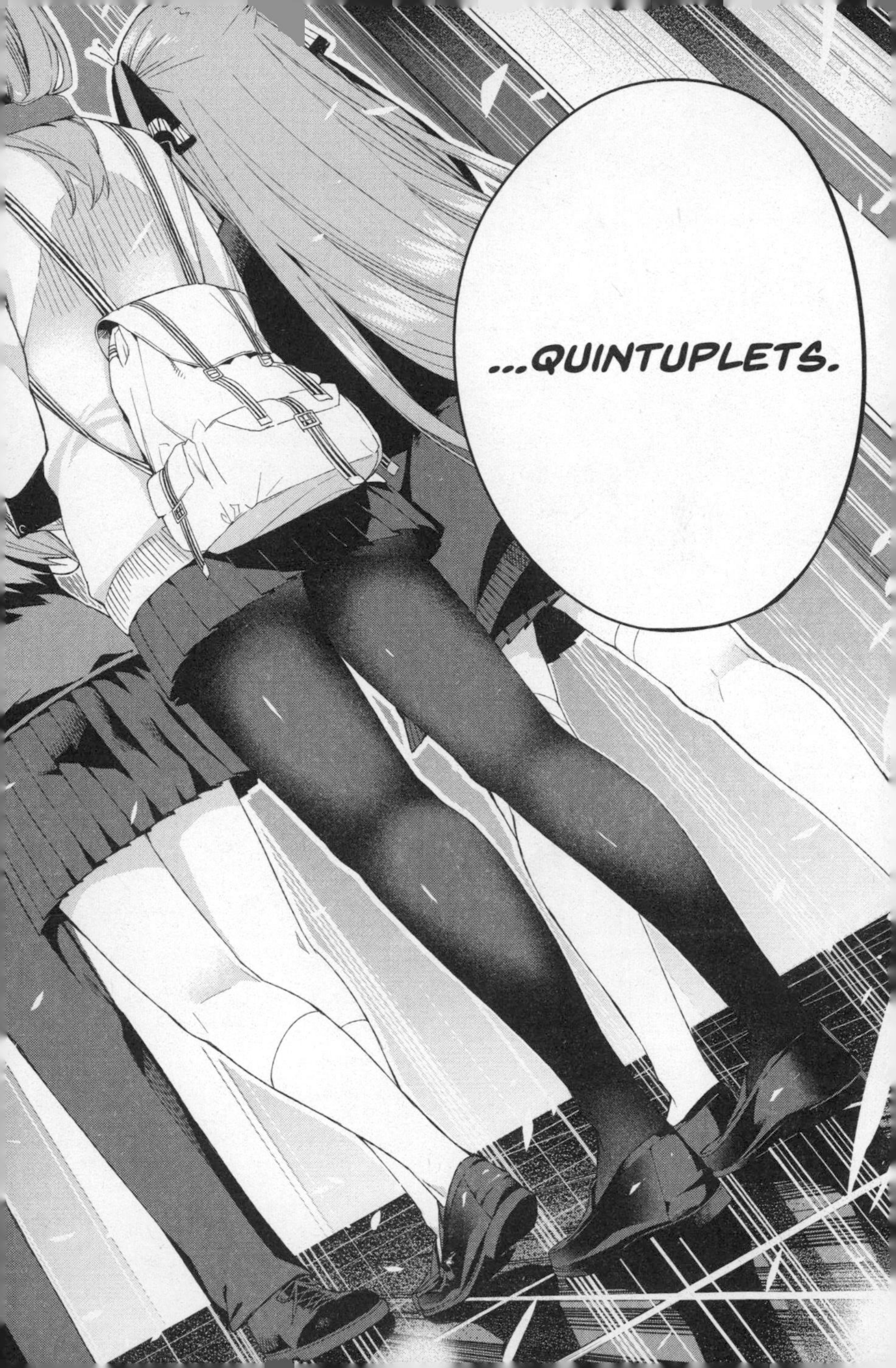
...QUINTUPLETS.

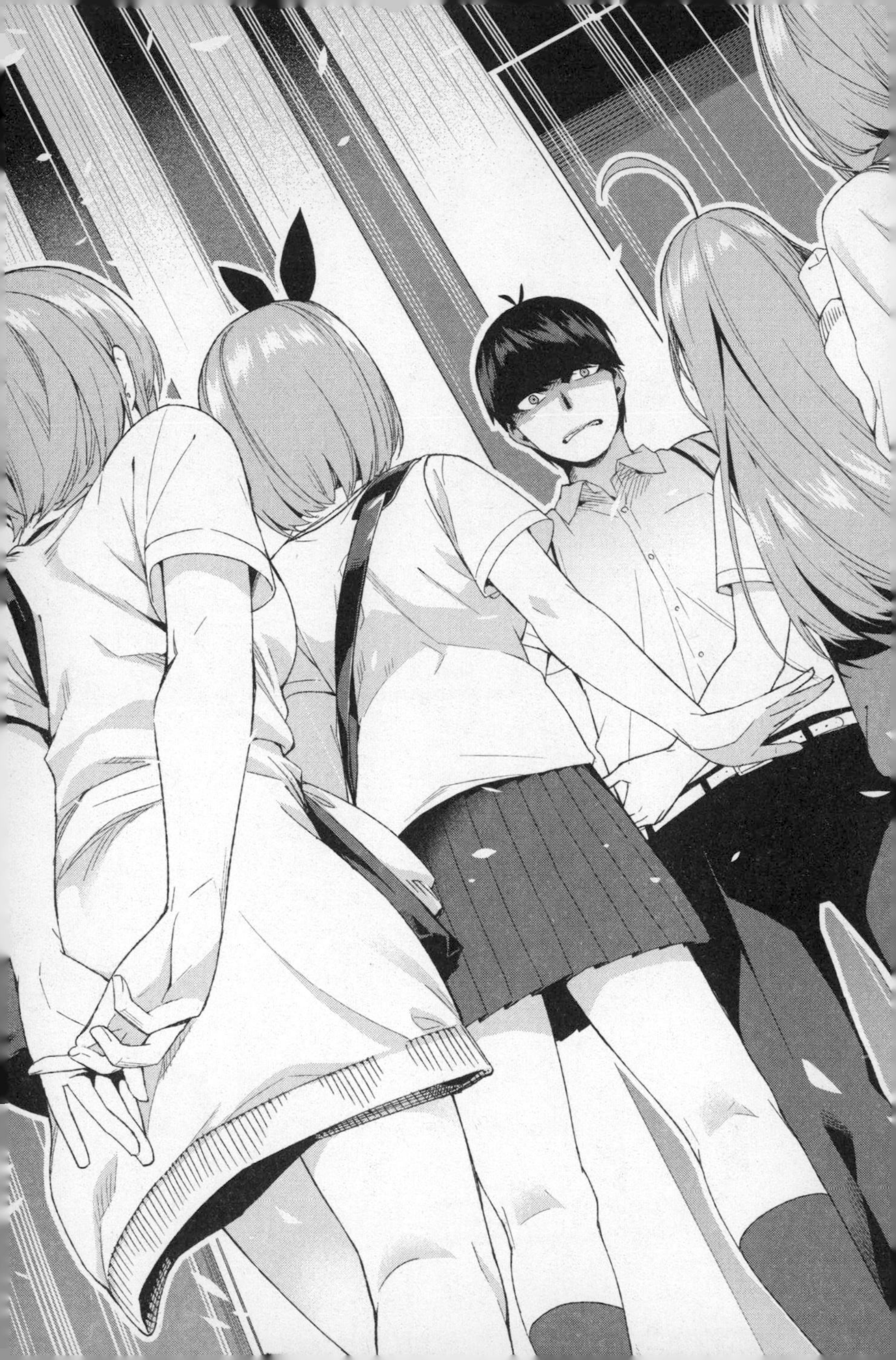

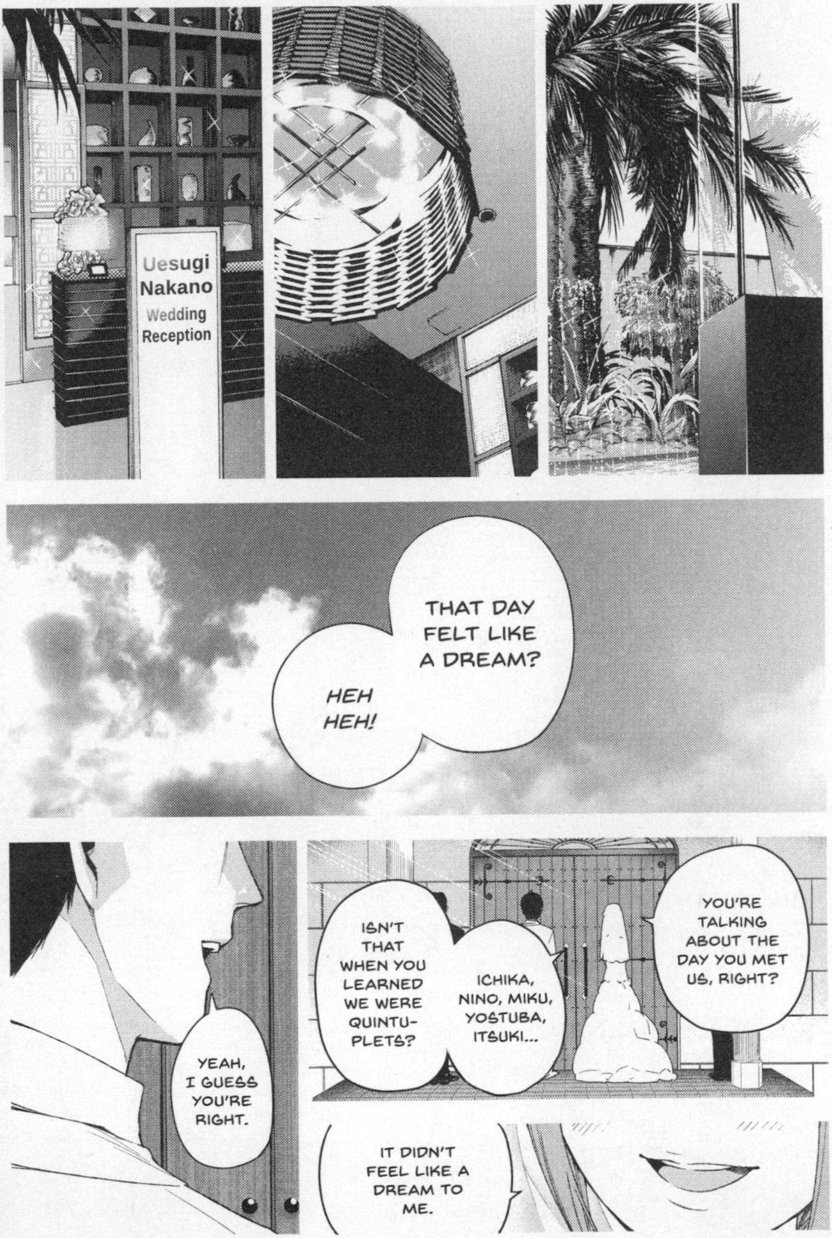
Uesugi Nakano Wedding Reception
THAT DAY FELT LIKE A DREAM?
HEH HEH!
YOU'RE TALKING ABOUT THE DAY YOU MET US, RIGHT?
ICHIKA, NINO, MIKU, YOSTUBA, ITSUKI...
ISN'T THAT WHEN YOU LEARNED WE WERE QUINTU-PLETS?
IT DIDN'T FEEL LIKE A DREAM TO ME.
YEAH, I GUESS YOU'RE RIGHT.

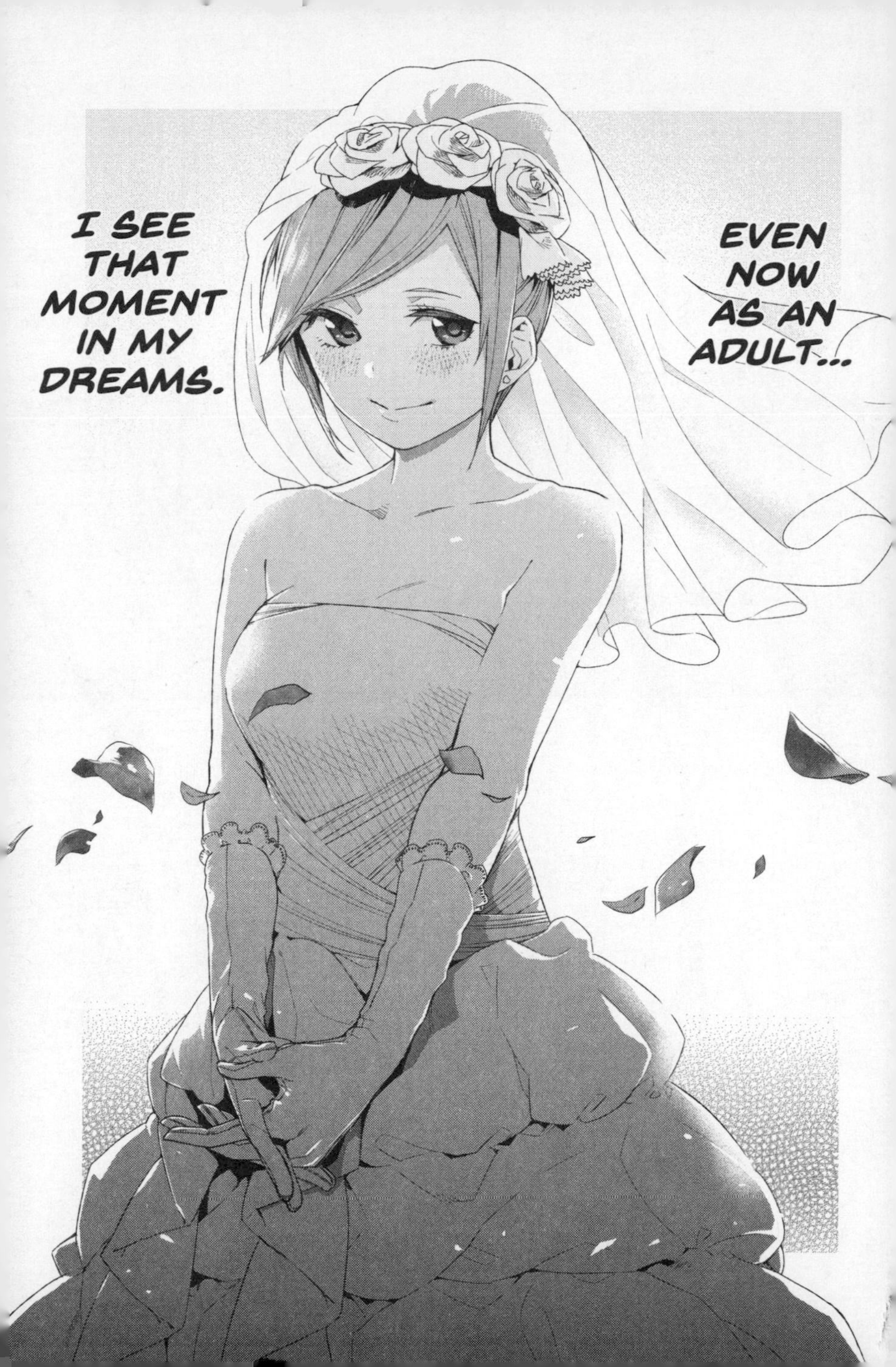
EVEN NOW AS AN ADULT...
I SEE THAT MOMENT IN MY DREAMS.

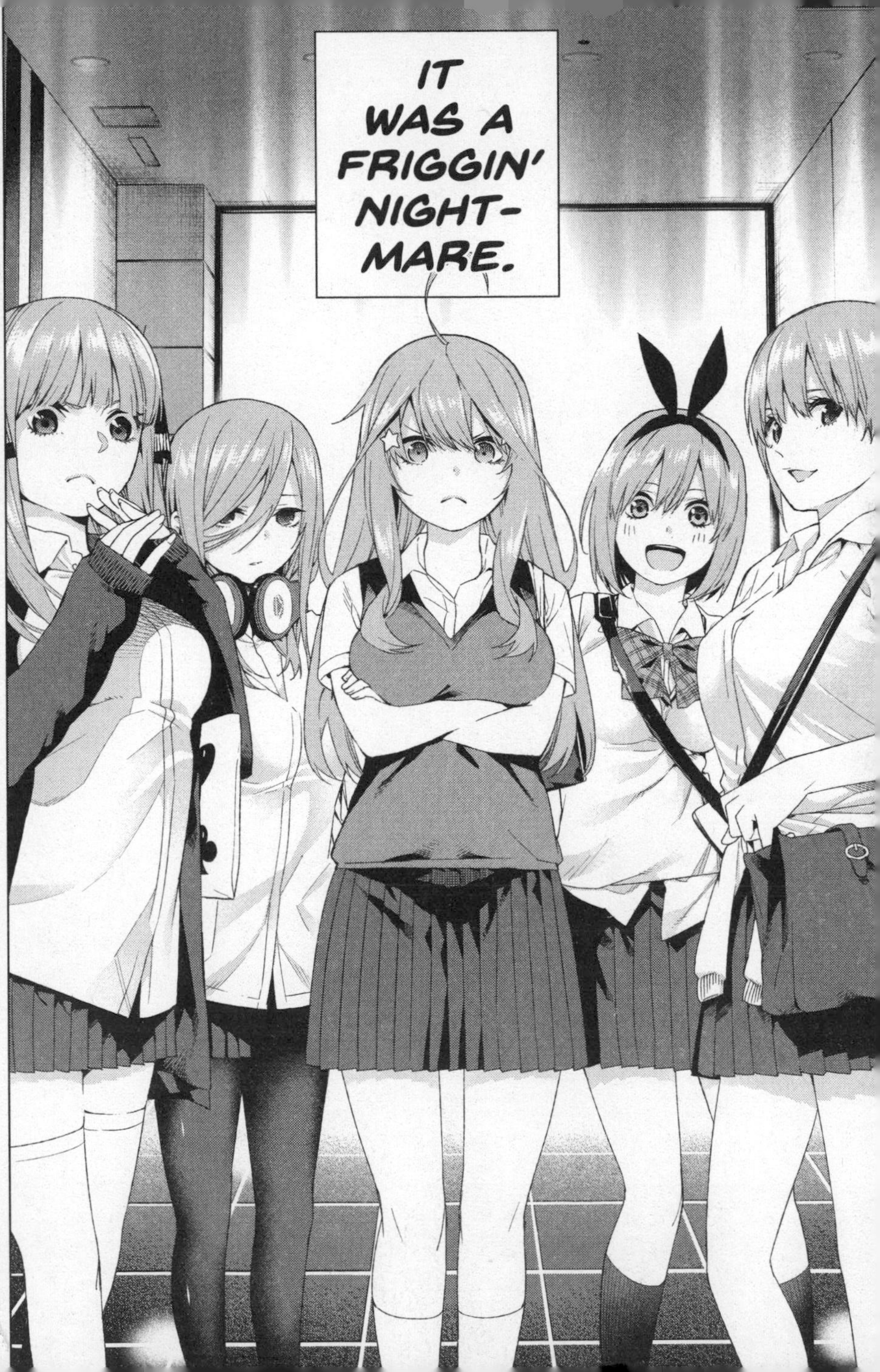
IT WAS A FRIGGIN' NIGHT-MARE.

CHAPTER 2 HOME VISIT

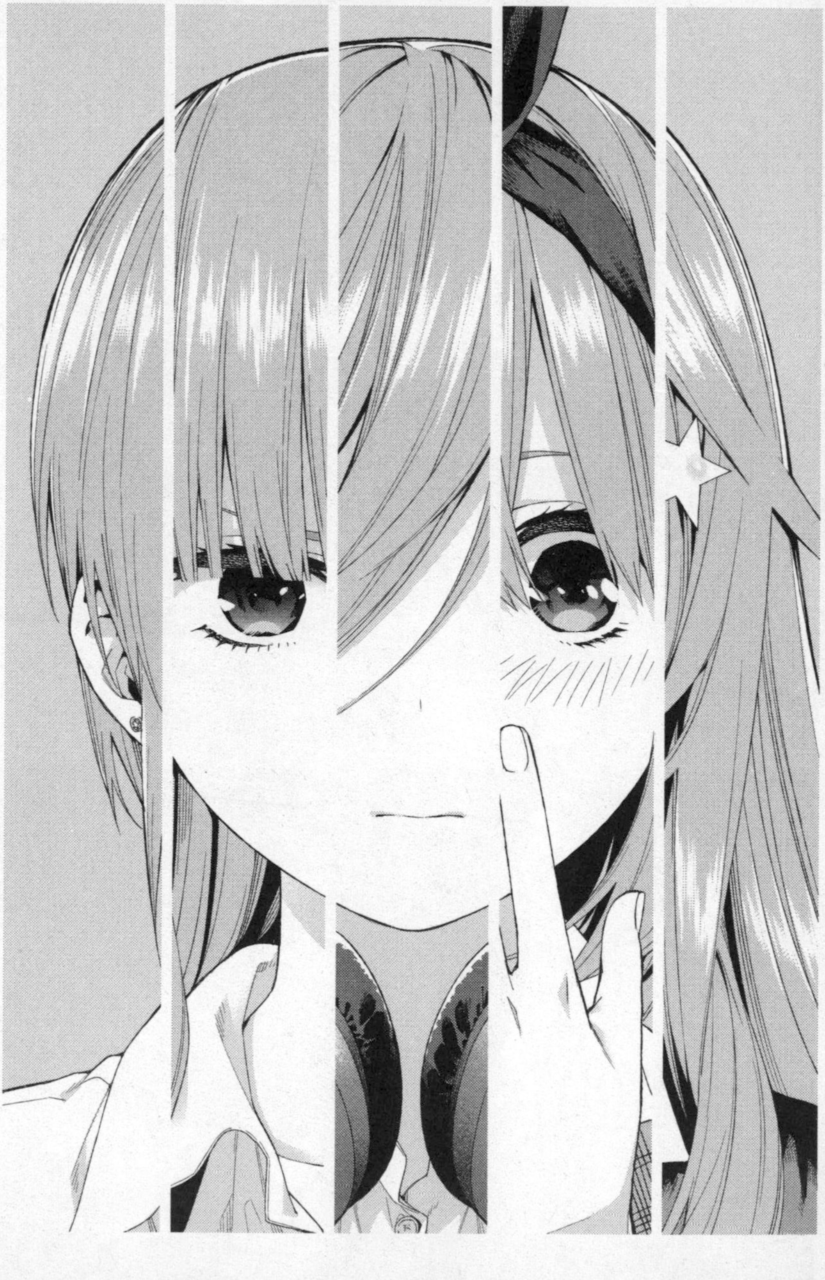

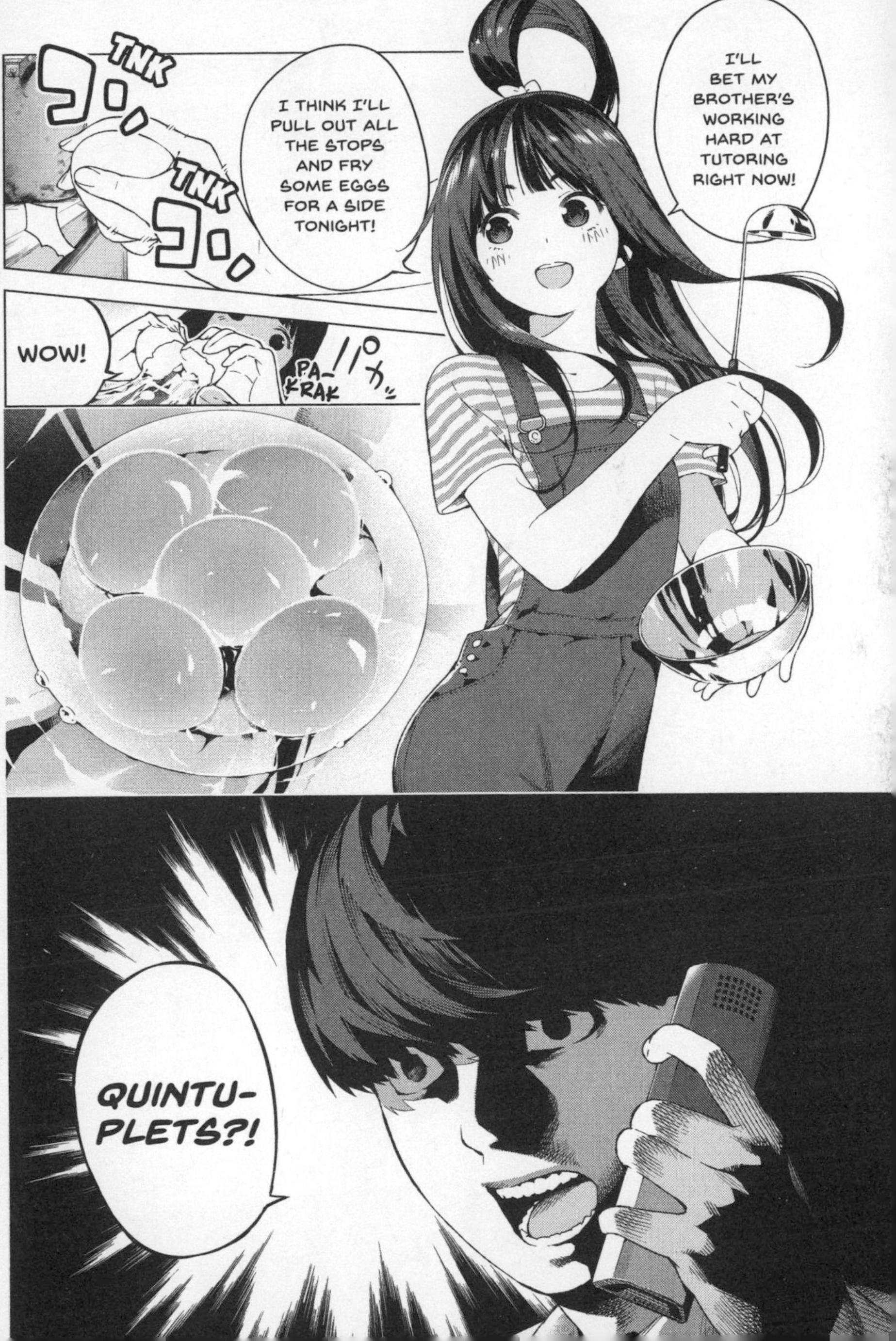
I'LL BET MY BROTHER'S WORKING HARD AT TUTORING RIGHT NOW!
I THINK I'LL PULL OUT ALL THE STOPS AND FRY SOME EGGS FOR A SIDE TONIGHT!
TNK
TNK
WOW!
PA-KRAK
QUINTU-PLETS?!

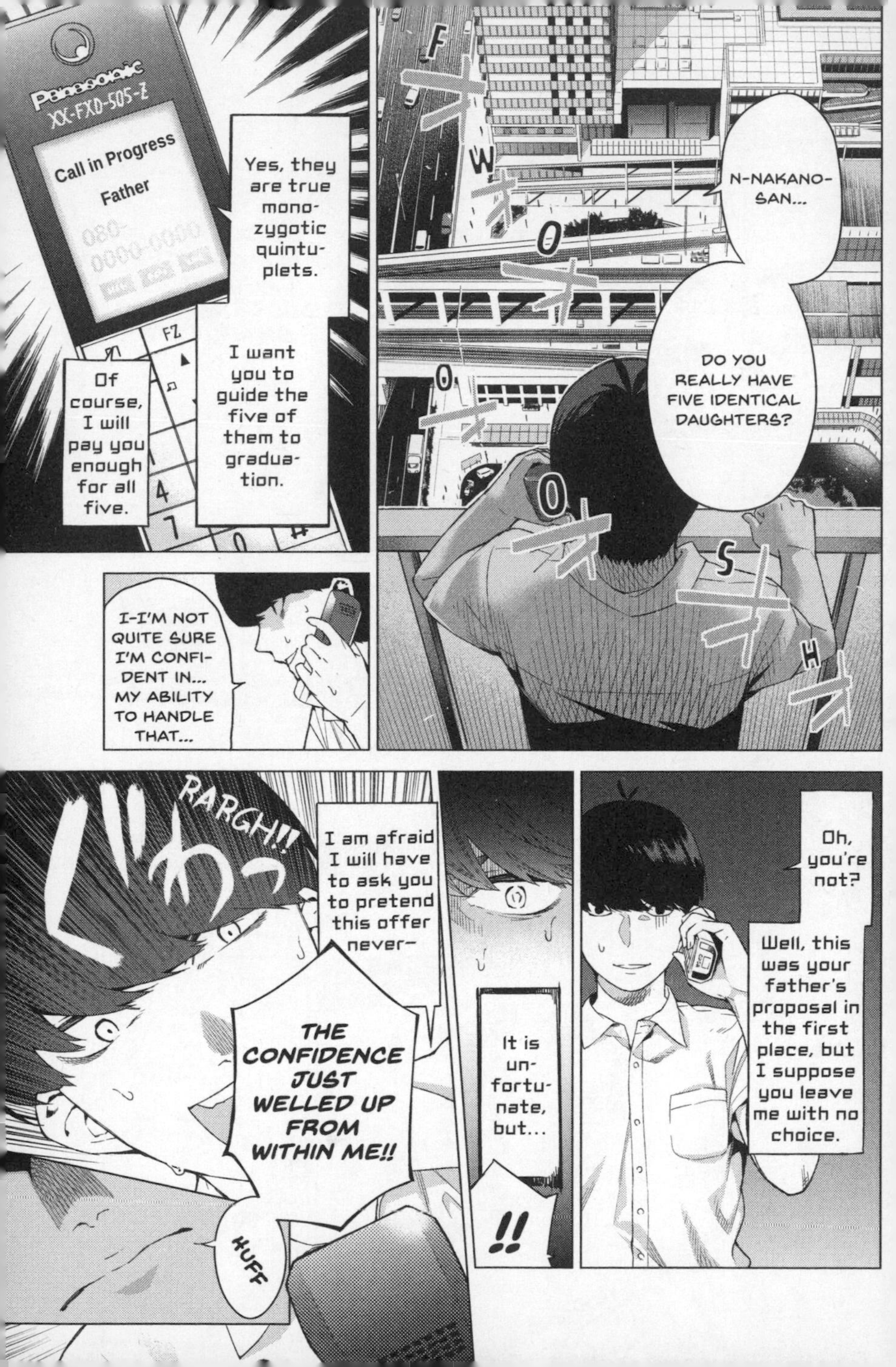

F W O O O S H
N-NAKANO-SAN...
DO YOU REALLY HAVE FIVE IDENTICAL DAUGHTERS?
XX-FXD-505-Z
Call in Progress
Father
Yes, they are true monozygotic quintuplets.
I want you to guide the five of them to graduation.
Of course, I will pay you enough for all five.
I-I'M NOT QUITE SURE I'M CONFIDENT IN... MY ABILITY TO HANDLE THAT...
Oh, you're not?
Well, this was your father's proposal in the first place, but I suppose you leave me with no choice.
It is unfortunate, but...
!!
I am afraid I will have to ask you to pretend this offer never—
RARGH!!
THE CONFIDENCE JUST WELLED UP FROM WITHIN ME!!
HUFF

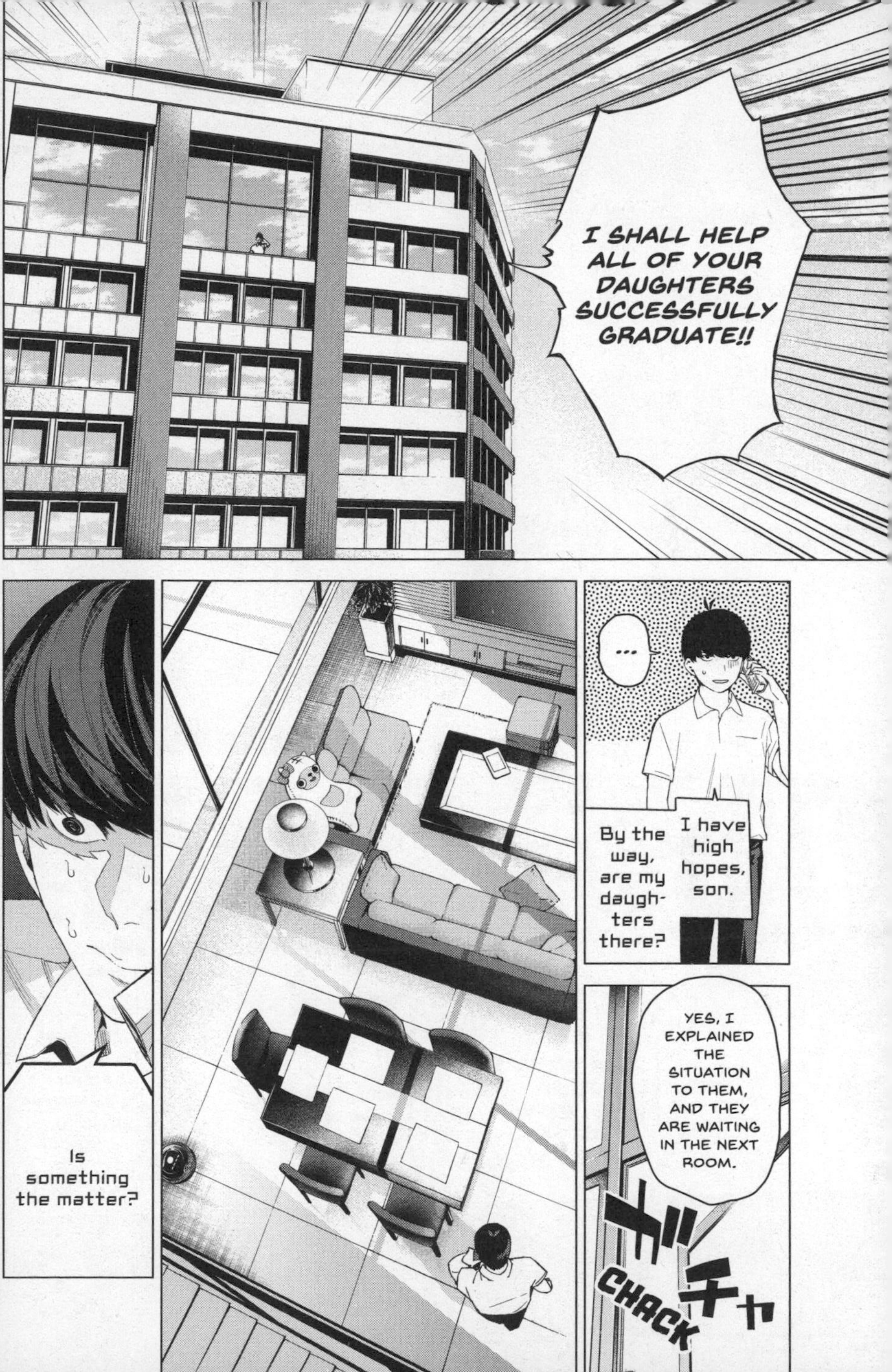
I SHALL HELP ALL OF YOUR DAUGHTERS SUCCESSFULLY GRADUATE!!
...
I have high hopes, son.
By the way, are my daughters there?
YES, I EXPLAINED THE SITUATION TO THEM, AND THEY ARE WAITING IN THE NEXT ROOM.
ガチャ
CHACK
Is something the matter?

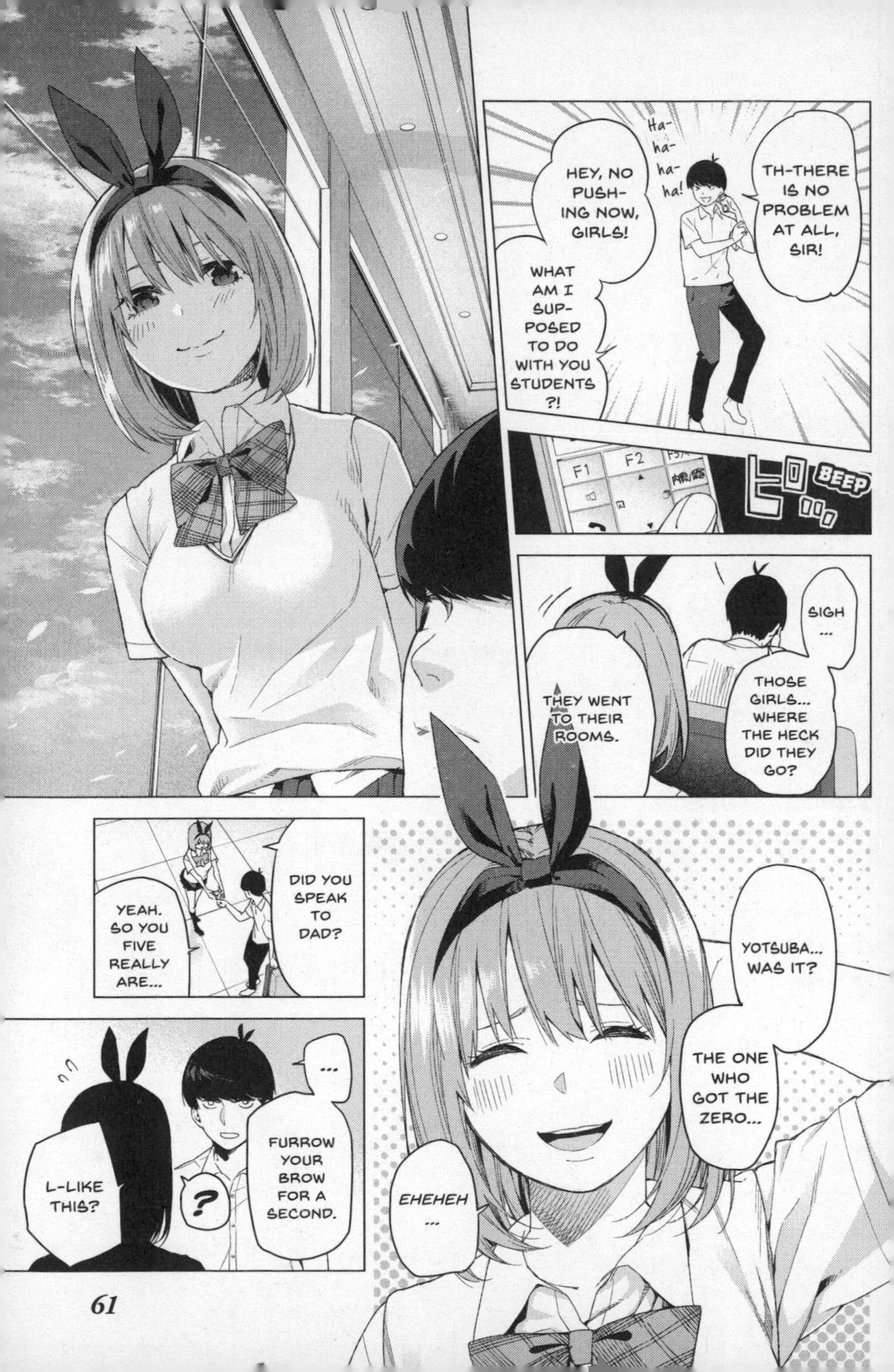
TH-THERE IS NO PROBLEM AT ALL, SIR!
Ha-ha-ha-ha!
HEY, NO PUSHING NOW, GIRLS!
WHAT AM I SUPPOSED TO DO WITH YOU STUDENTS?!
BEEP
SIGH...
THOSE GIRLS... WHERE THE HECK DID THEY GO?
THEY WENT TO THEIR ROOMS.
YOTSUBA... WAS IT?
THE ONE WHO GOT THE ZERO...
EHEHEH...
DID YOU SPEAK TO DAD?
YEAH. SO YOU FIVE REALLY ARE...
...
FURROW YOUR BROW FOR A SECOND.
?
L-LIKE THIS?

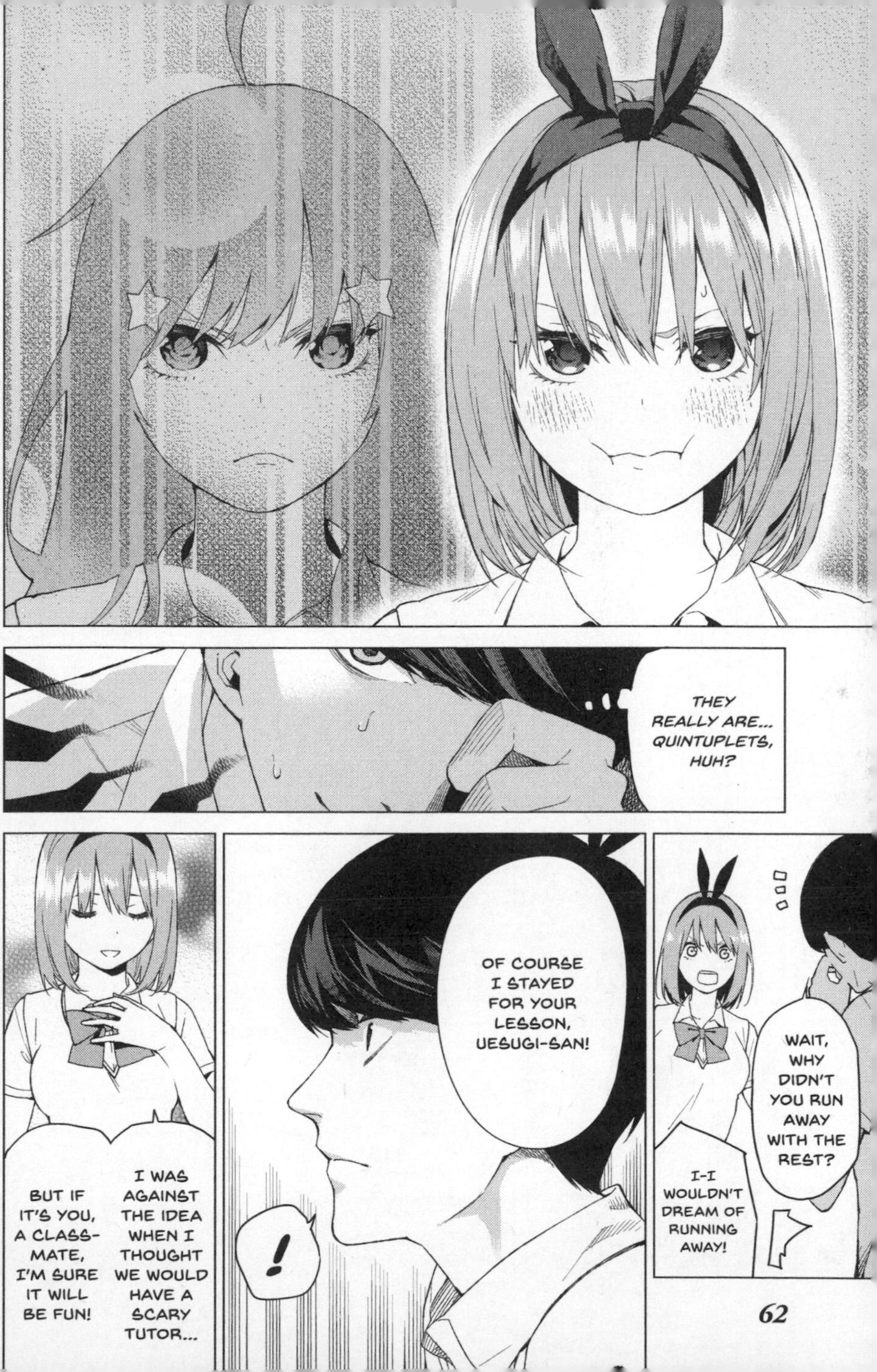
...
THEY REALLY ARE... QUINTUPLETS, HUH?
WAIT, WHY DIDN'T YOU RUN AWAY WITH THE REST?
I-I WOULDN'T DREAM OF RUNNING AWAY!
OF COURSE I STAYED FOR YOUR LESSON, UESUGI-SAN!
!
I WAS AGAINST THE IDEA WHEN I THOUGHT WE WOULD HAVE A SCARY TUTOR...
BUT IF IT'S YOU, A CLASS-MATE, I'M SURE IT WILL BE FUN!

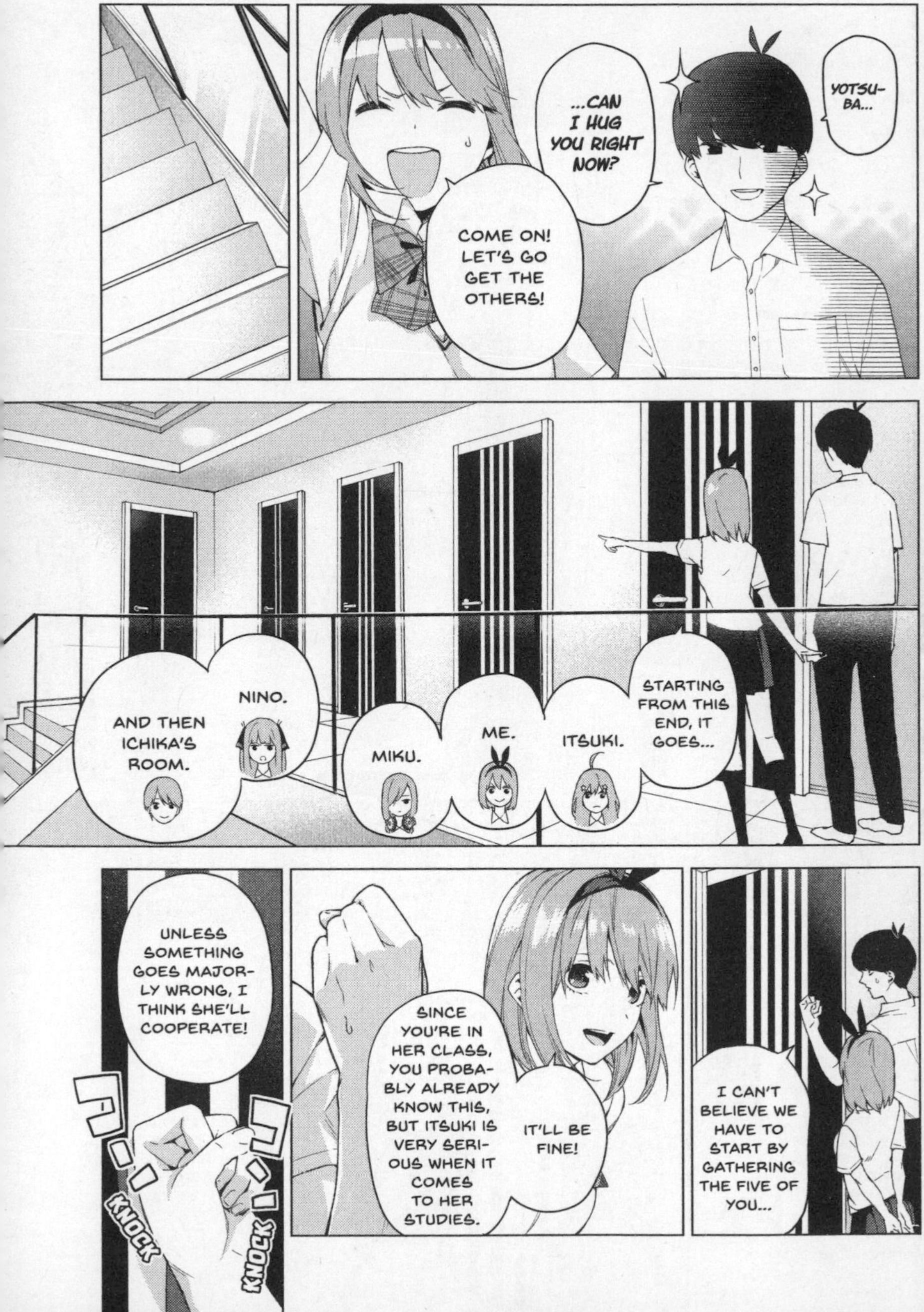
YOTSU-BA...
...CAN I HUG YOU RIGHT NOW?
COME ON! LET'S GO GET THE OTHERS!
STARTING FROM THIS END, IT GOES...
ITSUKI.
ME.
MIKU.
NINO.
AND THEN ICHIKA'S ROOM.
I CAN'T BELIEVE WE HAVE TO START BY GATHERING THE FIVE OF YOU...
SINCE YOU'RE IN HER CLASS, YOU PROBABLY ALREADY KNOW THIS, BUT ITSUKI IS VERY SERI-OUS WHEN IT COMES TO HER STUDIES.
IT'LL BE FINE!
UNLESS SOMETHING GOES MAJOR-LY WRONG, I THINK SHE'LL COOPERATE!
KNOCK
KNOCK

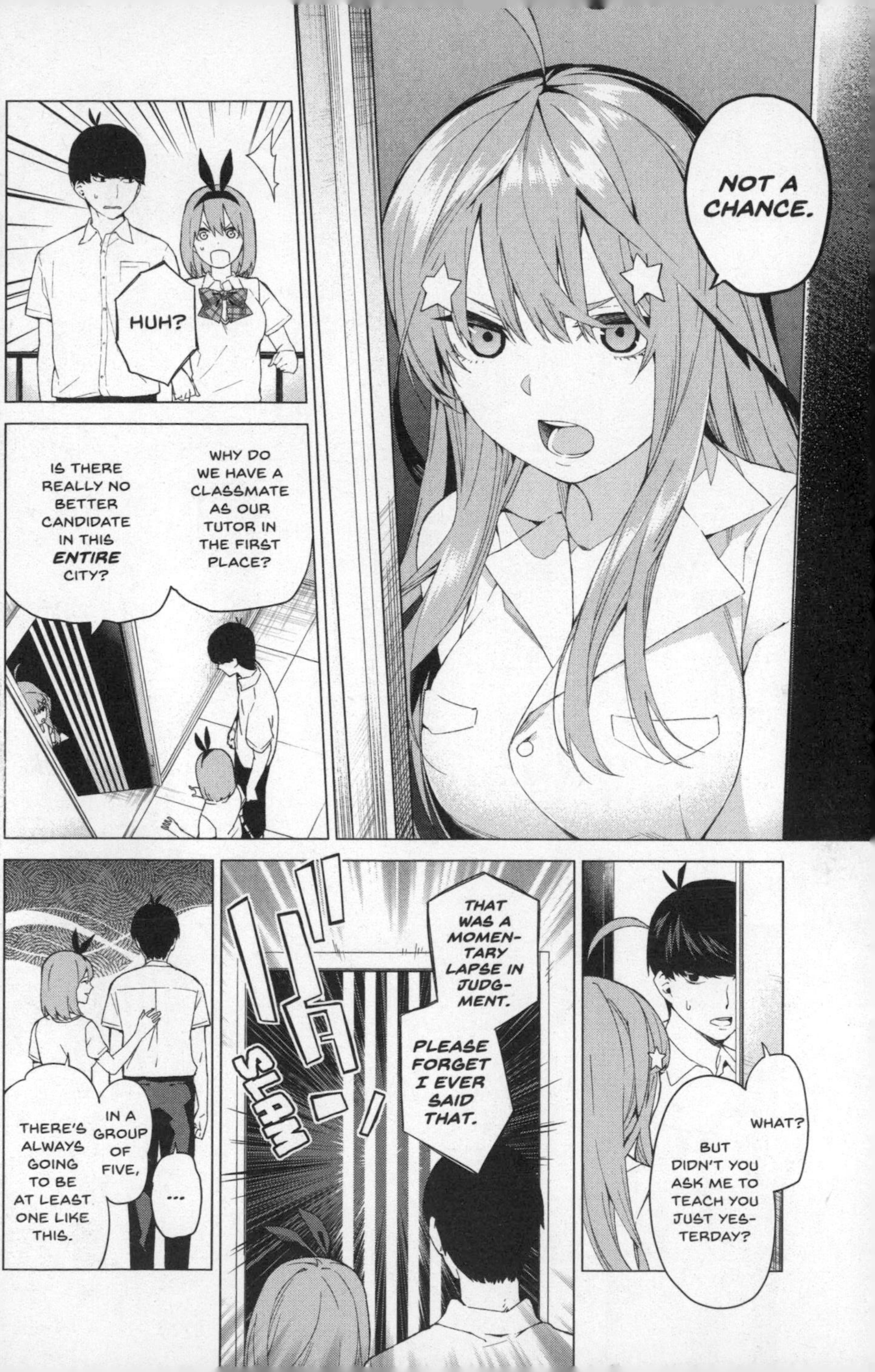
NOT A CHANCE.
HUH?
WHY DO WE HAVE A CLASSMATE AS OUR TUTOR IN THE FIRST PLACE?
IS THERE REALLY NO BETTER CANDIDATE IN THIS ENTIRE CITY?
WHAT?
BUT DIDN'T YOU ASK ME TO TEACH YOU JUST YES-TERDAY?
THAT WAS A MOMENTARY LAPSE IN JUDGMENT.
PLEASE FORGET I EVER SAID THAT.
SLAM
IN A GROUP OF FIVE,
THERE'S ALWAYS GOING TO BE AT LEAST ONE LIKE THIS.
...

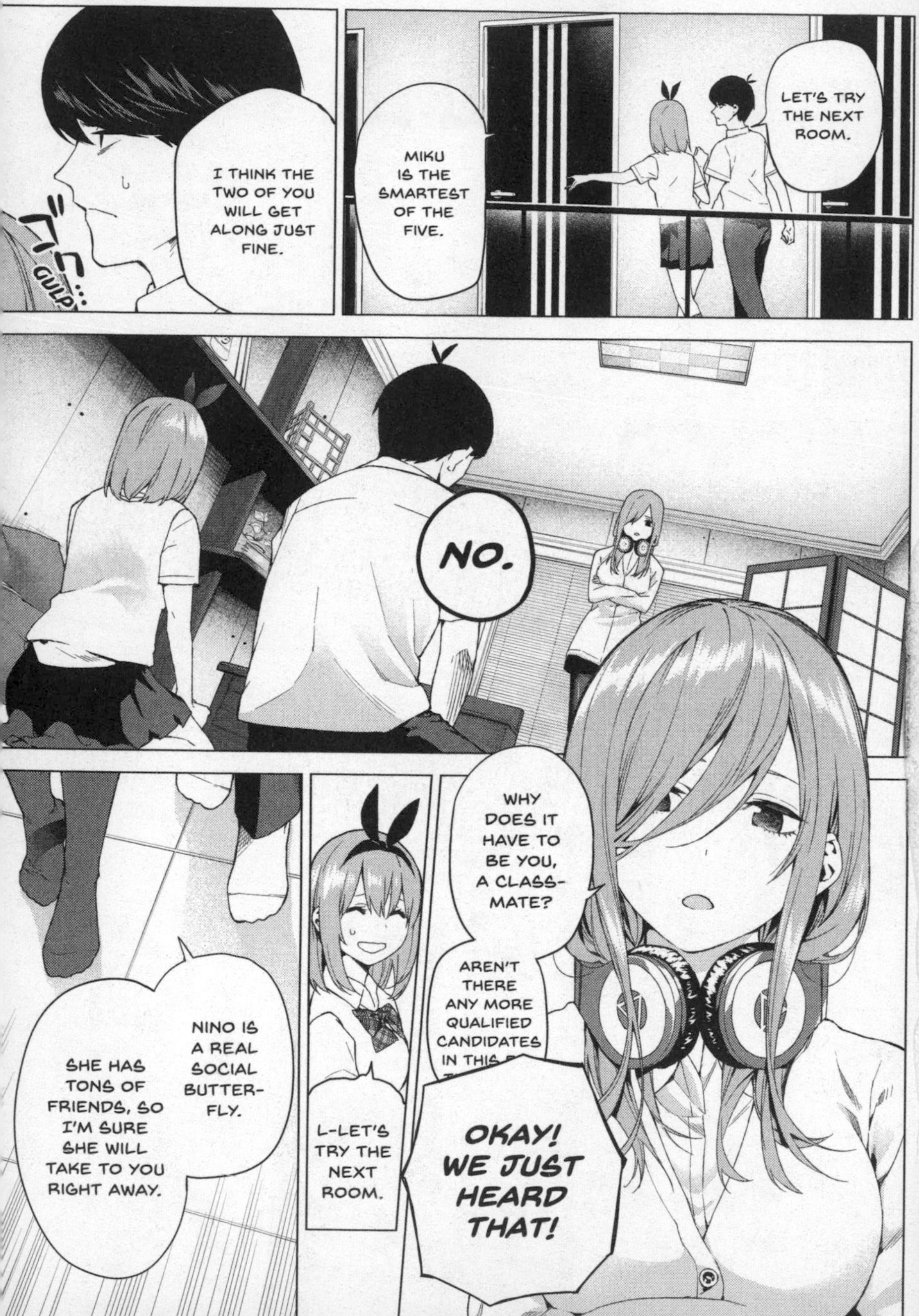
LET'S TRY THE NEXT ROOM.
MIKU IS THE SMARTEST OF THE FIVE.
I THINK THE TWO OF YOU WILL GET ALONG JUST FINE.
GULP...
NO.
WHY DOES IT HAVE TO BE YOU, A CLASSMATE?
AREN'T THERE ANY MORE QUALIFIED CANDIDATES IN THIS
OKAY! WE JUST HEARD THAT!
L-LET'S TRY THE NEXT ROOM.
NINO IS A REAL SOCIAL BUTTERFLY.
SHE HAS TONS OF FRIENDS, SO I'M SURE SHE WILL TAKE TO YOU RIGHT AWAY.

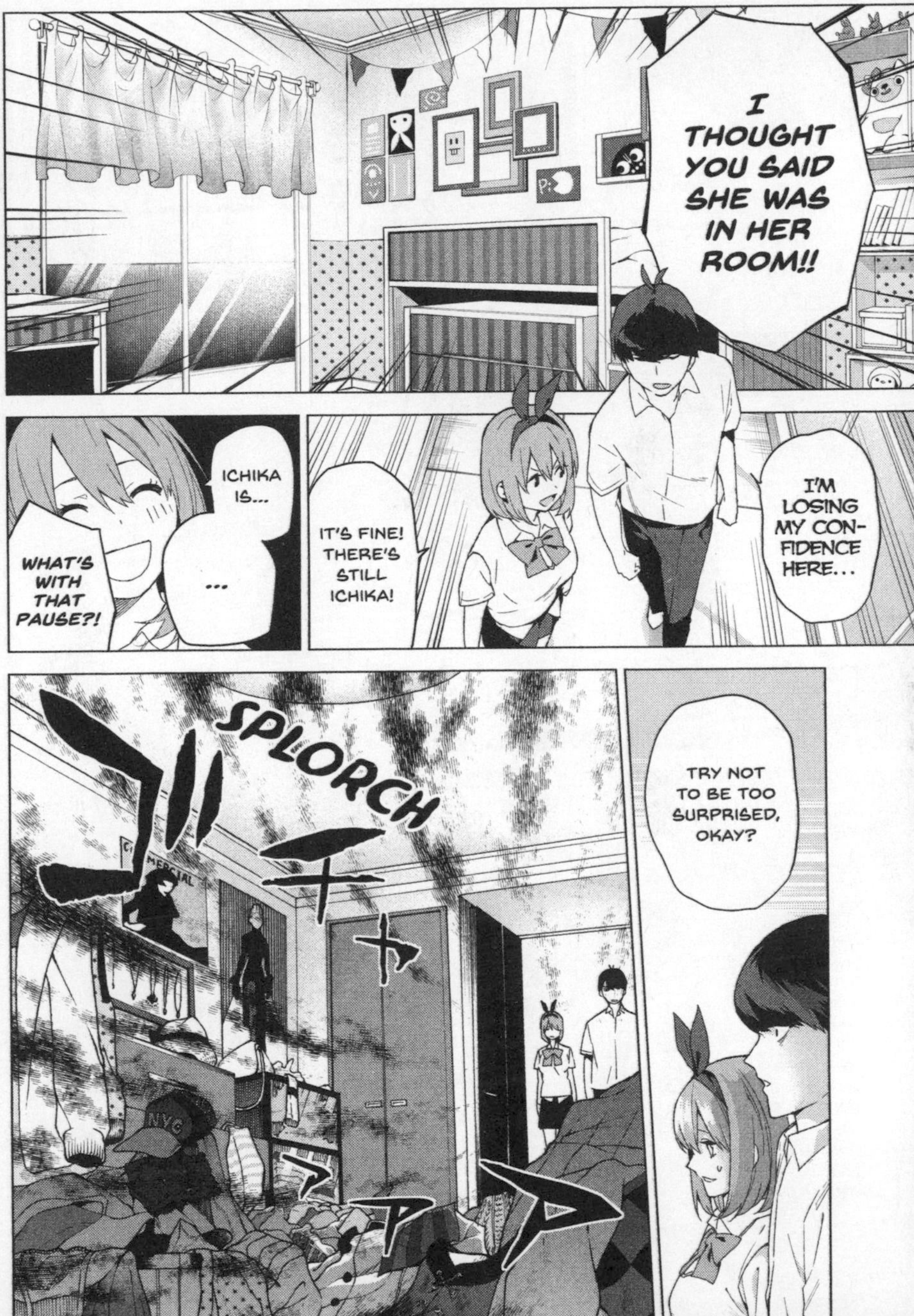
I THOUGHT YOU SAID SHE WAS IN HER ROOM!!
I'M LOSING MY CON-FIDENCE HERE...
IT'S FINE! THERE'S STILL ICHIKA!
ICHIKA IS...
...
WHAT'S WITH THAT PAUSE?!
TRY NOT TO BE TOO SURPRISED, OKAY?
SPLORCH

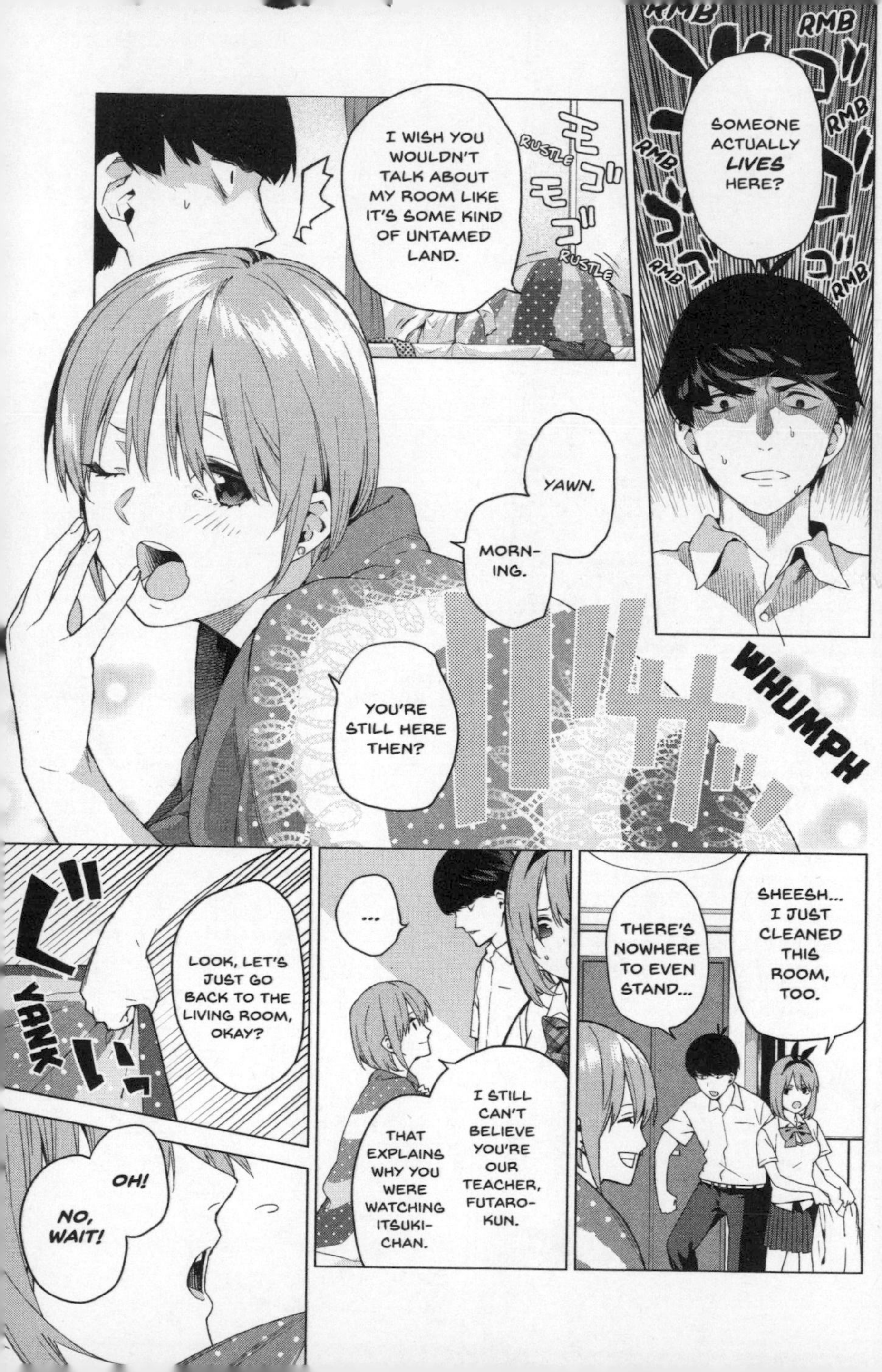
RMB
RMB
RMB
RMB
RMB
RMB
SOMEONE ACTUALLY LIVES HERE?
RUSTLE
RUSTLE
I WISH YOU WOULDN'T TALK ABOUT MY ROOM LIKE IT'S SOME KIND OF UNTAMED LAND.
YAWN.
MORN-ING.
YOU'RE STILL HERE THEN?
WHUMPH
SHEESH... I JUST CLEANED THIS ROOM, TOO.
THERE'S NOWHERE TO EVEN STAND...
...
I STILL CAN'T BELIEVE YOU'RE OUR TEACHER, FUTARO-KUN.
THAT EXPLAINS WHY YOU WERE WATCHING ITSUKI-CHAN.
YANK
LOOK, LET'S JUST GO BACK TO THE LIVING ROOM, OKAY?
OH!
NO, WAIT!

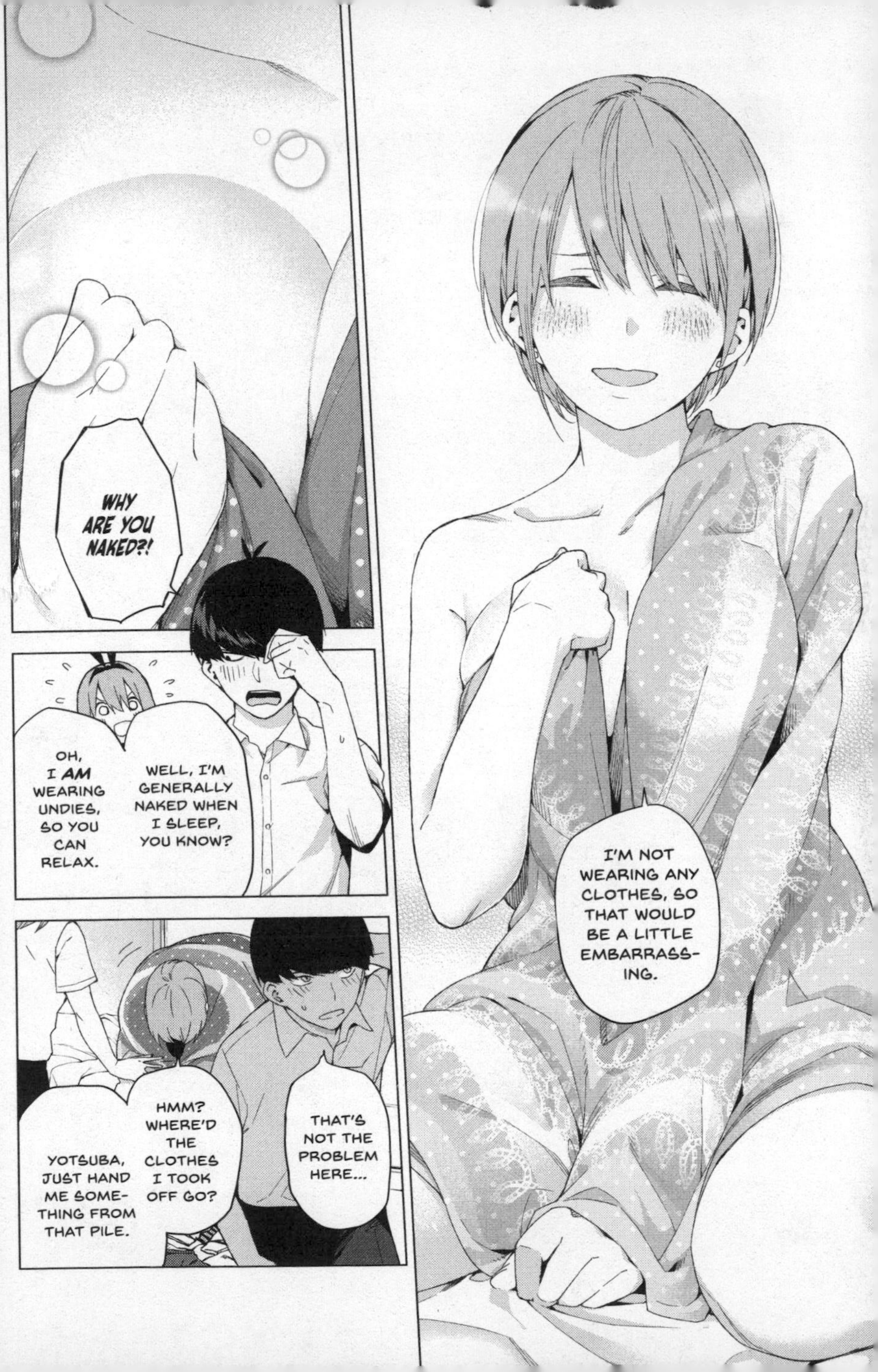
I'M NOT WEARING ANY CLOTHES, SO THAT WOULD BE A LITTLE EMBARRASS-ING.
WHY ARE YOU NAKED?!
WELL, I'M GENERALLY NAKED WHEN I SLEEP, YOU KNOW?
OH, I **AM** WEARING UNDIES, SO YOU CAN RELAX.
THAT'S NOT THE PROBLEM HERE...
HMM? WHERE'D THE CLOTHES I TOOK OFF GO?
YOTSUBA, JUST HAND ME SOME-THING FROM THAT PILE.

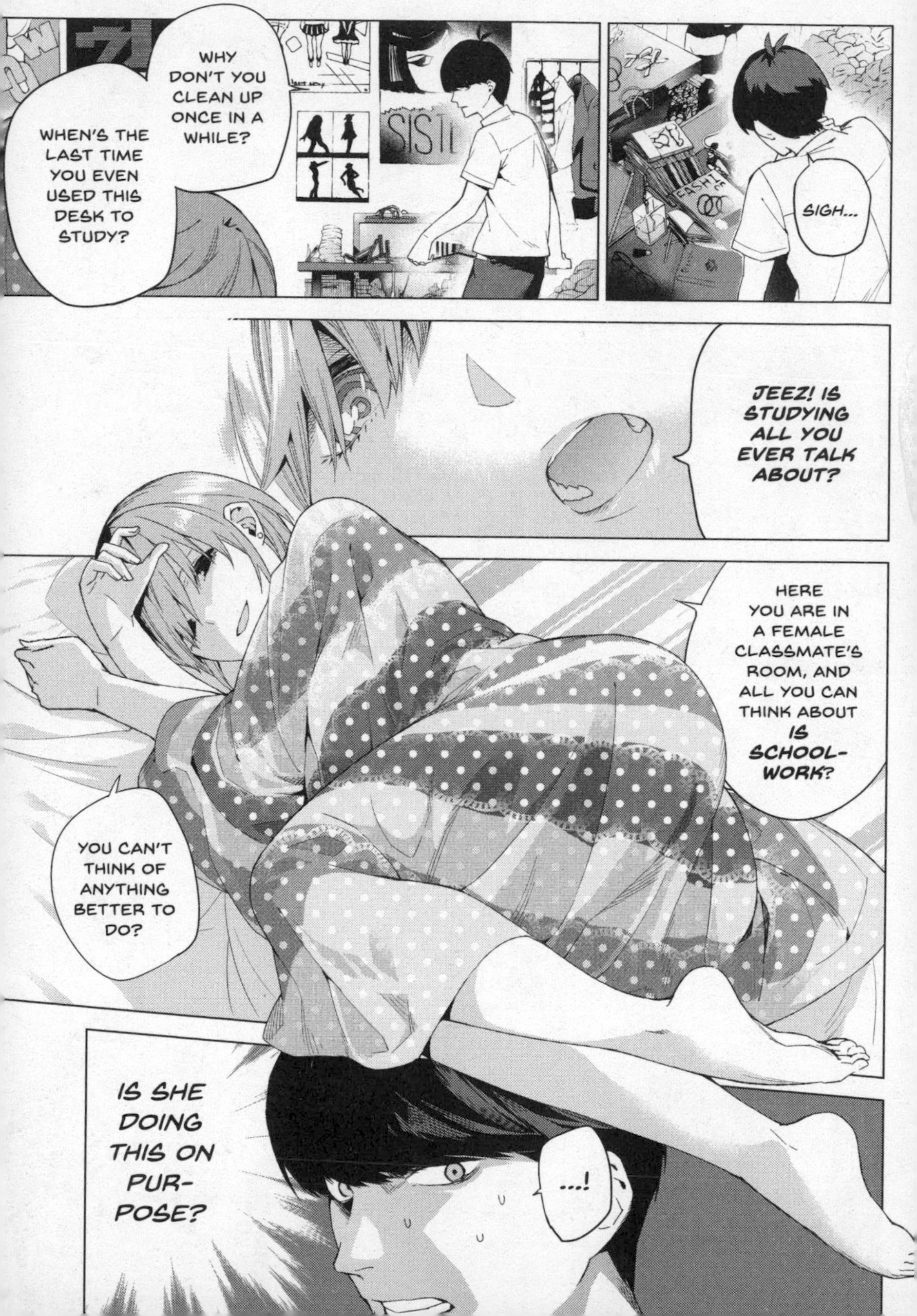
SIGH...
WHY DON'T YOU CLEAN UP ONCE IN A WHILE?
WHEN'S THE LAST TIME YOU EVEN USED THIS DESK TO STUDY?
JEEZ! IS STUDYING ALL YOU EVER TALK ABOUT?
HERE YOU ARE IN A FEMALE CLASSMATE'S ROOM, AND ALL YOU CAN THINK ABOUT IS SCHOOL-WORK?
YOU CAN'T THINK OF ANYTHING BETTER TO DO?
...!
IS SHE DOING THIS ON PUR-POSE?

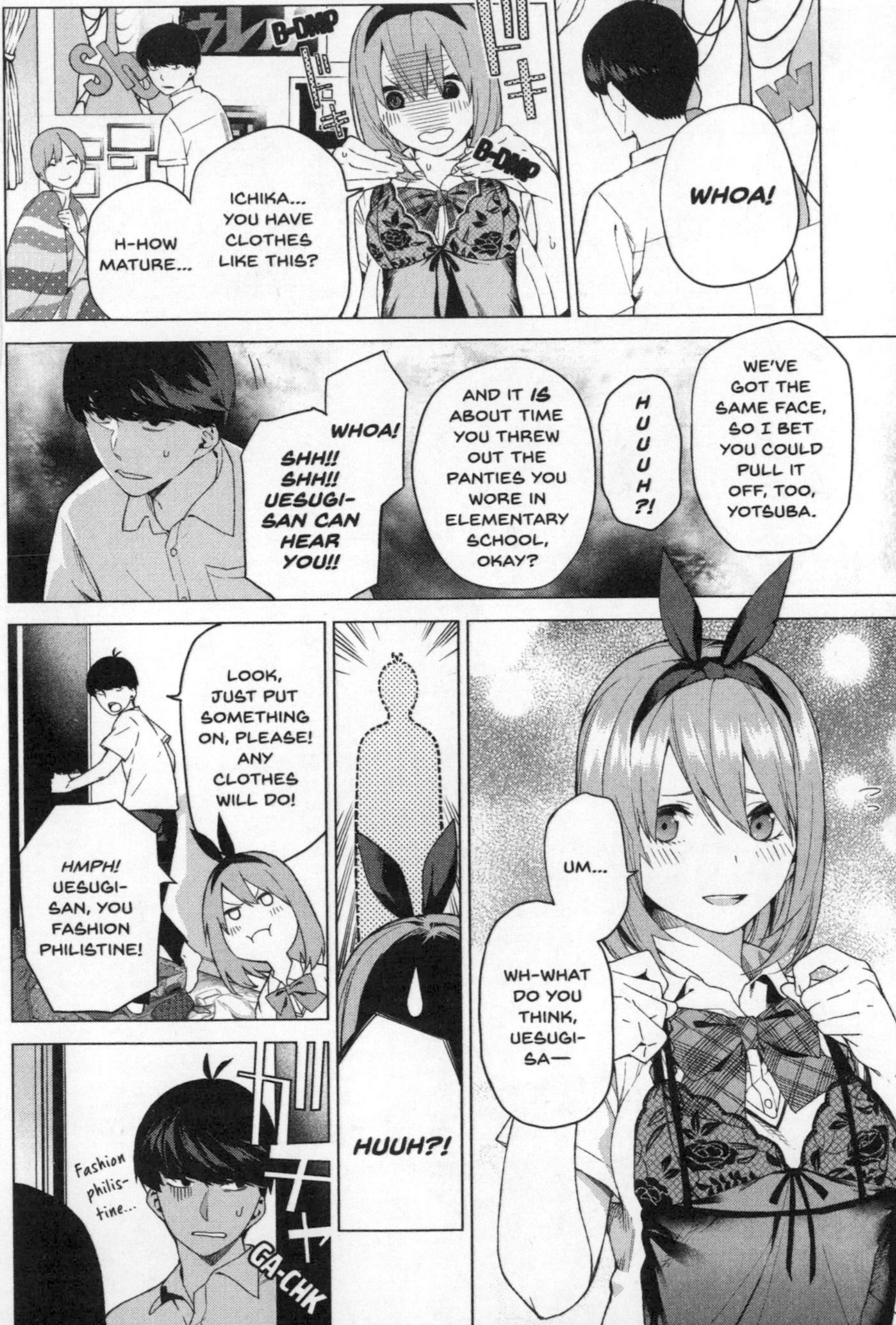
WHOA!
B-DMP
ICHIKA... YOU HAVE CLOTHES LIKE THIS?
H-HOW MATURE...
B-DMP
WE'VE GOT THE SAME FACE, SO I BET YOU COULD PULL IT OFF, TOO, YOTSUBA.
HUUUUH?!
AND IT IS ABOUT TIME YOU THREW OUT THE PANTIES YOU WORE IN ELEMENTARY SCHOOL, OKAY?
WHOA!
SHH!! SHH!! UESUGI-SAN CAN HEAR YOU!!
UM...
WH-WHAT DO YOU THINK, UESUGI-SA—
HUUH?!
LOOK, JUST PUT SOMETHING ON, PLEASE! ANY CLOTHES WILL DO!
HMPH! UESUGI-SAN, YOU FASHION PHILISTINE!
Fashion philis-tine...
GA-CHK

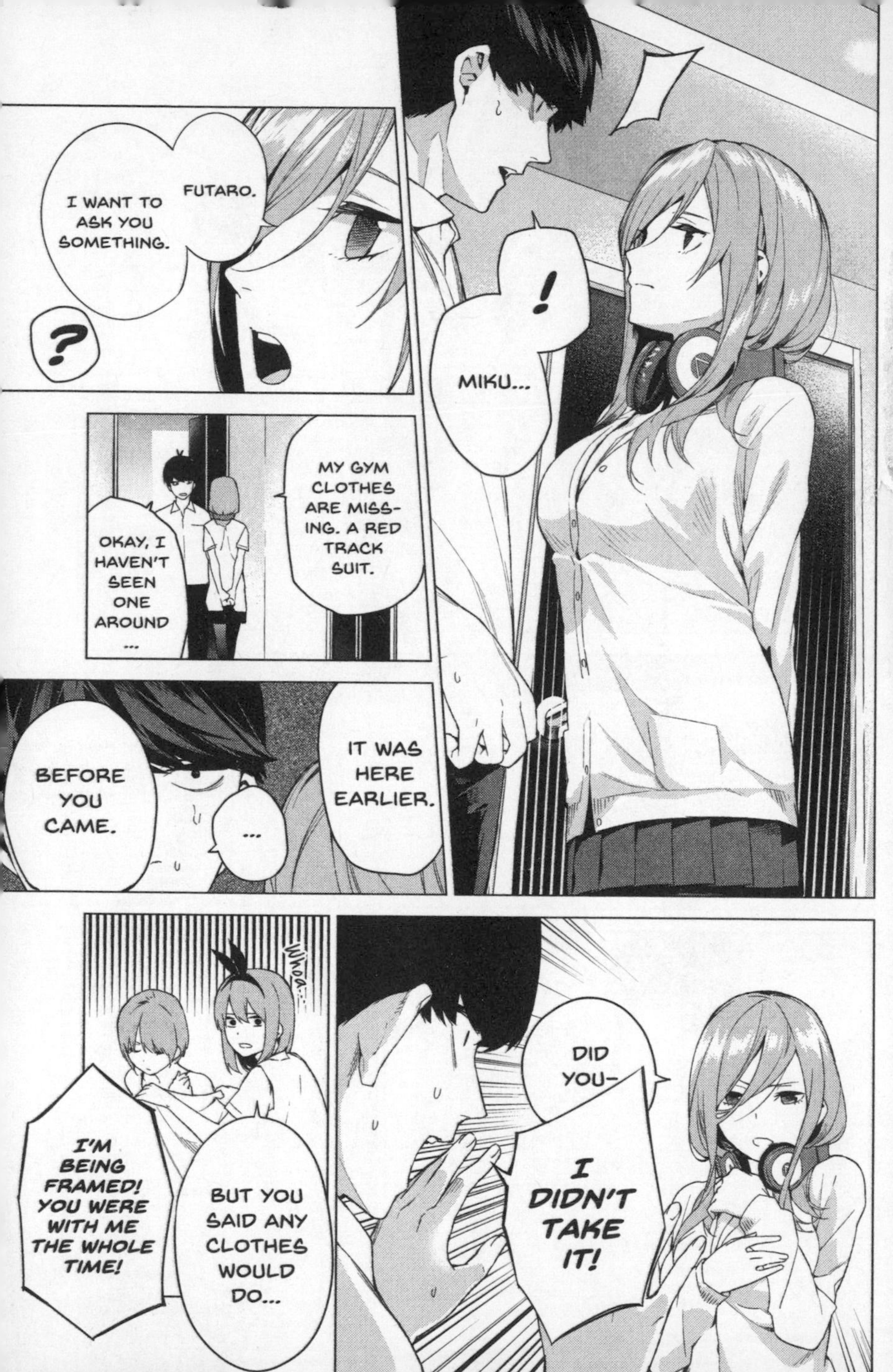
!
MIKU...
FUTARO.
I WANT TO ASK YOU SOMETHING.
?
MY GYM CLOTHES ARE MISS-ING. A RED TRACK SUIT.
OKAY, I HAVEN'T SEEN ONE AROUND...
IT WAS HERE EARLIER.
...
BEFORE YOU CAME.
DID YOU-
I DIDN'T TAKE IT!
Whoa...
BUT YOU SAID ANY CLOTHES WOULD DO...
I'M BEING FRAMED! YOU WERE WITH ME THE WHOLE TIME!

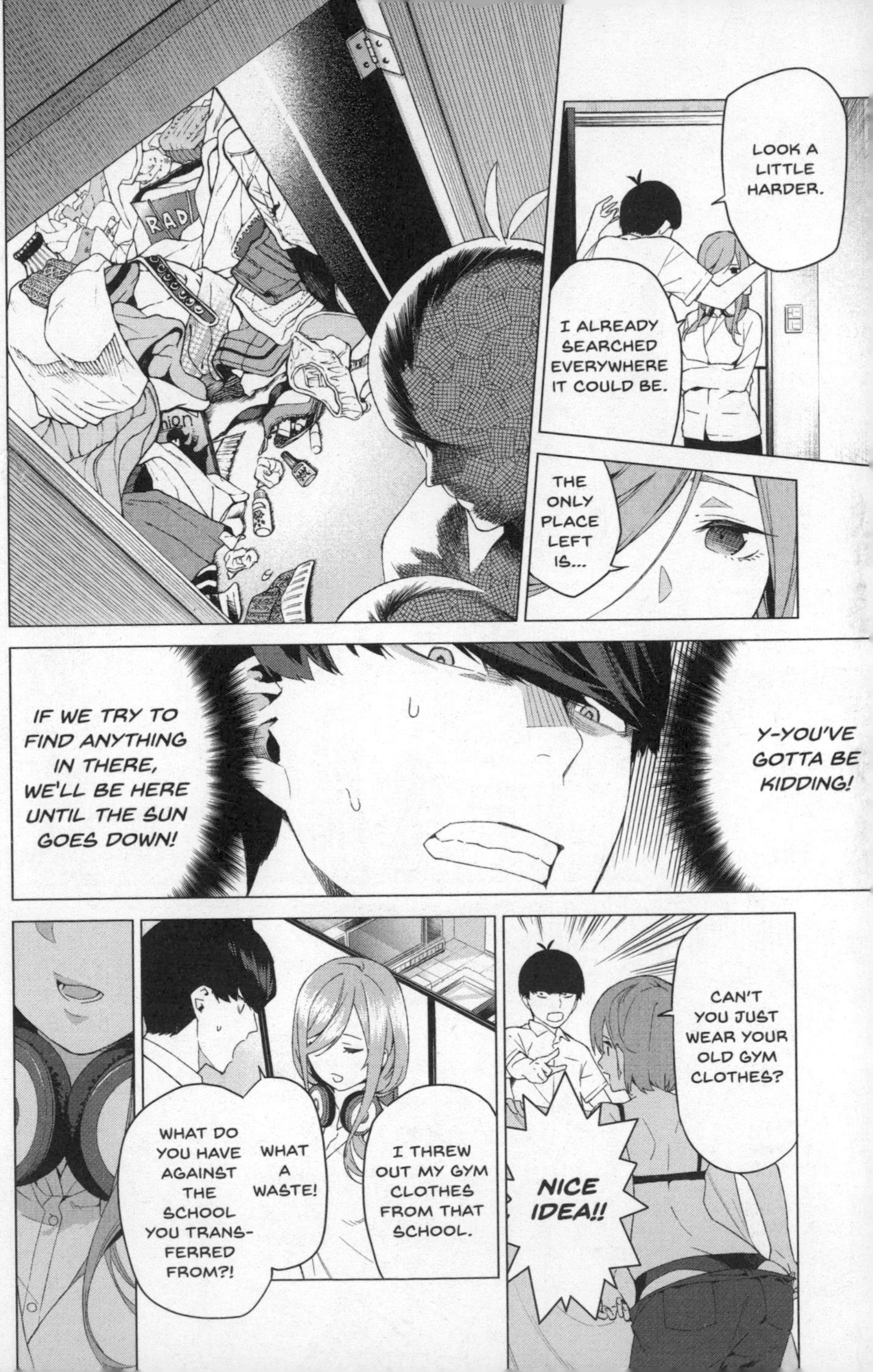
LOOK A LITTLE HARDER.
I ALREADY SEARCHED EVERYWHERE IT COULD BE.
THE ONLY PLACE LEFT IS...
Y-YOU'VE GOTTA BE KIDDING!
IF WE TRY TO FIND ANYTHING IN THERE, WE'LL BE HERE UNTIL THE SUN GOES DOWN!
CAN'T YOU JUST WEAR YOUR OLD GYM CLOTHES?
NICE IDEA!!
I THREW OUT MY GYM CLOTHES FROM THAT SCHOOL.
WHAT A WASTE!
WHAT DO YOU HAVE AGAINST THE SCHOOL YOU TRANS-FERRED FROM?!

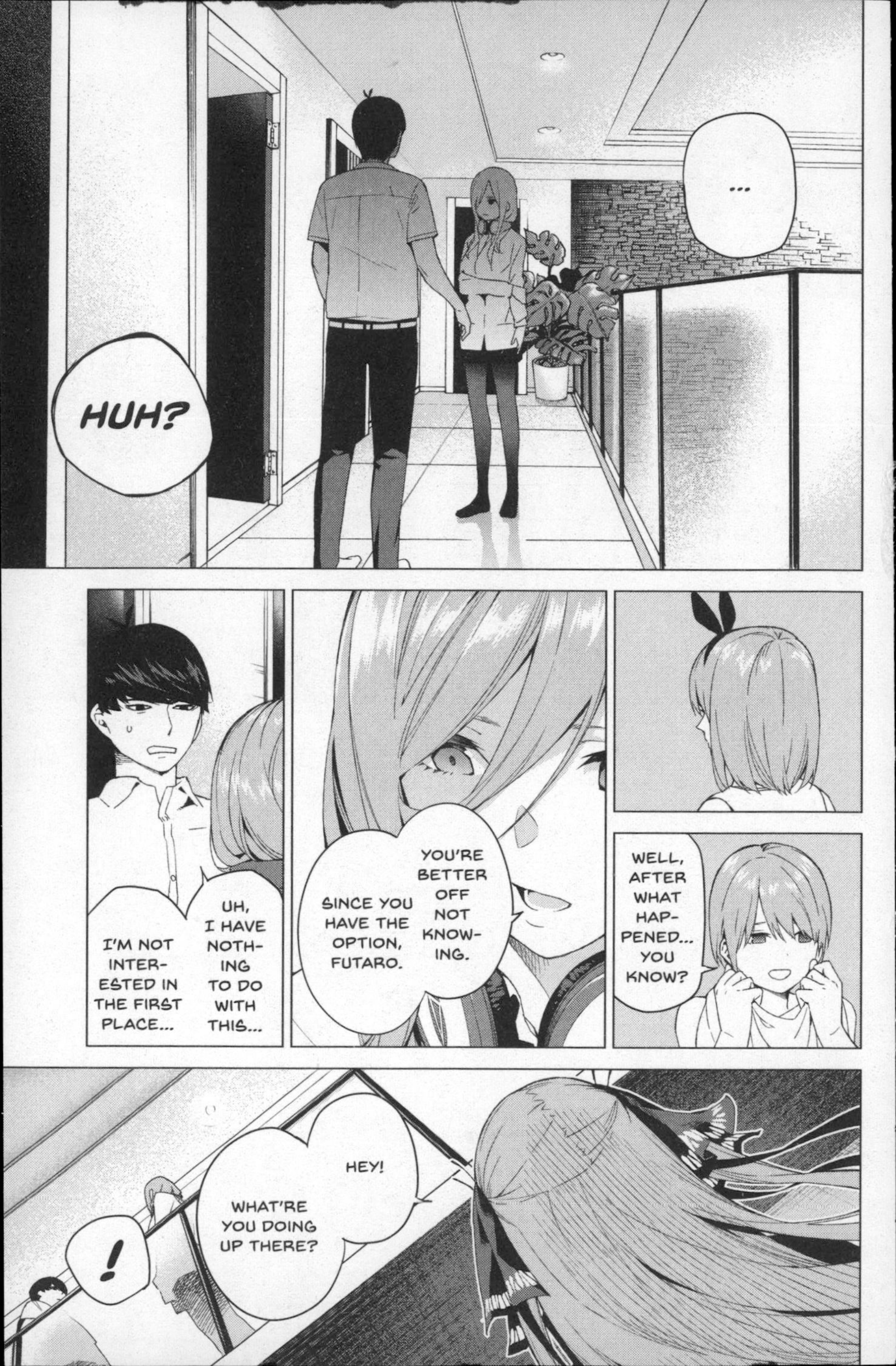
...
HUH?
WELL, AFTER WHAT HAPPENED... YOU KNOW?
YOU'RE BETTER OFF NOT KNOWING.
SINCE YOU HAVE THE OPTION, FUTARO.
UH, I HAVE NOTHING TO DO WITH THIS...
I'M NOT INTERESTED IN THE FIRST PLACE...
HEY! WHAT'RE YOU DOING UP THERE?
!

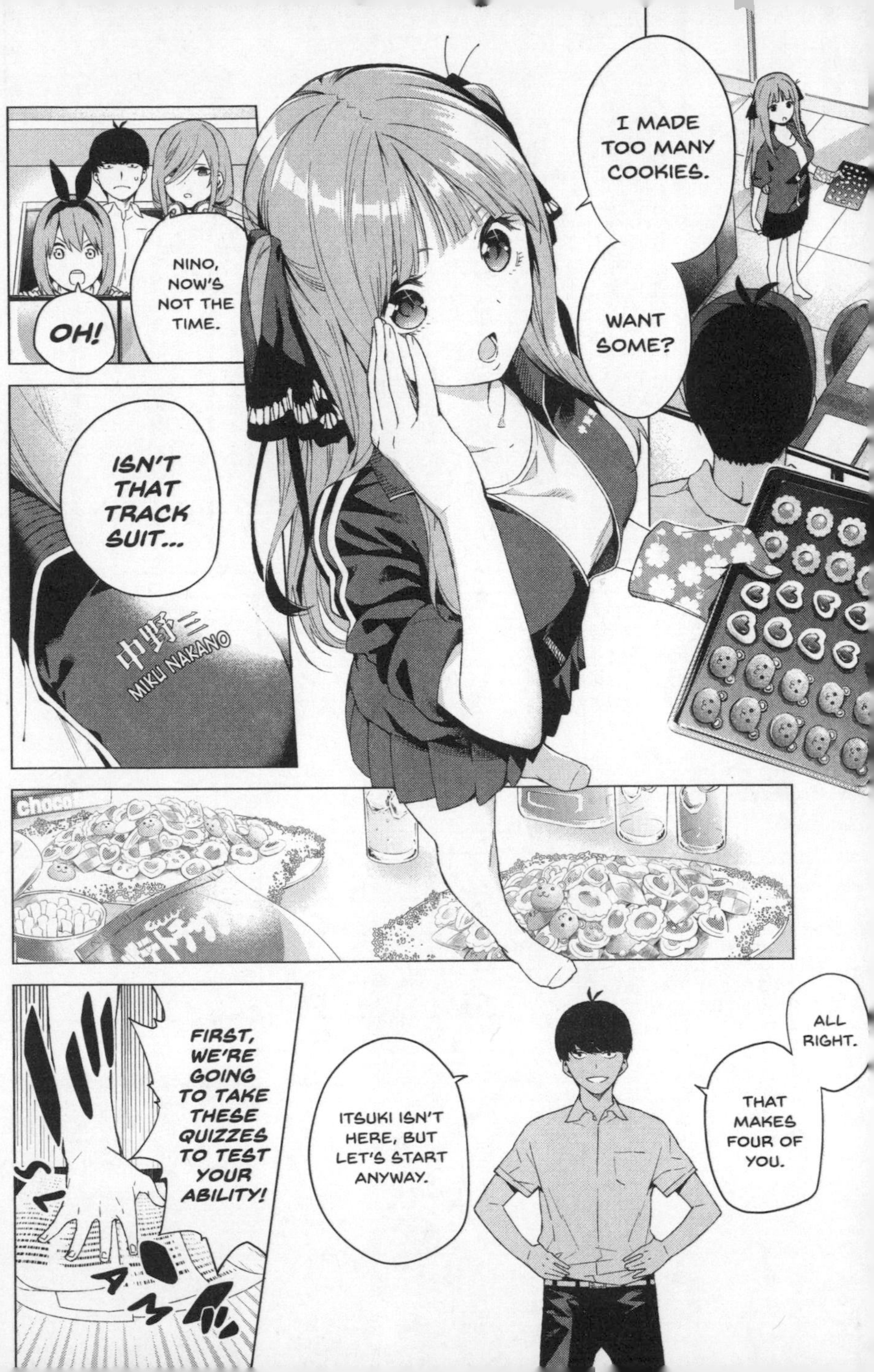

I MADE TOO MANY COOKIES.
WANT SOME?
NINO, NOW'S NOT THE TIME.
OH!
ISN'T THAT TRACK SUIT...
中野三
MIKU NAKANO
choco
ALL RIGHT.
THAT MAKES FOUR OF YOU.
ITSUKI ISN'T HERE, BUT LET'S START ANYWAY.
FIRST, WE'RE GOING TO TAKE THESE QUIZZES TO TEST YOUR ABILITY!
SLAM

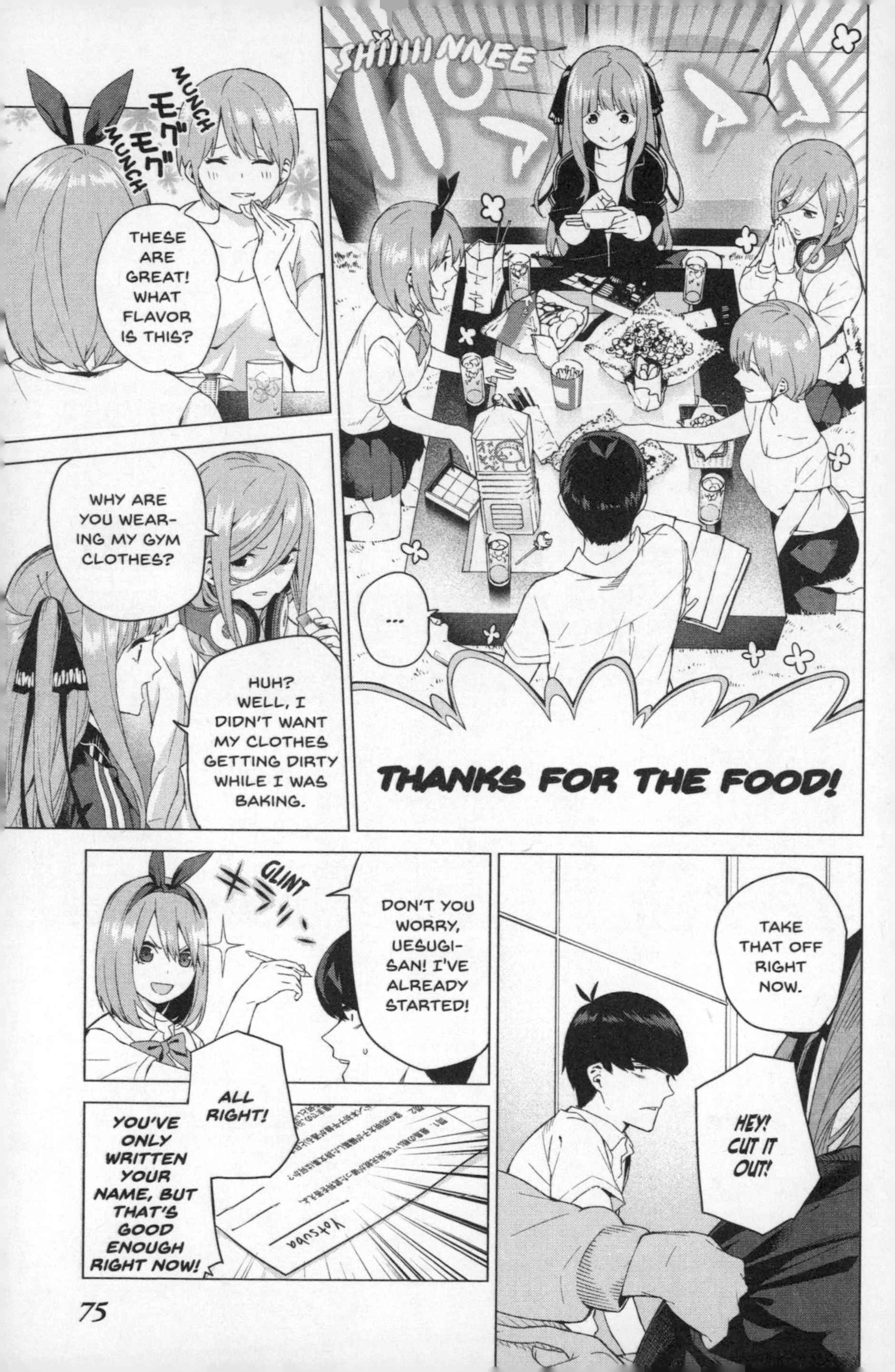
SHIIIIINNEE
...
THANKS FOR THE FOOD!
MUNCH モグ MUNCH モグ
THESE ARE GREAT! WHAT FLAVOR IS THIS?
WHY ARE YOU WEAR-ING MY GYM CLOTHES?
HUH? WELL, I DIDN'T WANT MY CLOTHES GETTING DIRTY WHILE I WAS BAKING.
TAKE THAT OFF RIGHT NOW.
HEY! CUT IT OUT!
GLINT
DON'T YOU WORRY, UESUGI-SAN! I'VE ALREADY STARTED!
ALL RIGHT!
YOU'VE ONLY WRITTEN YOUR NAME, BUT THAT'S GOOD ENOUGH RIGHT NOW!
Yotsuba

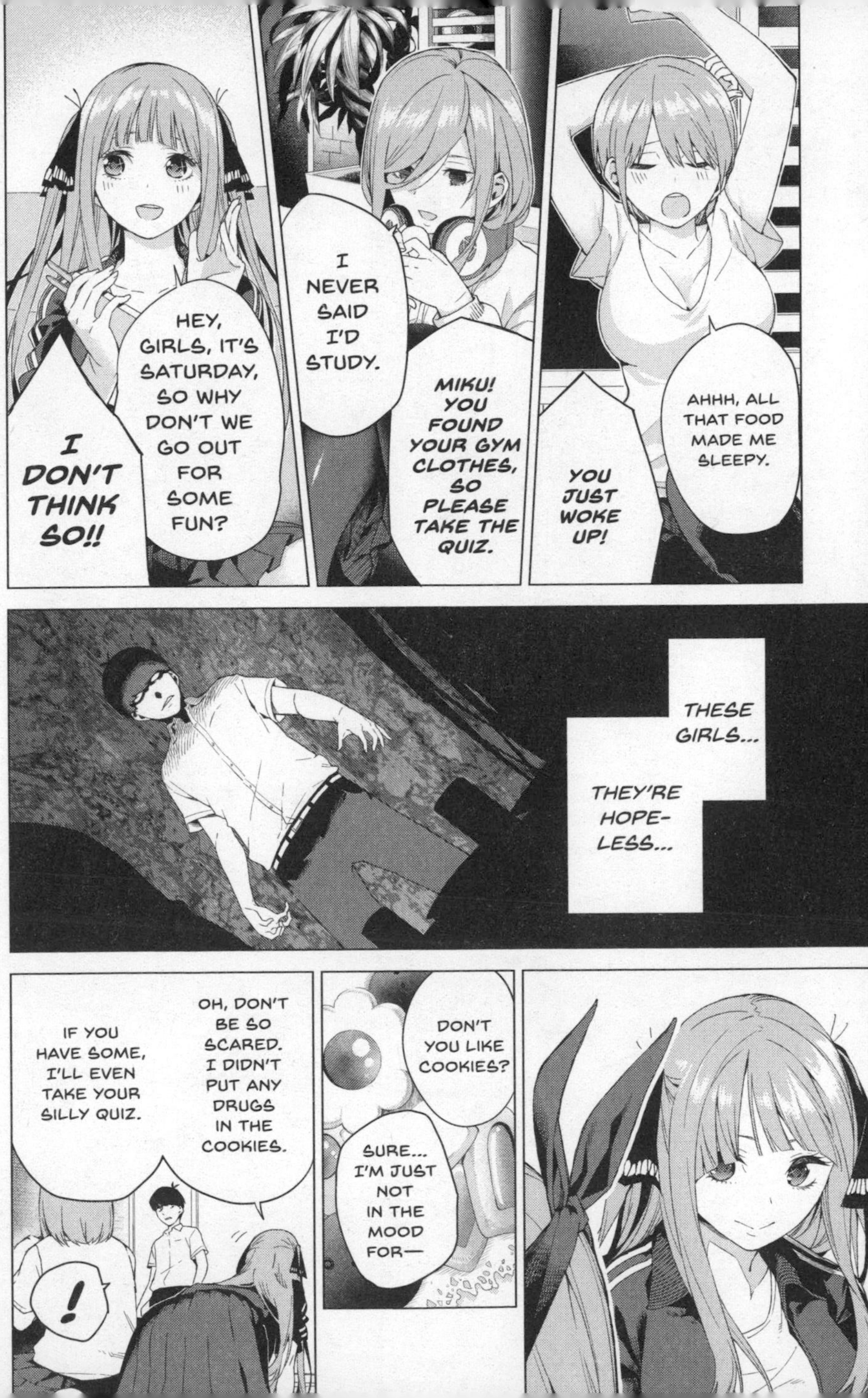
AHHH, ALL THAT FOOD MADE ME SLEEPY.
YOU JUST WOKE UP!
I NEVER SAID I'D STUDY.
MIKU! YOU FOUND YOUR GYM CLOTHES, SO PLEASE TAKE THE QUIZ.
HEY, GIRLS, IT'S SATURDAY, SO WHY DON'T WE GO OUT FOR SOME FUN?
I DON'T THINK SO!!
THESE GIRLS...
THEY'RE HOPE-LESS...
DON'T YOU LIKE COOKIES?
SURE... I'M JUST NOT IN THE MOOD FOR—
OH, DON'T BE SO SCARED. I DIDN'T PUT ANY DRUGS IN THE COOKIES.
IF YOU HAVE SOME, I'LL EVEN TAKE YOUR SILLY QUIZ.
!

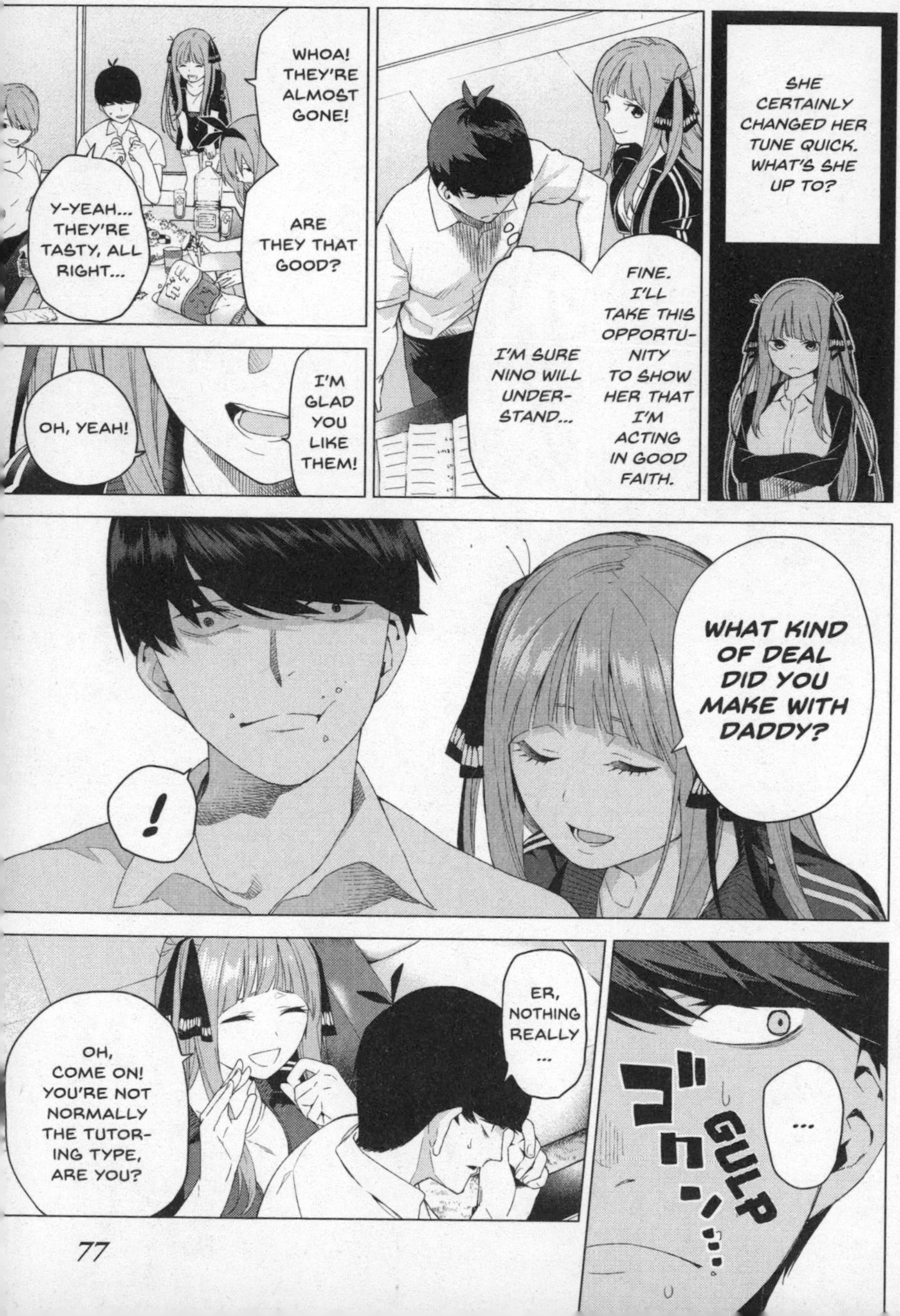
SHE CERTAINLY CHANGED HER TUNE QUICK. WHAT'S SHE UP TO?
FINE. I'LL TAKE THIS OPPORTUNITY TO SHOW HER THAT I'M ACTING IN GOOD FAITH.
I'M SURE NINO WILL UNDERSTAND...
WHOA! THEY'RE ALMOST GONE!
ARE THEY THAT GOOD?
Y-YEAH... THEY'RE TASTY, ALL RIGHT...
I'M GLAD YOU LIKE THEM!
OH, YEAH!
WHAT KIND OF DEAL DID YOU MAKE WITH DADDY?
!
...
GULP
ER, NOTHING REALLY ...
OH, COME ON! YOU'RE NOT NORMALLY THE TUTORING TYPE, ARE YOU?

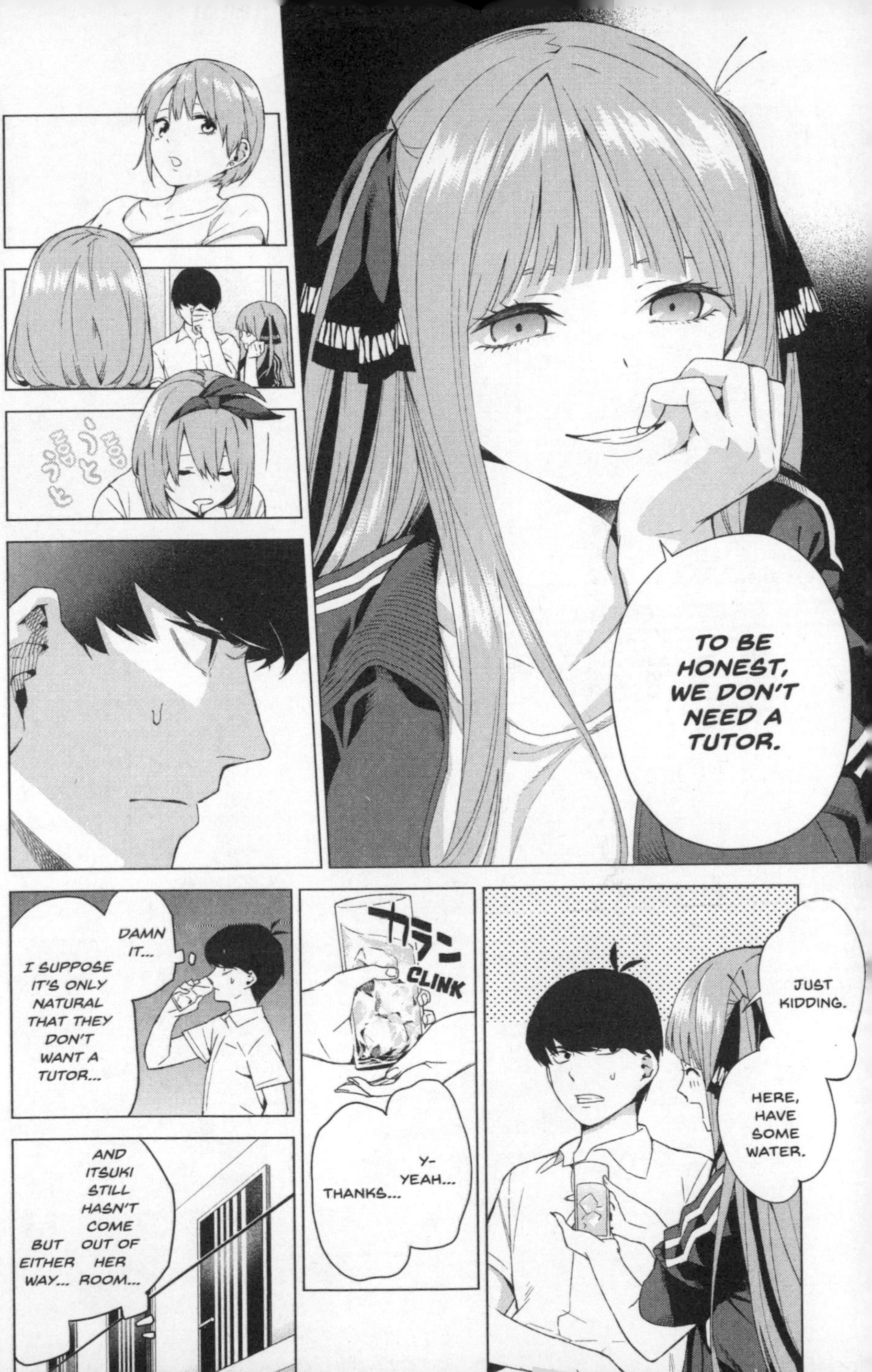
TO BE HONEST, WE DON'T NEED A TUTOR.
うとうと
JUST KIDDING.
HERE, HAVE SOME WATER.
カラン
CLINK
Y- YEAH... THANKS...
DAMN IT...
I SUPPOSE IT'S ONLY NATURAL THAT THEY DON'T WANT A TUTOR...
AND ITSUKI STILL HASN'T COME OUT OF HER ROOM...
BUT EITHER WAY...

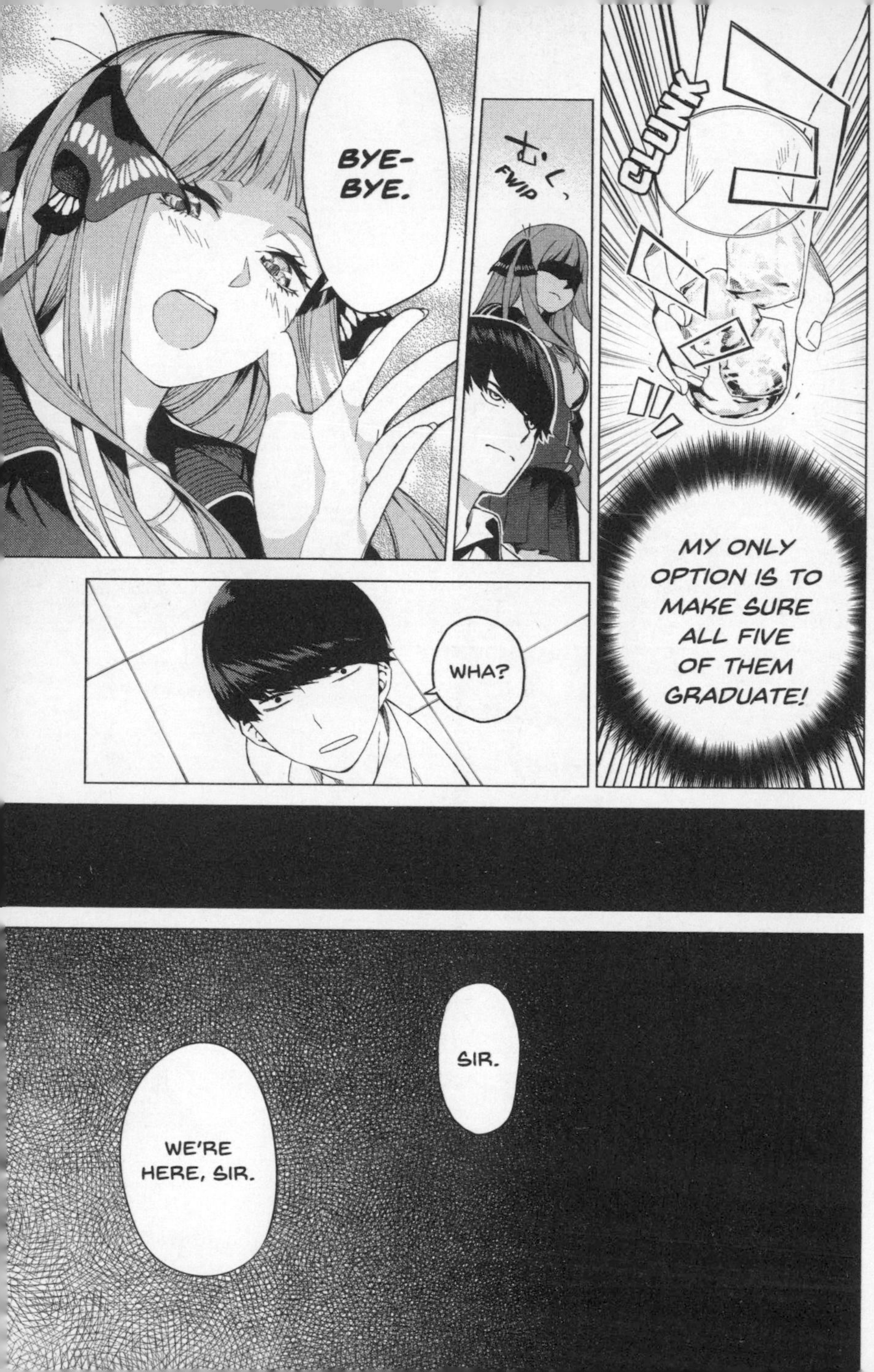
CLUNK
MY ONLY OPTION IS TO MAKE SURE ALL FIVE OF THEM GRADUATE!
FWIP
BYE-BYE.
WHA?
SIR.
WE'RE HERE, SIR.

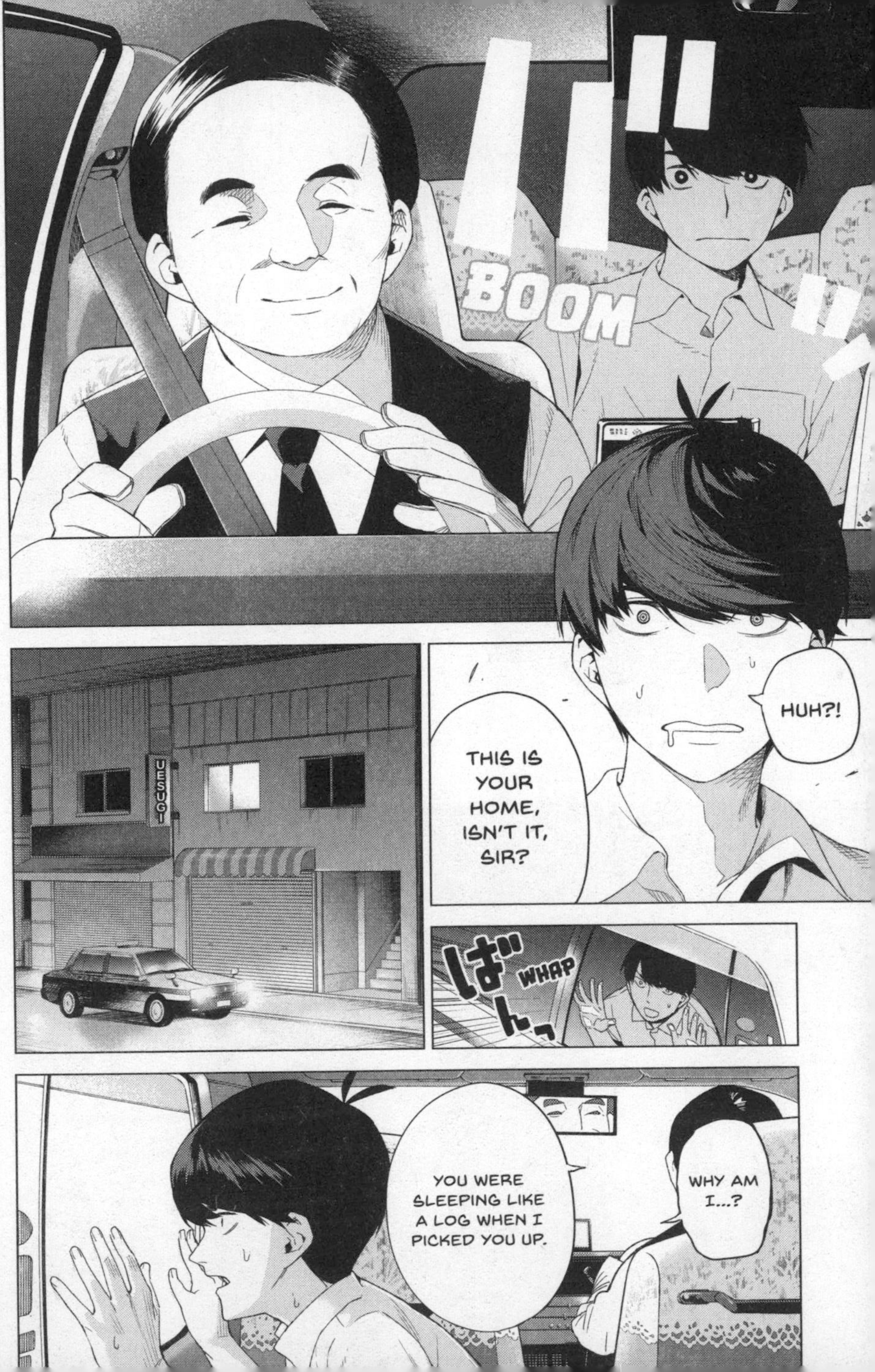
BOOM
HUH?!
THIS IS YOUR HOME, ISN'T IT, SIR?
ばんっ
WHAP
UESUGI
WHY AM I...?
YOU WERE SLEEPING LIKE A LOG WHEN I PICKED YOU UP.

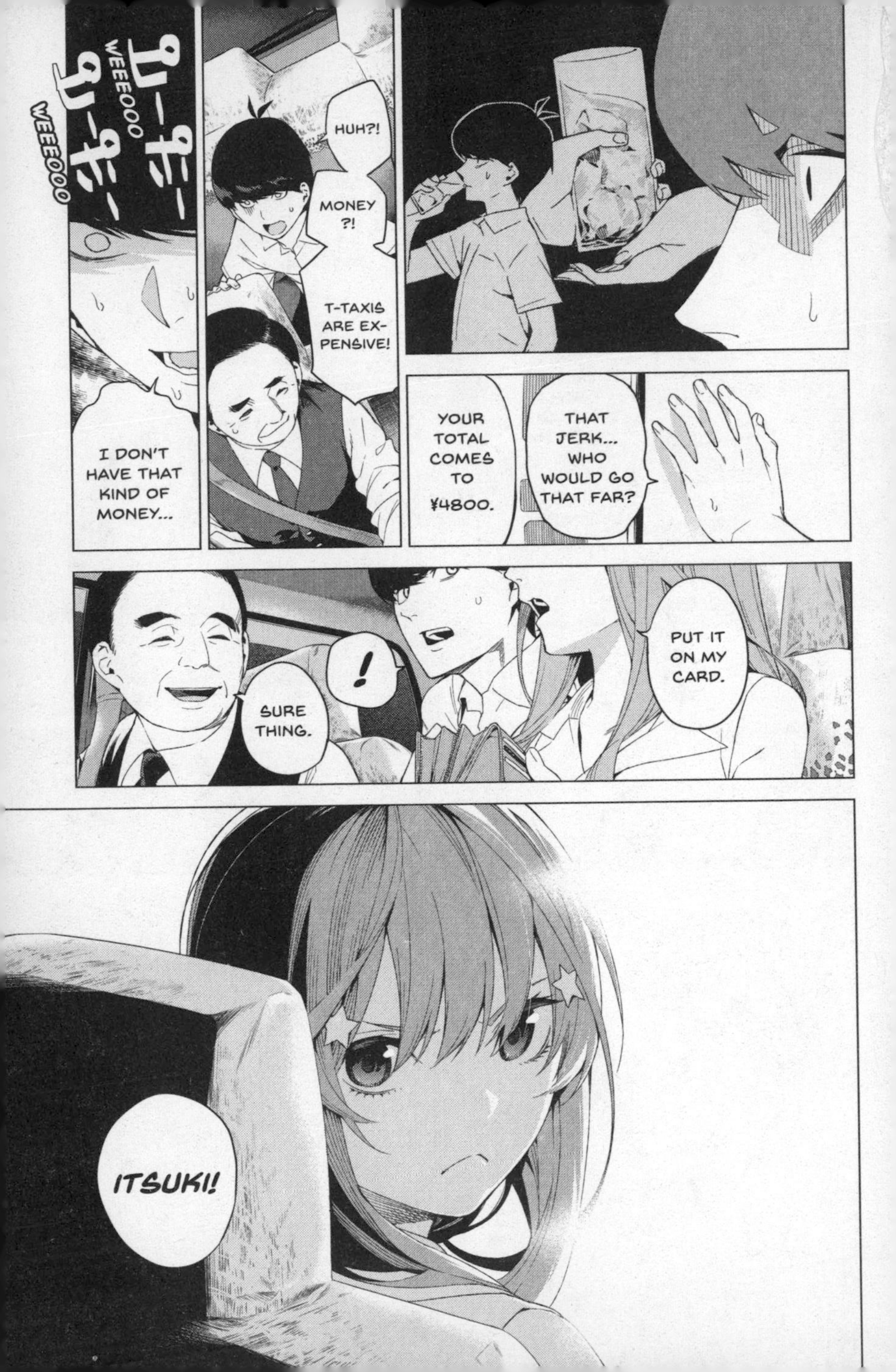
THAT JERK... WHO WOULD GO THAT FAR?
YOUR TOTAL COMES TO ¥4800.
HUH?!
MONEY?!
T-TAXIS ARE EX-PENSIVE!
WEEEOOO
WEEEOOO
I DON'T HAVE THAT KIND OF MONEY...
PUT IT ON MY CARD.
!
SURE THING.
ITSUKI!

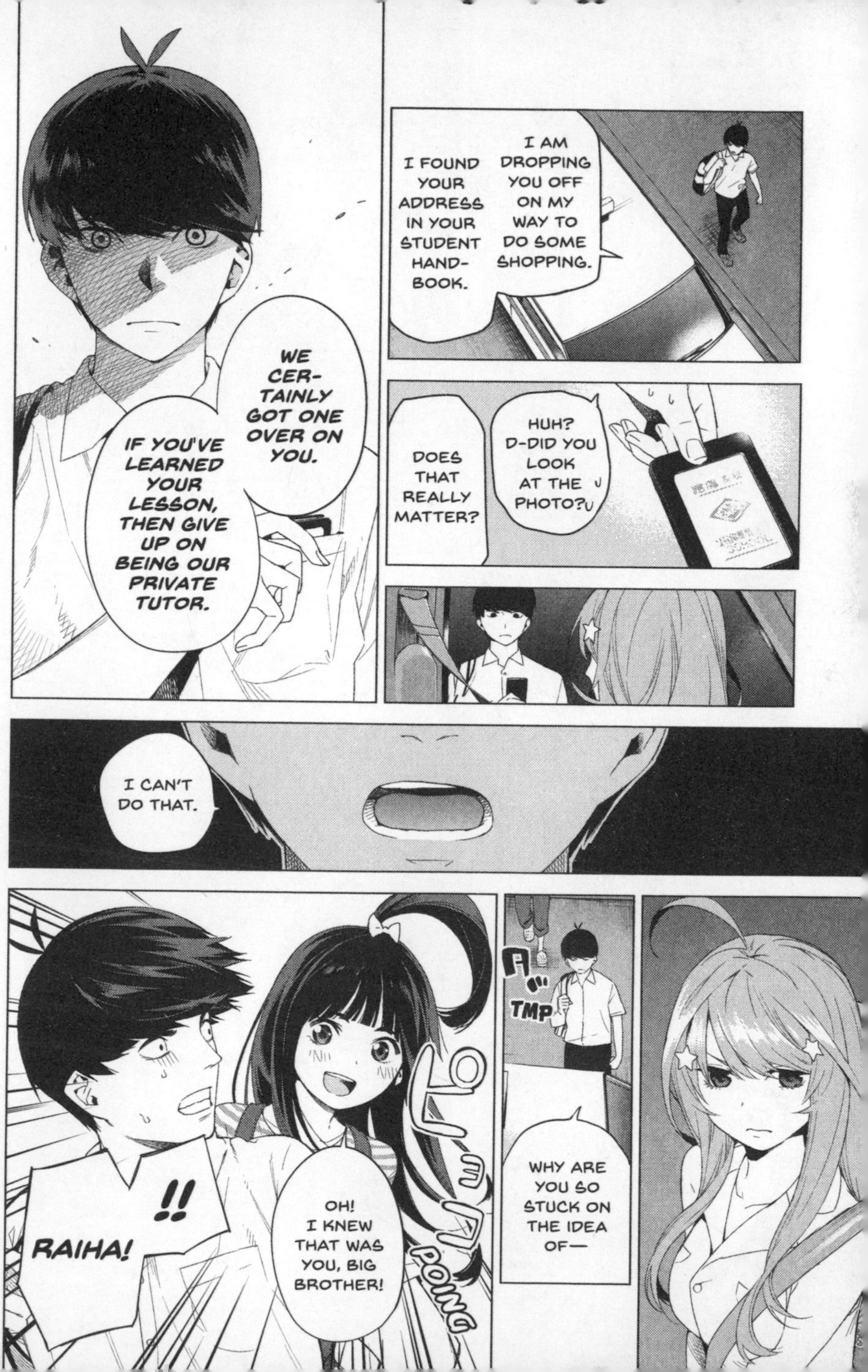
I AM DROPPING YOU OFF ON MY WAY TO DO SOME SHOPPING.
I FOUND YOUR ADDRESS IN YOUR STUDENT HANDBOOK.
HUH? D-DID YOU LOOK AT THE PHOTO?
DOES THAT REALLY MATTER?
WE CERTAINLY GOT ONE OVER ON YOU.
IF YOU'VE LEARNED YOUR LESSON, THEN GIVE UP ON BEING OUR PRIVATE TUTOR.
I CAN'T DO THAT.
WHY ARE YOU SO STUCK ON THE IDEA OF—
TMP
POING
OH! I KNEW THAT WAS YOU, BIG BROTHER!
!!
RAIHA!

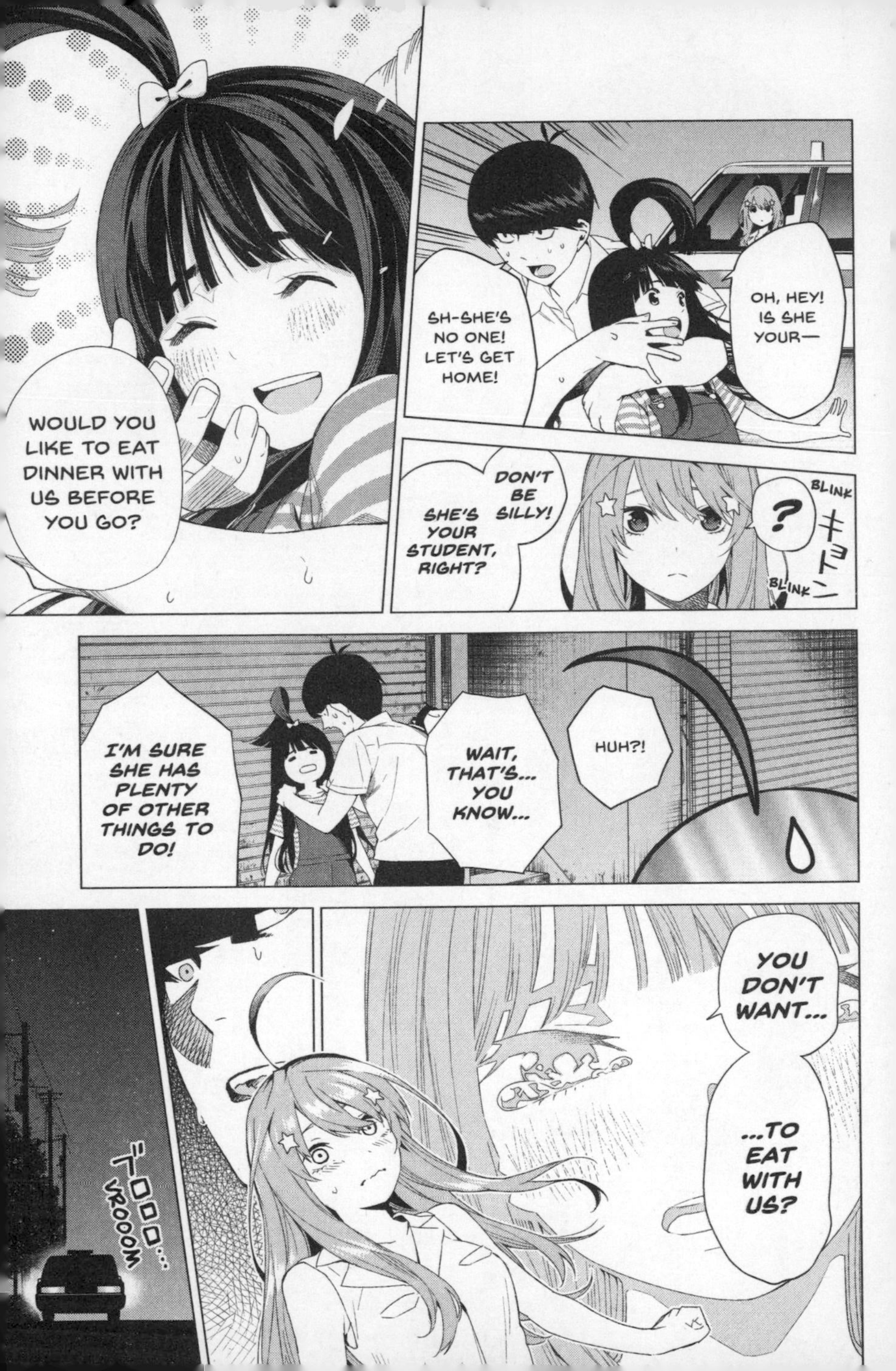
OH, HEY! IS SHE YOUR—
SH-SHE'S NO ONE! LET'S GET HOME!
?
BLINK
キョトン
BLINK
DON'T BE SILLY!
SHE'S YOUR STUDENT, RIGHT?
WOULD YOU LIKE TO EAT DINNER WITH US BEFORE YOU GO?
HUH?!
WAIT, THAT'S... YOU KNOW...
I'M SURE SHE HAS PLENTY OF OTHER THINGS TO DO!
YOU DON'T WANT...
...TO EAT WITH US?
ブロロロ…
VROOOM

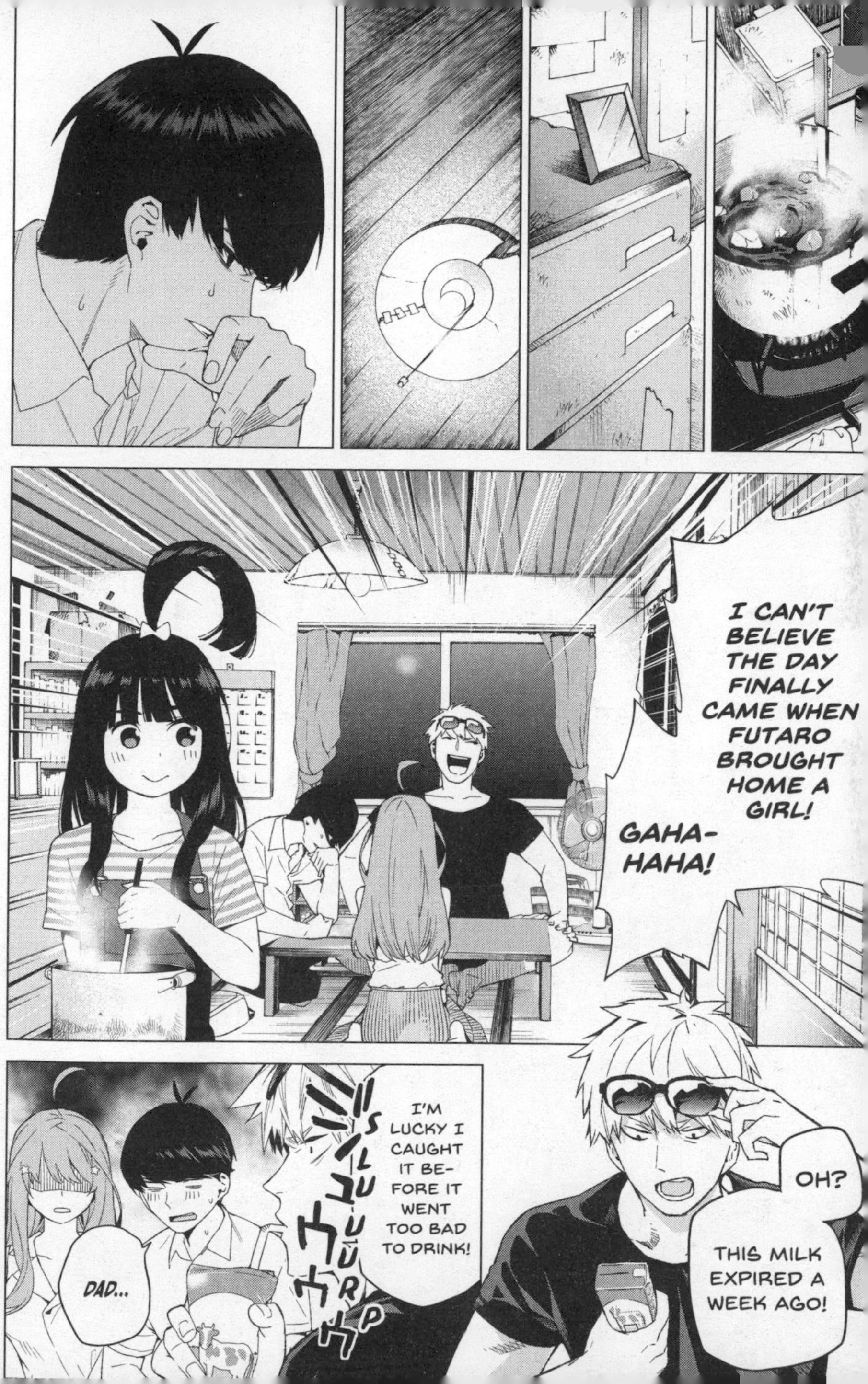
I CAN'T BELIEVE THE DAY FINALLY CAME WHEN FUTARO BROUGHT HOME A GIRL!
GAHA-HAHA!
OH?
THIS MILK EXPIRED A WEEK AGO!
I'M LUCKY I CAUGHT IT BEFORE IT WENT TOO BAD TO DRINK!
SLU-UURP
DAD...

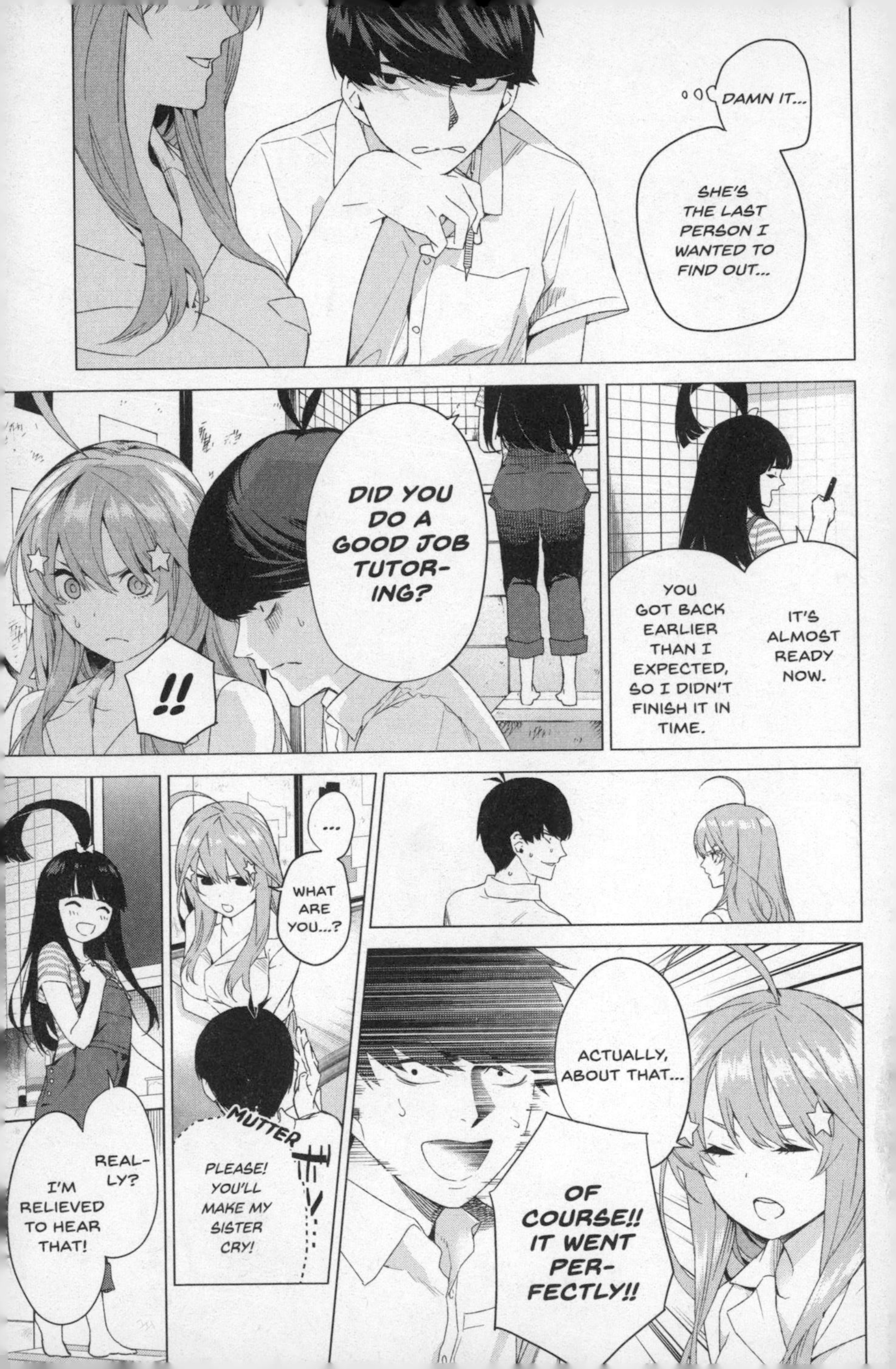
DAMN IT...
SHE'S THE LAST PERSON I WANTED TO FIND OUT...
YOU GOT BACK EARLIER THAN I EXPECTED, SO I DIDN'T FINISH IT IN TIME. IT'S ALMOST READY NOW.
DID YOU DO A GOOD JOB TUTOR-ING?
!!
ACTUALLY, ABOUT THAT...
OF COURSE!! IT WENT PER-FECTLY!!
...
WHAT ARE YOU...?
MUTTER
PLEASE! YOU'LL MAKE MY SISTER CRY!
REAL-LY? I'M RELIEVED TO HEAR THAT!

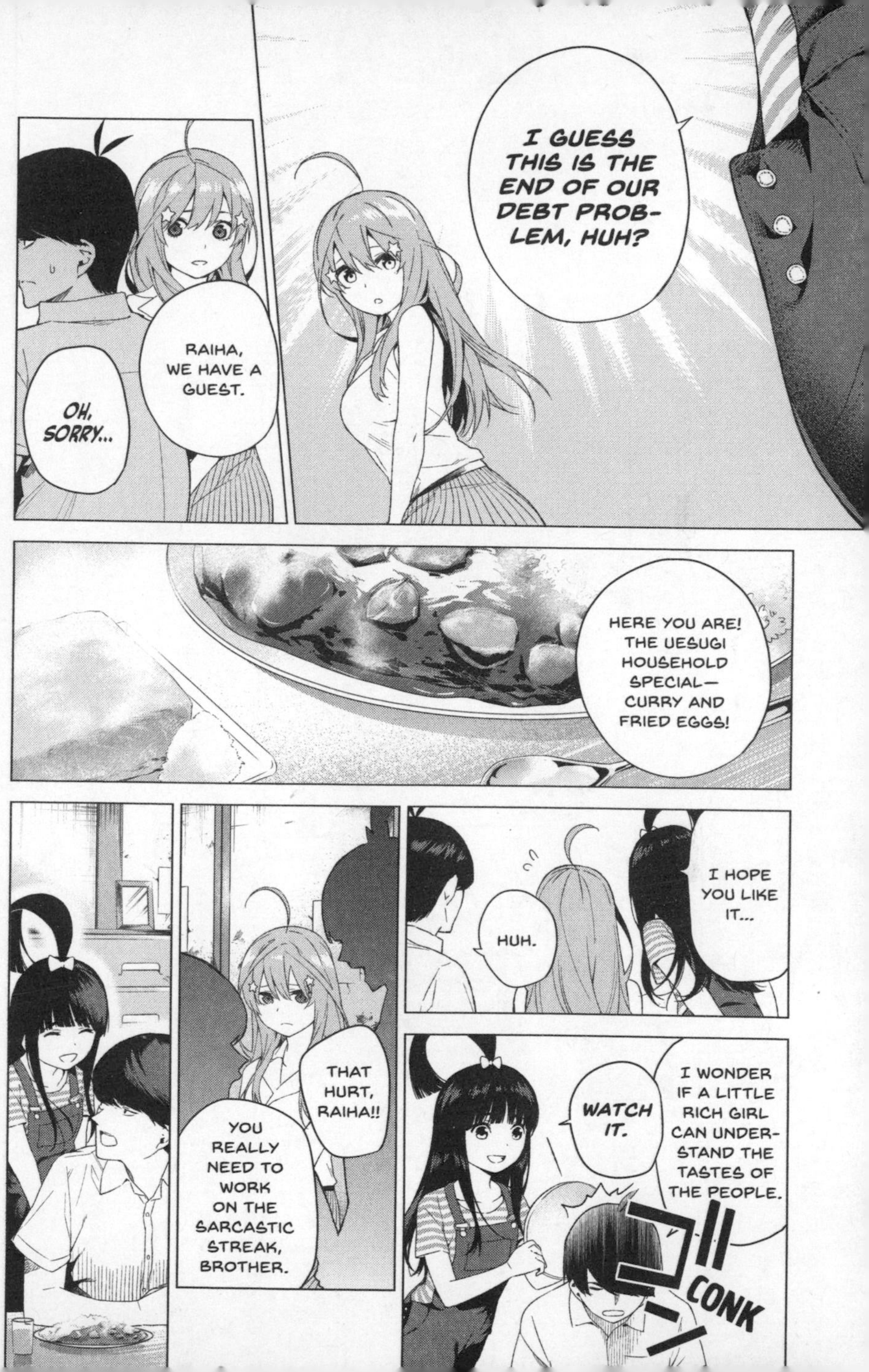
I GUESS THIS IS THE END OF OUR DEBT PROB-LEM, HUH?
RAIHA, WE HAVE A GUEST.
OH, SORRY...
HERE YOU ARE! THE UESUGI HOUSEHOLD SPECIAL— CURRY AND FRIED EGGS!
I HOPE YOU LIKE IT...
HUH.
I WONDER IF A LITTLE RICH GIRL CAN UNDER-STAND THE TASTES OF THE PEOPLE.
WATCH IT.
CONK
THAT HURT, RAIHA!!
YOU REALLY NEED TO WORK ON THE SARCASTIC STREAK, BROTHER.

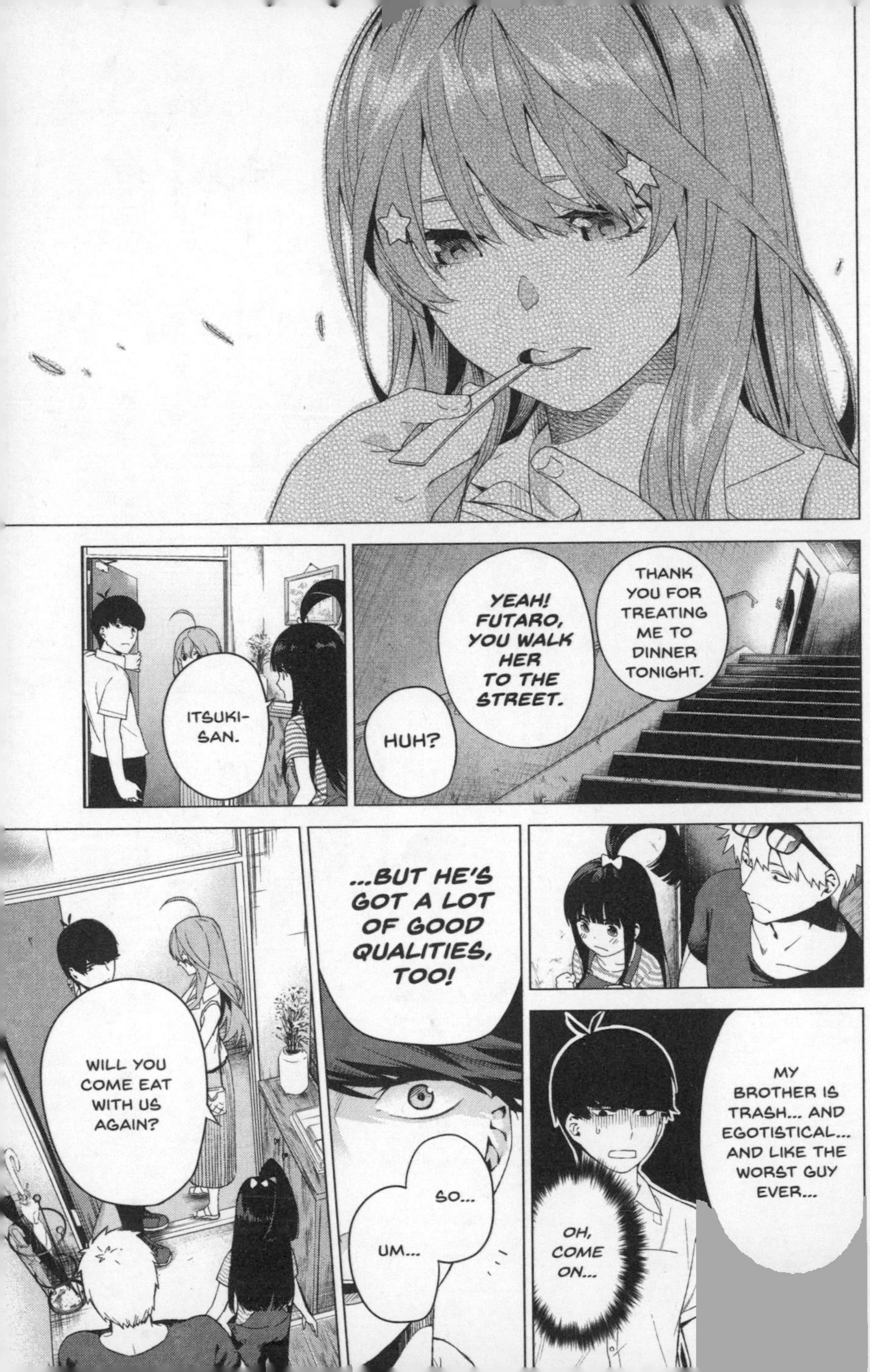
THANK YOU FOR TREATING ME TO DINNER TONIGHT.
YEAH! FUTARO, YOU WALK HER TO THE STREET.
HUH?
ITSUKI-SAN.
MY BROTHER IS TRASH... AND EGOTISTICAL... AND LIKE THE WORST GUY EVER...
OH, COME ON...
...BUT HE'S GOT A LOT OF GOOD QUALITIES, TOO!
SO...
UM...
WILL YOU COME EAT WITH US AGAIN?

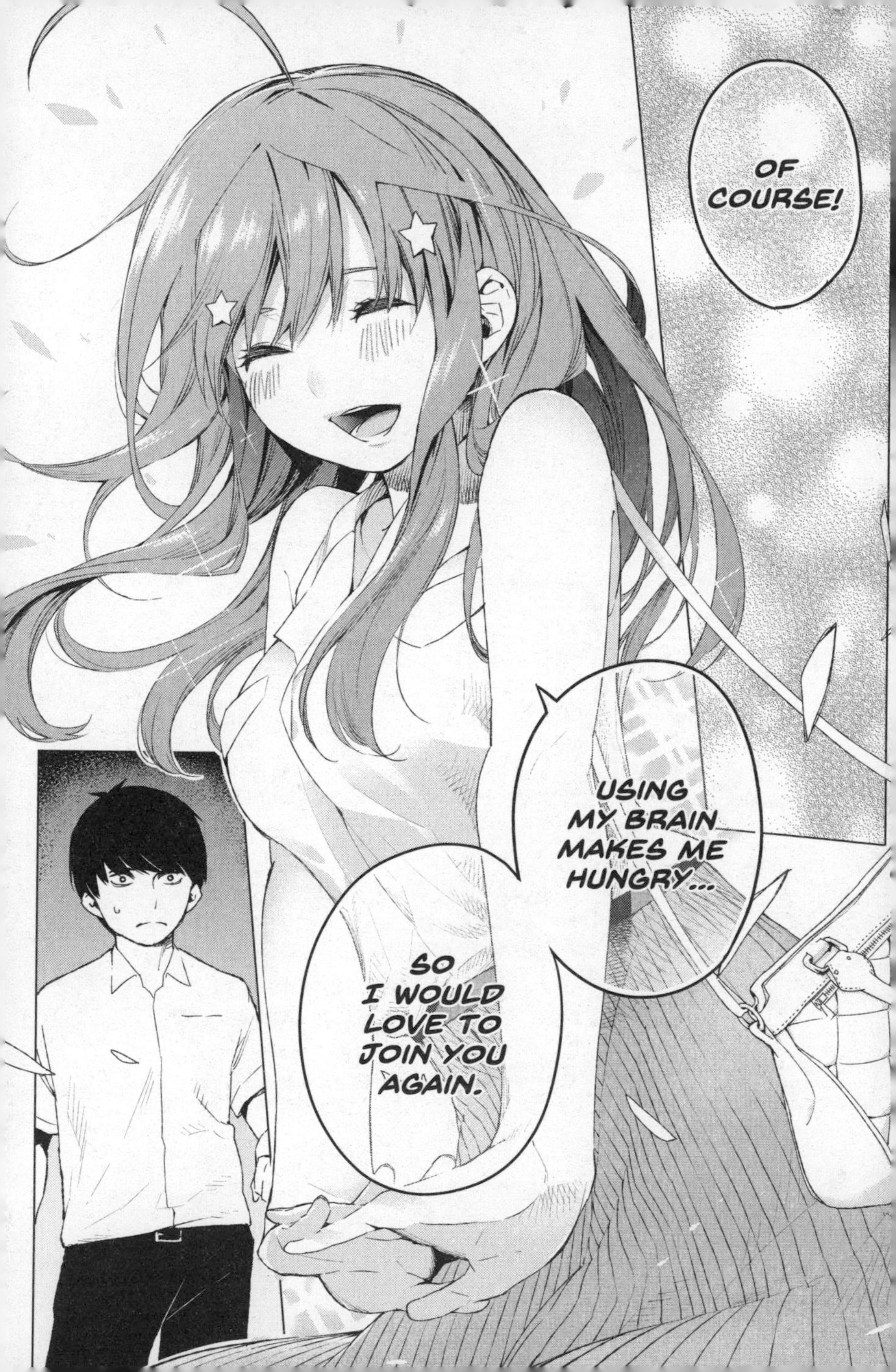
OF COURSE!
USING MY BRAIN MAKES ME HUNGRY...
SO I WOULD LOVE TO JOIN YOU AGAIN.

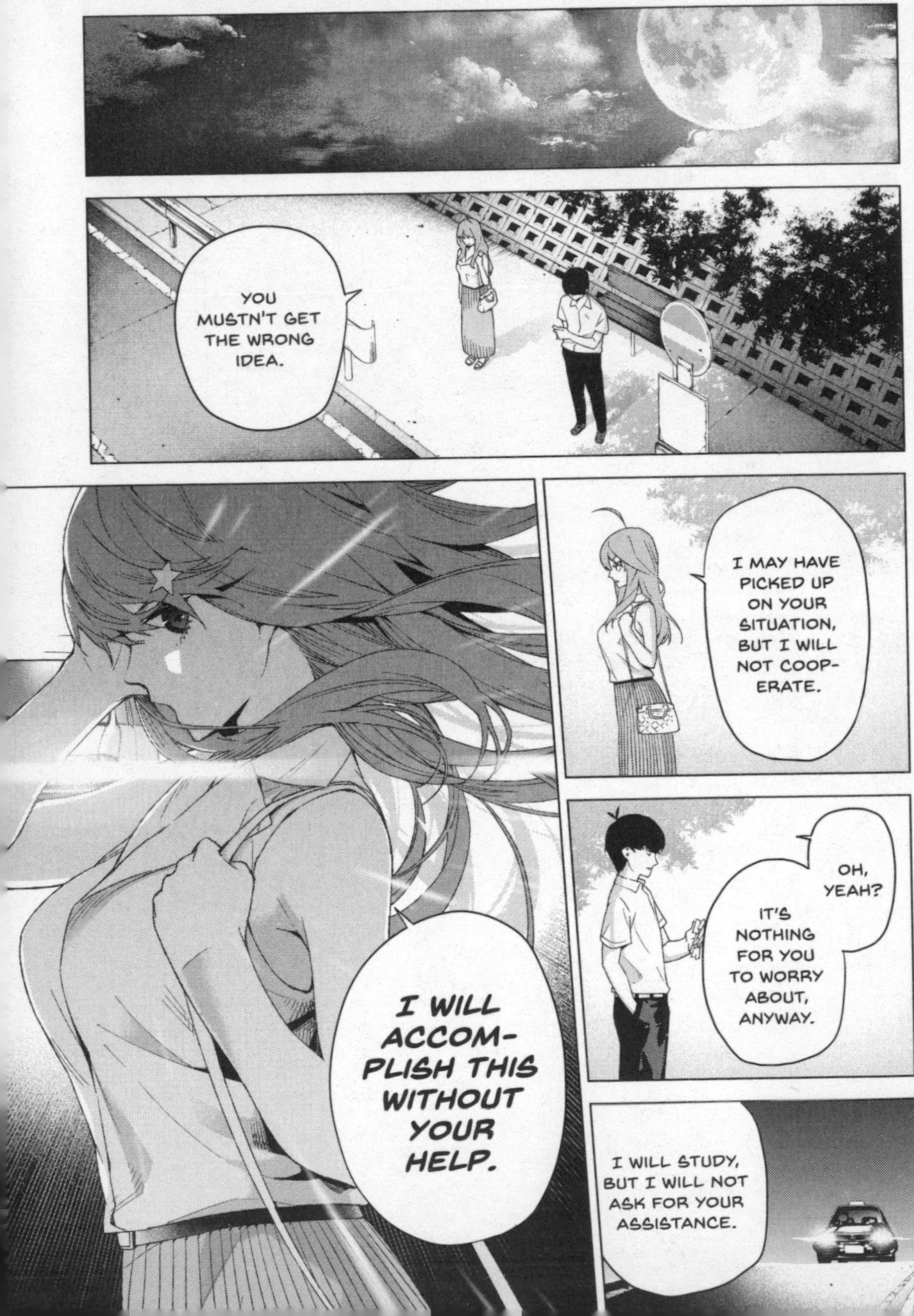
YOU MUSTN'T GET THE WRONG IDEA.
I MAY HAVE PICKED UP ON YOUR SITUATION, BUT I WILL NOT COOP-ERATE.
OH, YEAH?
IT'S NOTHING FOR YOU TO WORRY ABOUT, ANYWAY.
I WILL STUDY, BUT I WILL NOT ASK FOR YOUR ASSISTANCE.
I WILL ACCOM-PLISH THIS WITHOUT YOUR HELP.

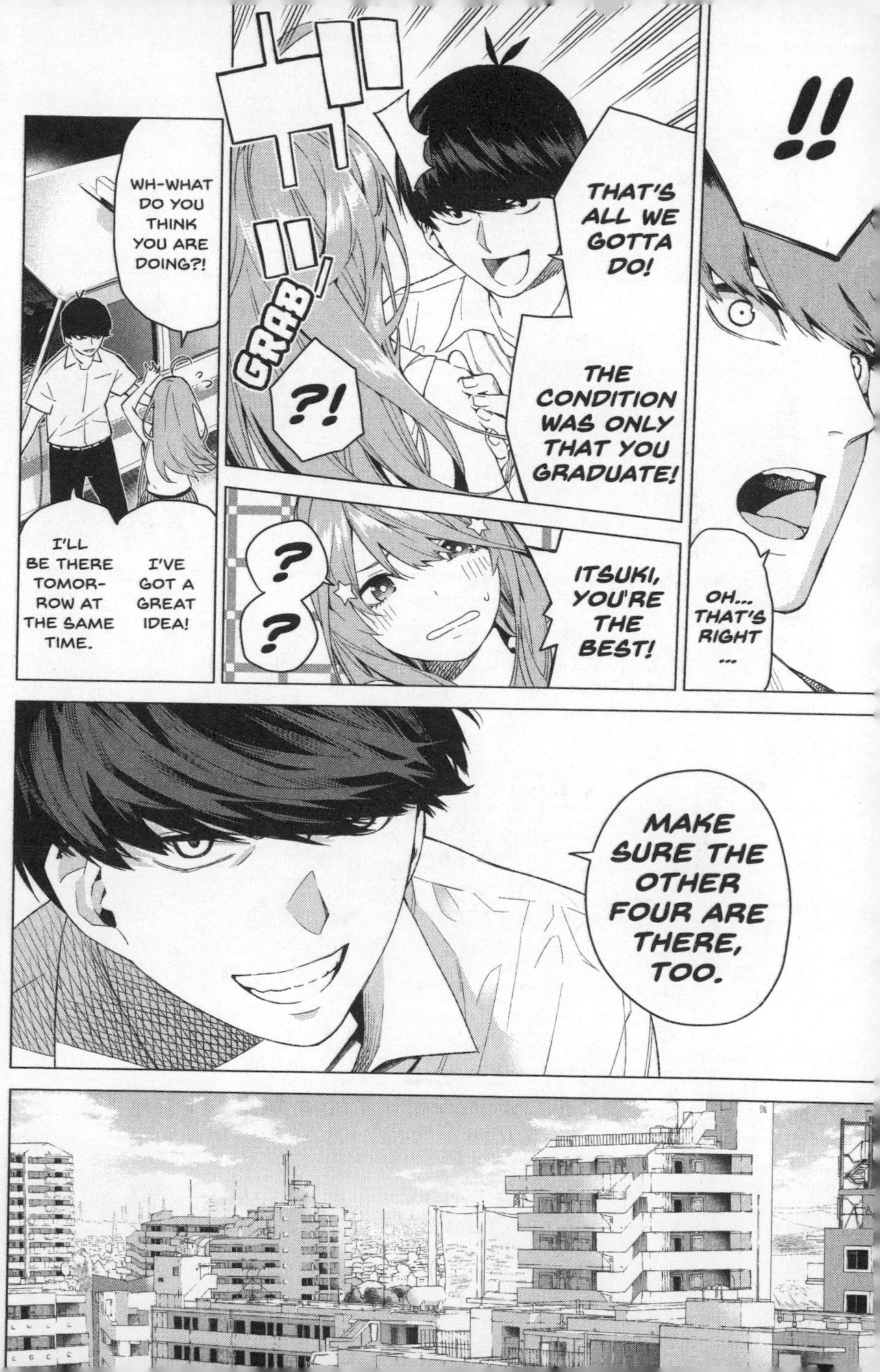
!!
OH... THAT'S RIGHT ...
THAT'S ALL WE GOTTA DO!
THE CONDITION WAS ONLY THAT YOU GRADUATE!
GRAB
?!
ITSUKI, YOU'RE THE BEST!
??
WH-WHAT DO YOU THINK YOU ARE DOING?!
I'VE GOT A GREAT IDEA!
I'LL BE THERE TOMOR-ROW AT THE SAME TIME.
MAKE SURE THE OTHER FOUR ARE THERE, TOO.

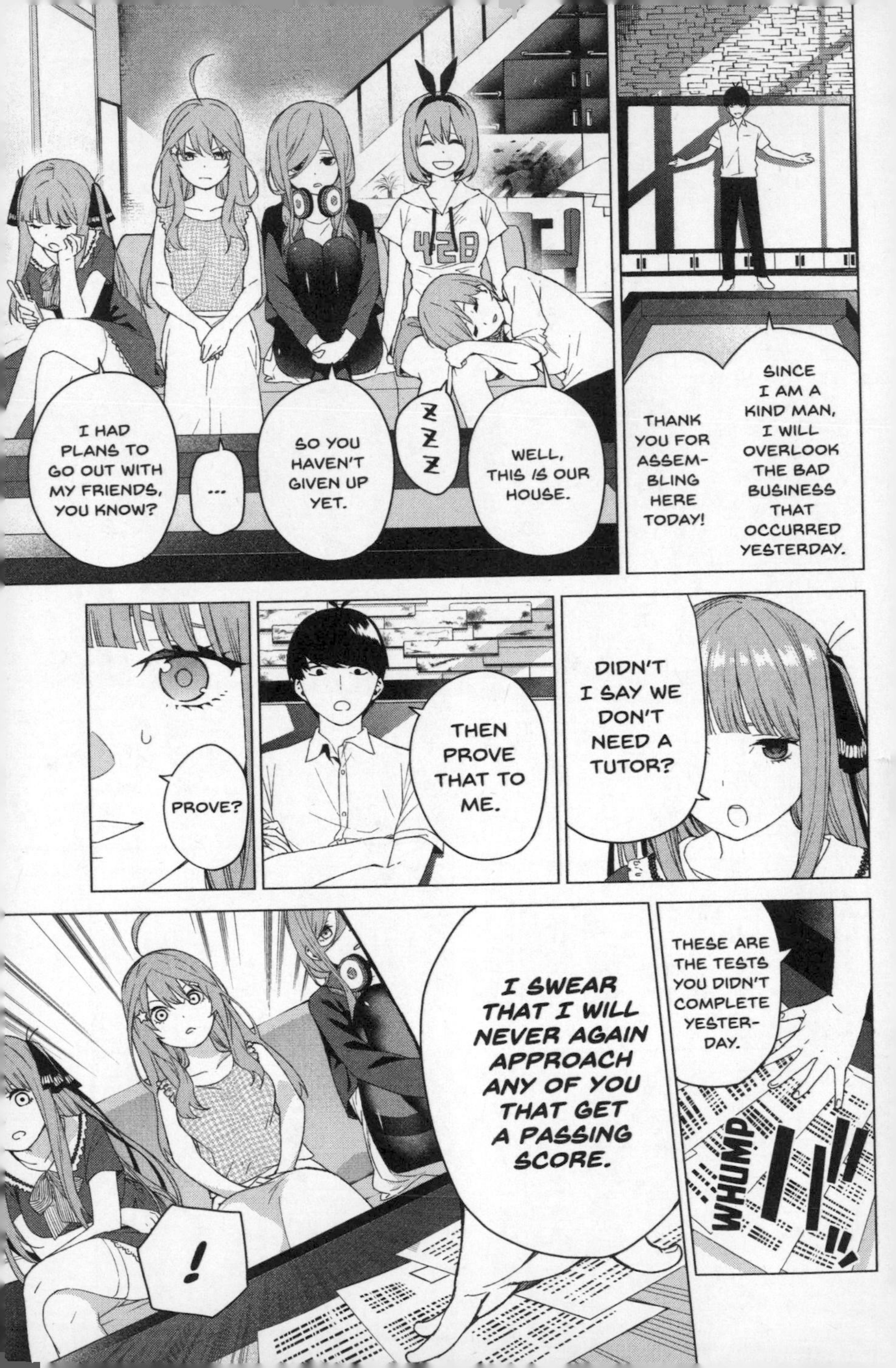
THANK YOU FOR ASSEMBLING HERE TODAY!
SINCE I AM A KIND MAN, I WILL OVERLOOK THE BAD BUSINESS THAT OCCURRED YESTERDAY.
WELL, THIS IS OUR HOUSE.
ZZZ
SO YOU HAVEN'T GIVEN UP YET.
...
I HAD PLANS TO GO OUT WITH MY FRIENDS, YOU KNOW?
DIDN'T I SAY WE DON'T NEED A TUTOR?
THEN PROVE THAT TO ME.
PROVE?
THESE ARE THE TESTS YOU DIDN'T COMPLETE YESTERDAY.
WHUMP!!!
I SWEAR THAT I WILL NEVER AGAIN APPROACH ANY OF YOU THAT GET A PASSING SCORE.
!

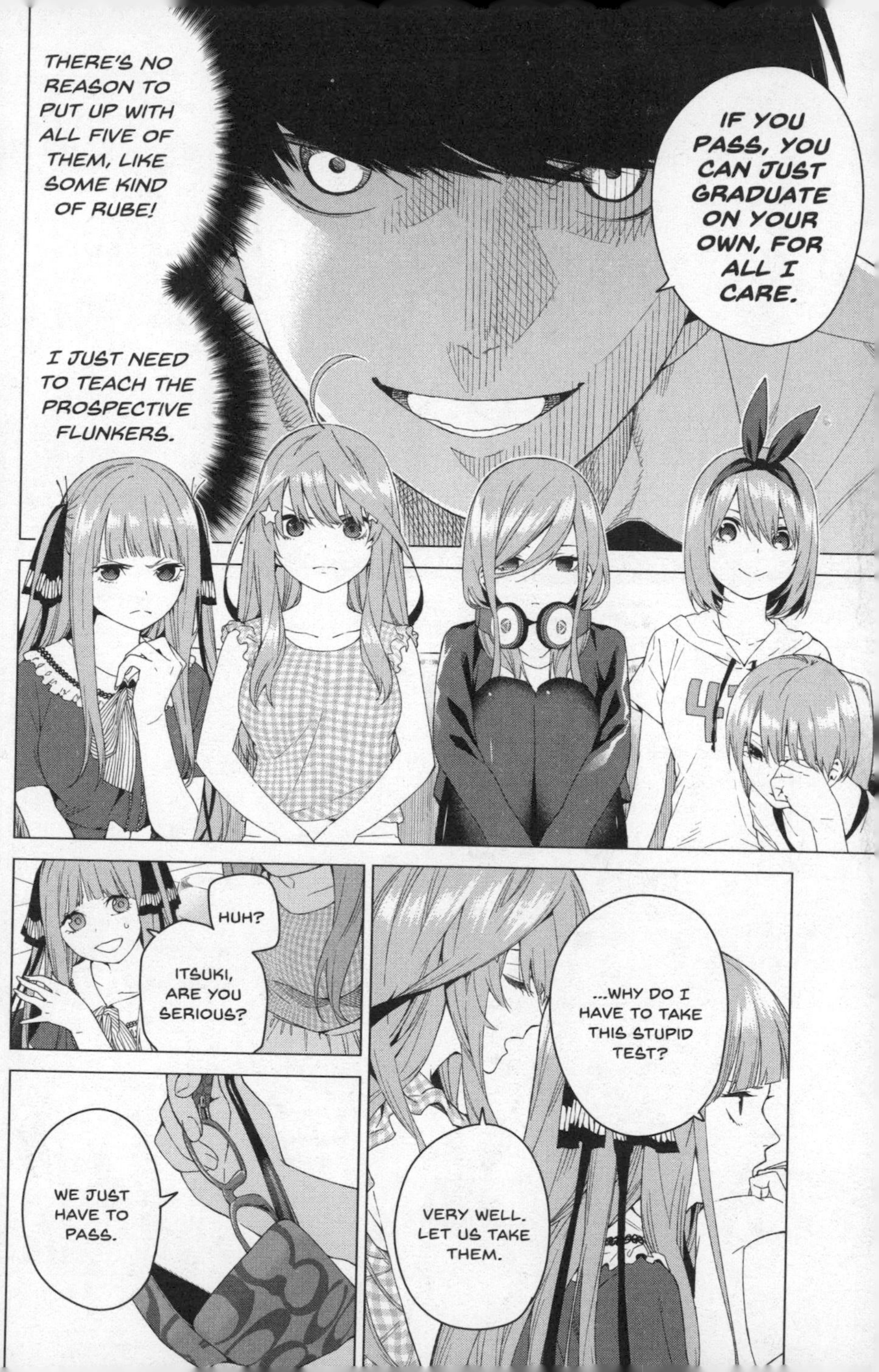
IF YOU PASS, YOU CAN JUST GRADUATE ON YOUR OWN, FOR ALL I CARE.
THERE'S NO REASON TO PUT UP WITH ALL FIVE OF THEM, LIKE SOME KIND OF RUBE!
I JUST NEED TO TEACH THE PROSPECTIVE FLUNKERS.
...WHY DO I HAVE TO TAKE THIS STUPID TEST?
VERY WELL. LET US TAKE THEM.
HUH?
ITSUKI, ARE YOU SERIOUS?
WE JUST HAVE TO PASS.

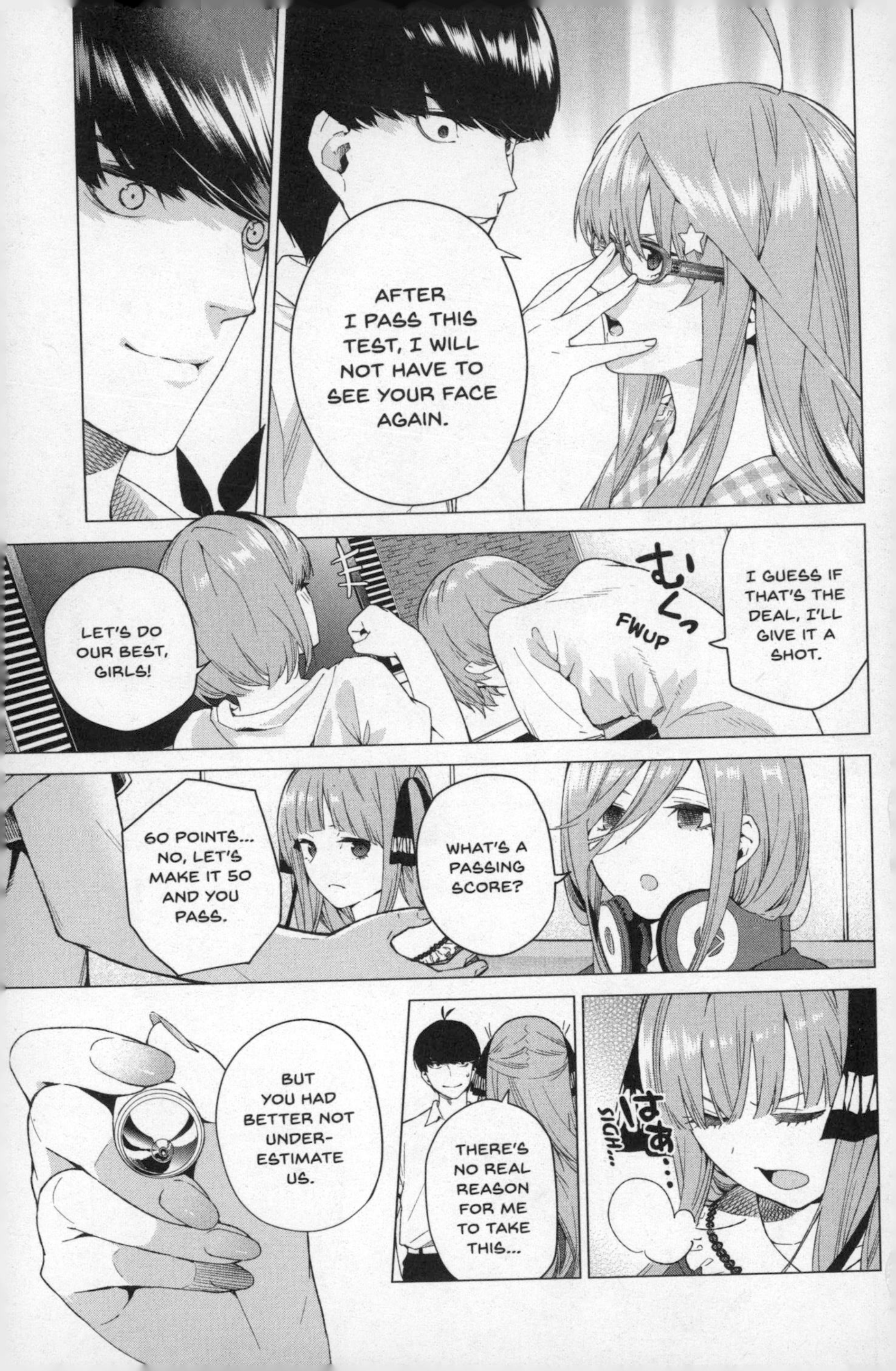
AFTER I PASS THIS TEST, I WILL NOT HAVE TO SEE YOUR FACE AGAIN.
むくっ
FWUP
I GUESS IF THAT'S THE DEAL, I'LL GIVE IT A SHOT.
LET'S DO OUR BEST, GIRLS!
WHAT'S A PASSING SCORE?
60 POINTS... NO, LET'S MAKE IT 50 AND YOU PASS.
はあ…
SIGH...
THERE'S NO REAL REASON FOR ME TO TAKE THIS...
BUT YOU HAD BETTER NOT UNDER-ESTIMATE US.

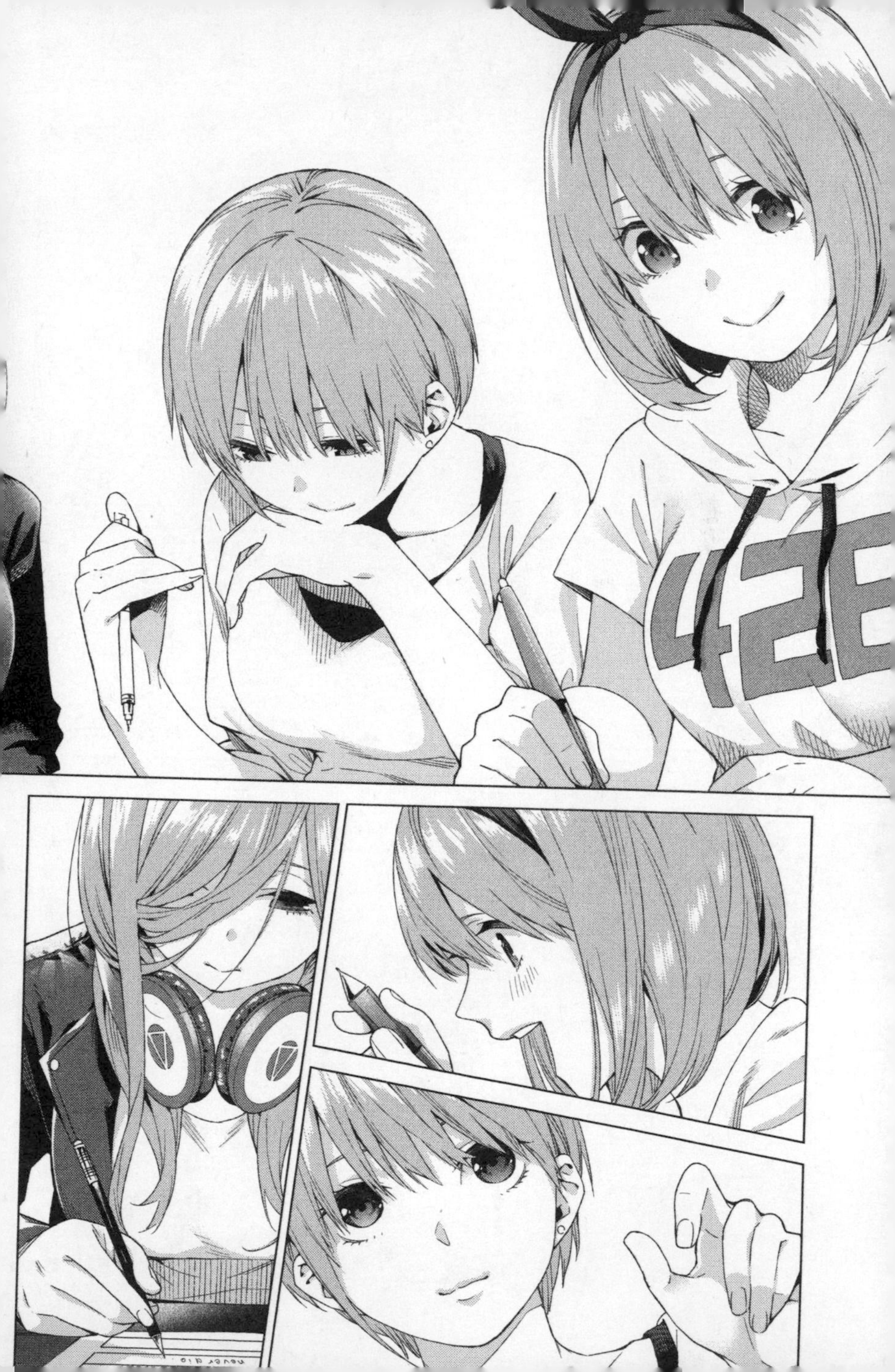

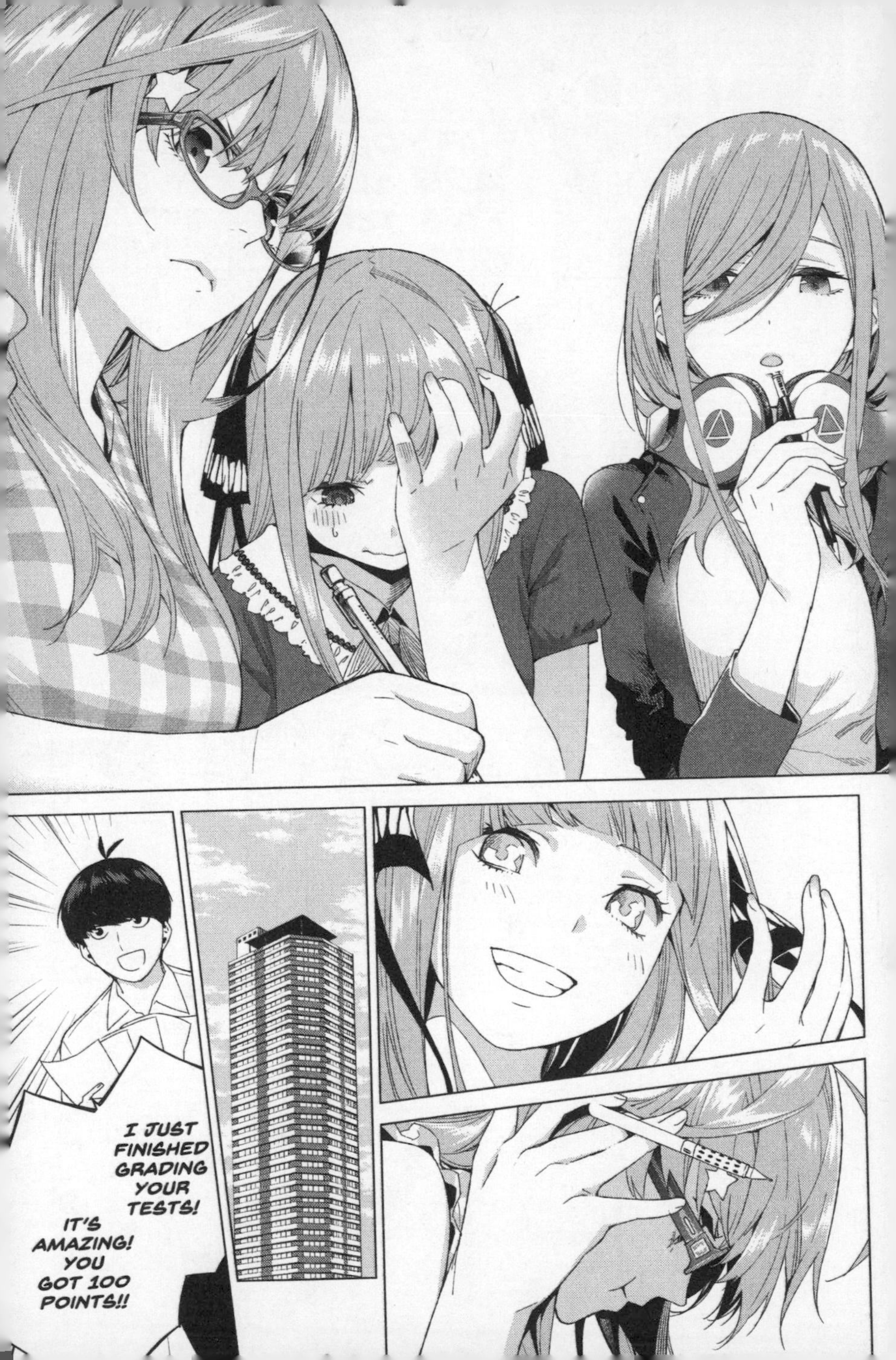
I JUST FINISHED GRADING YOUR TESTS!
IT'S AMAZING! YOU GOT 100 POINTS!!

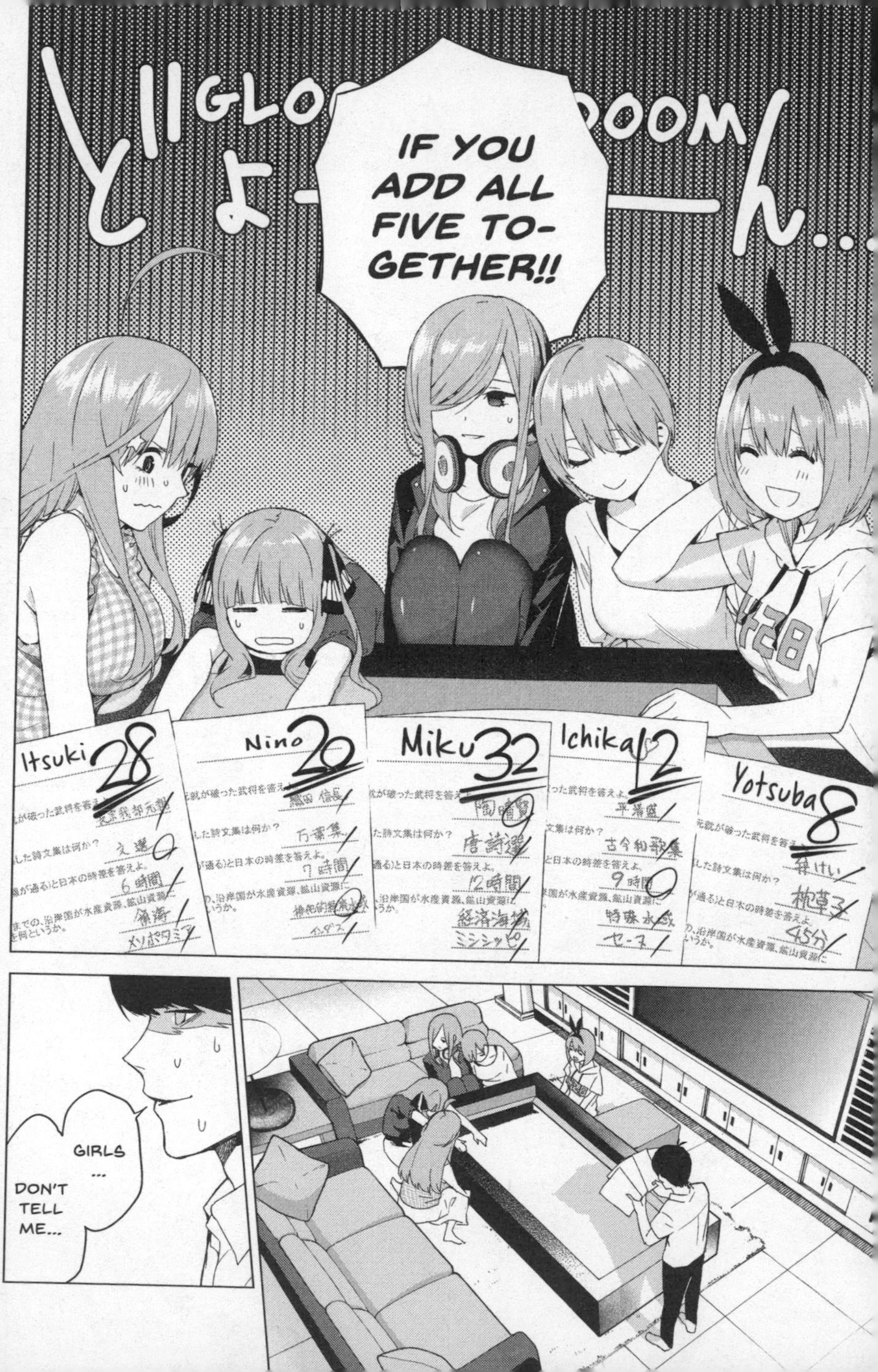
とよーーーん…
GLOO
OOOM
IF YOU ADD ALL FIVE TO-GETHER!!
Itsuki 28
Nino 20
Miku 32
Ichika 12
Yotsuba 8
GIRLS... DON'T TELL ME...

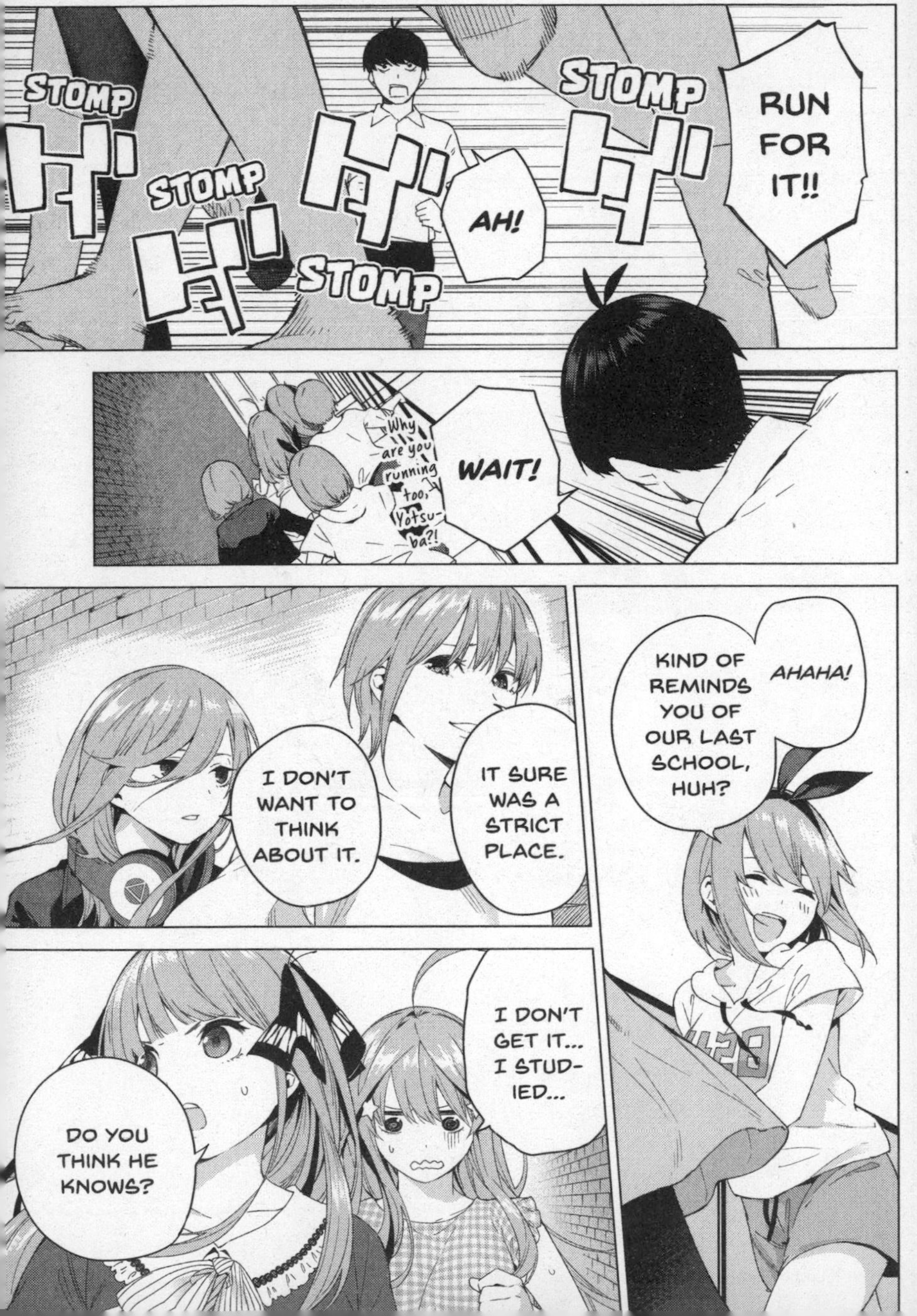
RUN FOR IT!!
STOMP
AH!
STOMP
STOMP
STOMP
WAIT!
Why are you running too, Yotsuba?!
AHAHA!
KIND OF REMINDS YOU OF OUR LAST SCHOOL, HUH?
IT SURE WAS A STRICT PLACE.
I DON'T WANT TO THINK ABOUT IT.
I DON'T GET IT... I STUDIED...
DO YOU THINK HE KNOWS?

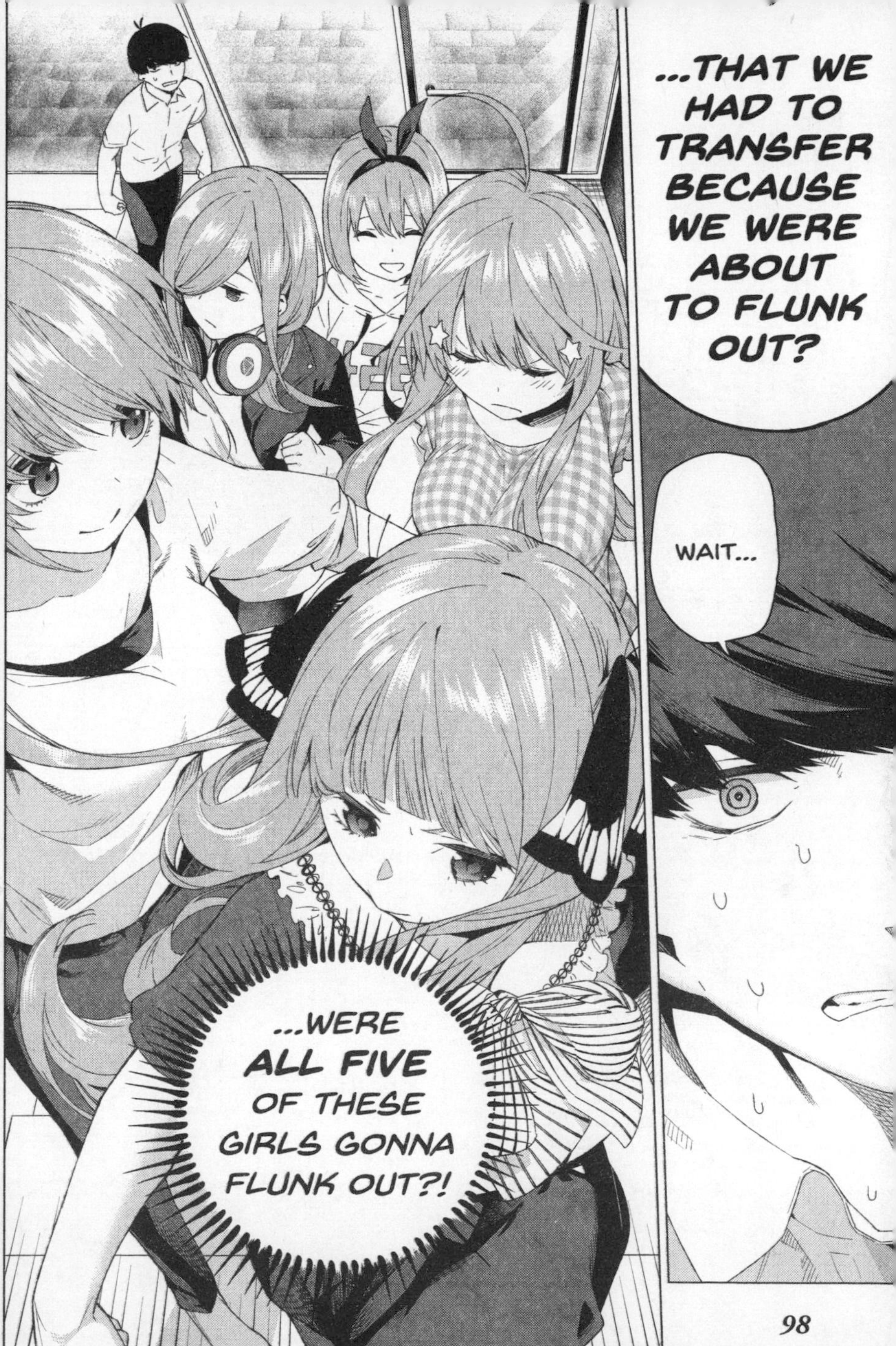
...THAT WE HAD TO TRANSFER BECAUSE WE WERE ABOUT TO FLUNK OUT?
WAIT...
...WERE ALL FIVE OF THESE GIRLS GONNA FLUNK OUT?!

CHAPTER 3
ROOFTOP CONFESSION

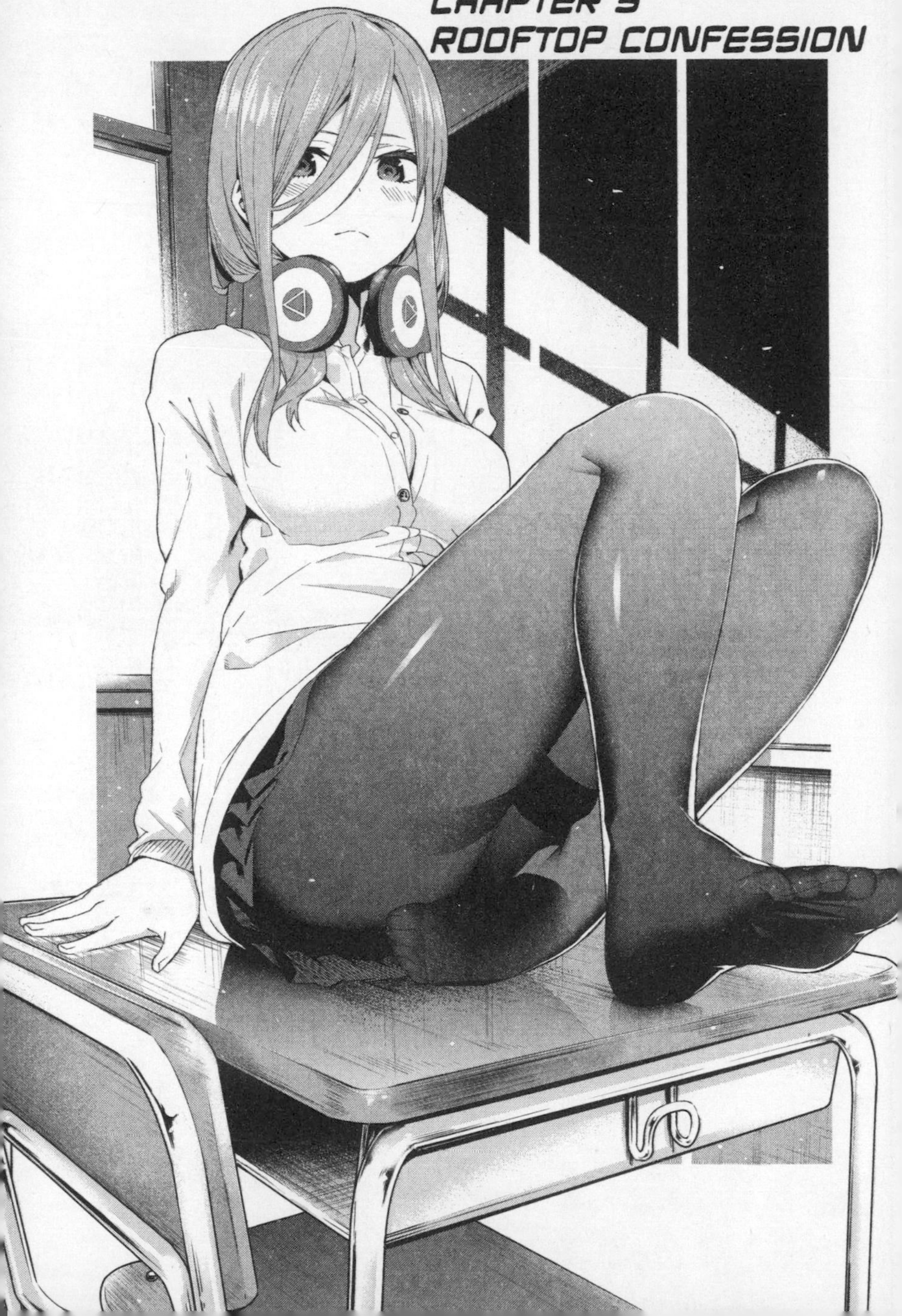

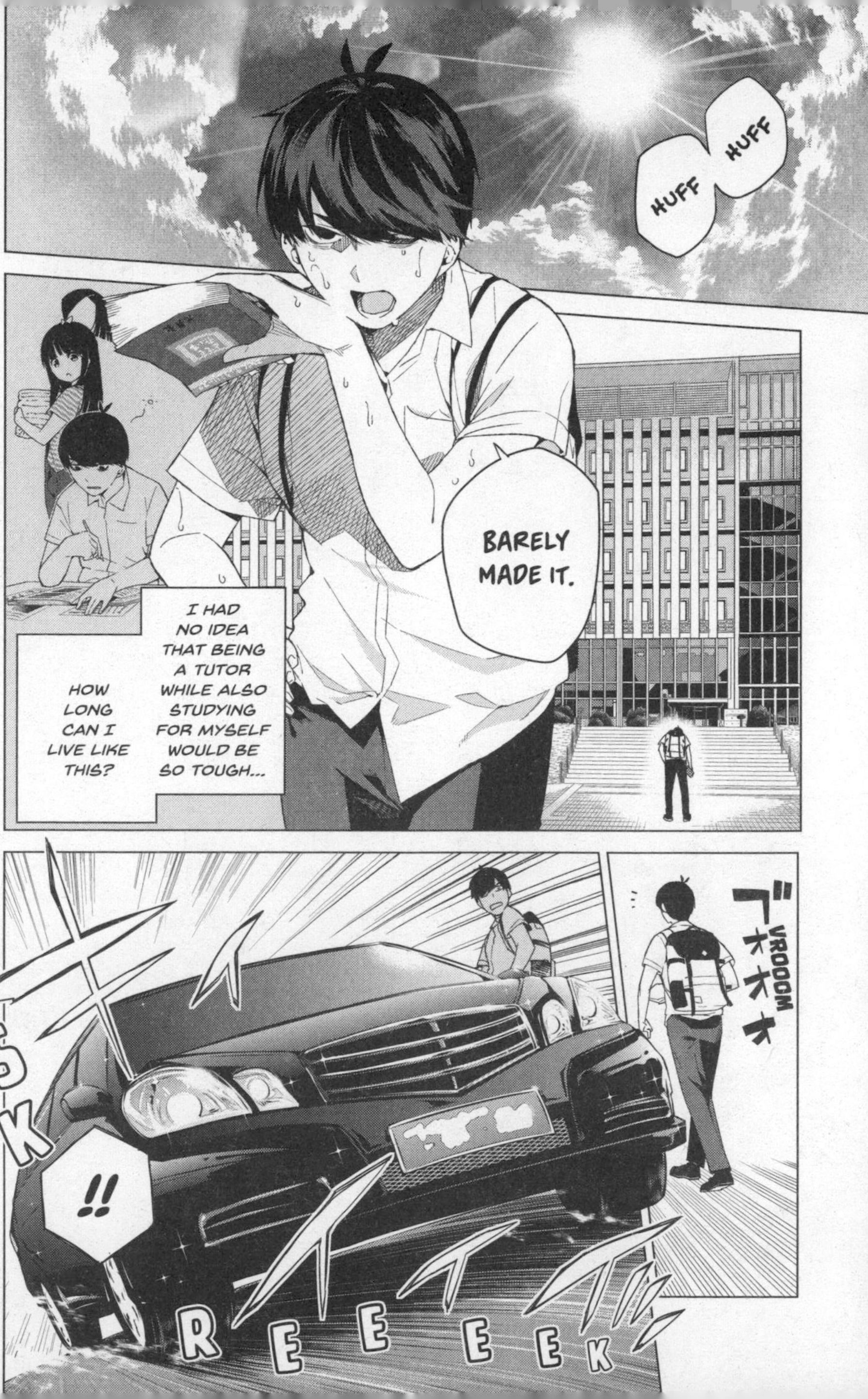
HUFF HUFF
BARELY MADE IT.
I HAD NO IDEA THAT BEING A TUTOR WHILE ALSO STUDYING FOR MYSELF WOULD BE SO TOUGH...
HOW LONG CAN I LIVE LIKE THIS?
VROOOM
SKREEEEK
!!

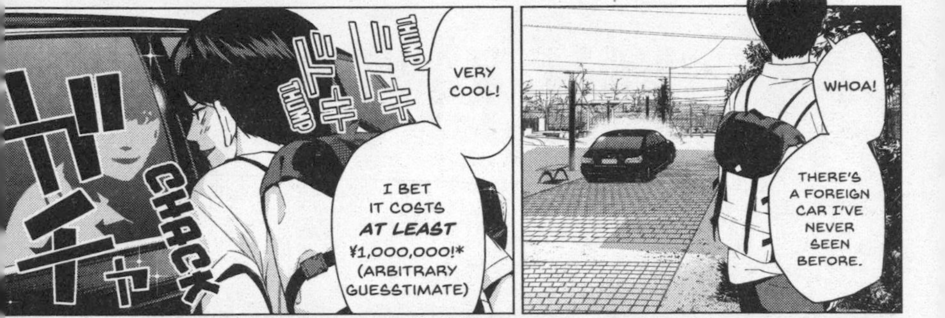
WHOA!
THERE'S A FOREIGN CAR I'VE NEVER SEEN BEFORE.
VERY COOL!
ドキドキ
THUMP THUMP
I BET IT COSTS AT LEAST ¥1,000,000!* (ARBITRARY GUESSTIMATE)
ガチャ
CHACK

*Approximately $10,000.

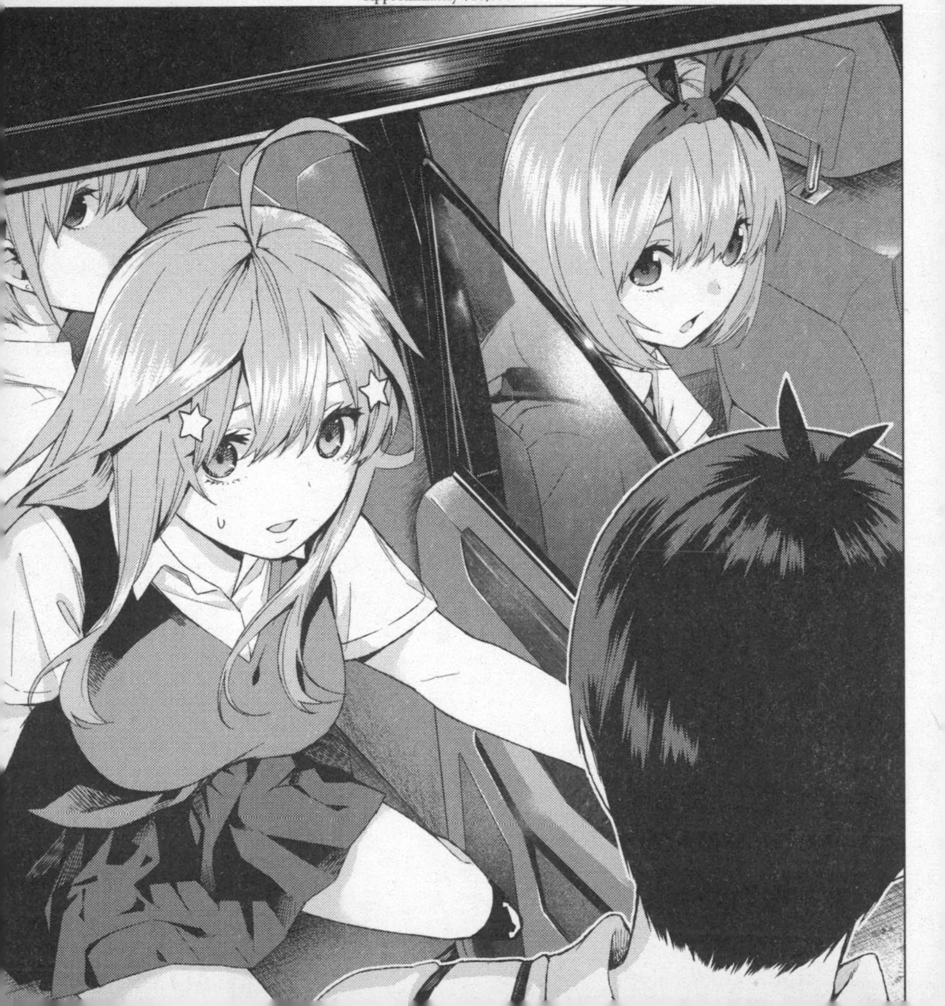

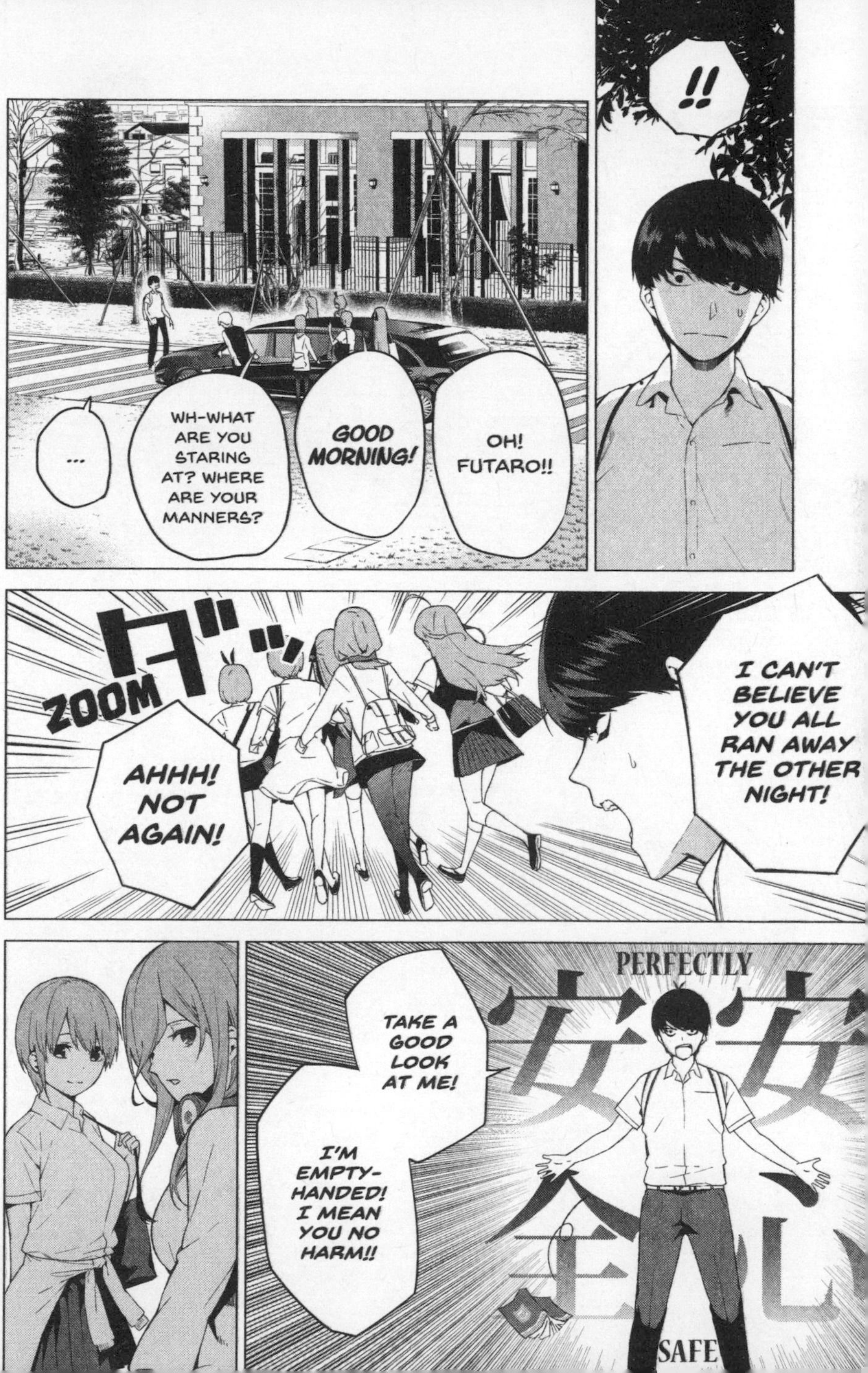
!!
OH! FUTARO!!
GOOD MORNING!
WH-WHAT ARE YOU STARING AT? WHERE ARE YOUR MANNERS?
...
I CAN'T BELIEVE YOU ALL RAN AWAY THE OTHER NIGHT!
ZOOM
AHHH! NOT AGAIN!
PERFECTLY
TAKE A GOOD LOOK AT ME!
I'M EMPTY-HANDED! I MEAN YOU NO HARM!!
SAFE

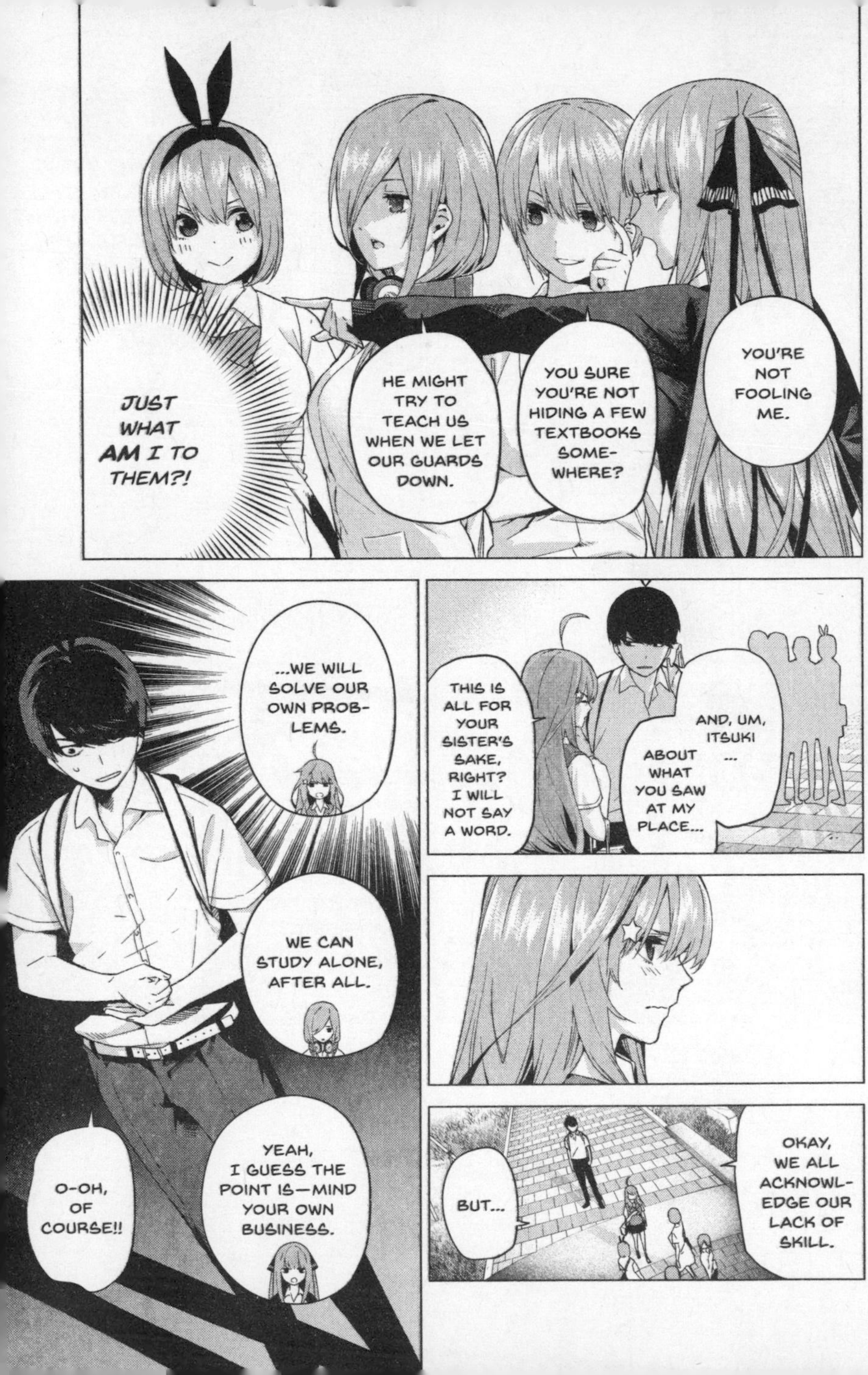
YOU'RE NOT FOOLING ME.
YOU SURE YOU'RE NOT HIDING A FEW TEXTBOOKS SOMEWHERE?
HE MIGHT TRY TO TEACH US WHEN WE LET OUR GUARDS DOWN.
JUST WHAT AM I TO THEM?!
AND, UM, ITSUKI...
ABOUT WHAT YOU SAW AT MY PLACE...
THIS IS ALL FOR YOUR SISTER'S SAKE, RIGHT? I WILL NOT SAY A WORD.
OKAY, WE ALL ACKNOWLEDGE OUR LACK OF SKILL.
BUT...
...WE WILL SOLVE OUR OWN PROBLEMS.
WE CAN STUDY ALONE, AFTER ALL.
YEAH, I GUESS THE POINT IS—MIND YOUR OWN BUSINESS.
O-OH, OF COURSE!!

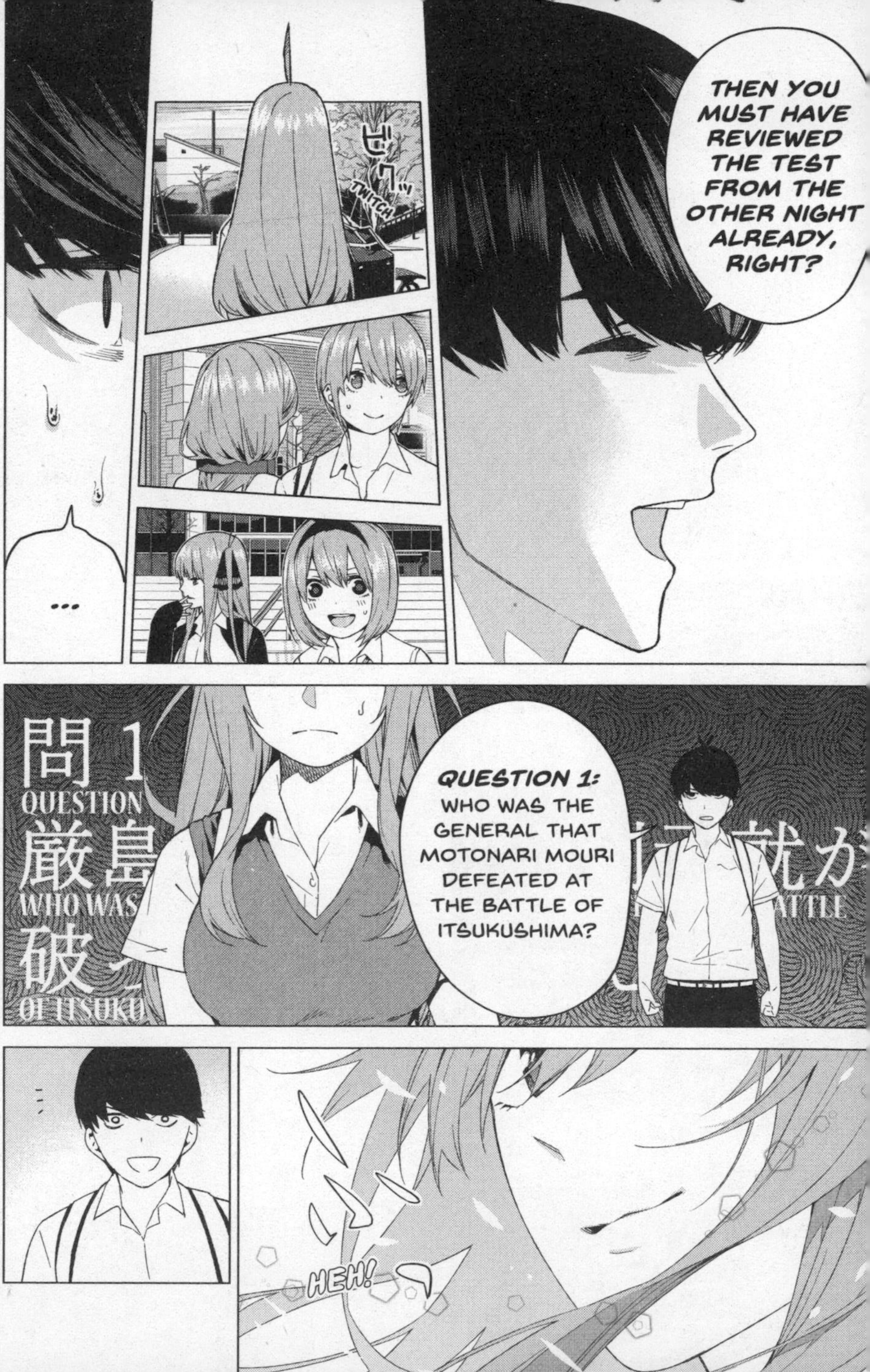
THEN YOU MUST HAVE REVIEWED THE TEST FROM THE OTHER NIGHT ALREADY, RIGHT?
ビクッ
TWITCH
...
QUESTION 1: WHO WAS THE GENERAL THAT MOTONARI MOURI DEFEATED AT THE BATTLE OF ITSUKUSHIMA?
HEH!

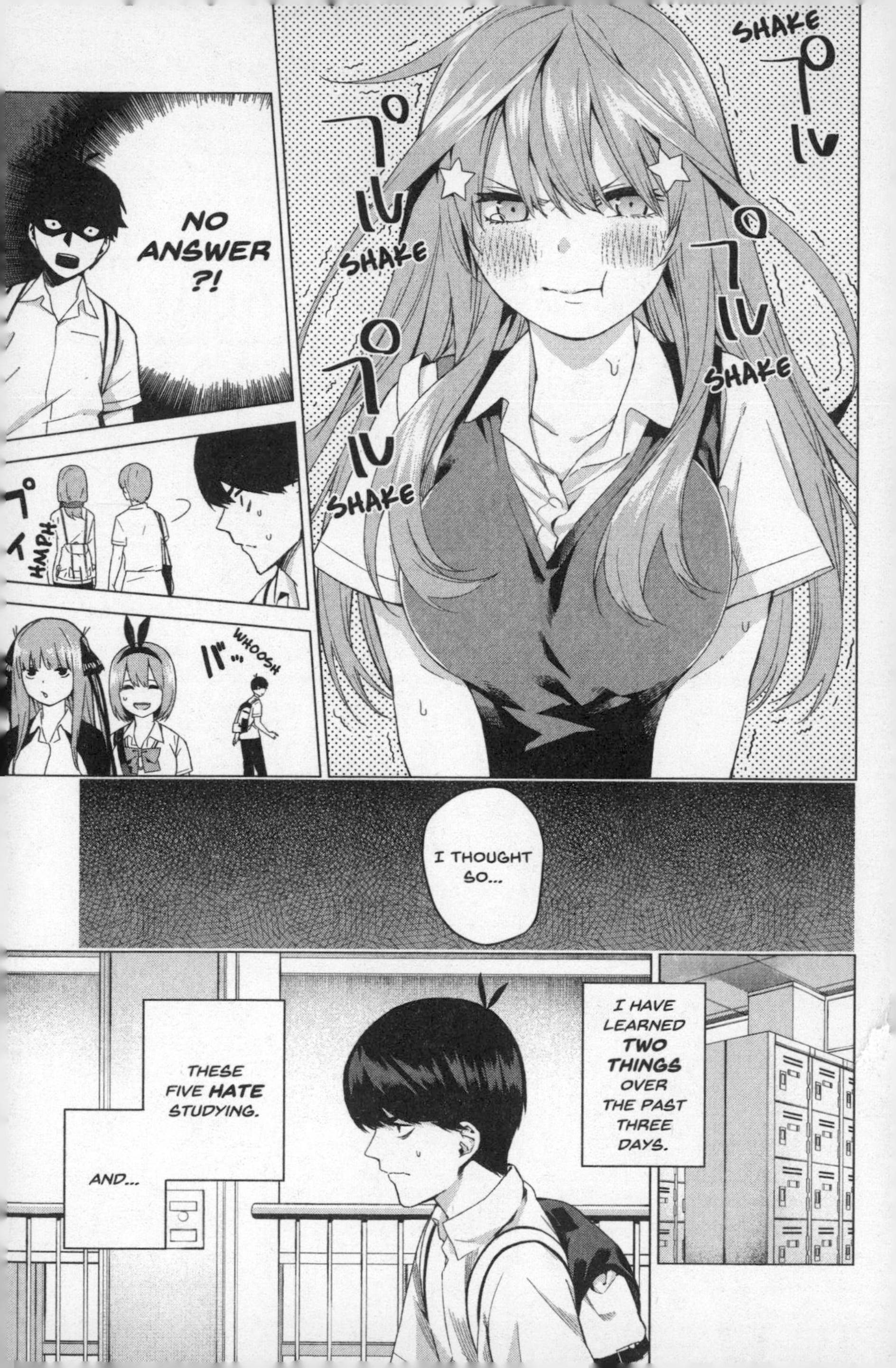

SHAKE
プル
プル
SHAKE
プル
SHAKE
プル
SHAKE
NO ANSWER ?!
プイ
HMPH
バッ
WHOOSH
I THOUGHT SO...
I HAVE LEARNED **TWO THINGS** OVER THE PAST THREE DAYS.
THESE FIVE **HATE** STUDYING.
AND...

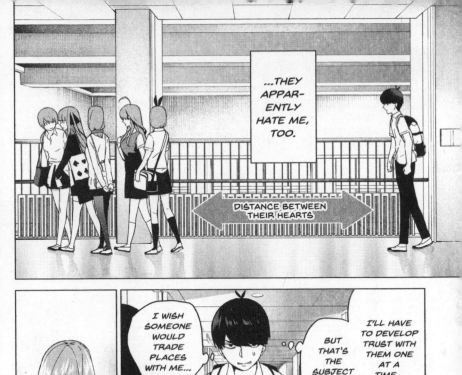

...THEY APPARENTLY HATE ME, TOO.

DISTANCE BETWEEN THEIR HEARTS

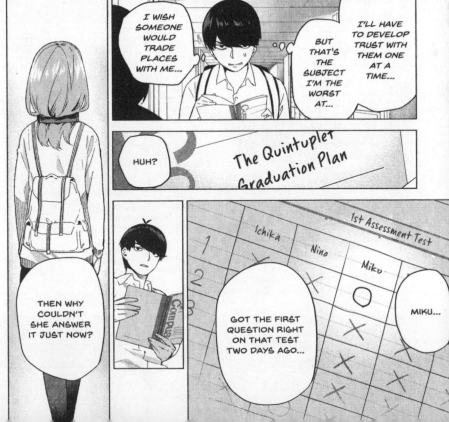

I WISH SOMEONE WOULD TRADE PLACES WITH ME...

BUT THAT'S THE SUBJECT I'M THE WORST AT...

I'LL HAVE TO DEVELOP TRUST WITH THEM ONE AT A TIME...

HUH?

The Quintuplet Graduation Plan

THEN WHY COULDN'T SHE ANSWER IT JUST NOW?

GOT THE FIRST QUESTION RIGHT ON THAT TEST TWO DAYS AGO...

MIKU...

1st Assessment Test

	Ichika	Nino	Miku
1	×	×	○
2		×	
3	×		×
			×

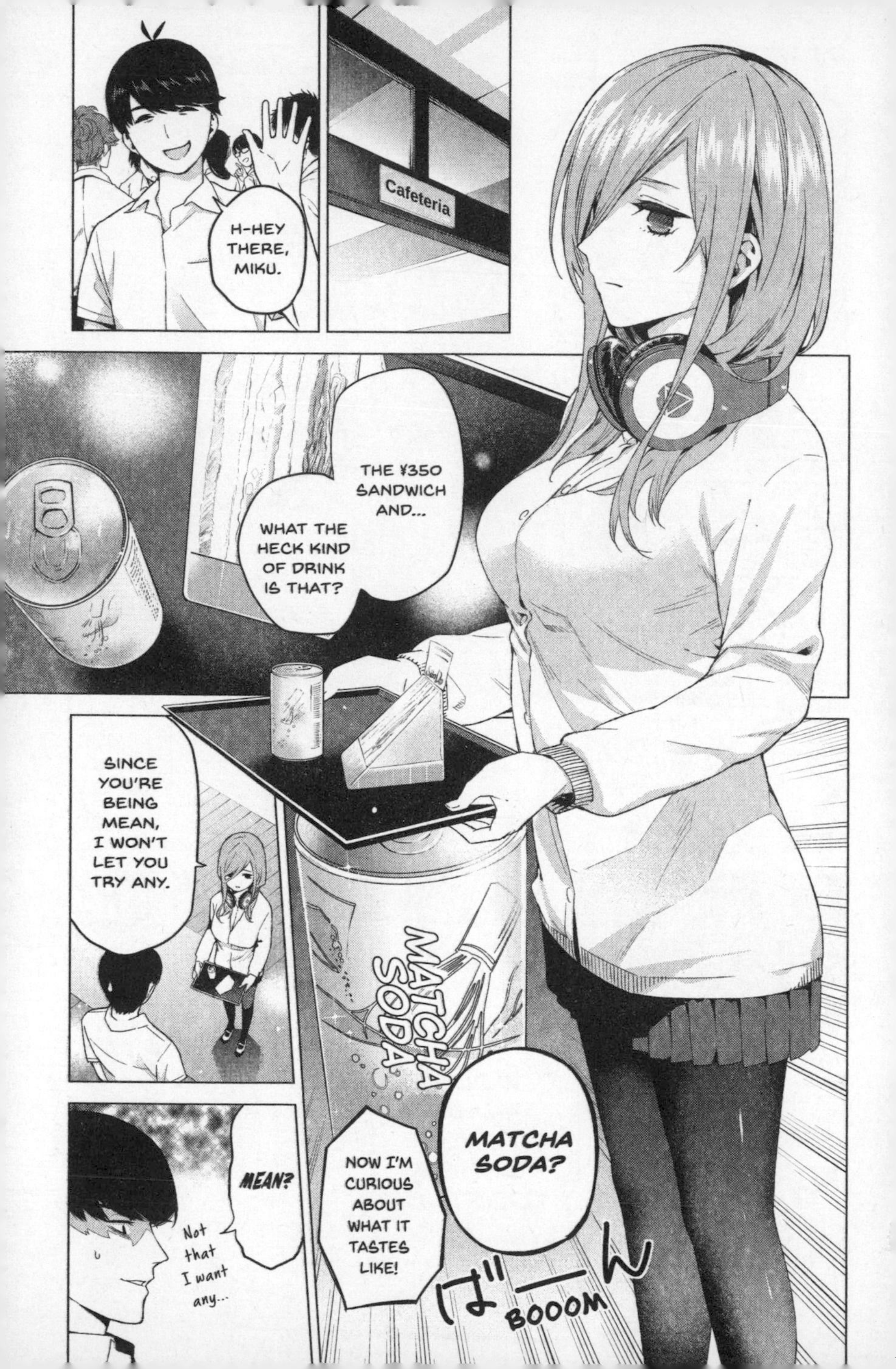
Cafeteria
H-HEY THERE, MIKU.
THE ¥350 SANDWICH AND...
WHAT THE HECK KIND OF DRINK IS THAT?
MATCHA SODA
MATCHA SODA?
NOW I'M CURIOUS ABOUT WHAT IT TASTES LIKE!
ばーん
BOOOM
SINCE YOU'RE BEING MEAN, I WON'T LET YOU TRY ANY.
MEAN?
Not that I want any...

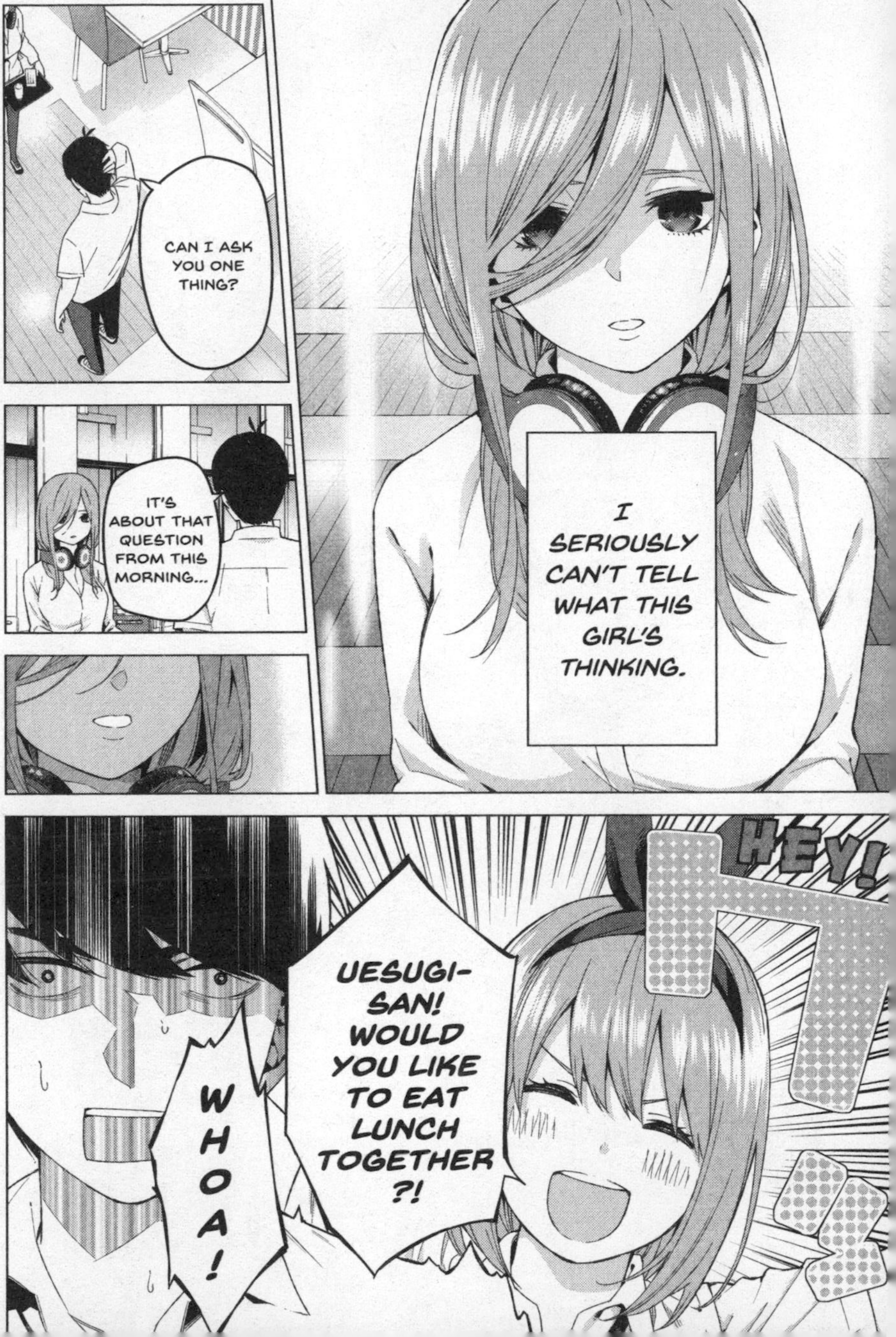
I SERIOUSLY CAN'T TELL WHAT THIS GIRL'S THINKING.
CAN I ASK YOU ONE THING?
IT'S ABOUT THAT QUESTION FROM THIS MORNING...
HEY!
UESUGI-SAN! WOULD YOU LIKE TO EAT LUNCH TOGETHER?!
WHOA!

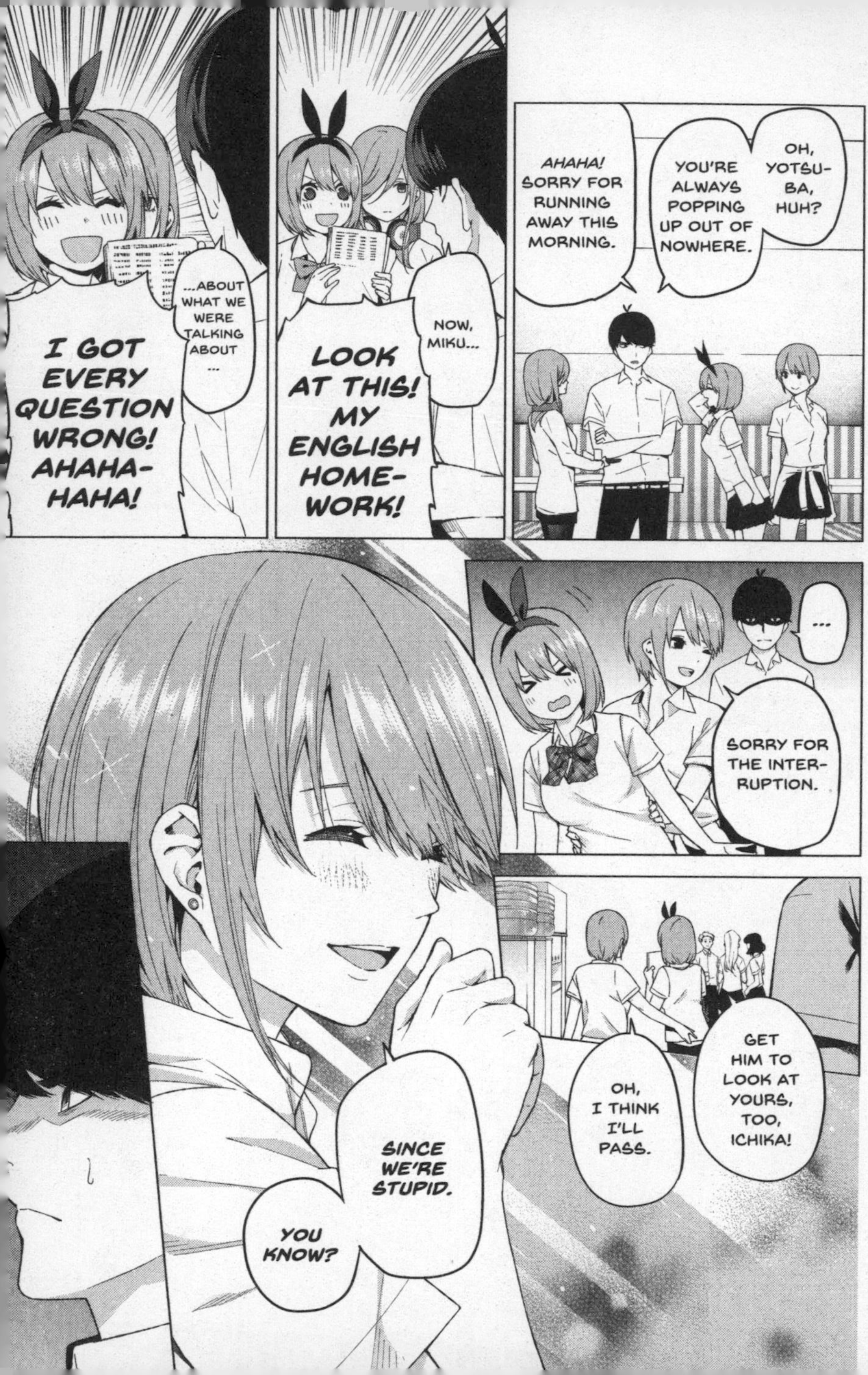
OH, YOTSUBA, HUH?
YOU'RE ALWAYS POPPING UP OUT OF NOWHERE.
AHAHA! SORRY FOR RUNNING AWAY THIS MORNING.
NOW, MIKU...
LOOK AT THIS! MY ENGLISH HOMEWORK!
...ABOUT WHAT WE WERE TALKING ABOUT...
I GOT EVERY QUESTION WRONG! AHAHAHAHA!
...
SORRY FOR THE INTERRUPTION.
GET HIM TO LOOK AT YOURS, TOO, ICHIKA!
OH, I THINK I'LL PASS.
SINCE WE'RE STUPID.
YOU KNOW?

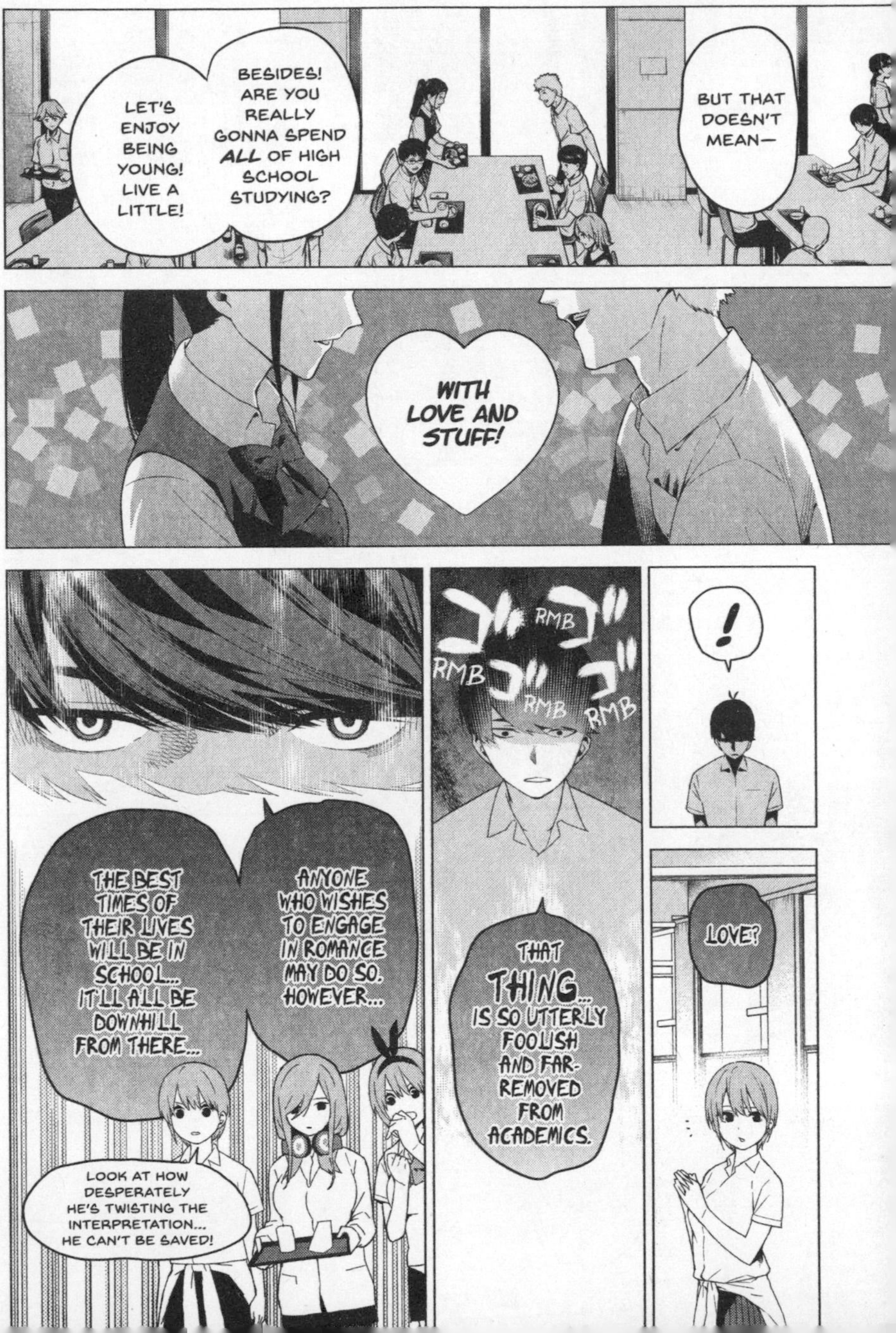
BUT THAT DOESN'T MEAN—
BESIDES! ARE YOU REALLY GONNA SPEND ALL OF HIGH SCHOOL STUDYING?
LET'S ENJOY BEING YOUNG! LIVE A LITTLE!
WITH LOVE AND STUFF!
!
LOVE?
RMB RMB RMB RMB
THAT THING... IS SO UTTERLY FOOLISH AND FAR-REMOVED FROM ACADEMICS.
ANYONE WHO WISHES TO ENGAGE IN ROMANCE MAY DO SO. HOWEVER...
THE BEST TIMES OF THEIR LIVES WILL BE IN SCHOOL... IT'LL ALL BE DOWNHILL FROM THERE...
LOOK AT HOW DESPERATELY HE'S TWISTING THE INTERPRETATION... HE CAN'T BE SAVED!

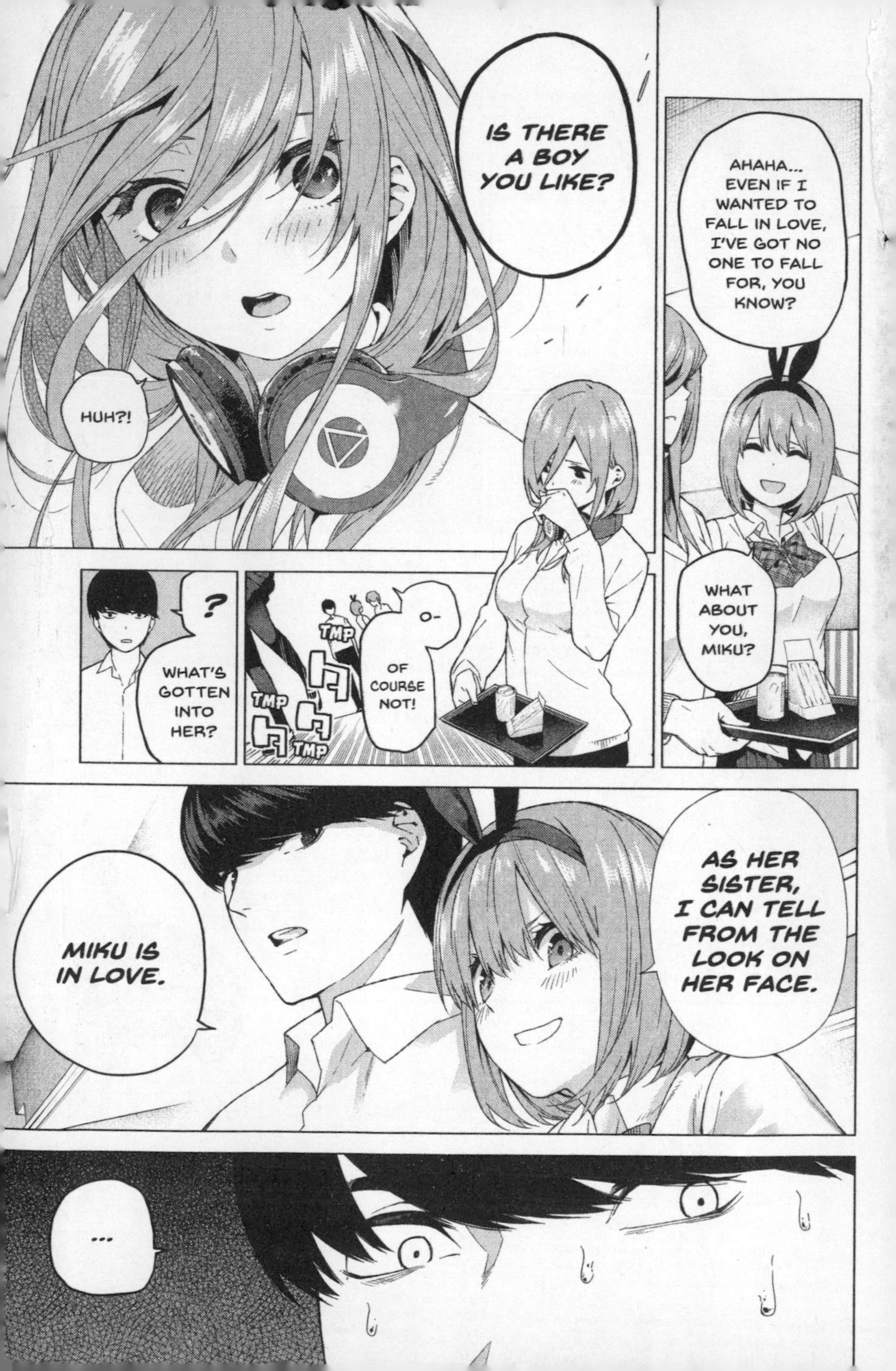
AHAHA... EVEN IF I WANTED TO FALL IN LOVE, I'VE GOT NO ONE TO FALL FOR, YOU KNOW?
WHAT ABOUT YOU, MIKU?
IS THERE A BOY YOU LIKE?
HUH?!
O-
OF COURSE NOT!
TMP
TMP
TMP
?
WHAT'S GOTTEN INTO HER?
AS HER SISTER, I CAN TELL FROM THE LOOK ON HER FACE.
MIKU IS IN LOVE.
...

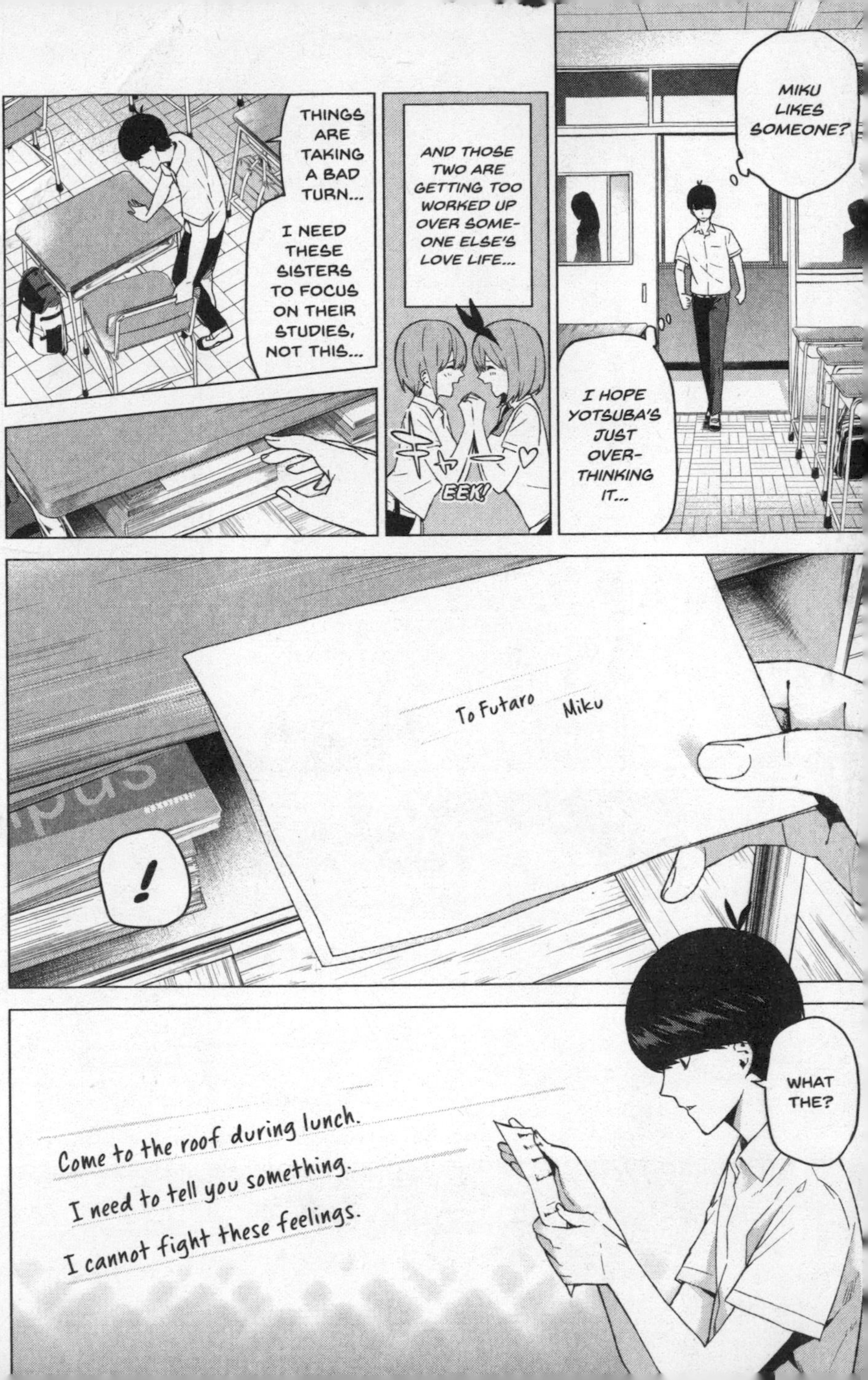

MIKU LIKES SOMEONE?
I HOPE YOTSUBA'S JUST OVER-THINKING IT...
AND THOSE TWO ARE GETTING TOO WORKED UP OVER SOME-ONE ELSE'S LOVE LIFE...
EEK!
THINGS ARE TAKING A BAD TURN...
I NEED THESE SISTERS TO FOCUS ON THEIR STUDIES, NOT THIS...
To Futaro Miku
!
WHAT THE?
Come to the roof during lunch.
I need to tell you something.
I cannot fight these feelings.

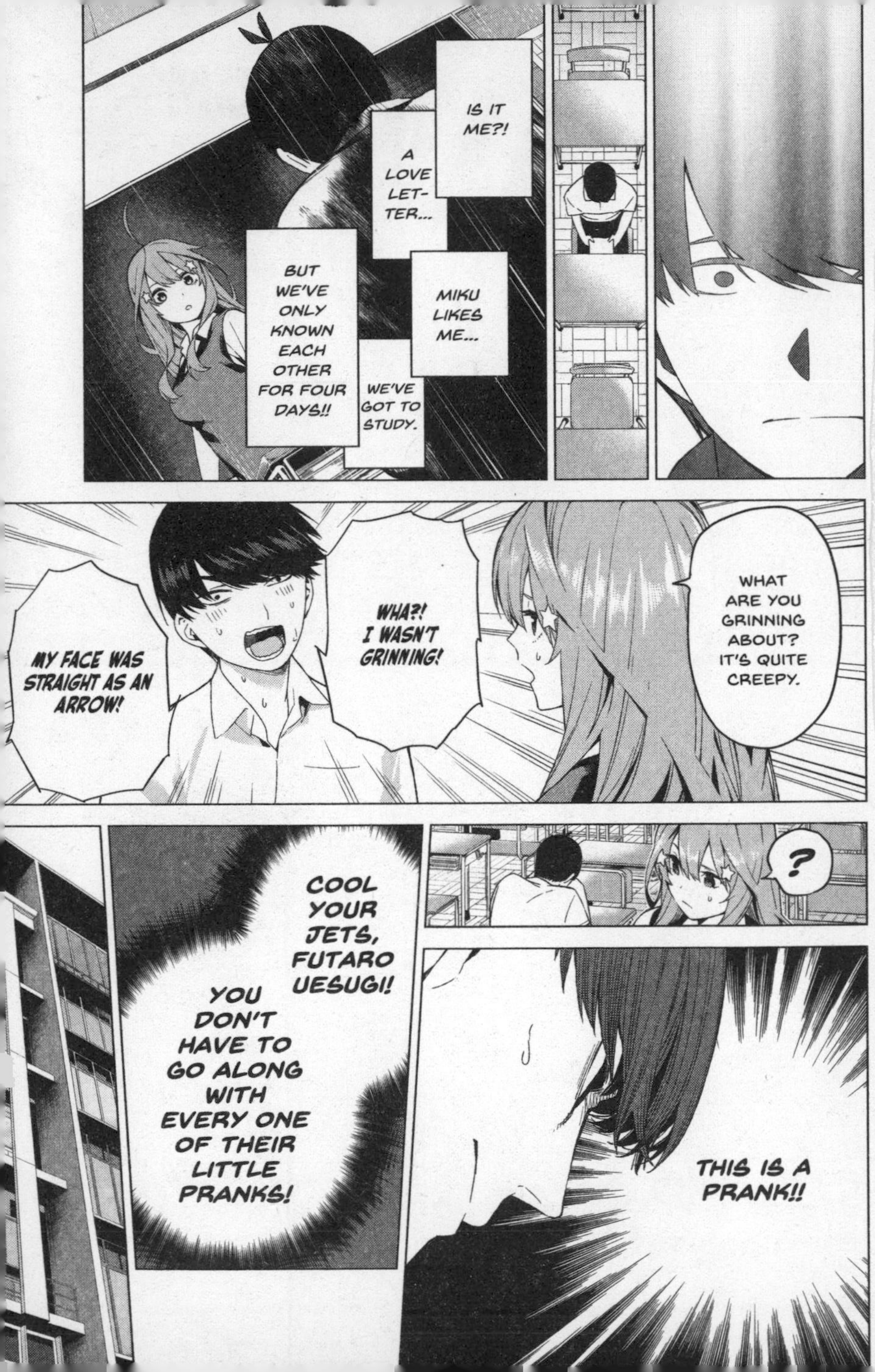
IS IT ME?!
A LOVE LETTER...
MIKU LIKES ME...
BUT WE'VE ONLY KNOWN EACH OTHER FOR FOUR DAYS!!
WE'VE GOT TO STUDY.
WHAT ARE YOU GRINNING ABOUT? IT'S QUITE CREEPY.
WHA?! I WASN'T GRINNING!
MY FACE WAS STRAIGHT AS AN ARROW!
?
THIS IS A PRANK!!
COOL YOUR JETS, FUTARO UESUGI!
YOU DON'T HAVE TO GO ALONG WITH EVERY ONE OF THEIR LITTLE PRANKS!

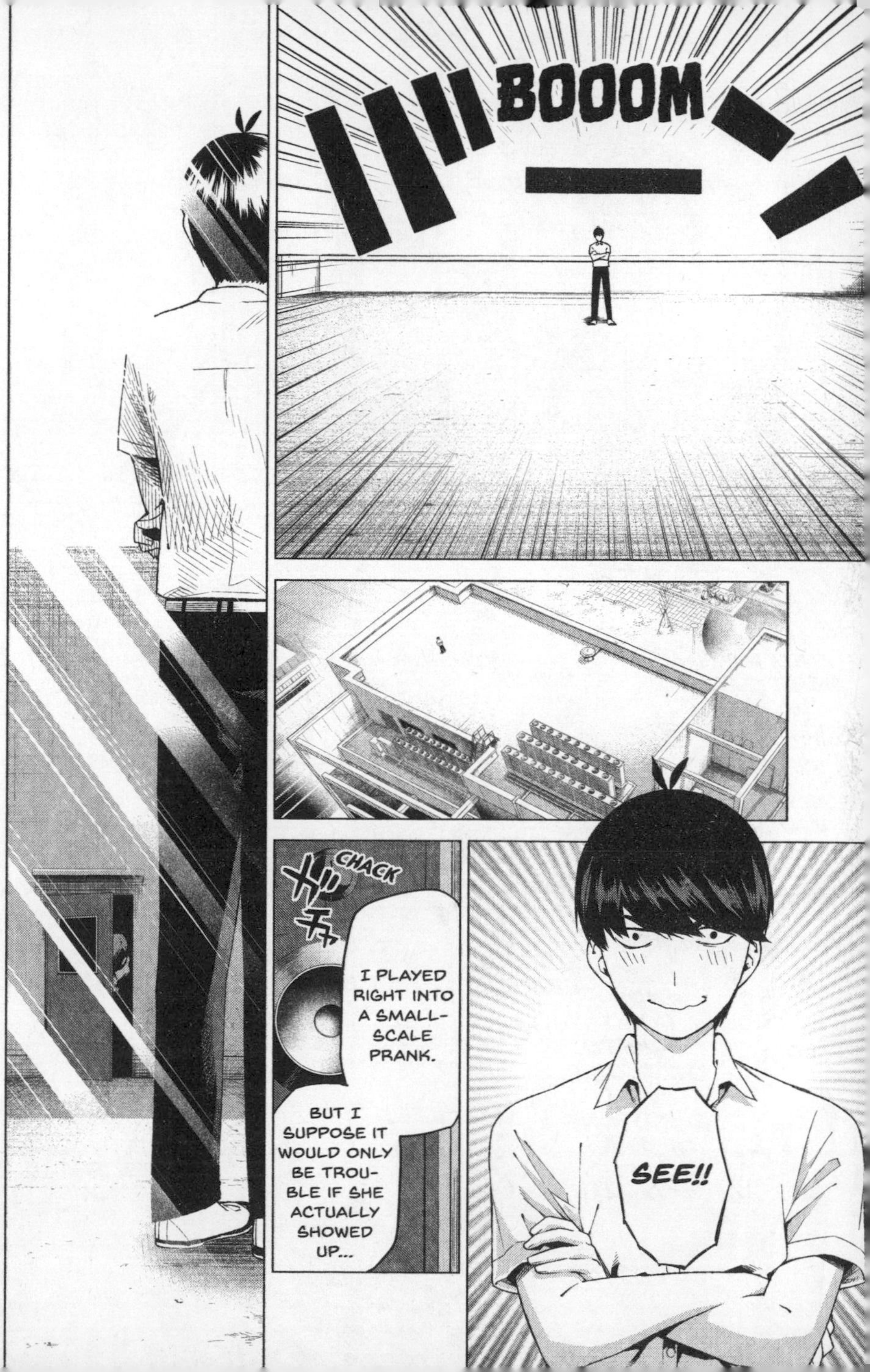
BOOOM
SEE!!
CHACK
I PLAYED RIGHT INTO A SMALL-SCALE PRANK.
BUT I SUPPOSE IT WOULD ONLY BE TROUBLE IF SHE ACTUALLY SHOWED UP...

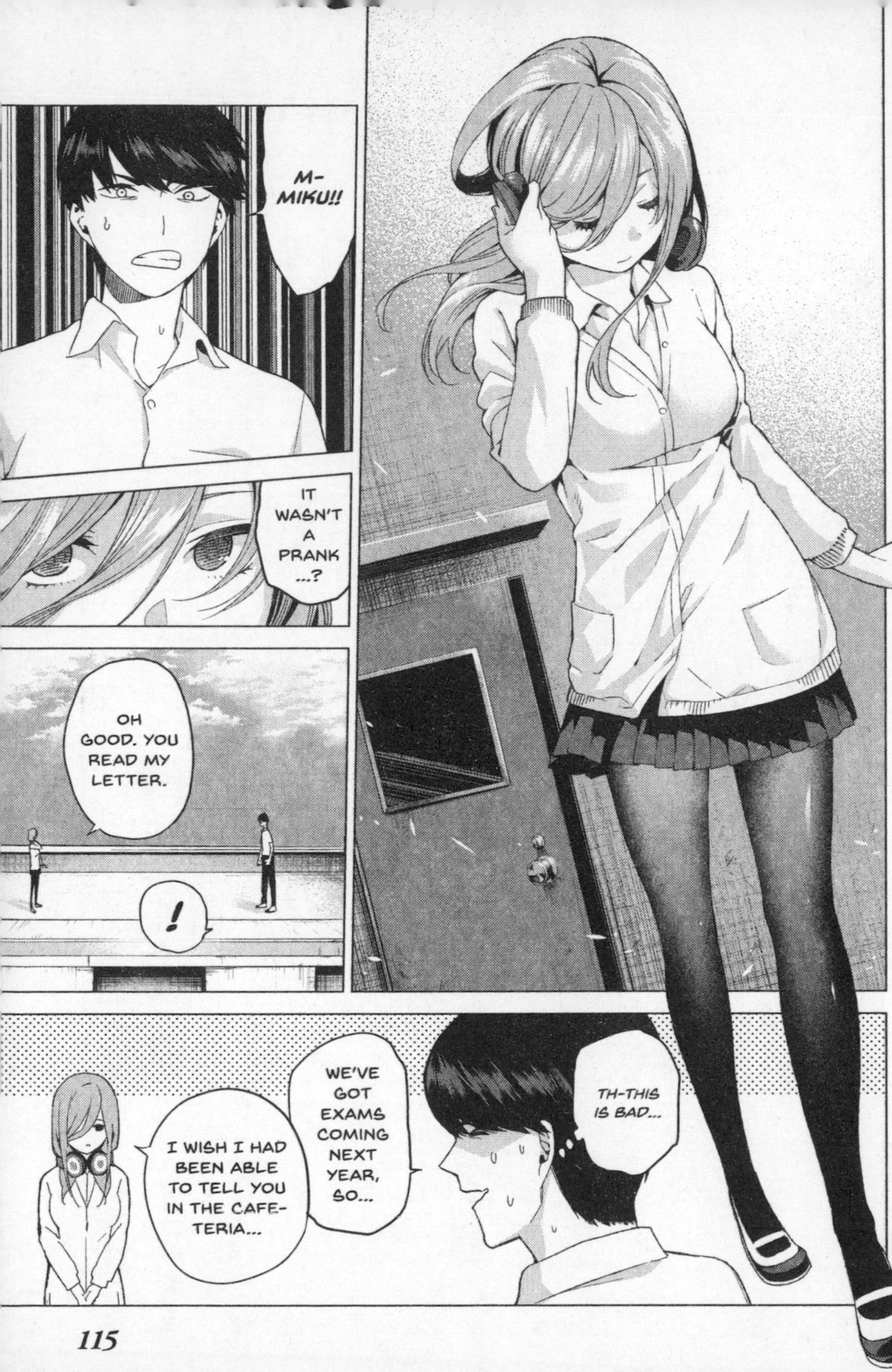
M-MIKU!!
IT WASN'T A PRANK ...?
OH GOOD. YOU READ MY LETTER.
!
TH-THIS IS BAD...
WE'VE GOT EXAMS COMING NEXT YEAR, SO...
I WISH I HAD BEEN ABLE TO TELL YOU IN THE CAFETERIA...

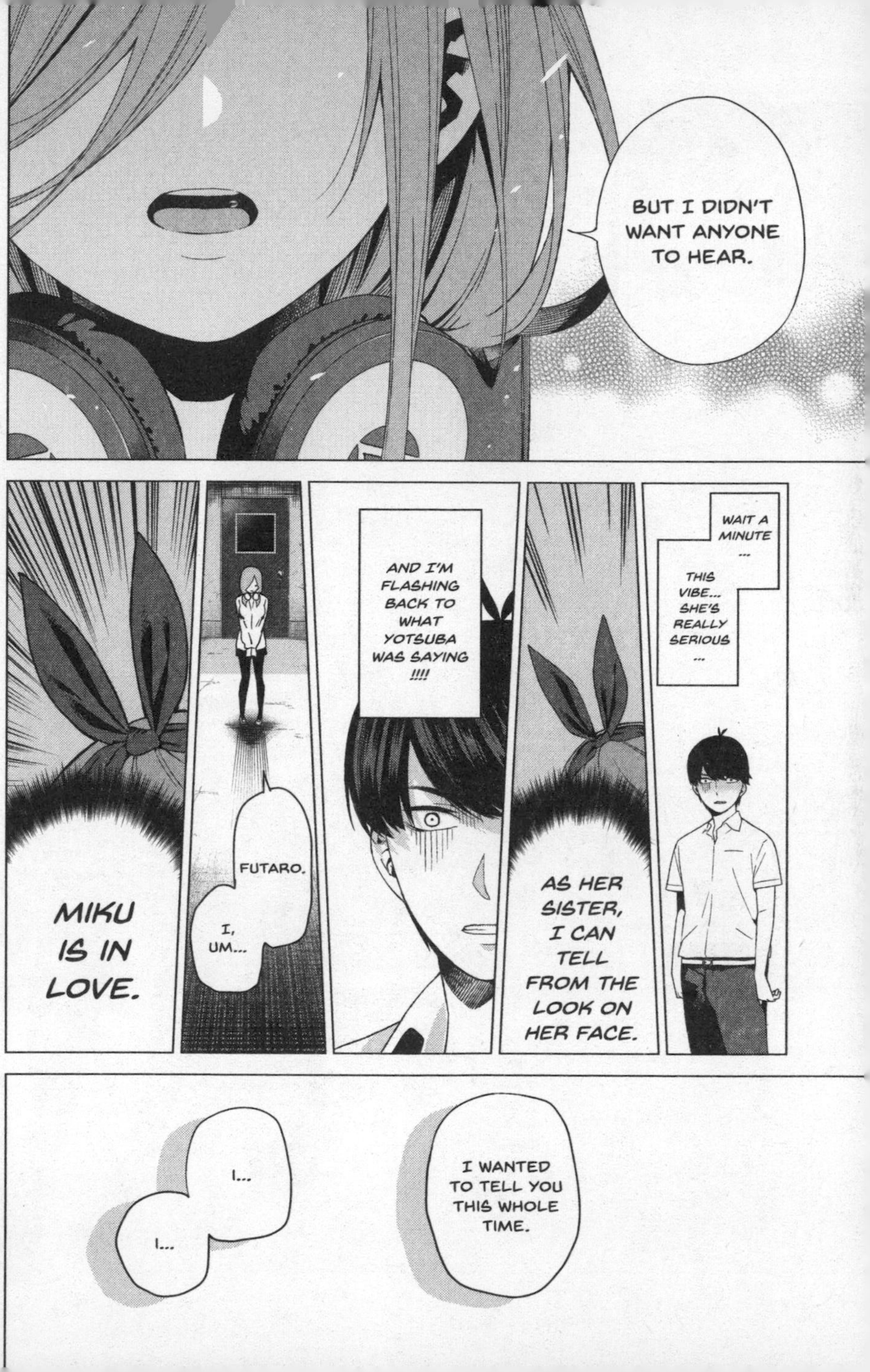
BUT I DIDN'T WANT ANYONE TO HEAR.
WAIT A MINUTE ...
THIS VIBE... SHE'S REALLY SERIOUS ...
AS HER SISTER, I CAN TELL FROM THE LOOK ON HER FACE.
AND I'M FLASHING BACK TO WHAT YOTSUBA WAS SAYING !!!!
FUTARO.
I, UM...
MIKU IS IN LOVE.
I WANTED TO TELL YOU THIS WHOLE TIME.
I...
I...

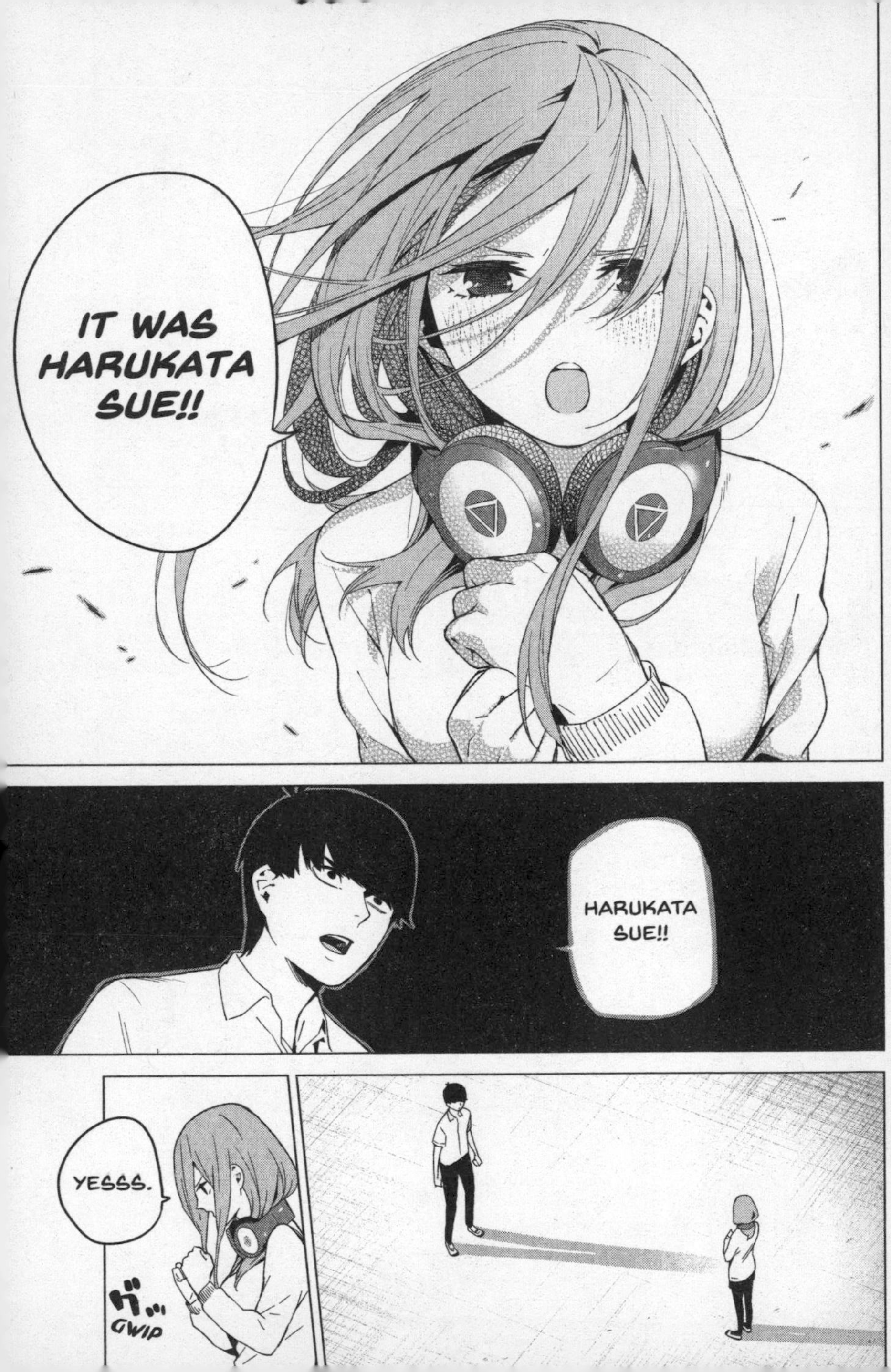
IT WAS HARUKATA SUE!!
HARUKATA SUE!!
YESSS.
GWIP

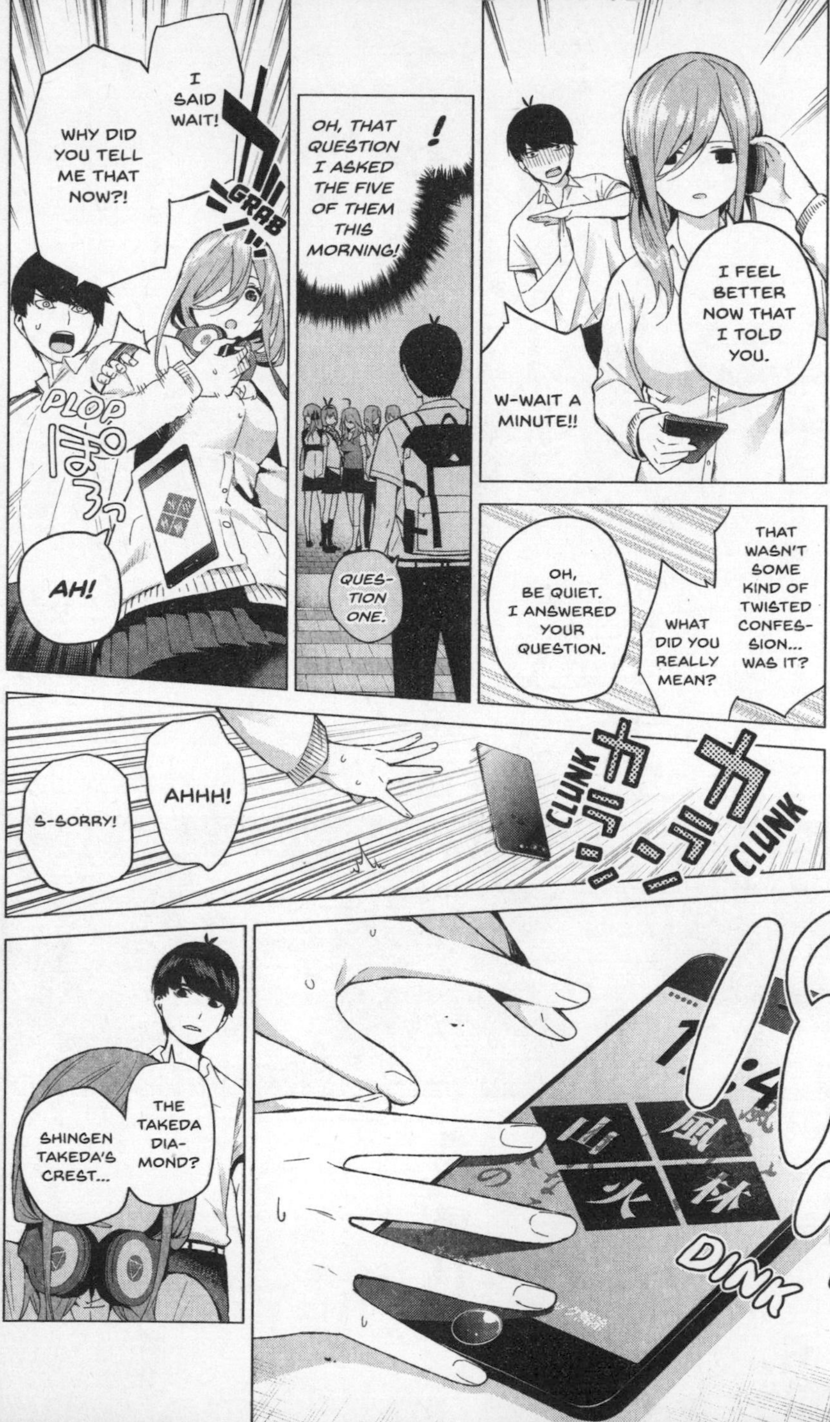
I FEEL BETTER NOW THAT I TOLD YOU.
W-WAIT A MINUTE!!
THAT WASN'T SOME KIND OF TWISTED CONFESSION... WAS IT?
WHAT DID YOU REALLY MEAN?
OH, BE QUIET. I ANSWERED YOUR QUESTION.
!
OH, THAT QUESTION I ASKED THE FIVE OF THEM THIS MORNING!
QUESTION ONE.
I SAID WAIT!
GRAB
WHY DID YOU TELL ME THAT NOW?!
PLOP
ぽろっ
AH!
CLUNK
カッ
CLUNK
カッ
AHHH!
S-SORRY!
?
DINK
風
林
火
山
THE TAKEDA DIAMOND?
SHINGEN TAKEDA'S CREST...

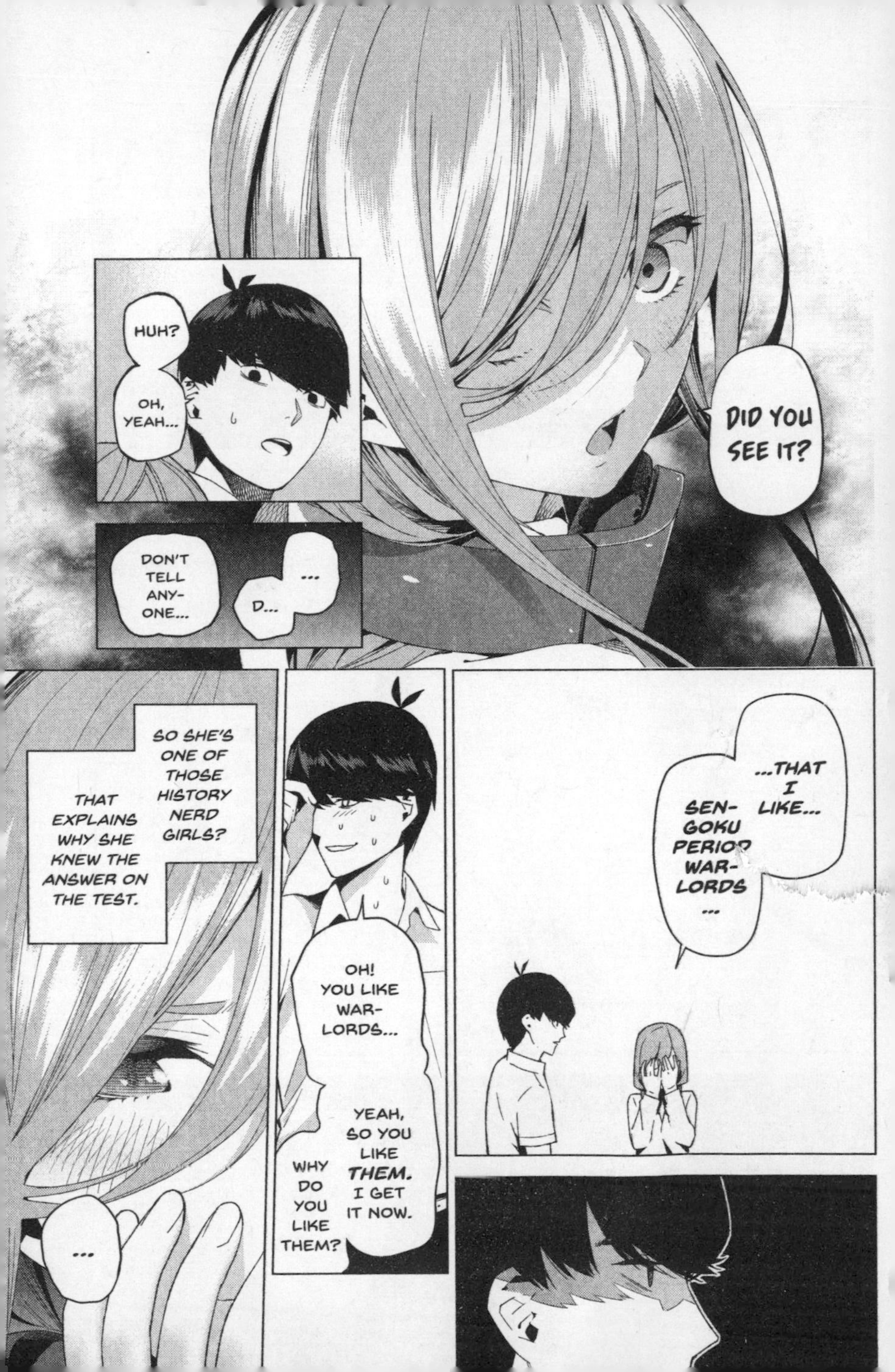
DID YOU SEE IT?
HUH?
OH, YEAH...
...
D...
DON'T TELL ANY-ONE...
...THAT I LIKE...
SEN-GOKU PERIOD WAR-LORDS...
OH! YOU LIKE WAR-LORDS...
YEAH, SO YOU LIKE *THEM.* I GET IT NOW.
WHY DO YOU LIKE THEM?
SO SHE'S ONE OF THOSE HISTORY NERD GIRLS?
THAT EXPLAINS WHY SHE KNEW THE ANSWER ON THE TEST.
...

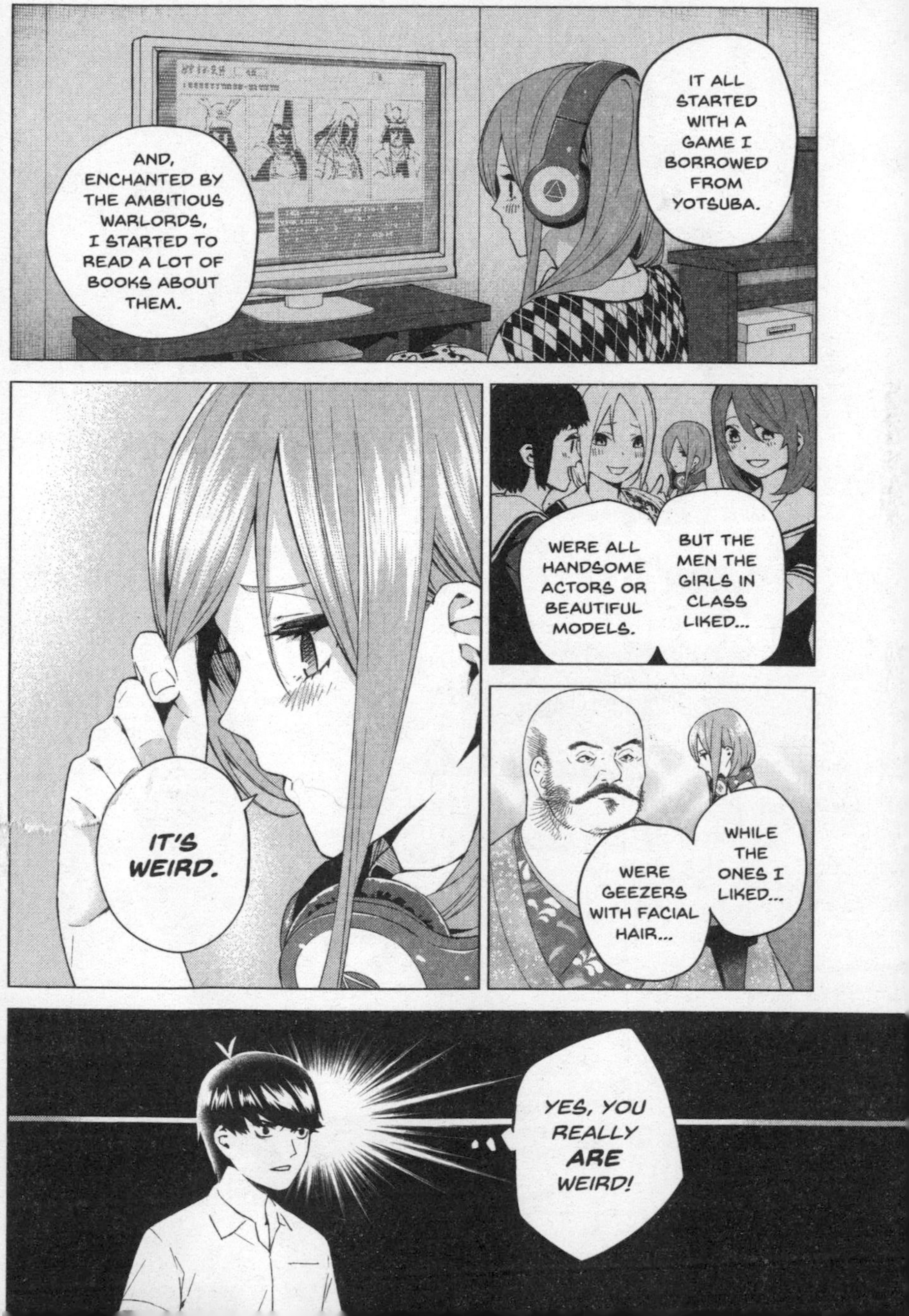
IT ALL STARTED WITH A GAME I BORROWED FROM YOTSUBA.
AND, ENCHANTED BY THE AMBITIOUS WARLORDS, I STARTED TO READ A LOT OF BOOKS ABOUT THEM.
BUT THE MEN THE GIRLS IN CLASS LIKED...
WERE ALL HANDSOME ACTORS OR BEAUTIFUL MODELS.
WHILE THE ONES I LIKED...
WERE GEEZERS WITH FACIAL HAIR...
IT'S WEIRD.
YES, YOU REALLY ARE WEIRD!

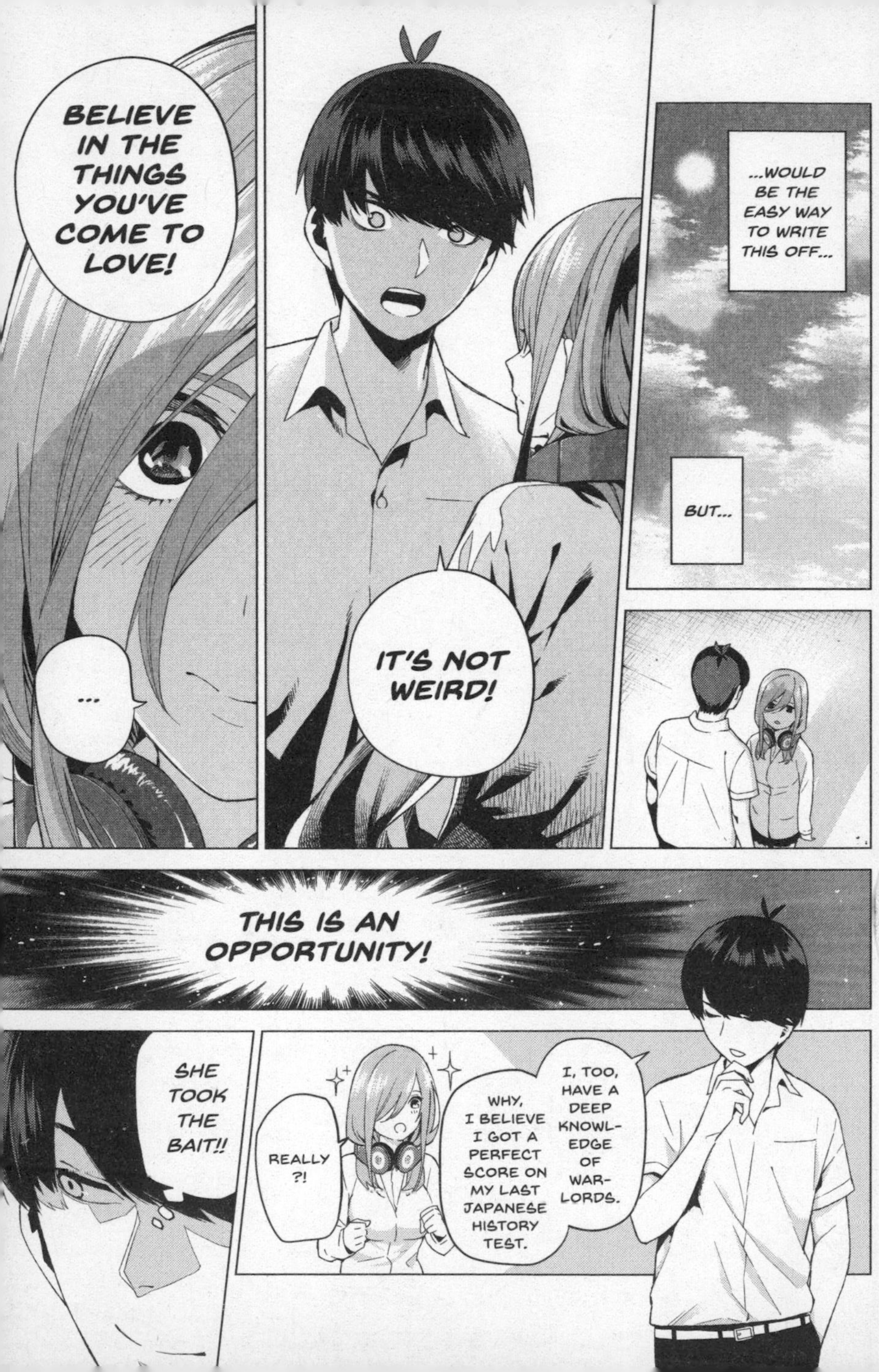
...WOULD BE THE EASY WAY TO WRITE THIS OFF...
BUT...
IT'S NOT WEIRD!
BELIEVE IN THE THINGS YOU'VE COME TO LOVE!
...
THIS IS AN OPPORTUNITY!
I, TOO, HAVE A DEEP KNOWL-EDGE OF WAR-LORDS.
WHY, I BELIEVE I GOT A PERFECT SCORE ON MY LAST JAPANESE HISTORY TEST.
REALLY?!
SHE TOOK THE BAIT!!

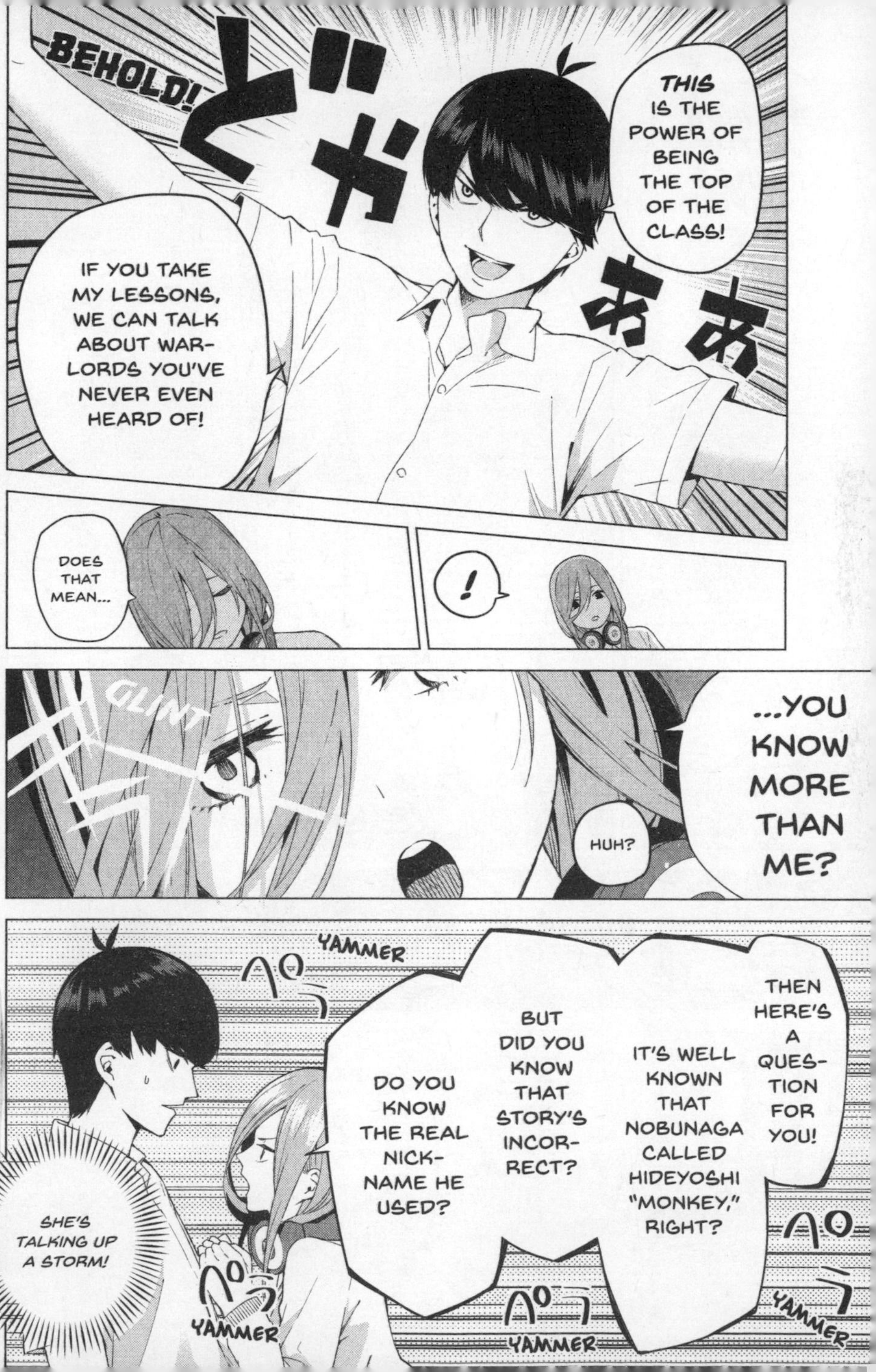
THIS IS THE POWER OF BEING THE TOP OF THE CLASS!
ああ
BEHOLD!
IF YOU TAKE MY LESSONS, WE CAN TALK ABOUT WAR-LORDS YOU'VE NEVER EVEN HEARD OF!
!
DOES THAT MEAN...
...YOU KNOW MORE THAN ME?
HUH?
GLINT
YAMMER
THEN HERE'S A QUES-TION FOR YOU!
IT'S WELL KNOWN THAT NOBUNAGA CALLED HIDEYOSHI "MONKEY," RIGHT?
BUT DID YOU KNOW THAT STORY'S INCOR-RECT?
DO YOU KNOW THE REAL NICK-NAME HE USED?
YAMMER
YAMMER
YAMMER
SHE'S TALKING UP A STORM!
YAMMER

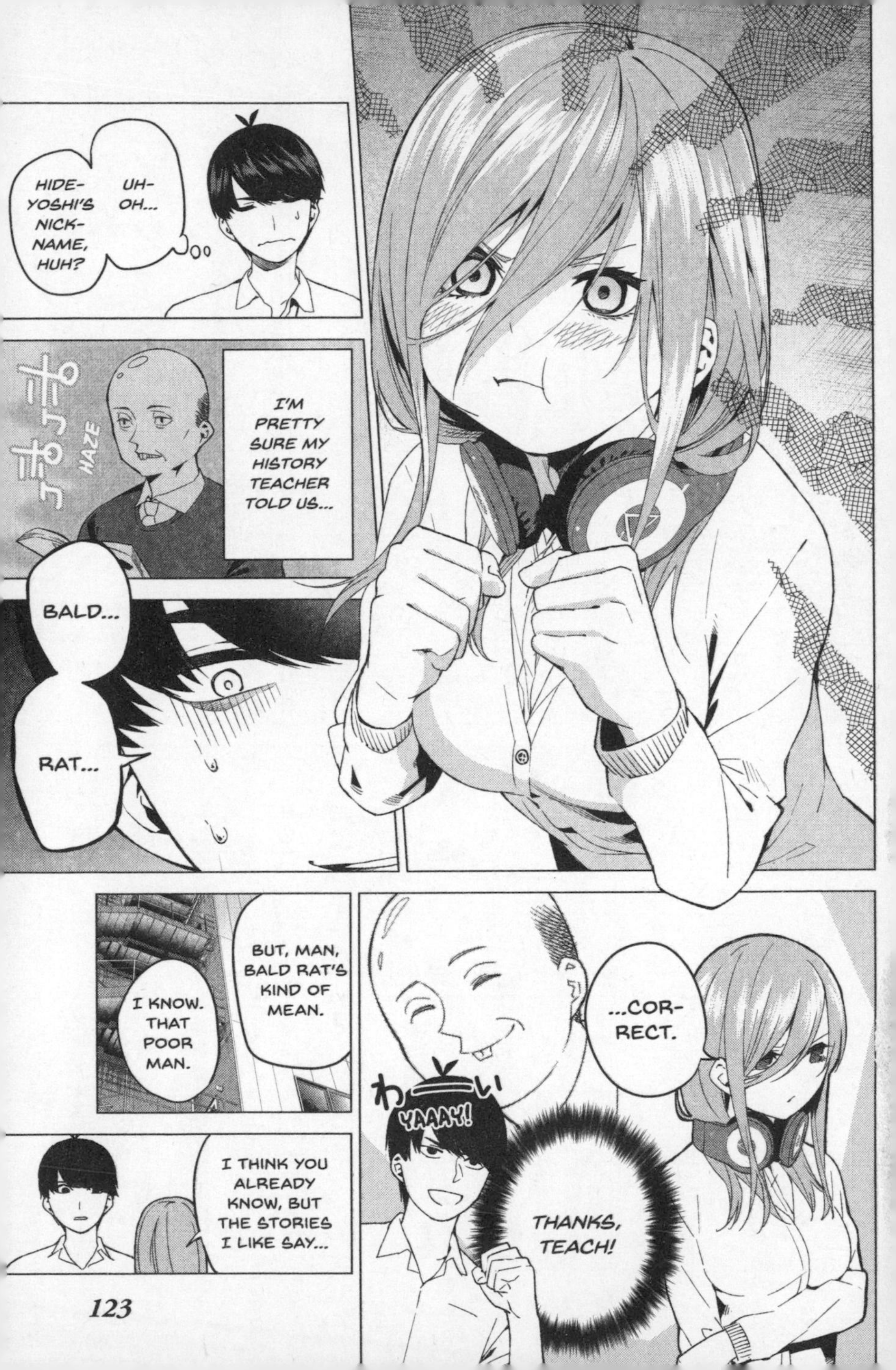
UH-OH...
HIDE-YOSHI'S NICK-NAME, HUH?
I'M PRETTY SURE MY HISTORY TEACHER TOLD US...
HAZE
BALD...
RAT...
...COR-RECT.
わーい
YAAAY!
THANKS, TEACH!
BUT, MAN, BALD RAT'S KIND OF MEAN.
I KNOW. THAT POOR MAN.
I THINK YOU ALREADY KNOW, BUT THE STORIES I LIKE SAY...

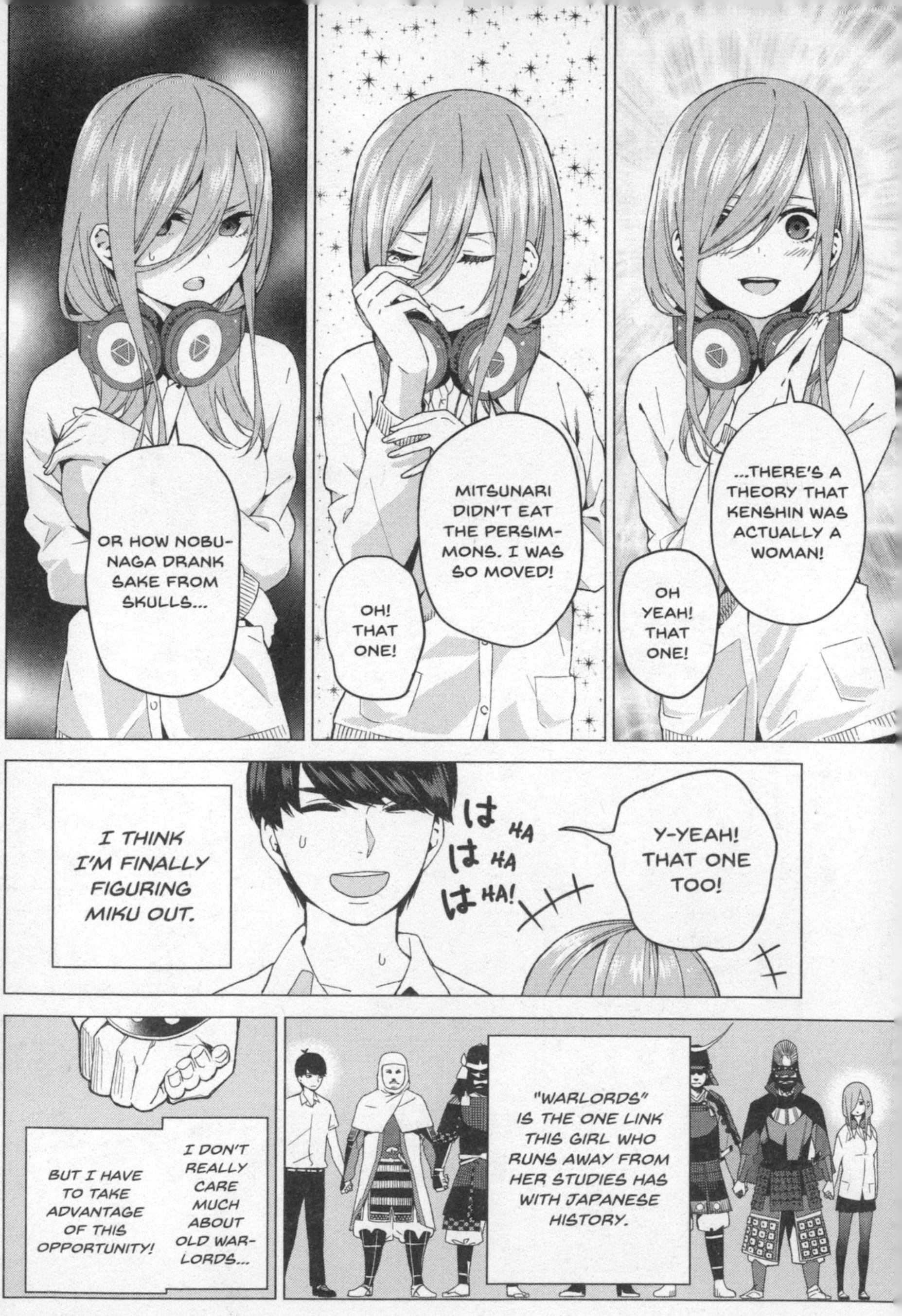
...THERE'S A THEORY THAT KENSHIN WAS ACTUALLY A WOMAN!
OH YEAH! THAT ONE!
MITSUNARI DIDN'T EAT THE PERSIMMONS. I WAS SO MOVED!
OH! THAT ONE!
OR HOW NOBUNAGA DRANK SAKE FROM SKULLS...
Y-YEAH! THAT ONE TOO!
はHA はHA はHA!
I THINK I'M FINALLY FIGURING MIKU OUT.
"WARLORDS" IS THE ONE LINK THIS GIRL WHO RUNS AWAY FROM HER STUDIES HAS WITH JAPANESE HISTORY.
I DON'T REALLY CARE MUCH ABOUT OLD WARLORDS...
BUT I HAVE TO TAKE ADVANTAGE OF THIS OPPORTUNITY!

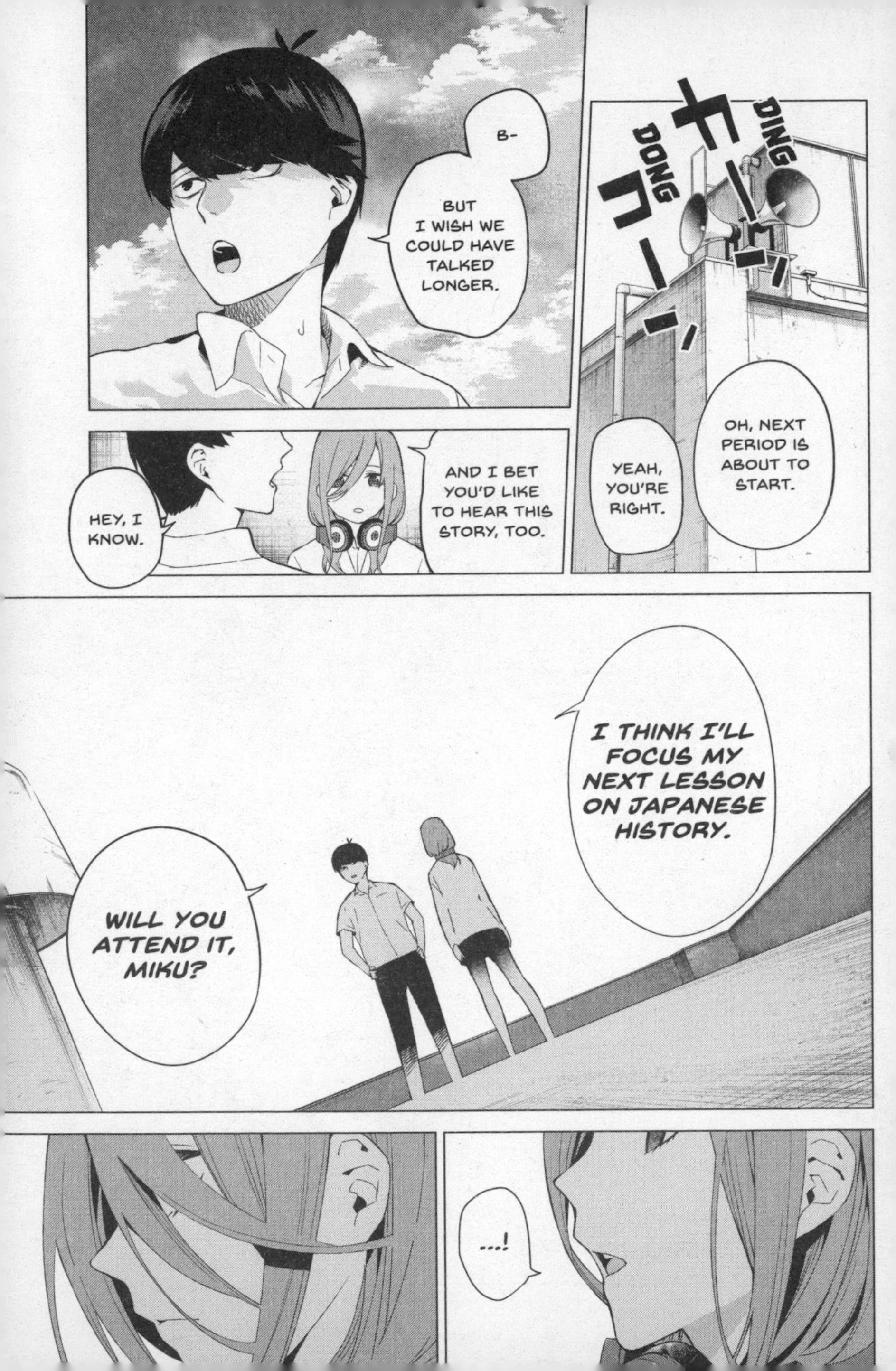
DING
DONG
OH, NEXT PERIOD IS ABOUT TO START.
YEAH, YOU'RE RIGHT.
B-
BUT I WISH WE COULD HAVE TALKED LONGER.
AND I BET YOU'D LIKE TO HEAR THIS STORY, TOO.
HEY, I KNOW.
I THINK I'LL FOCUS MY NEXT LESSON ON JAPANESE HISTORY.
WILL YOU ATTEND IT, MIKU?
...!

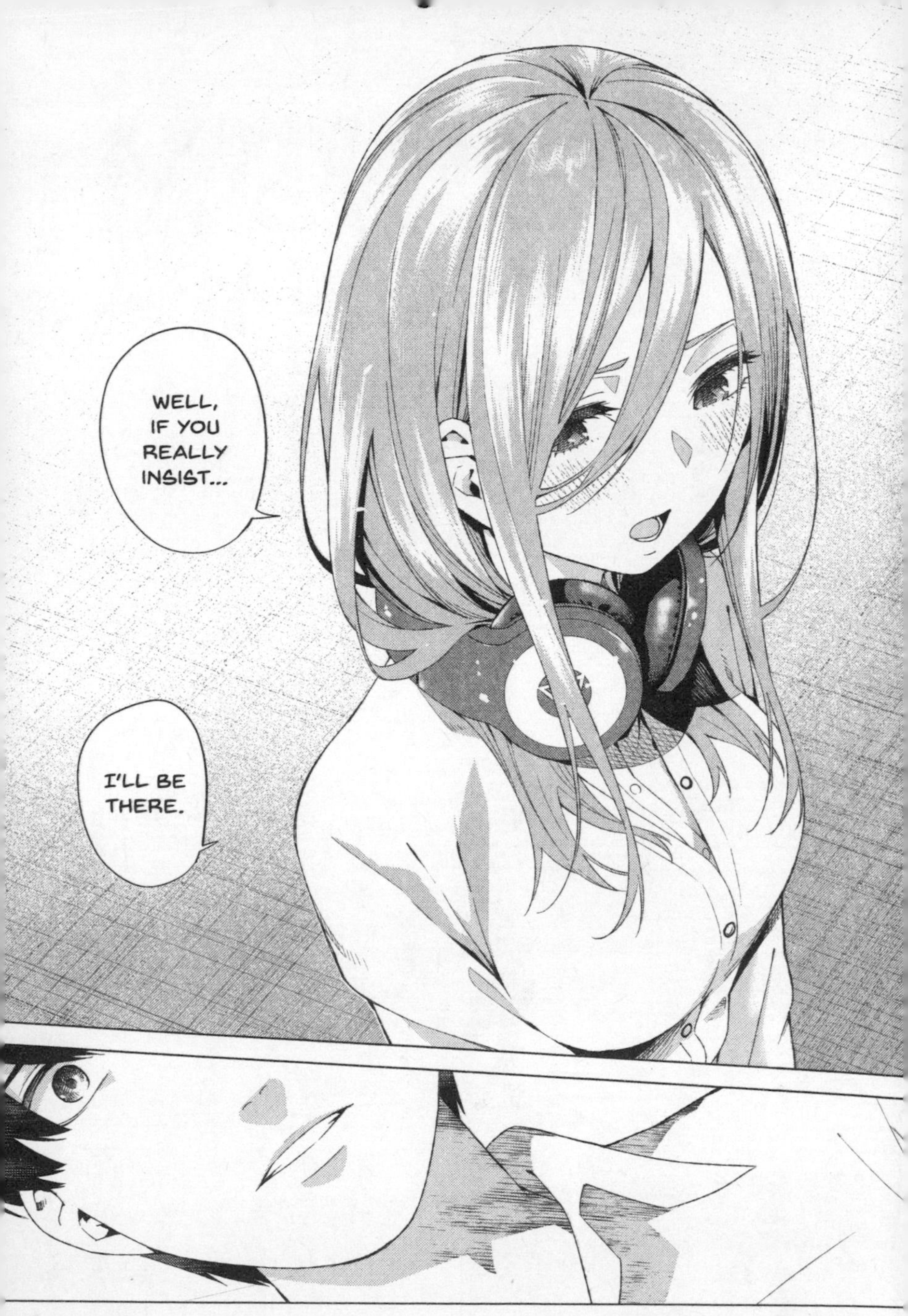
WELL, IF YOU REALLY INSIST...
I'LL BE THERE.

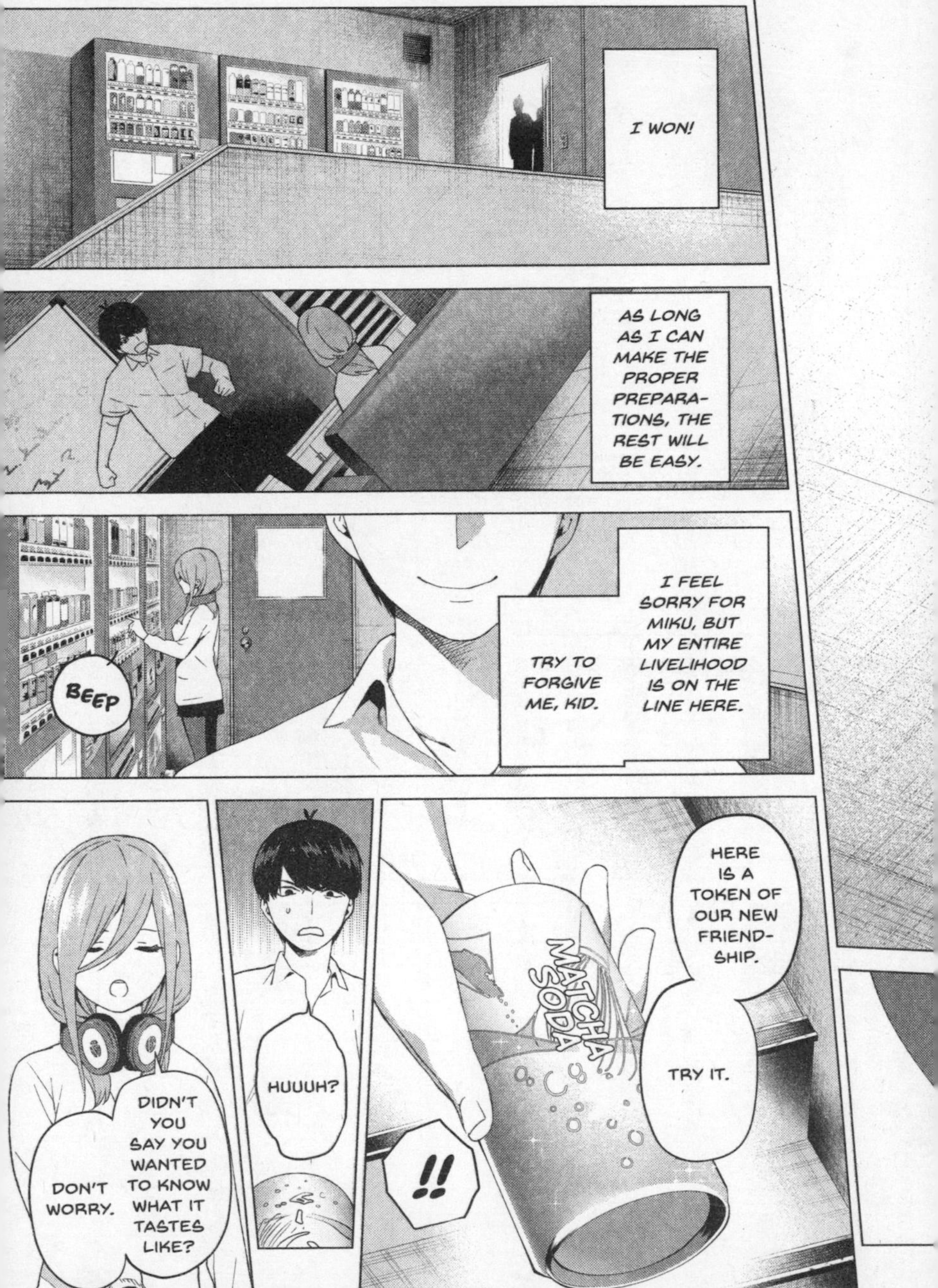
I WON!
AS LONG AS I CAN MAKE THE PROPER PREPARA-TIONS, THE REST WILL BE EASY.
I FEEL SORRY FOR MIKU, BUT MY ENTIRE LIVELIHOOD IS ON THE LINE HERE.
TRY TO FORGIVE ME, KID.
BEEP
HERE IS A TOKEN OF OUR NEW FRIEND-SHIP.
TRY IT.
MATCHA SODA
!!
HUUUH?
DIDN'T YOU SAY YOU WANTED TO KNOW WHAT IT TASTES LIKE?
DON'T WORRY.

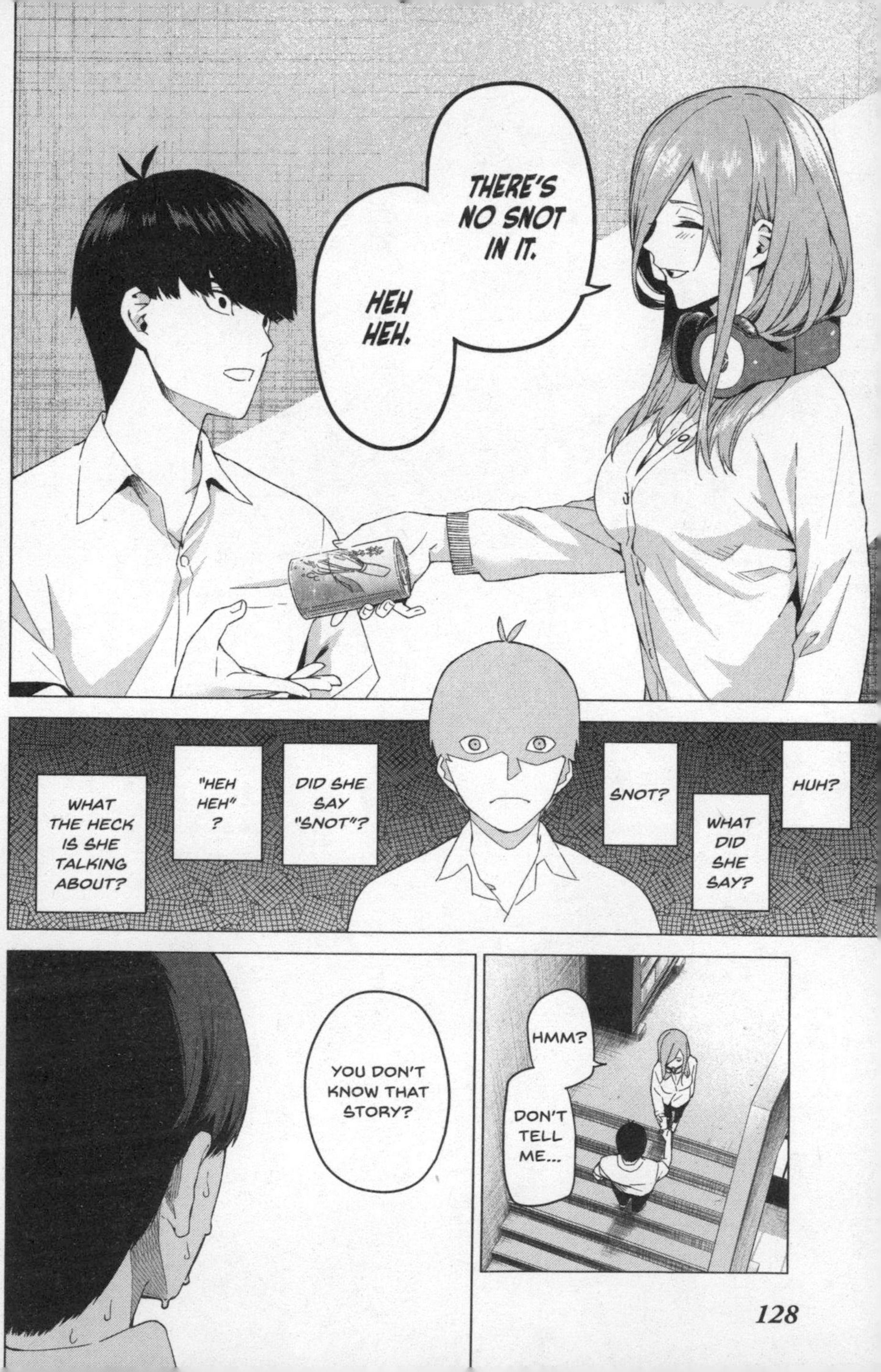
THERE'S NO SNOT IN IT.
HEH HEH.
HUH?
WHAT DID SHE SAY?
SNOT?
DID SHE SAY "SNOT"?
"HEH HEH"?
WHAT THE HECK IS SHE TALKING ABOUT?
HMM?
DON'T TELL ME...
YOU DON'T KNOW THAT STORY?

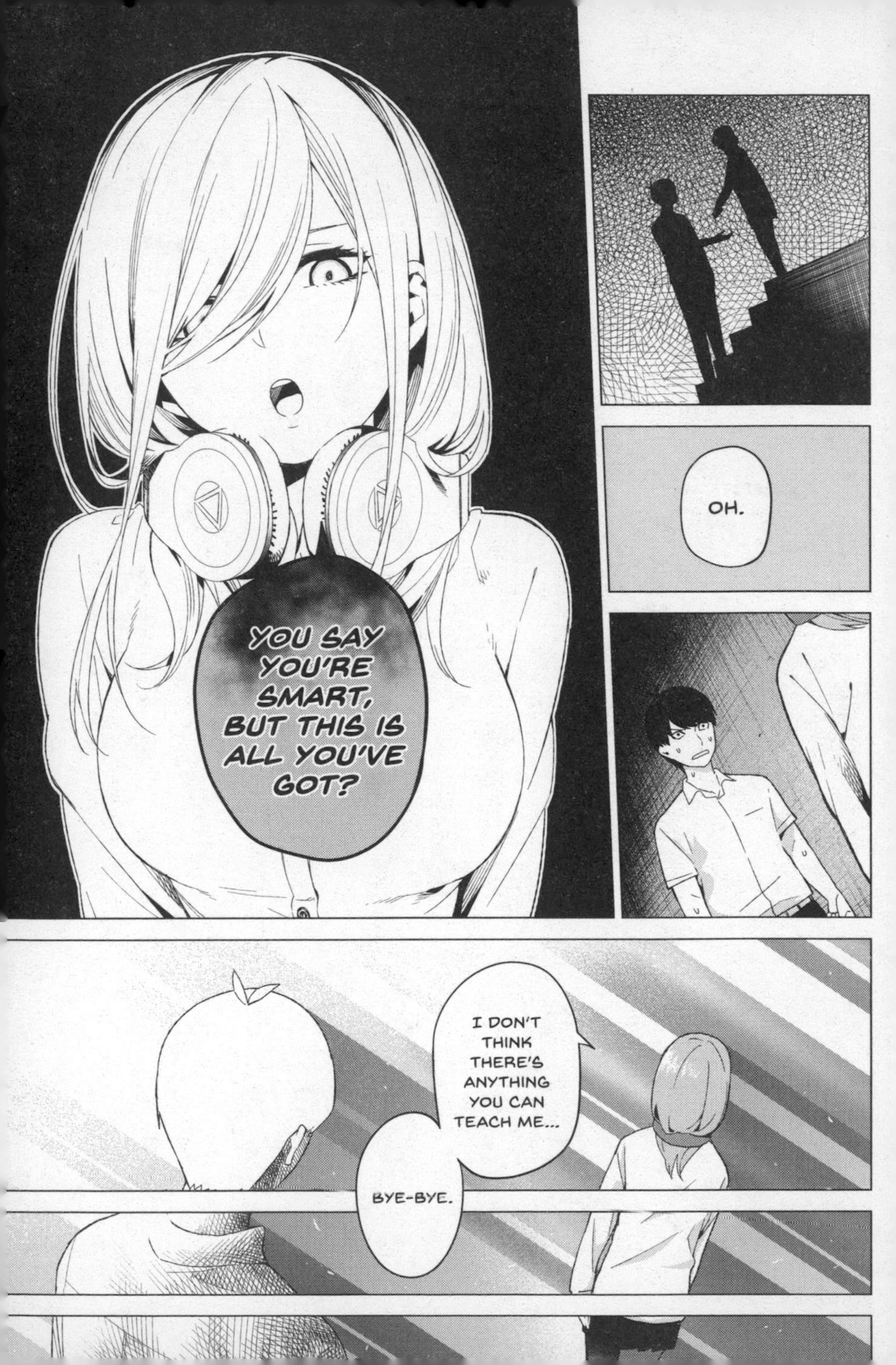
OH.
YOU SAY YOU'RE SMART, BUT THIS IS ALL YOU'VE GOT?
I DON'T THINK THERE'S ANYTHING YOU CAN TEACH ME...
BYE-BYE.

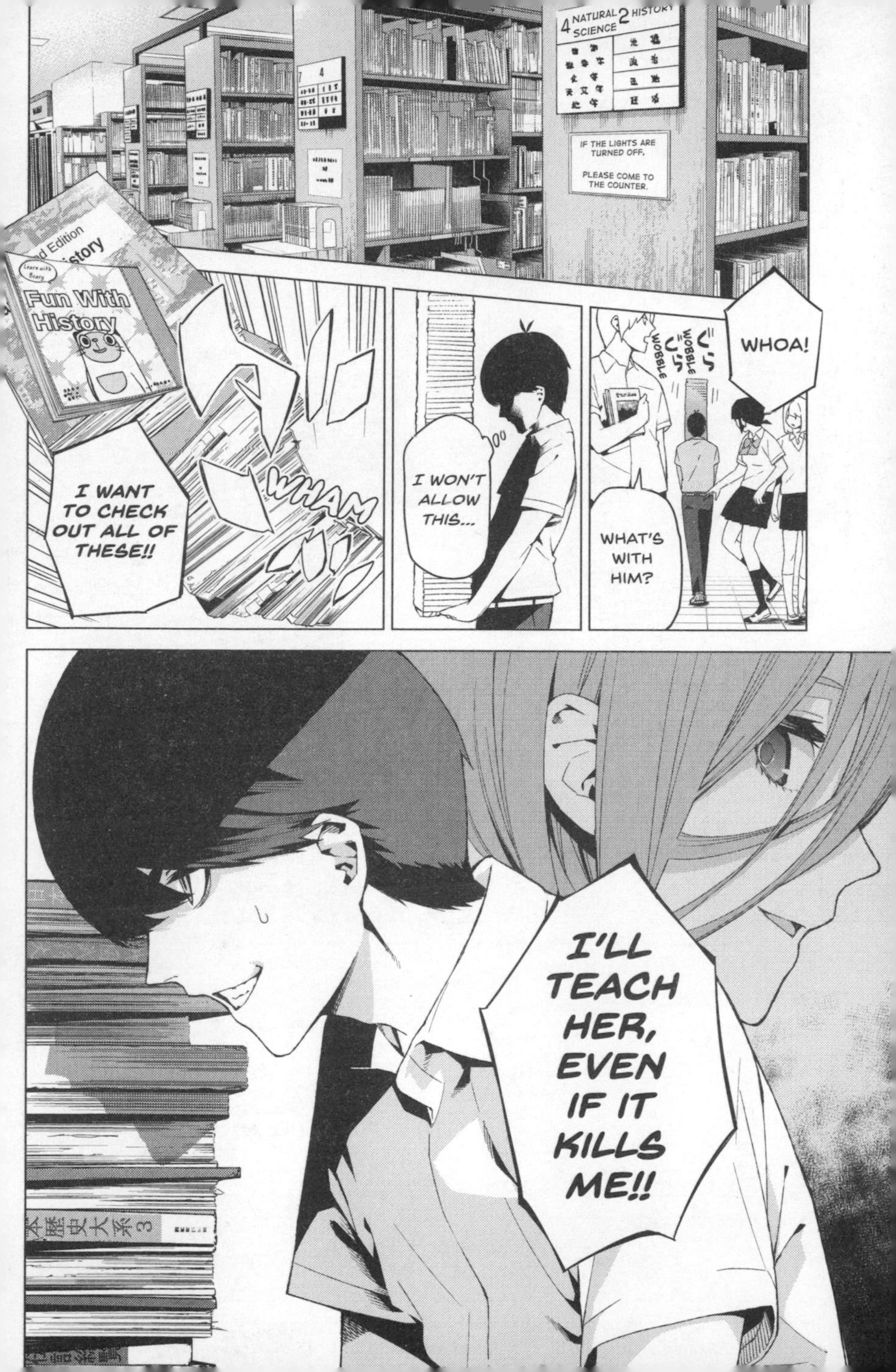
4 NATURAL SCIENCE 2 HISTORY
IF THE LIGHTS ARE TURNED OFF, PLEASE COME TO THE COUNTER.
WHOA!
WOBBLE WOBBLE
WHAT'S WITH HIM?
I WON'T ALLOW THIS...
WHAM
Learn with Beary
Fun With History
I WANT TO CHECK OUT ALL OF THESE!!
I'LL TEACH HER, EVEN IF IT KILLS ME!!

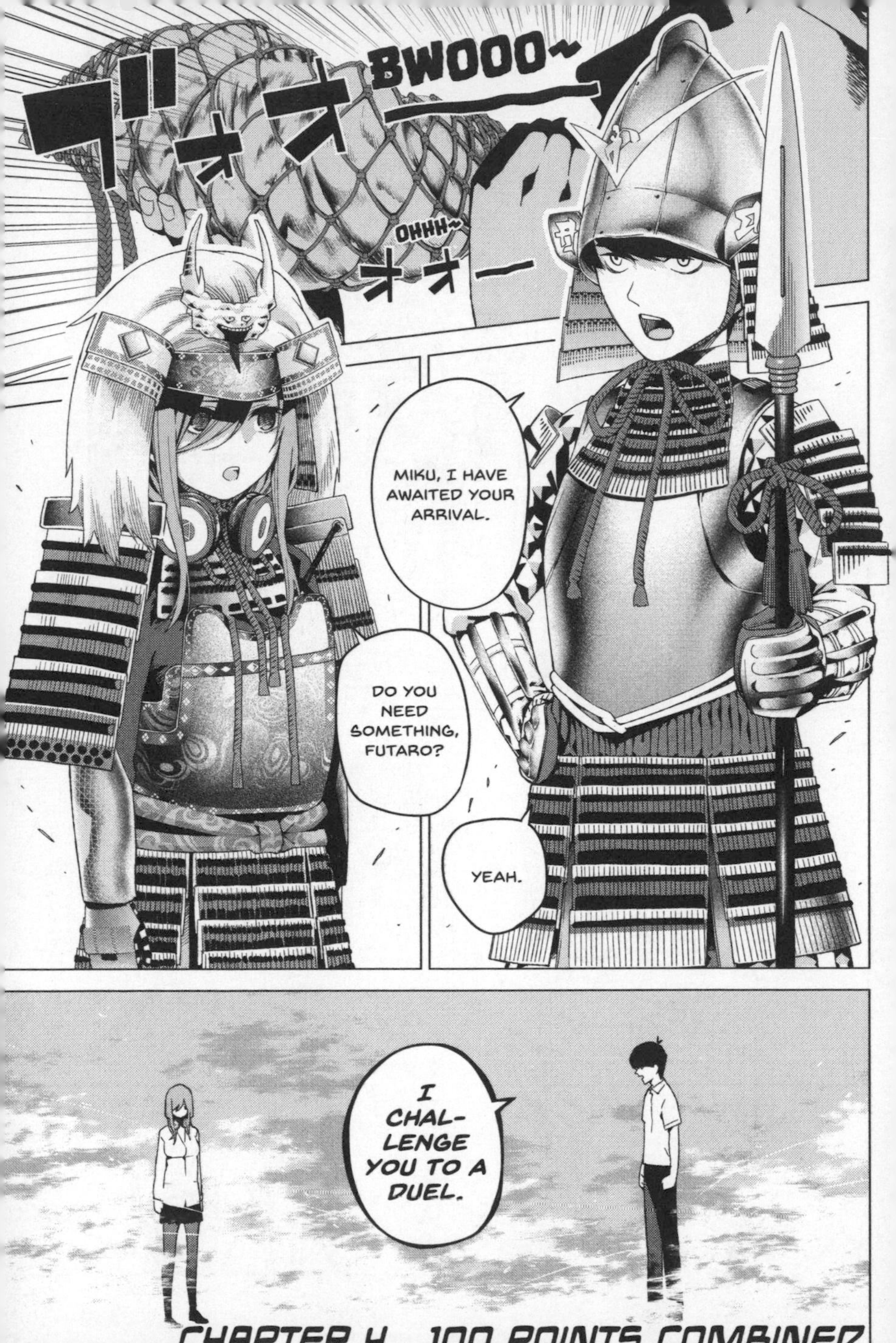
ブォオー
BWOOO~
オオー
OHHH~
MIKU, I HAVE AWAITED YOUR ARRIVAL.
DO YOU NEED SOMETHING, FUTARO?
YEAH.
I CHAL-LENGE YOU TO A DUEL.

CHAPTER 4 100 POINTS COMBINED

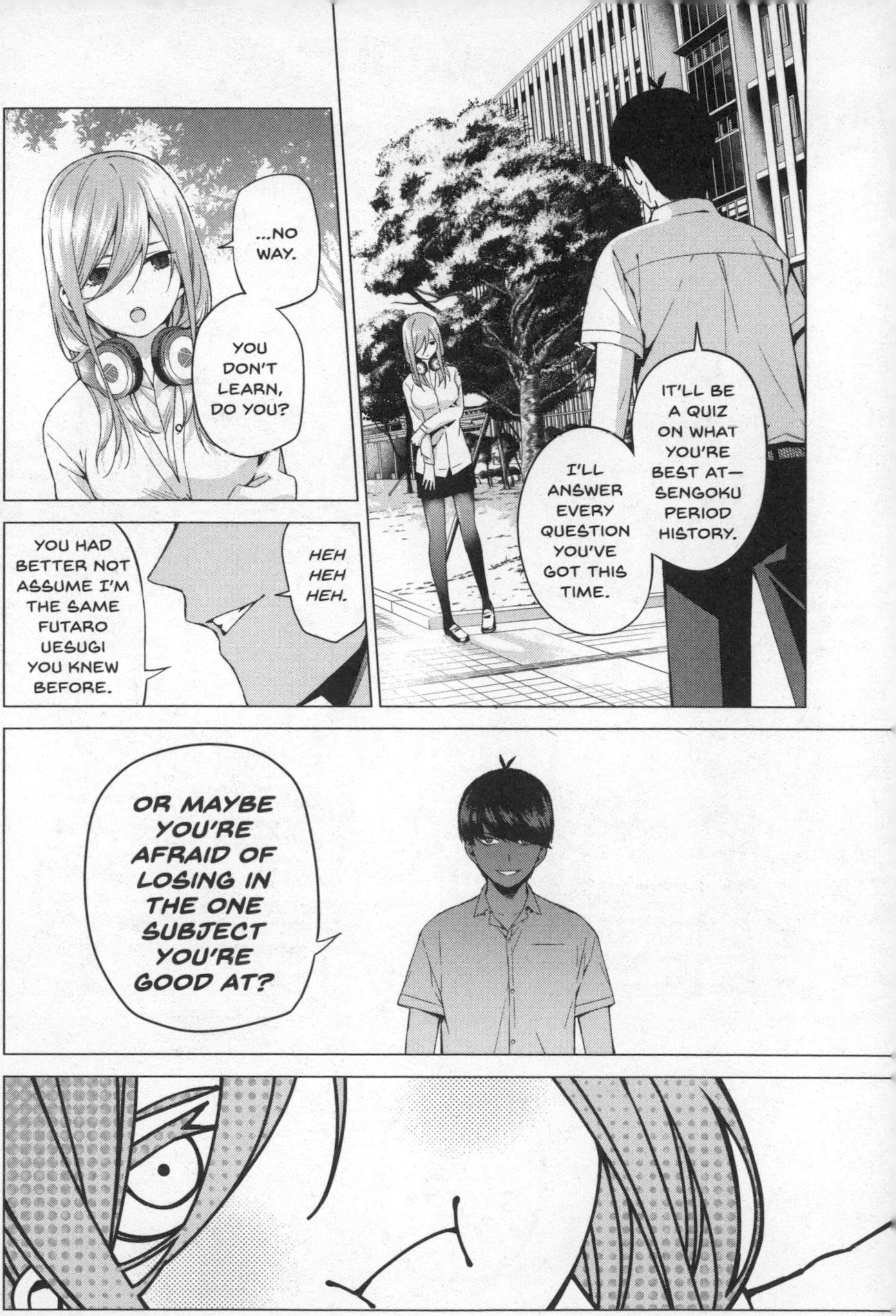
IT'LL BE A QUIZ ON WHAT YOU'RE BEST AT— SENGOKU PERIOD HISTORY.
I'LL ANSWER EVERY QUESTION YOU'VE GOT THIS TIME.
...NO WAY.
YOU DON'T LEARN, DO YOU?
HEH HEH HEH.
YOU HAD BETTER NOT ASSUME I'M THE SAME FUTARO UESUGI YOU KNEW BEFORE.
OR MAYBE YOU'RE AFRAID OF LOSING IN THE ONE SUBJECT YOU'RE GOOD AT?

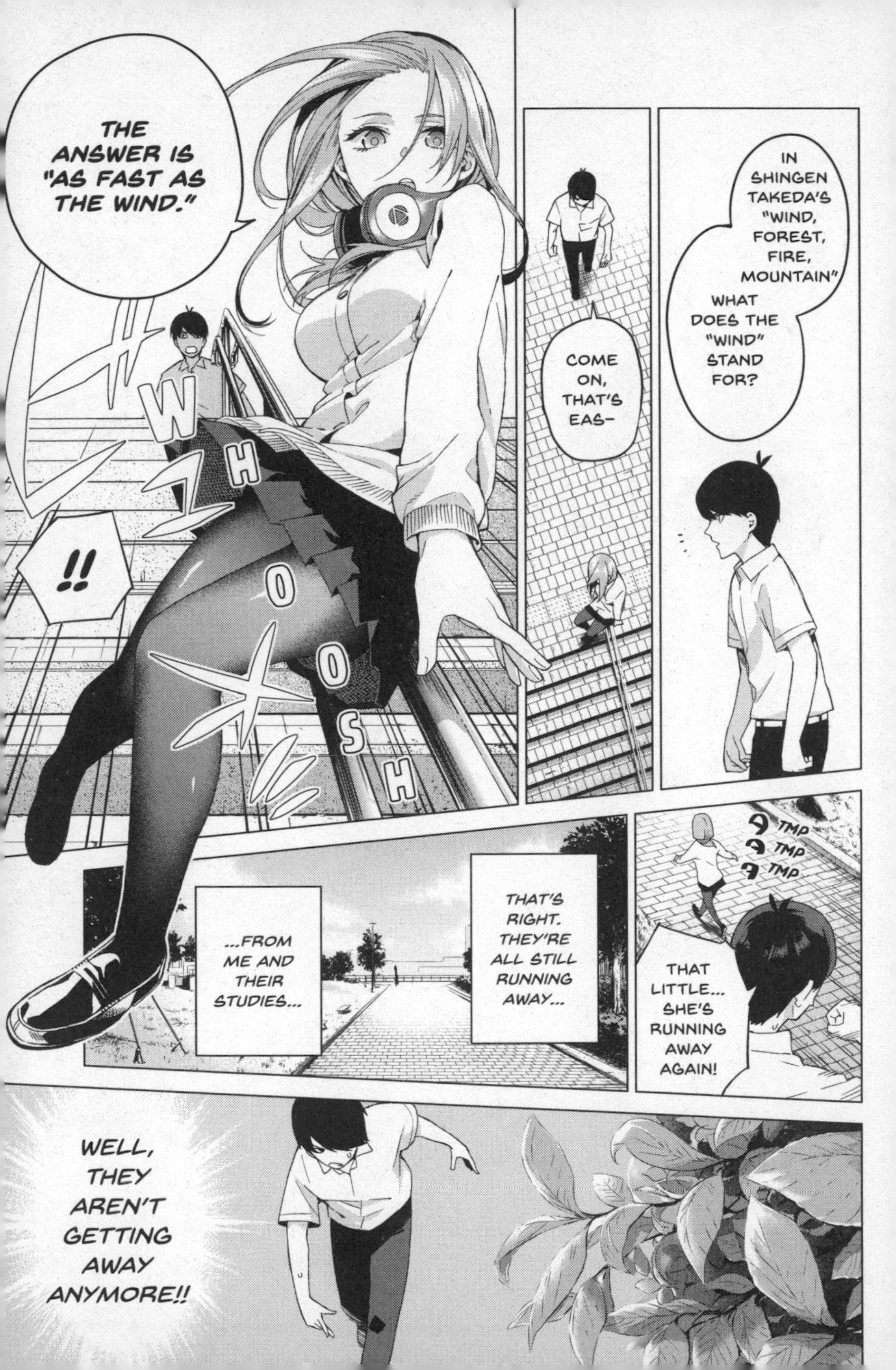
IN SHINGEN TAKEDA'S "WIND, FOREST, FIRE, MOUNTAIN"
WHAT DOES THE "WIND" STAND FOR?
COME ON, THAT'S EAS-
THE ANSWER IS "AS FAST AS THE WIND."
WHOOSH
!!
TMP TMP TMP
THAT LITTLE... SHE'S RUNNING AWAY AGAIN!
THAT'S RIGHT. THEY'RE ALL STILL RUNNING AWAY...
...FROM ME AND THEIR STUDIES...
WELL, THEY AREN'T GETTING AWAY ANYMORE!!

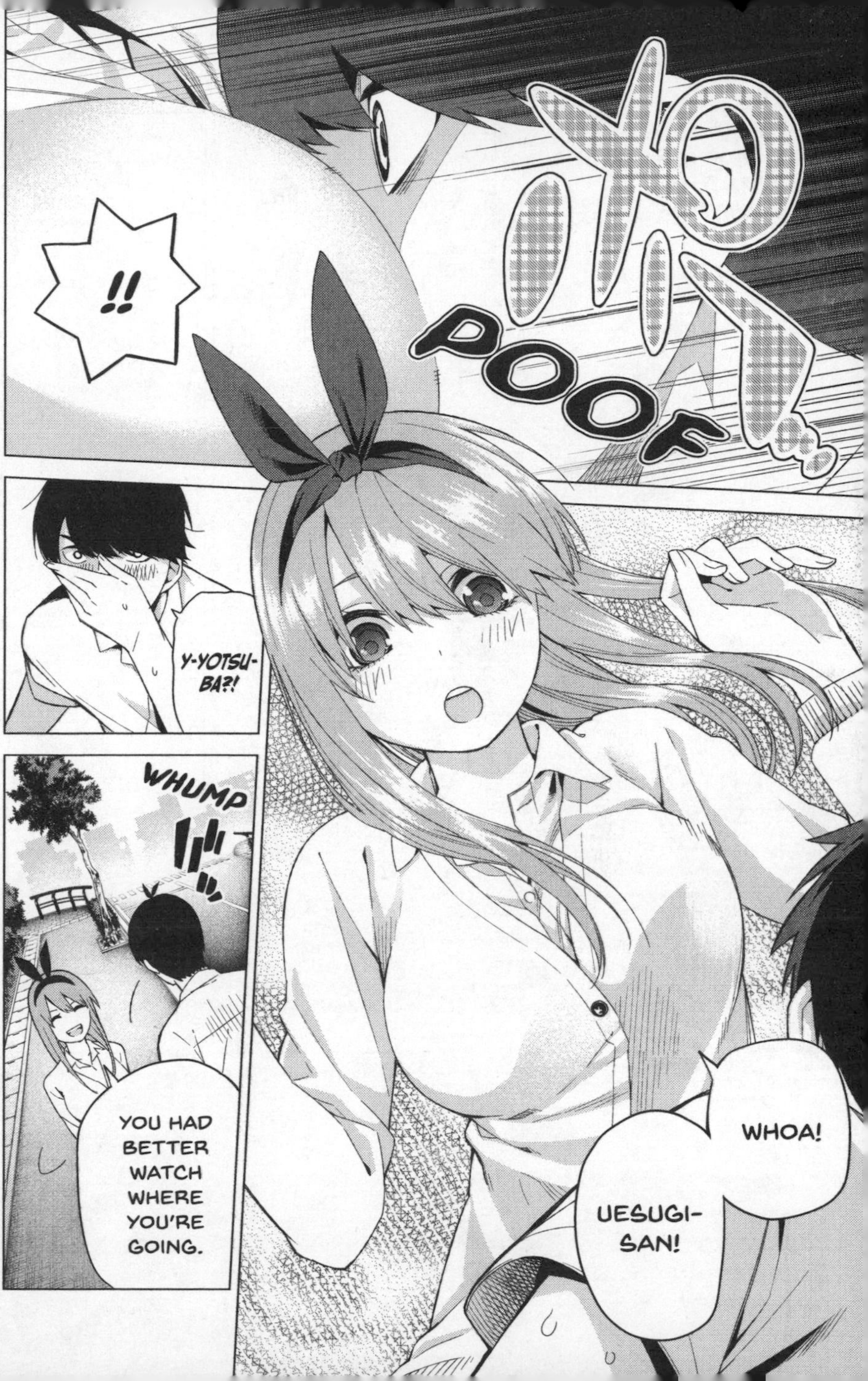
POOF
!!
WHOA!
UESUGI-SAN!
Y-YOTSUBA?!
WHUMP
YOU HAD BETTER WATCH WHERE YOU'RE GOING.

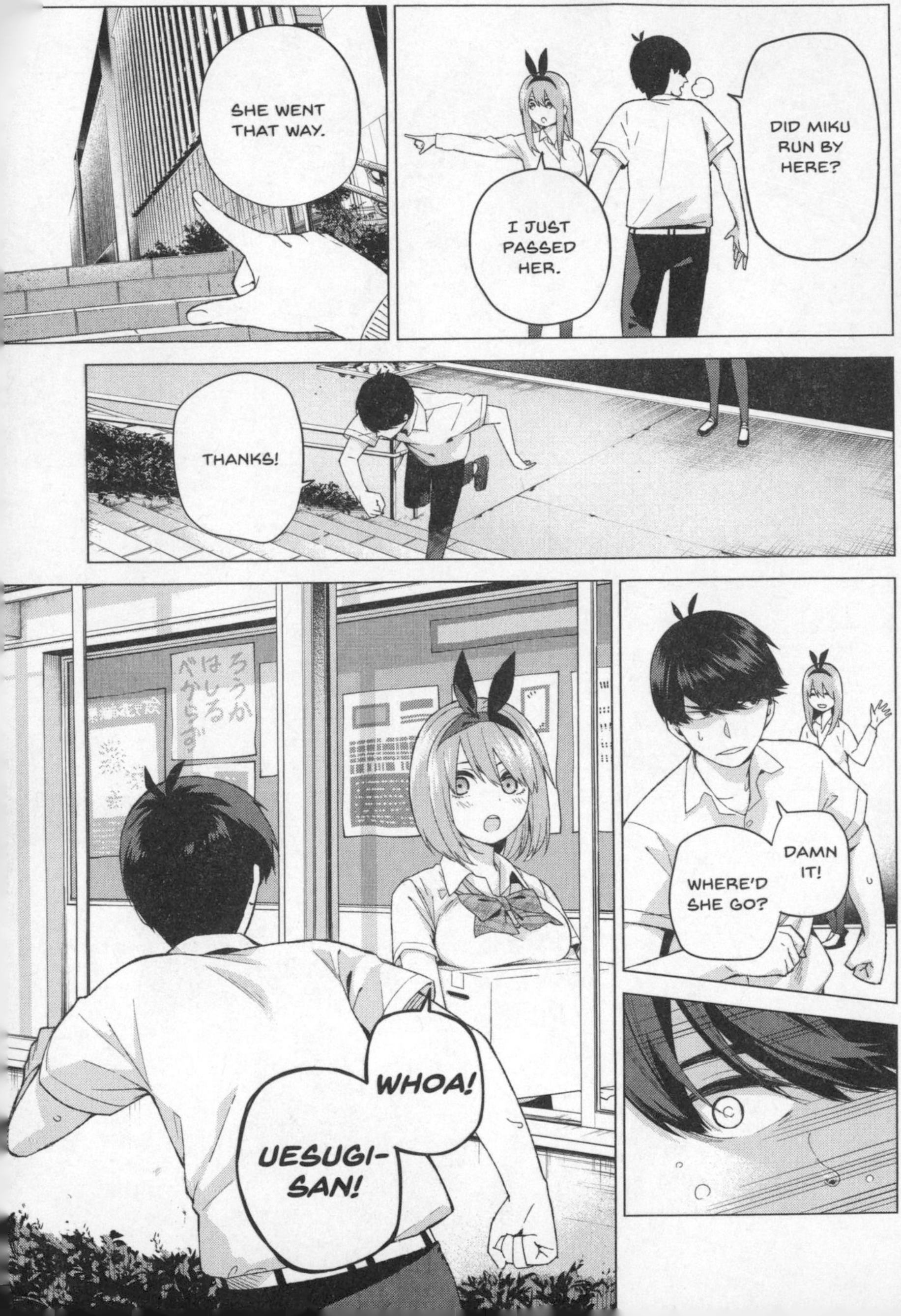
DID MIKU RUN BY HERE?
I JUST PASSED HER.
SHE WENT THAT WAY.
THANKS!
DAMN IT!
WHERE'D SHE GO?
ろうかはしるべからず
WHOA!
UESUGI-SAN!

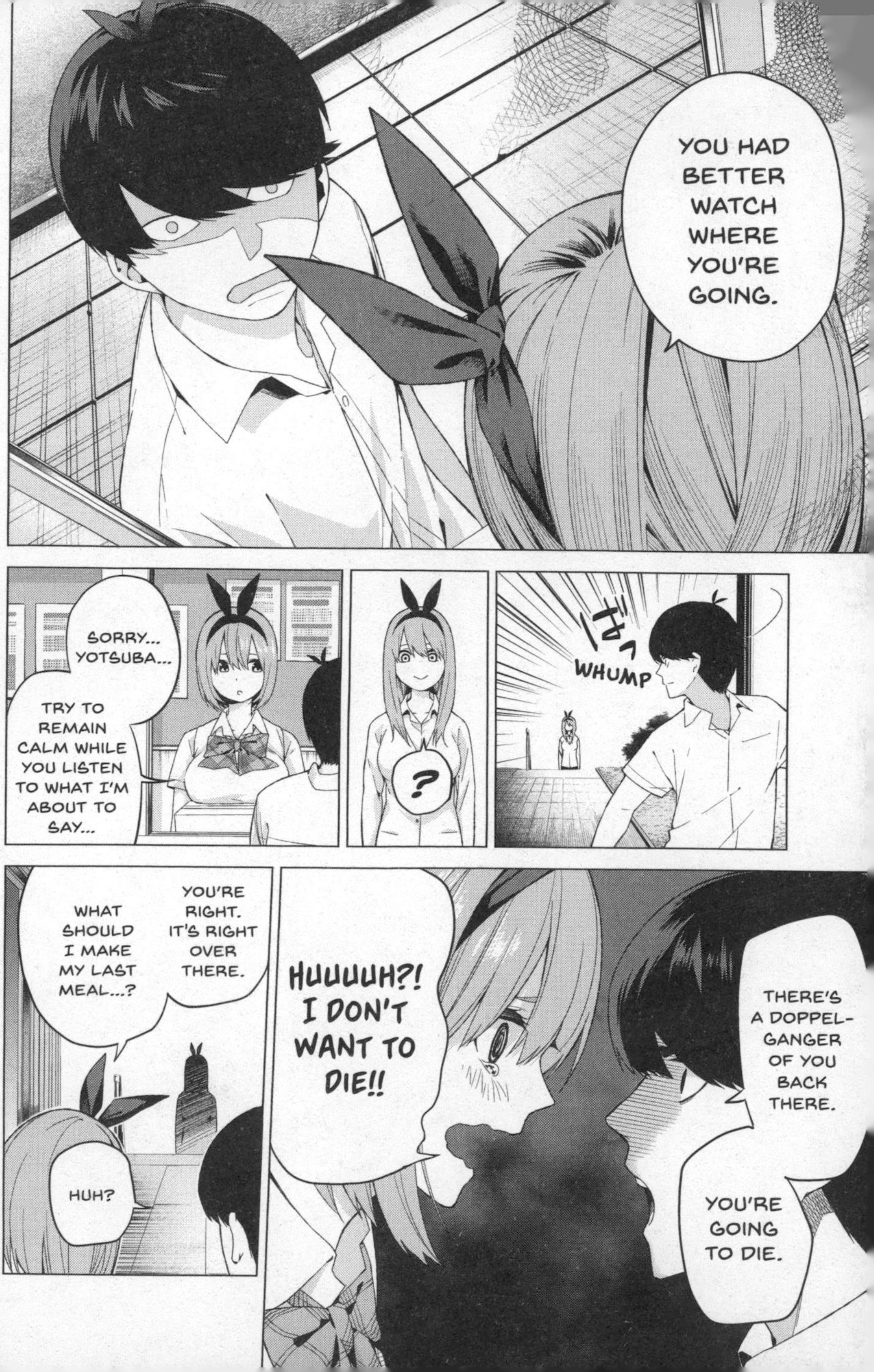

YOU HAD BETTER WATCH WHERE YOU'RE GOING.
ばっ
WHUMP
?
SORRY... YOTSUBA...
TRY TO REMAIN CALM WHILE YOU LISTEN TO WHAT I'M ABOUT TO SAY...
THERE'S A DOPPEL-GANGER OF YOU BACK THERE.
YOU'RE GOING TO DIE.
HUUUUH?! I DON'T WANT TO DIE!!
YOU'RE RIGHT. IT'S RIGHT OVER THERE.
WHAT SHOULD I MAKE MY LAST MEAL...?
HUH?

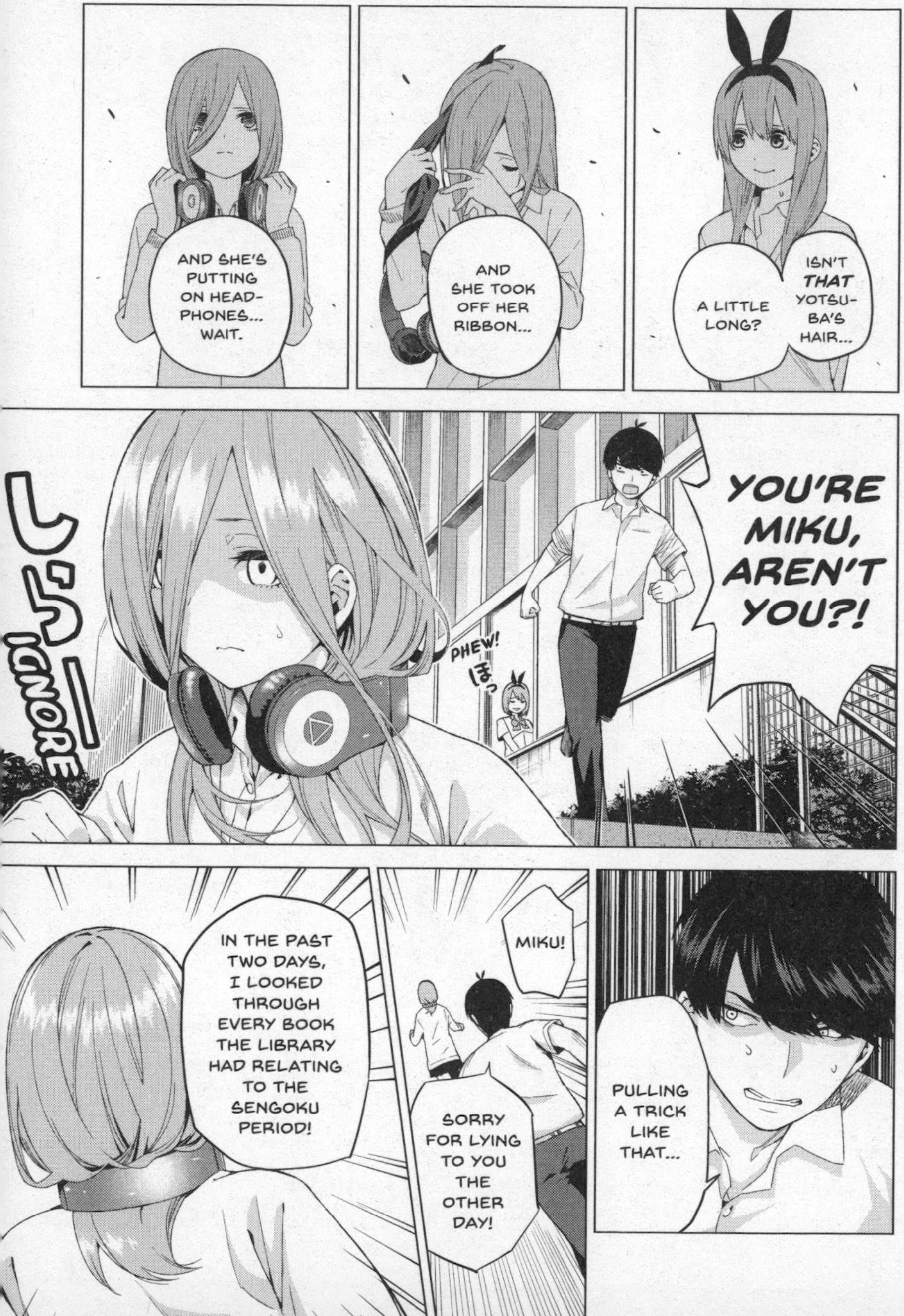
ISN'T THAT YOTSUBA'S HAIR...
A LITTLE LONG?
AND SHE TOOK OFF HER RIBBON...
AND SHE'S PUTTING ON HEAD-PHONES... WAIT.
YOU'RE MIKU, AREN'T YOU?!
PHEW! ほっ
しらー IGNORE
PULLING A TRICK LIKE THAT...
MIKU!
SORRY FOR LYING TO YOU THE OTHER DAY!
IN THE PAST TWO DAYS, I LOOKED THROUGH EVERY BOOK THE LIBRARY HAD RELATING TO THE SENGOKU PERIOD!

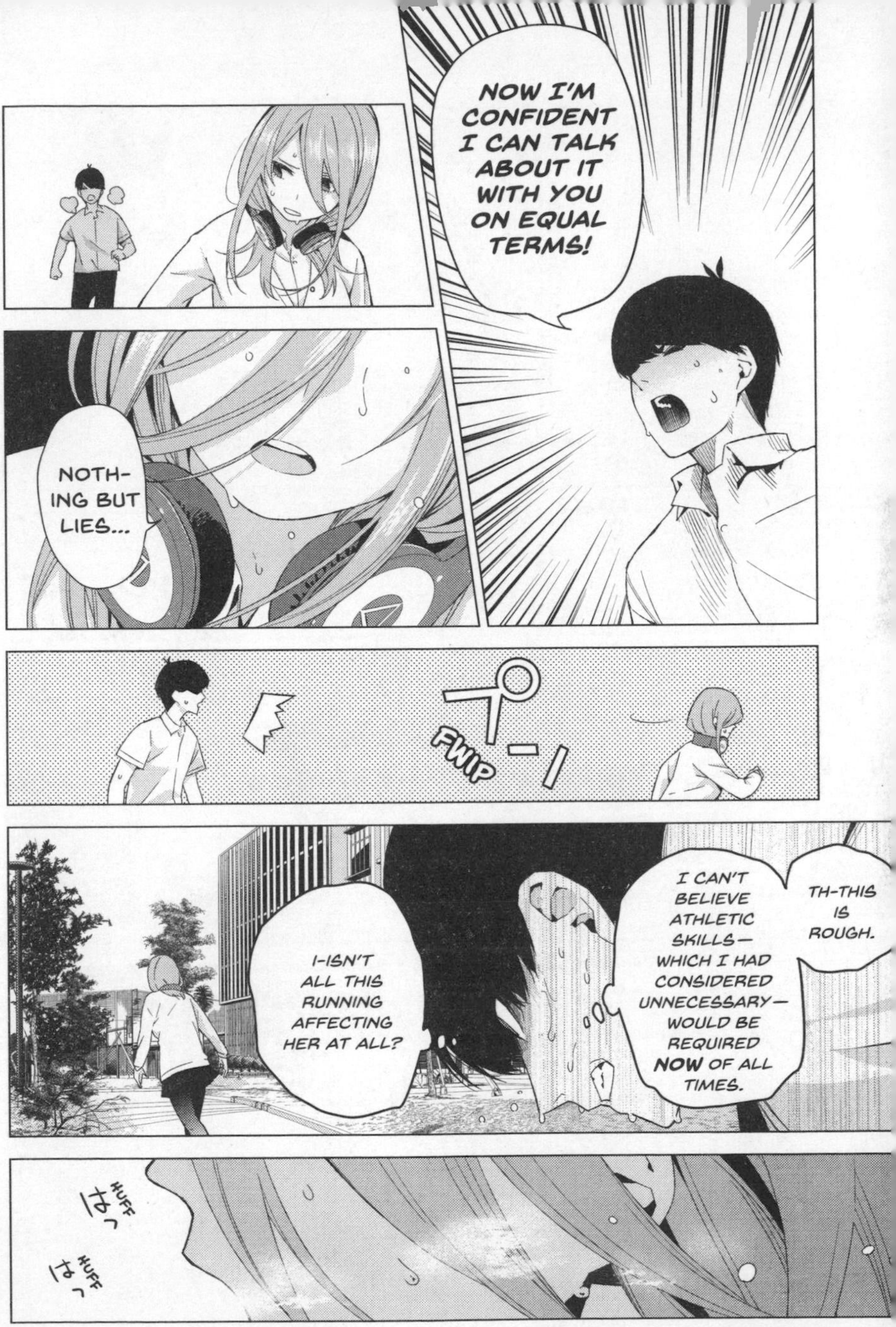
NOW I'M CONFIDENT I CAN TALK ABOUT IT WITH YOU ON EQUAL TERMS!
NOTH-ING BUT LIES...
FWIP
TH-THIS IS ROUGH.
I CAN'T BELIEVE ATHLETIC SKILLS— WHICH I HAD CONSIDERED UNNECESSARY— WOULD BE REQUIRED NOW OF ALL TIMES.
I-ISN'T ALL THIS RUNNING AFFECTING HER AT ALL?
HUFF
HUFF

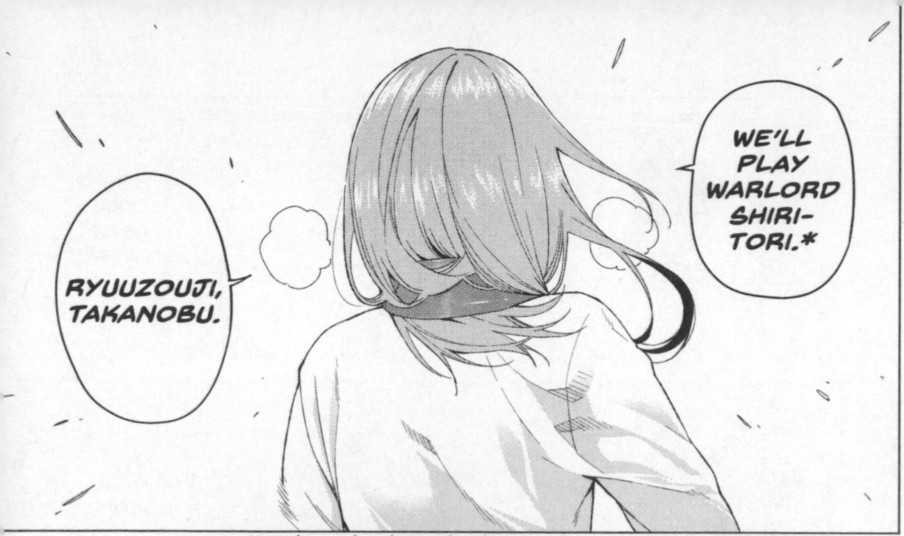
WE'LL PLAY WARLORD SHIRI-TORI.*
RYUUZOUJI, TAKANOBU.

*A word game where the next player has to start their word with the last syllable of the previous word.

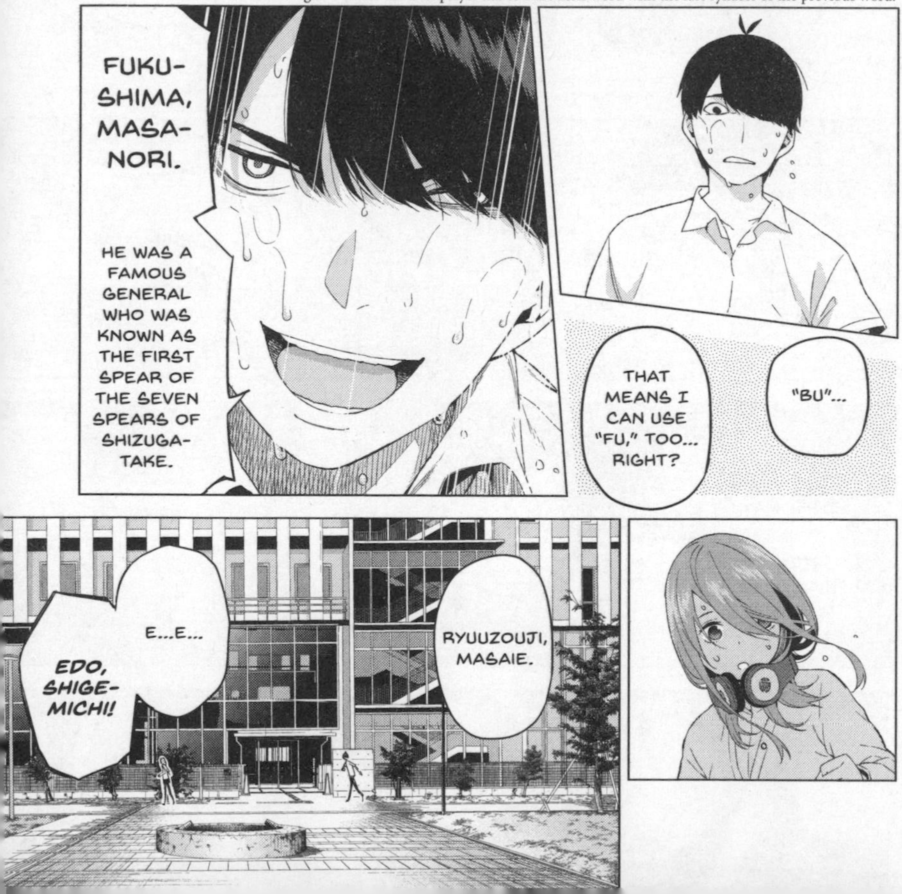
"BU"...
THAT MEANS I CAN USE "FU," TOO... RIGHT?
FUKU-SHIMA, MASA-NORI.
HE WAS A FAMOUS GENERAL WHO WAS KNOWN AS THE FIRST SPEAR OF THE SEVEN SPEARS OF SHIZUGA-TAKE.
RYUUZOUJI, MASAIE.
E...E...
EDO, SHIGE-MICHI!

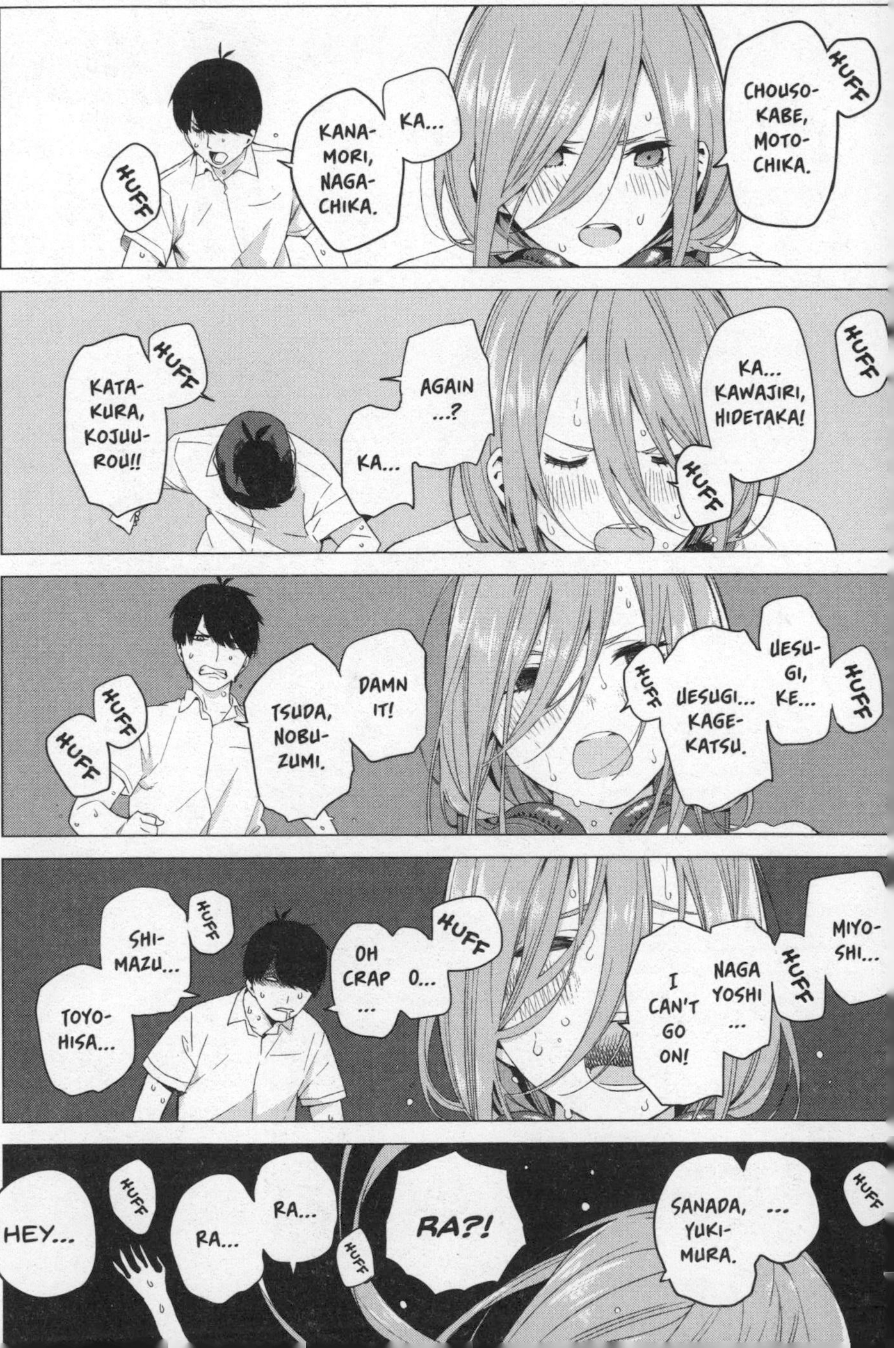
HUFF
CHOUSO-KABE, MOTO-CHIKA.
KA...
KANA-MORI, NAGA-CHIKA.
HUFF
HUFF
KA... KAWAJIRI, HIDETAKA!
HUFF
AGAIN ...?
KA...
HUFF
KATA-KURA, KOJUU-ROU!!
UESUGI, KE...
HUFF
HUFF
UESUGI... KAGE-KATSU.
DAMN IT!
TSUDA, NOBU-ZUMI.
HUFF
HUFF
MIYO-SHI...
HUFF
NAGA YOSHI ...
I CAN'T GO ON!
HUFF
O...
OH CRAP ...
HUFF
SHI-MAZU...
TOYO-HISA...
HUFF
...
SANADA, YUKI-MURA.
RA?!
HUFF
RA...
RA...
HUFF
HEY...

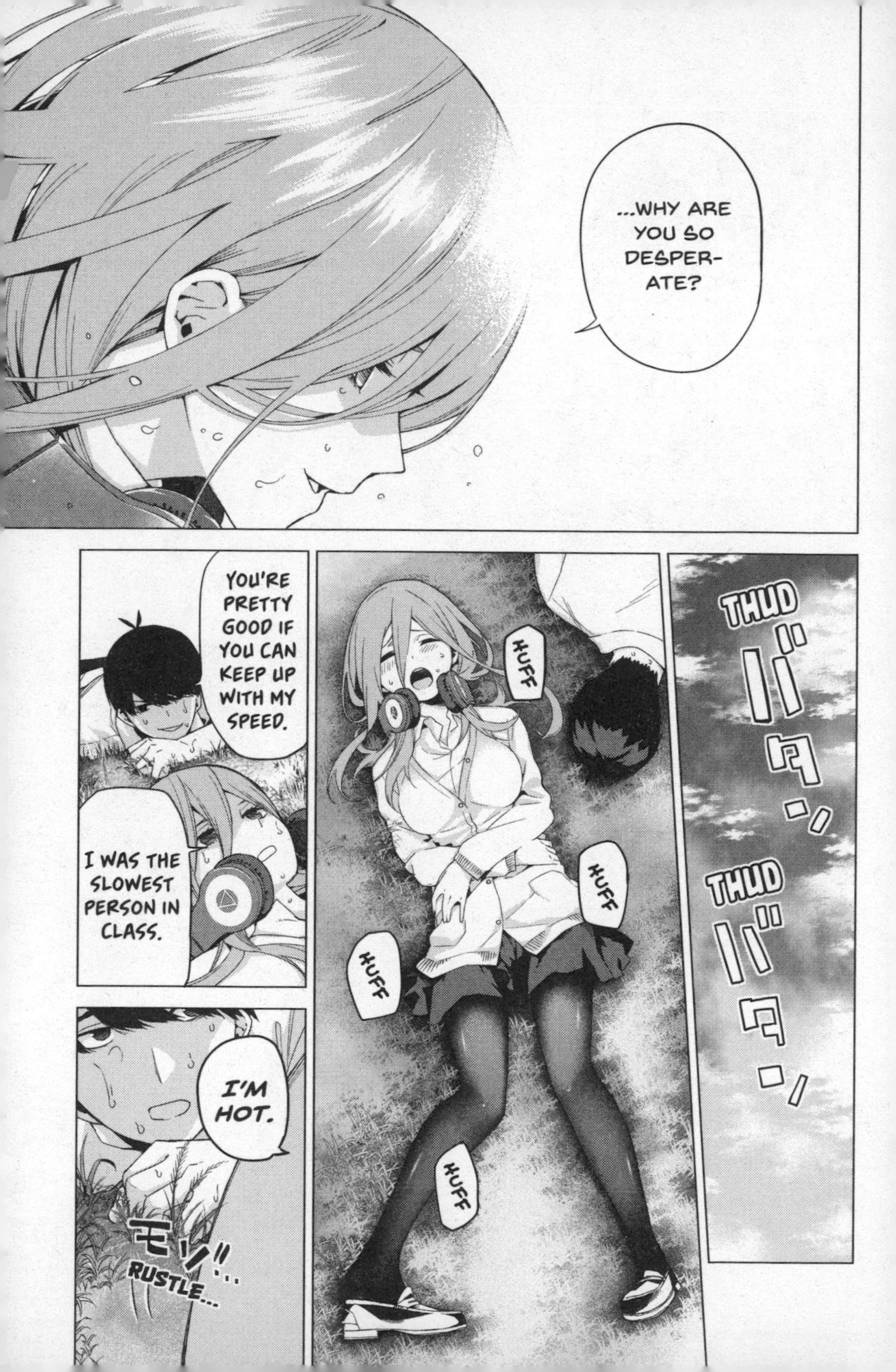
...WHY ARE YOU SO DESPER-ATE?
THUD
THUD
HUFF
HUFF
HUFF
HUFF
YOU'RE PRETTY GOOD IF YOU CAN KEEP UP WITH MY SPEED.
I WAS THE SLOWEST PERSON IN CLASS.
I'M HOT.
RUSTLE...

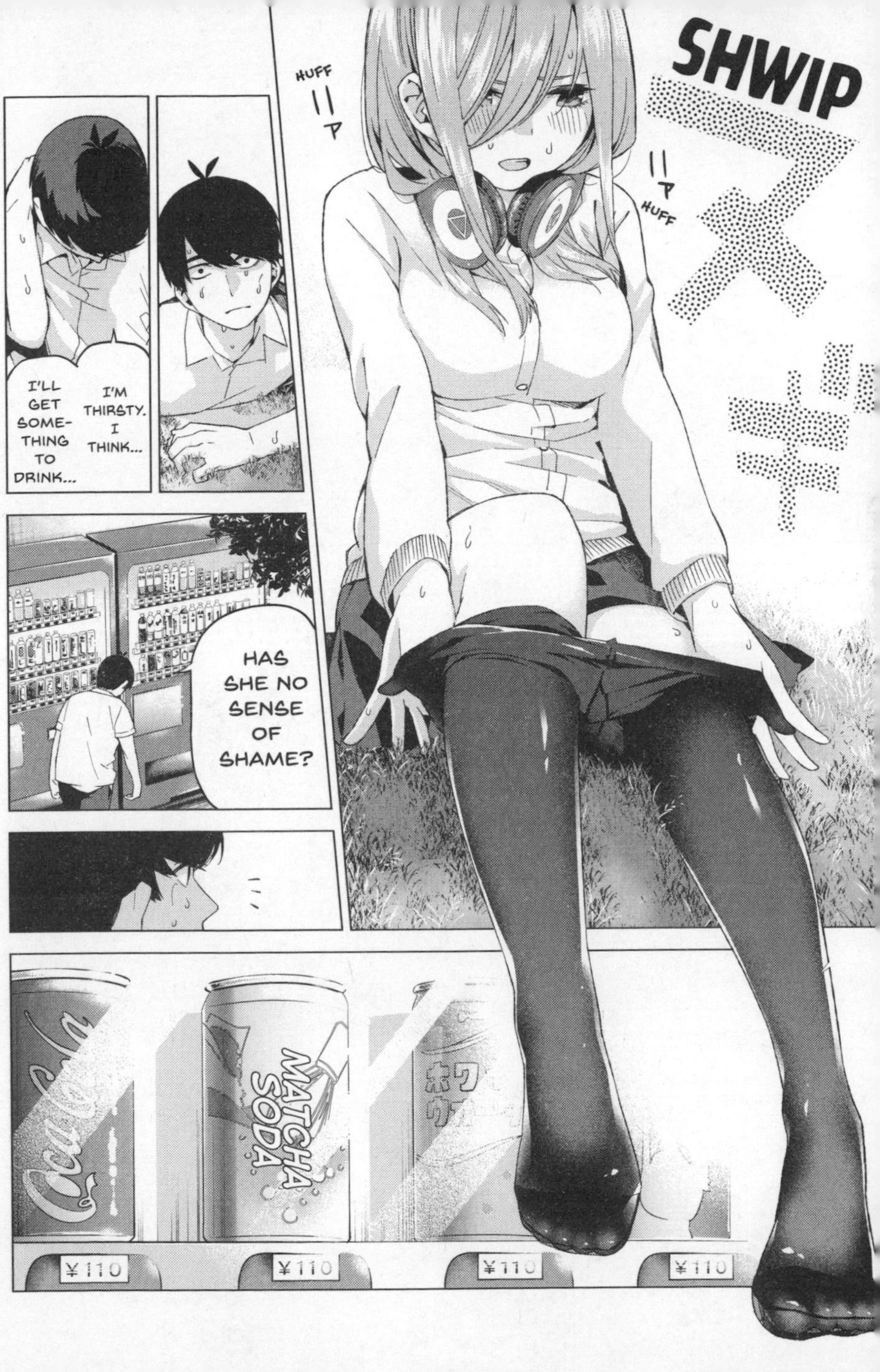
SHWIP
HUFF
HUFF
I'M THIRSTY. I THINK...
I'LL GET SOMETHING TO DRINK...
HAS SHE NO SENSE OF SHAME?
MATCHA SODA
¥110
¥110
¥110
¥110

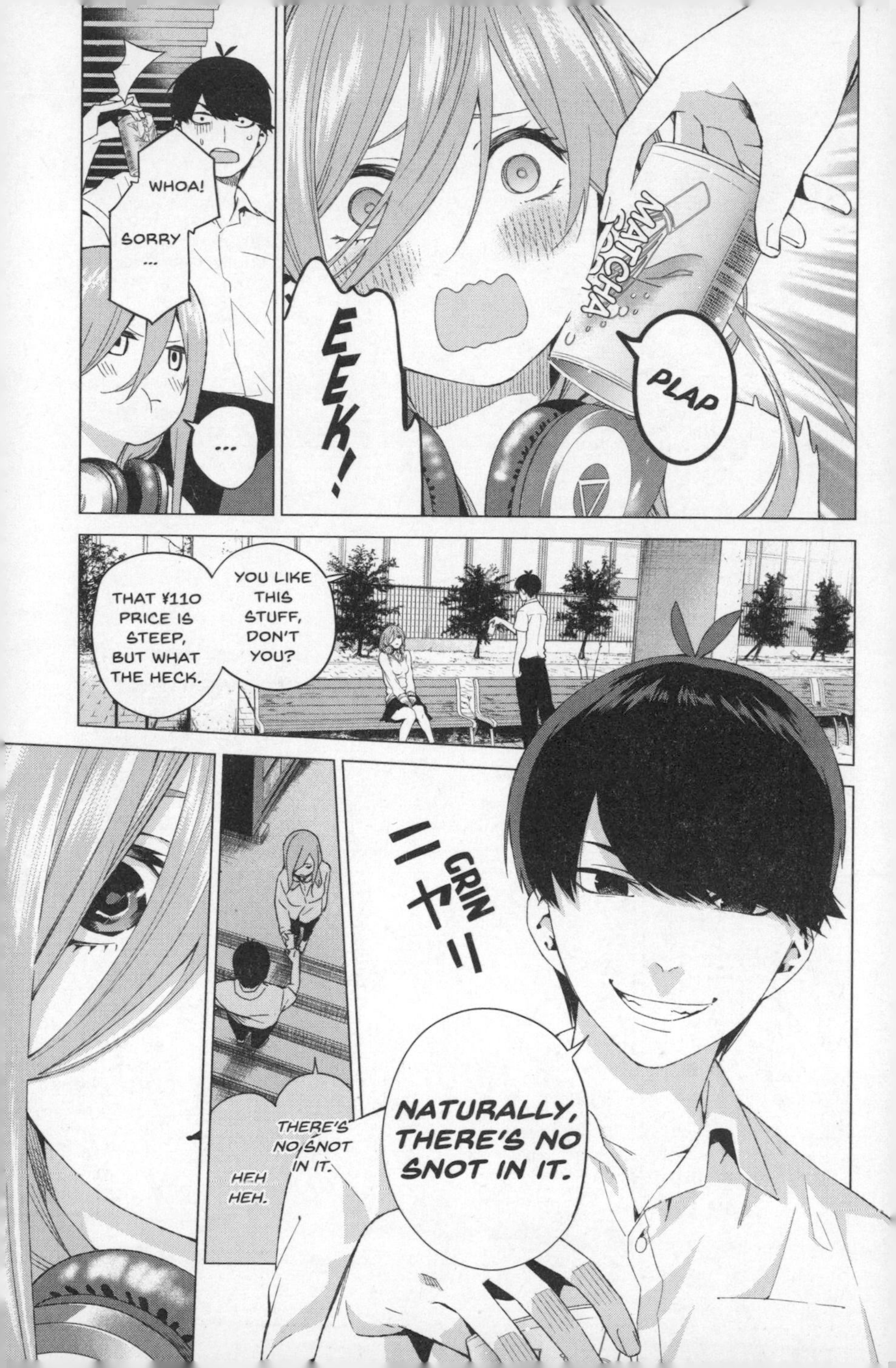
MATCHA SODA
PLAP
EEK!
WHOA!
SORRY ...
...
YOU LIKE THIS STUFF, DON'T YOU?
THAT ¥110 PRICE IS STEEP, BUT WHAT THE HECK.
ニヤッ
GRIN
NATURALLY, THERE'S NO SNOT IN IT.
THERE'S NO SNOT IN IT.
HEH HEH.

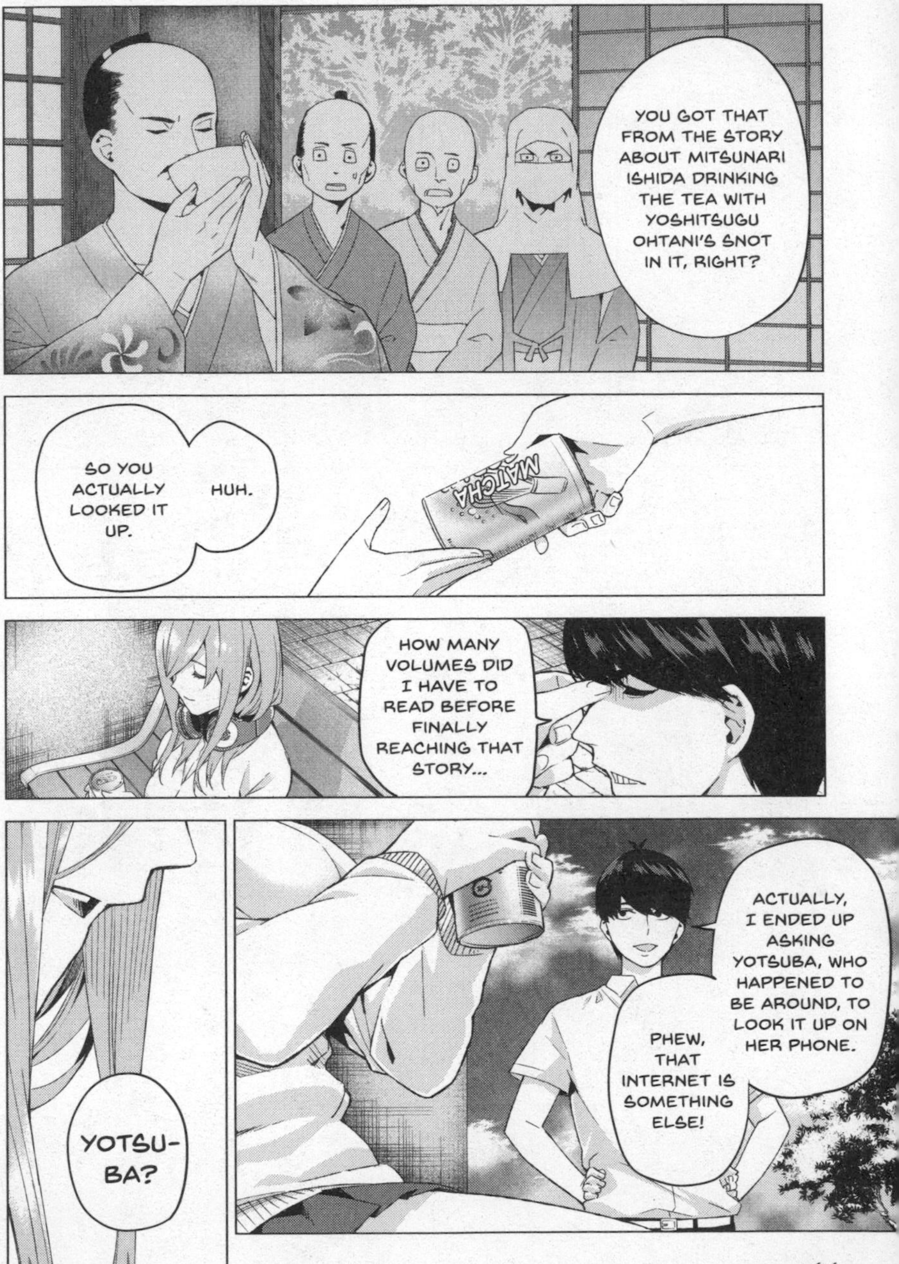
YOU GOT THAT FROM THE STORY ABOUT MITSUNARI ISHIDA DRINKING THE TEA WITH YOSHITSUGU OHTANI'S SNOT IN IT, RIGHT?
SO YOU ACTUALLY LOOKED IT UP. HUH.
MATCHA
HOW MANY VOLUMES DID I HAVE TO READ BEFORE FINALLY REACHING THAT STORY...
ACTUALLY, I ENDED UP ASKING YOTSUBA, WHO HAPPENED TO BE AROUND, TO LOOK IT UP ON HER PHONE.
PHEW, THAT INTERNET IS SOMETHING ELSE!
YOTSU-BA?

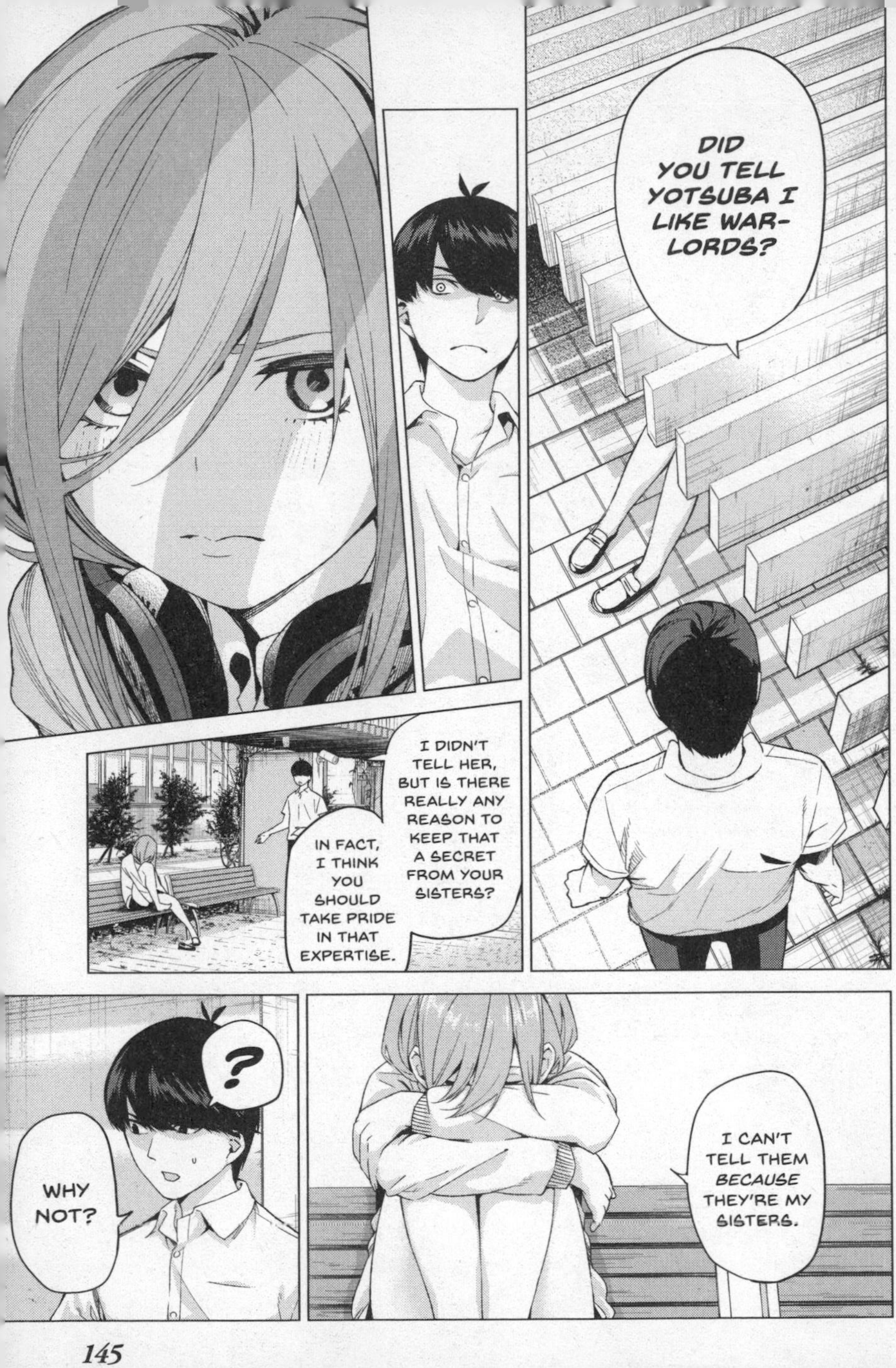
DID YOU TELL YOTSUBA I LIKE WAR-LORDS?
I DIDN'T TELL HER, BUT IS THERE REALLY ANY REASON TO KEEP THAT A SECRET FROM YOUR SISTERS?
IN FACT, I THINK YOU SHOULD TAKE PRIDE IN THAT EXPERTISE.
I CAN'T TELL THEM *BECAUSE* THEY'RE MY SISTERS.
?
WHY NOT?

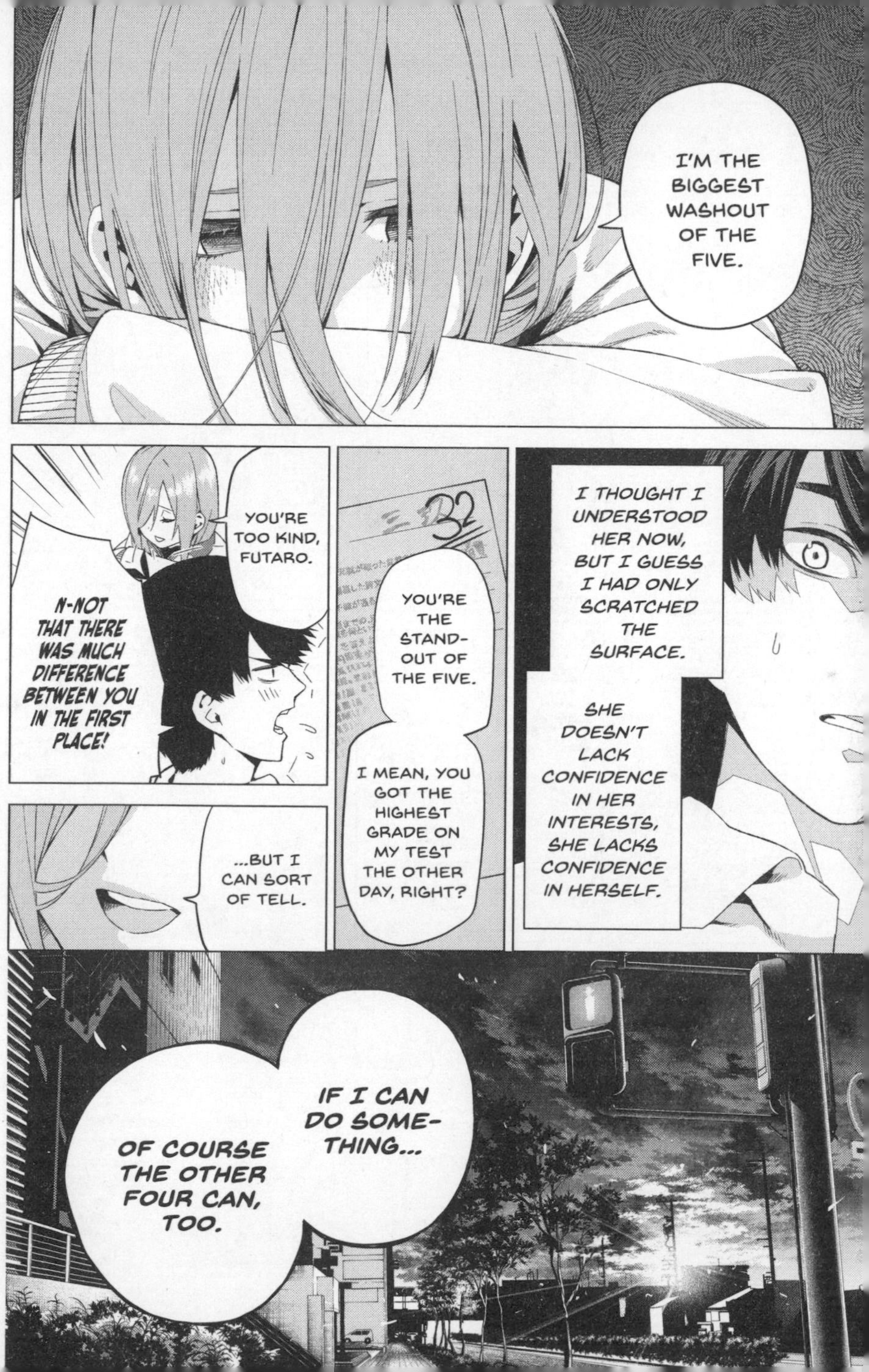
I'M THE BIGGEST WASHOUT OF THE FIVE.
I THOUGHT I UNDERSTOOD HER NOW, BUT I GUESS I HAD ONLY SCRATCHED THE SURFACE.
SHE DOESN'T LACK CONFIDENCE IN HER INTERESTS, SHE LACKS CONFIDENCE IN HERSELF.
YOU'RE THE STAND-OUT OF THE FIVE.
I MEAN, YOU GOT THE HIGHEST GRADE ON MY TEST THE OTHER DAY, RIGHT?
YOU'RE TOO KIND, FUTARO.
N-NOT THAT THERE WAS MUCH DIFFERENCE BETWEEN YOU IN THE FIRST PLACE!
...BUT I CAN SORT OF TELL.
IF I CAN DO SOME-THING...
OF COURSE THE OTHER FOUR CAN, TOO.

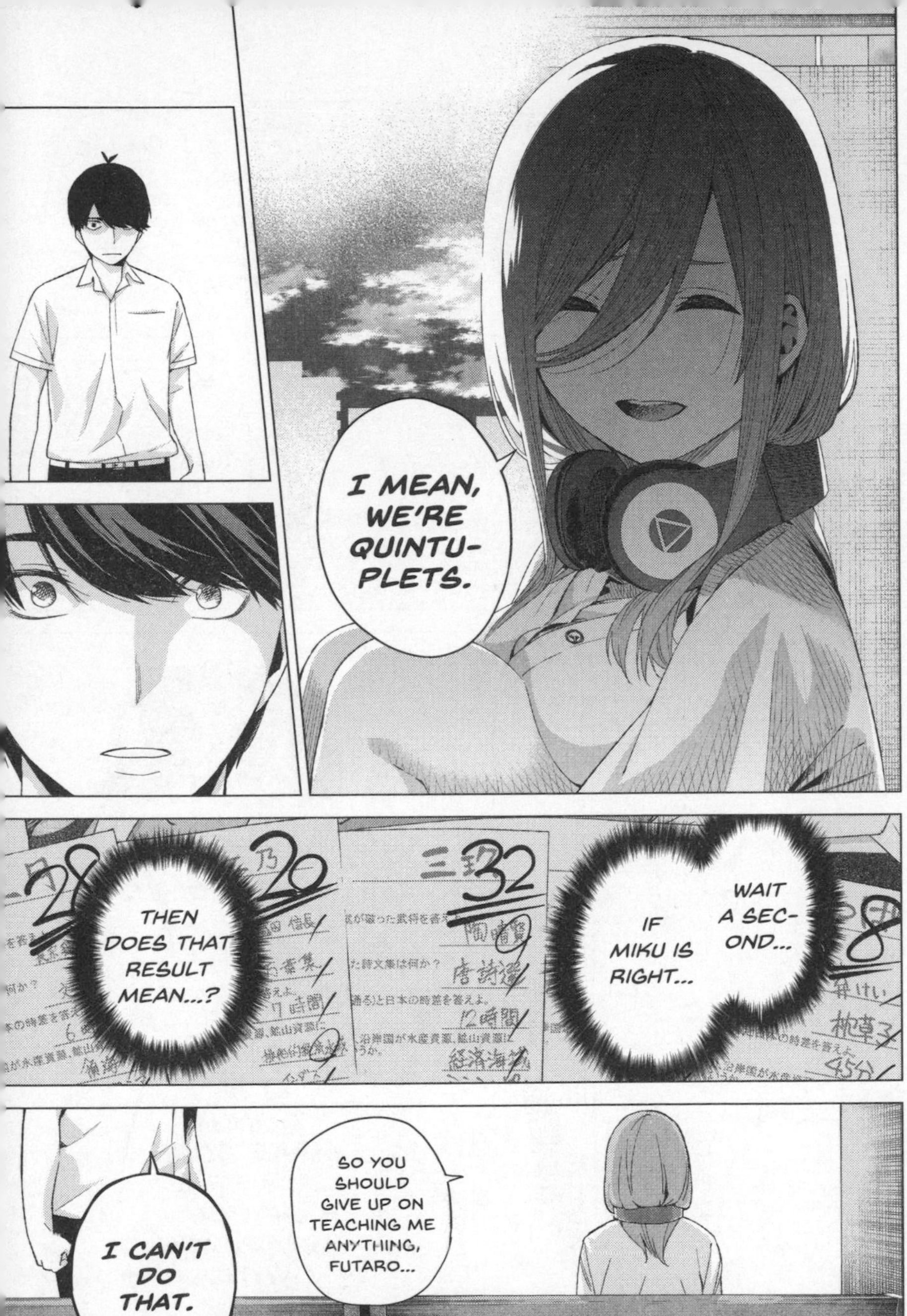
I MEAN, WE'RE QUINTU-PLETS.
WAIT A SEC-OND...
IF MIKU IS RIGHT...
THEN DOES THAT RESULT MEAN...?
SO YOU SHOULD GIVE UP ON TEACHING ME ANYTHING, FUTARO...
I CAN'T DO THAT.

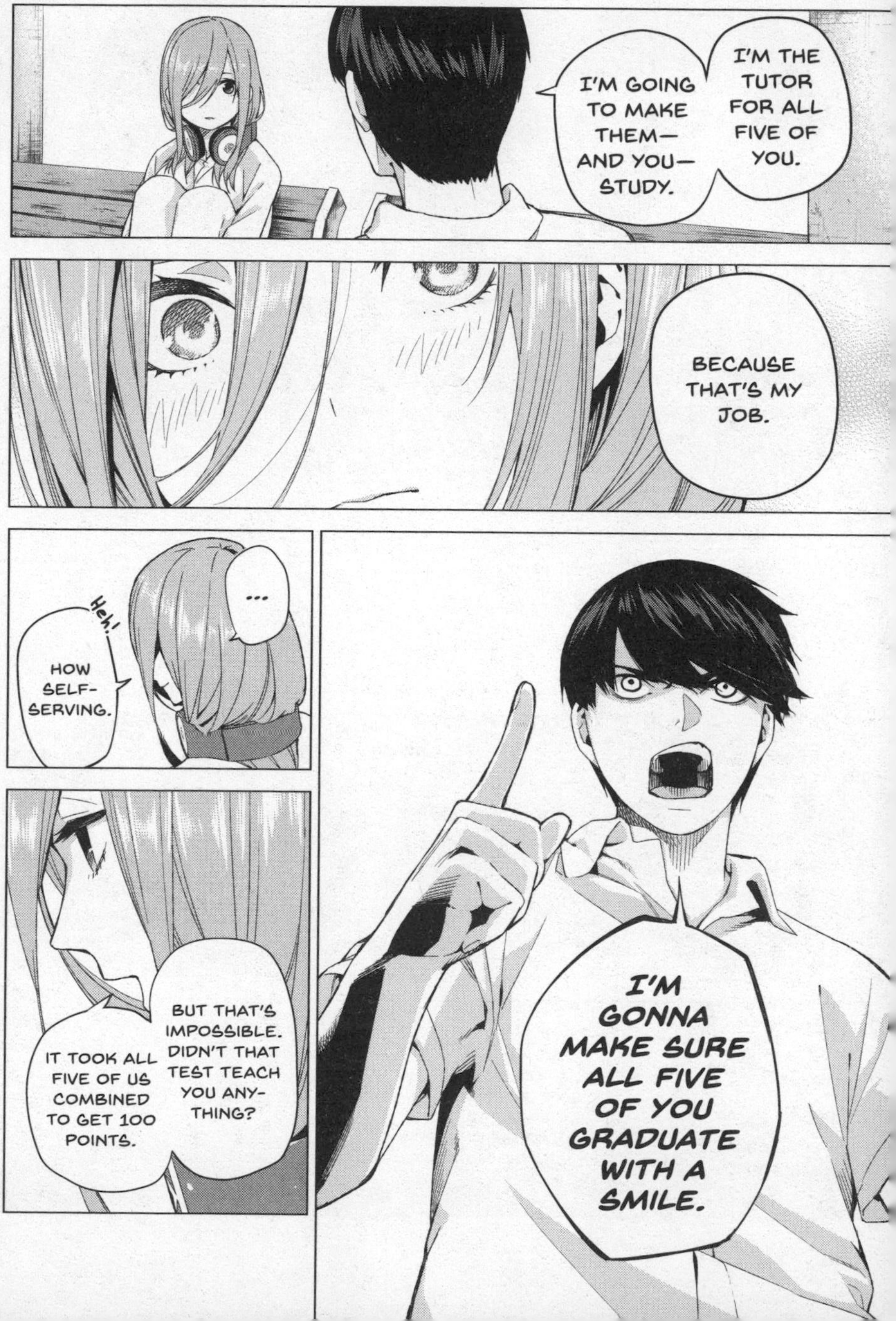
I'M THE TUTOR FOR ALL FIVE OF YOU.
I'M GOING TO MAKE THEM— AND YOU— STUDY.
BECAUSE THAT'S MY JOB.
I'M GONNA MAKE SURE ALL FIVE OF YOU GRADUATE WITH A SMILE.
...
Heh!
HOW SELF-SERVING.
BUT THAT'S IMPOSSIBLE. DIDN'T THAT TEST TEACH YOU ANYTHING?
IT TOOK ALL FIVE OF US COMBINED TO GET 100 POINTS.

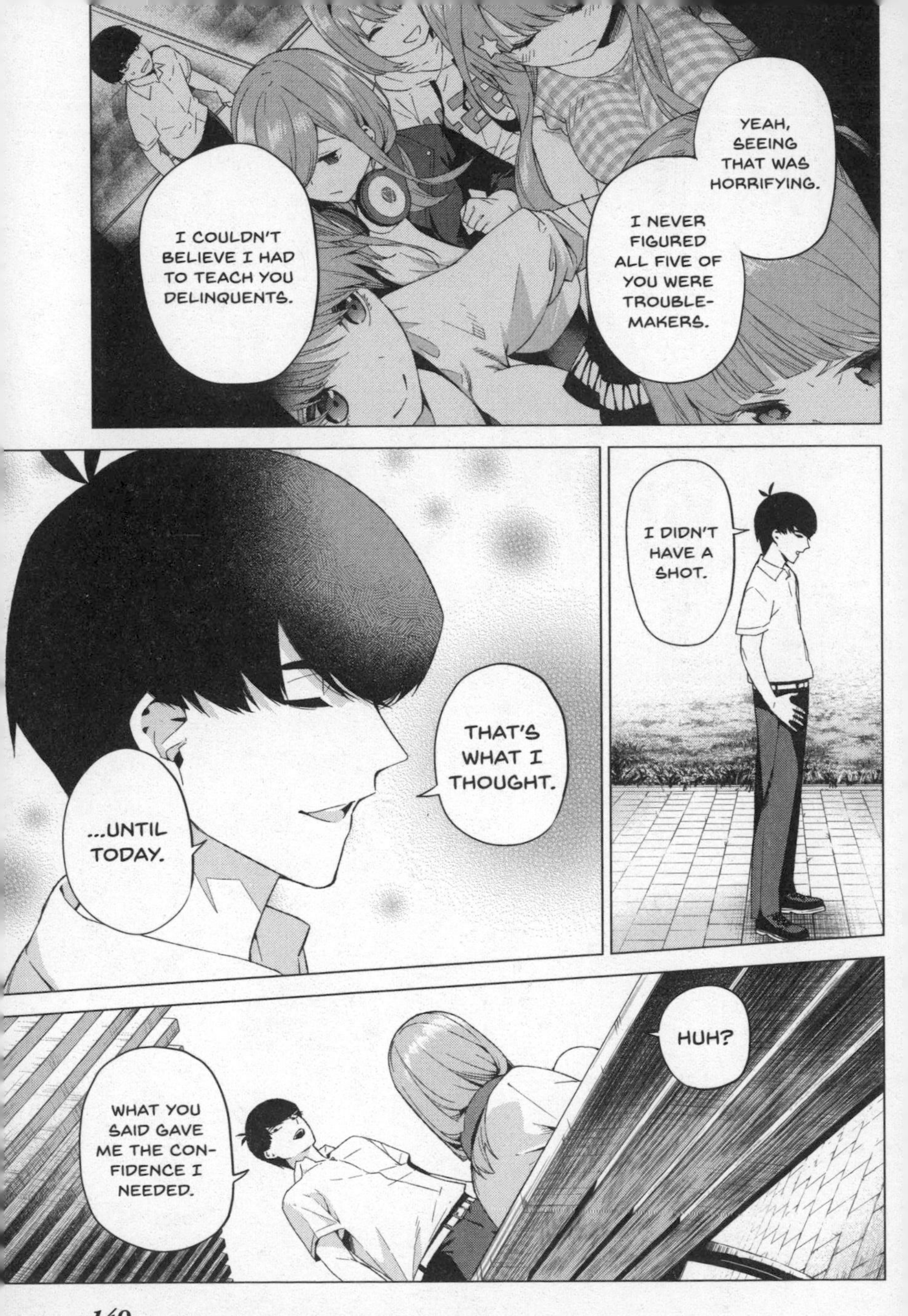
YEAH, SEEING THAT WAS HORRIFYING.
I NEVER FIGURED ALL FIVE OF YOU WERE TROUBLE-MAKERS.
I COULDN'T BELIEVE I HAD TO TEACH YOU DELINQUENTS.
I DIDN'T HAVE A SHOT.
THAT'S WHAT I THOUGHT.
...UNTIL TODAY.
HUH?
WHAT YOU SAID GAVE ME THE CON-FIDENCE I NEEDED.

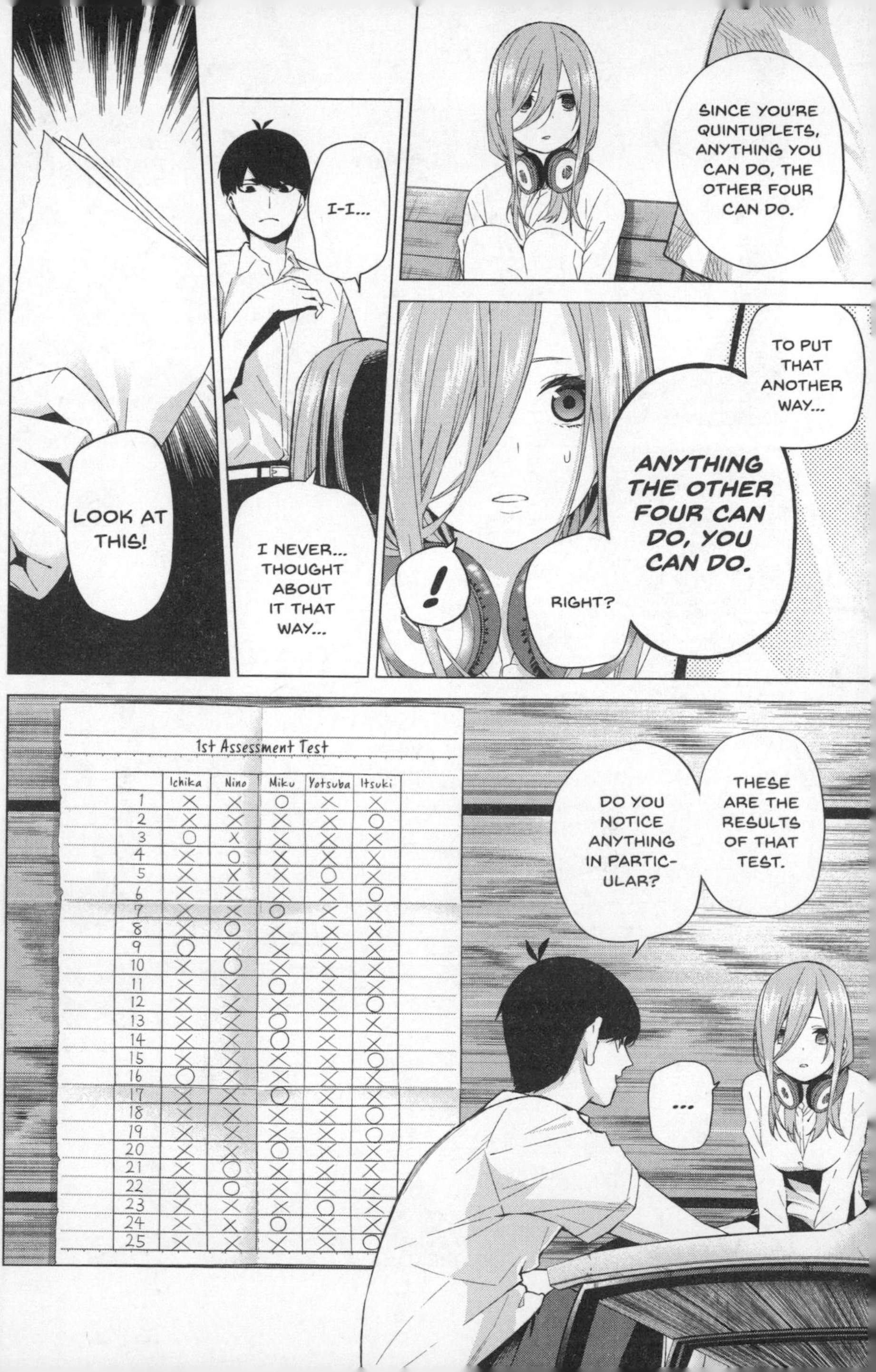
SINCE YOU'RE QUINTUPLETS, ANYTHING YOU CAN DO, THE OTHER FOUR CAN DO.
TO PUT THAT ANOTHER WAY...
ANYTHING THE OTHER FOUR CAN DO, YOU CAN DO.
!
RIGHT?
I-I...
I NEVER... THOUGHT ABOUT IT THAT WAY...
LOOK AT THIS!
THESE ARE THE RESULTS OF THAT TEST.
DO YOU NOTICE ANYTHING IN PARTIC-ULAR?
...
1st Assessment Test

	Ichika	Nino	Miku	Yotsuba	Itsuki
1	×	×	○	×	×
2	×	×	×	×	○
3	○	×	×	×	×
4	×	○	×	×	×
5	×	×	×	○	×
6	×	×	×	×	○
7	×	×	○	×	×
8	×	○	×	×	×
9	○	×	×	×	×
10	×	○	×	×	×
11	×	×	○	×	×
12	×	×	×	×	○
13	×	×	○	×	×
14	×	×	○	×	×
15	×	×	×	×	○
16	○	×	×	×	×
17	×	×	○	×	×
18	×	×	×	×	○
19	×	×	×	×	○
20	×	×	○	×	×
21	×	○	×	×	×
22	×	○	×	×	×
23	×	×	×	○	×
24	×	×	○	×	×
25	×	×	×	×	○

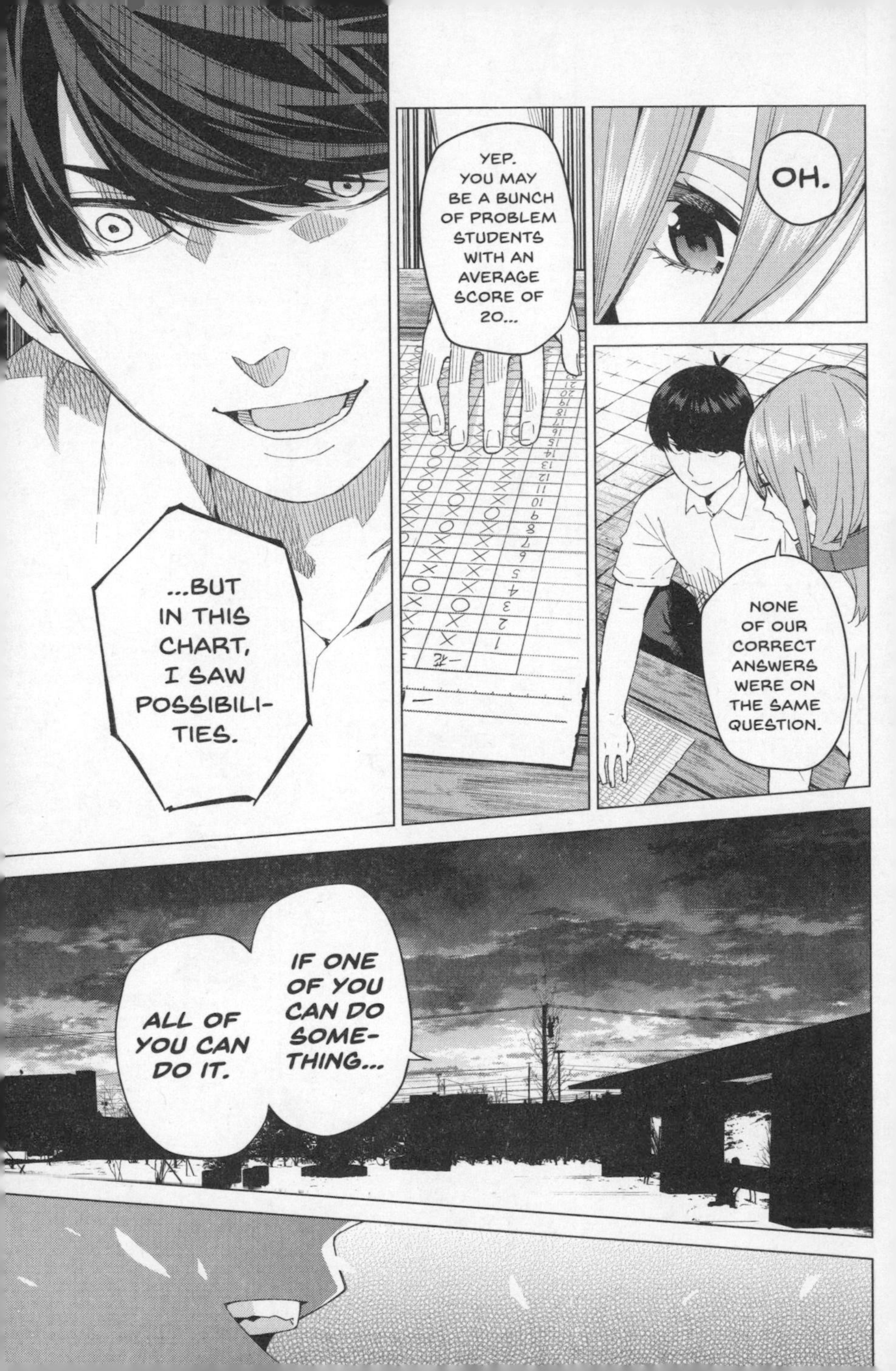
OH.
NONE OF OUR CORRECT ANSWERS WERE ON THE SAME QUESTION.
YEP. YOU MAY BE A BUNCH OF PROBLEM STUDENTS WITH AN AVERAGE SCORE OF 20...
...BUT IN THIS CHART, I SAW POSSIBILI- TIES.
IF ONE OF YOU CAN DO SOME- THING...
ALL OF YOU CAN DO IT.

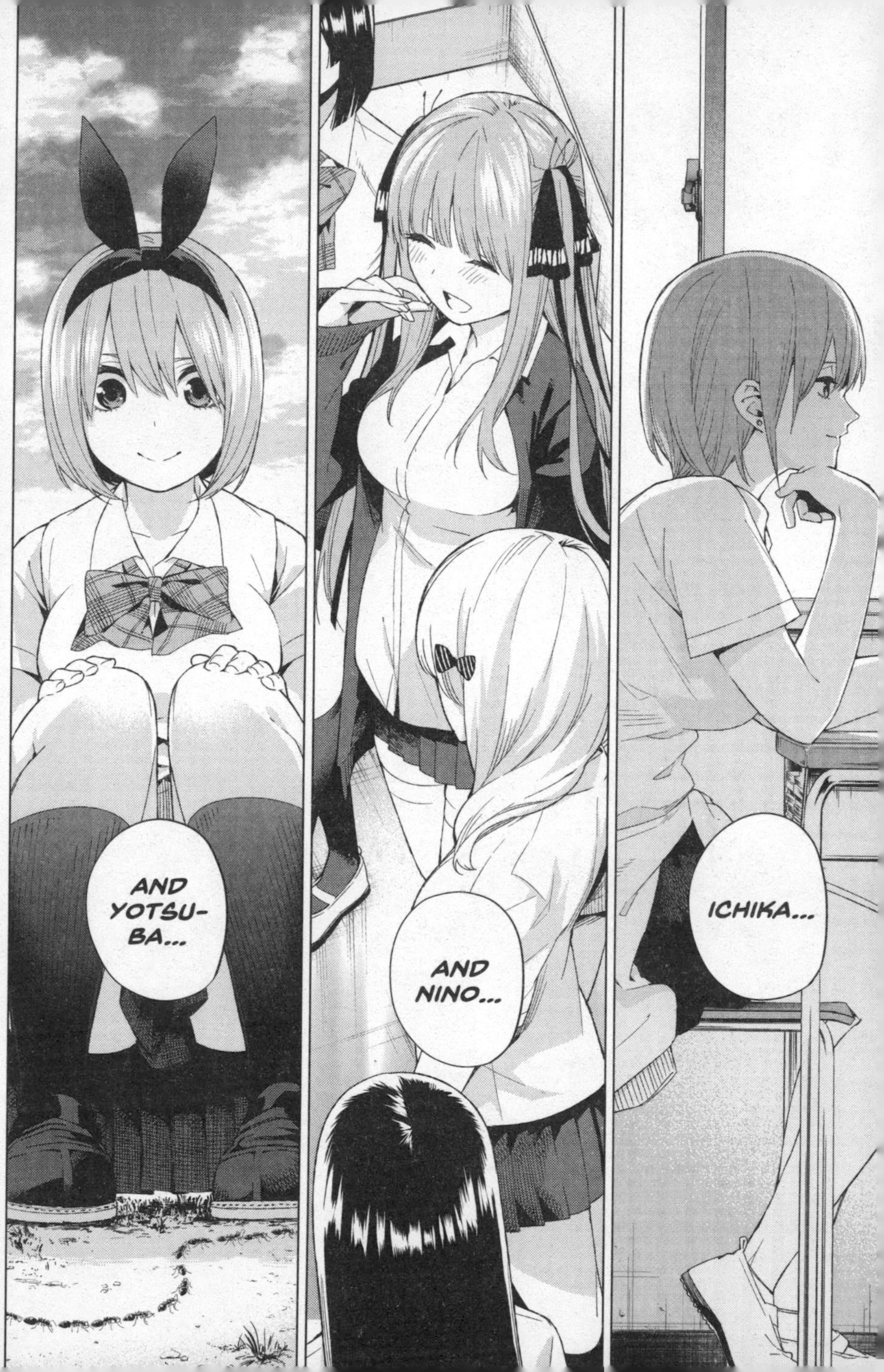
ICHIKA...
AND NINO...
AND YOTSU-BA...

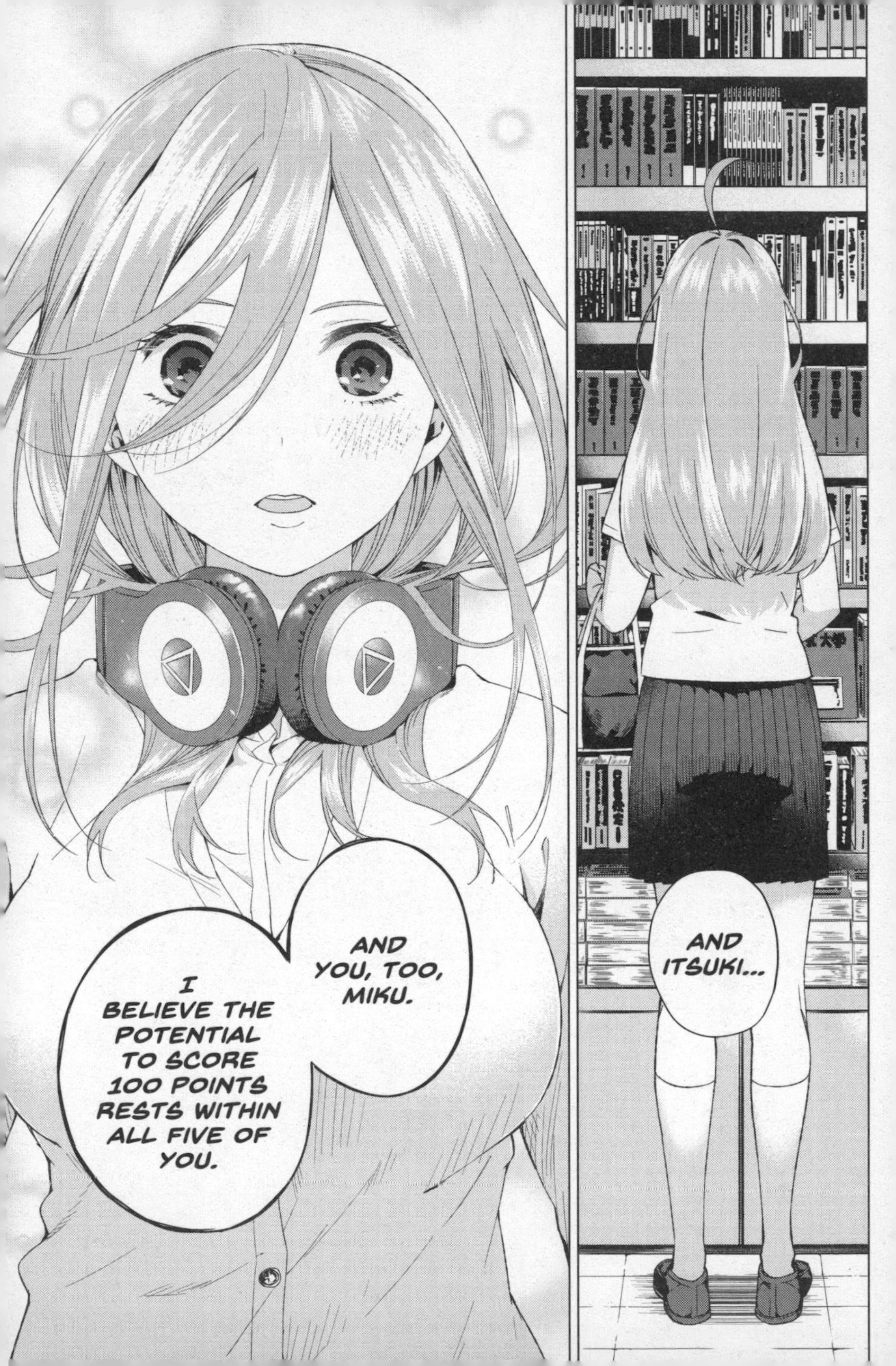
AND ITSUKI...
AND YOU, TOO, MIKU.
I BELIEVE THE POTENTIAL TO SCORE 100 POINTS RESTS WITHIN ALL FIVE OF YOU.

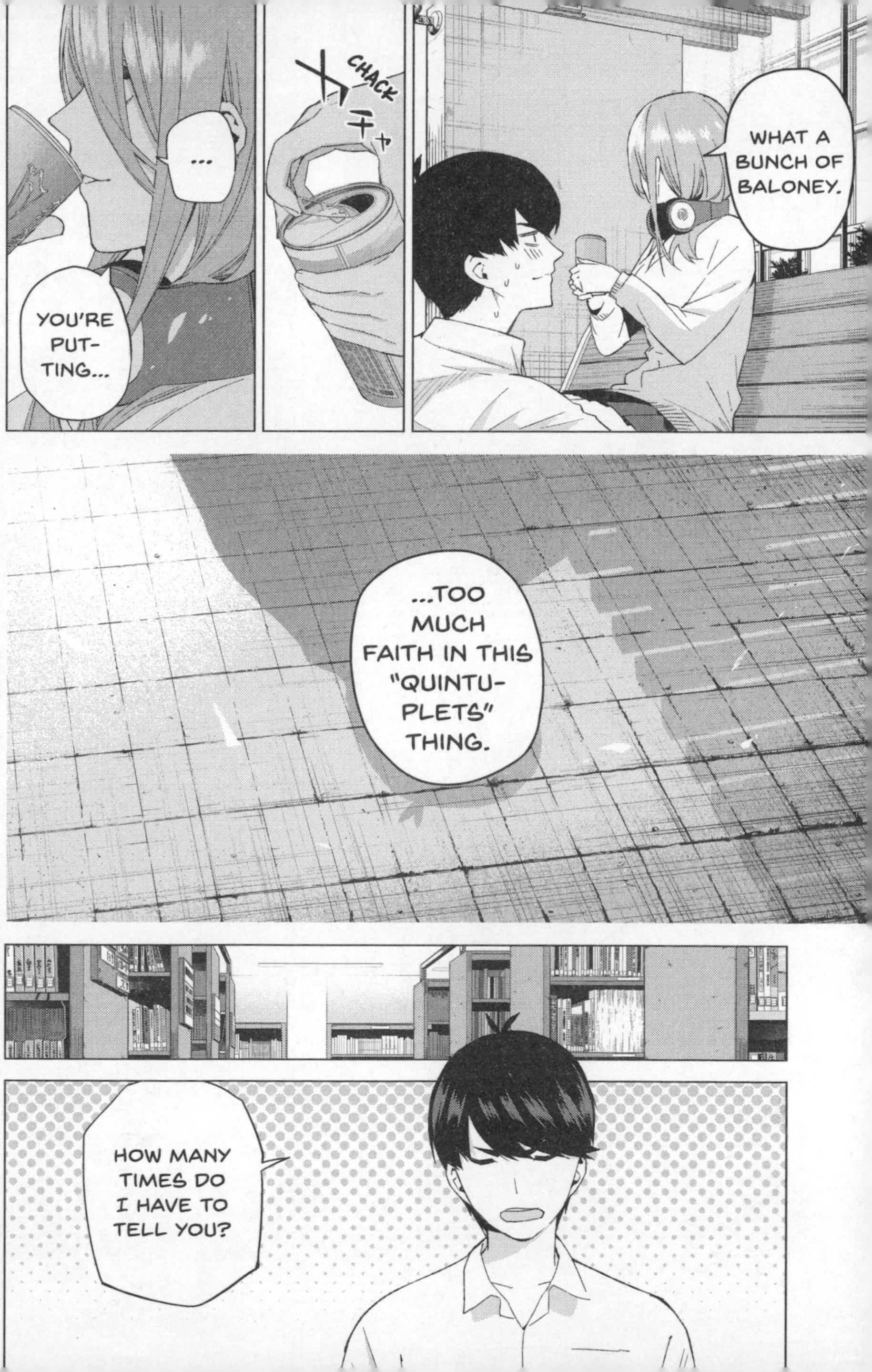
WHAT A BUNCH OF BALONEY.
CHACK
...
YOU'RE PUT-TING...
...TOO MUCH FAITH IN THIS "QUINTU-PLETS" THING.
HOW MANY TIMES DO I HAVE TO TELL YOU?

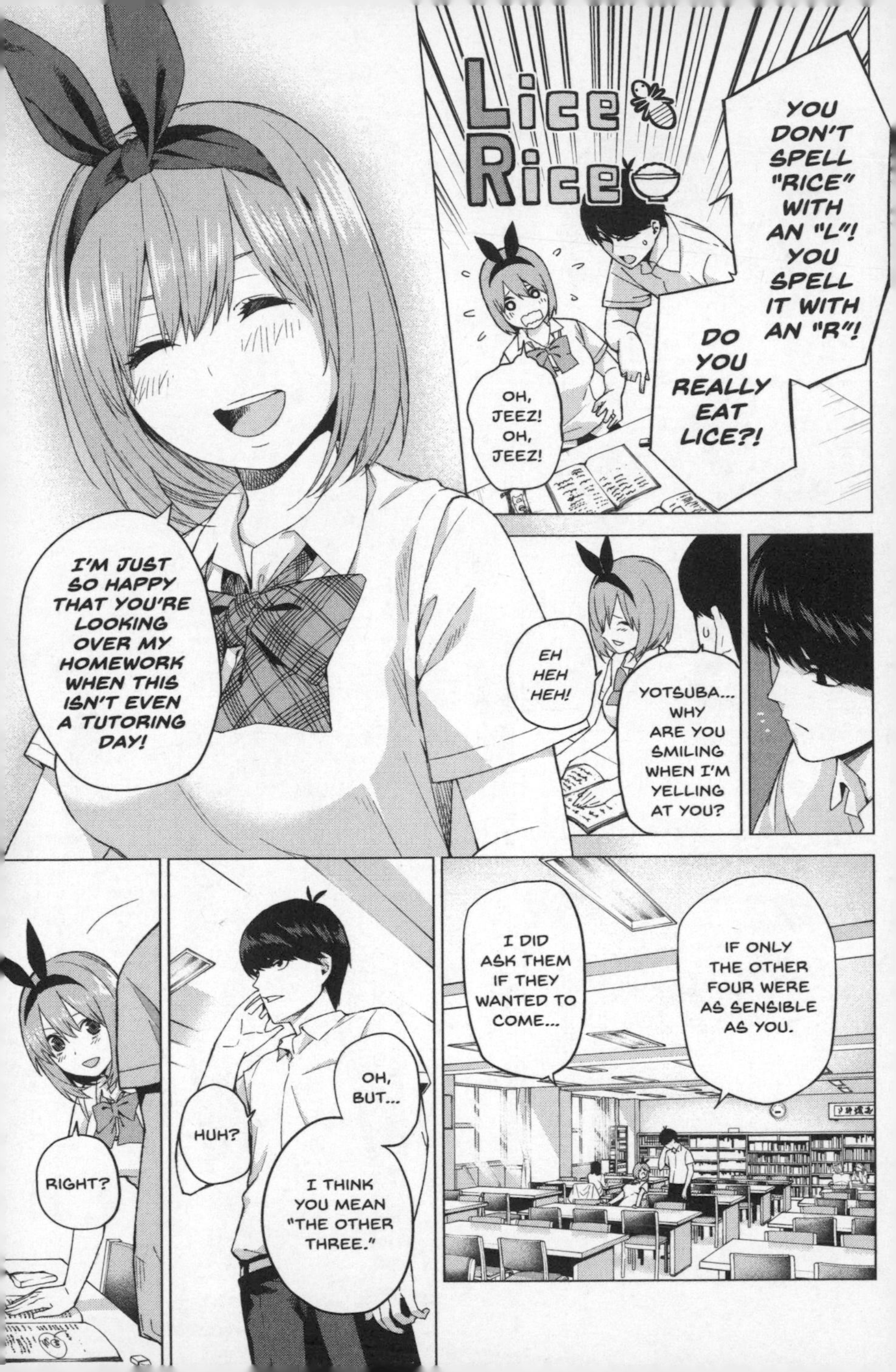

Lice
Rice
YOU DON'T SPELL "RICE" WITH AN "L"! YOU SPELL IT WITH AN "R"!
DO YOU REALLY EAT LICE?!
OH, JEEZ! OH, JEEZ!
YOTSUBA... WHY ARE YOU SMILING WHEN I'M YELLING AT YOU?
EH HEH HEH!
I'M JUST SO HAPPY THAT YOU'RE LOOKING OVER MY HOMEWORK WHEN THIS ISN'T EVEN A TUTORING DAY!
IF ONLY THE OTHER FOUR WERE AS SENSIBLE AS YOU.
I DID ASK THEM IF THEY WANTED TO COME...
OH, BUT...
I THINK YOU MEAN "THE OTHER THREE."
HUH?
RIGHT?

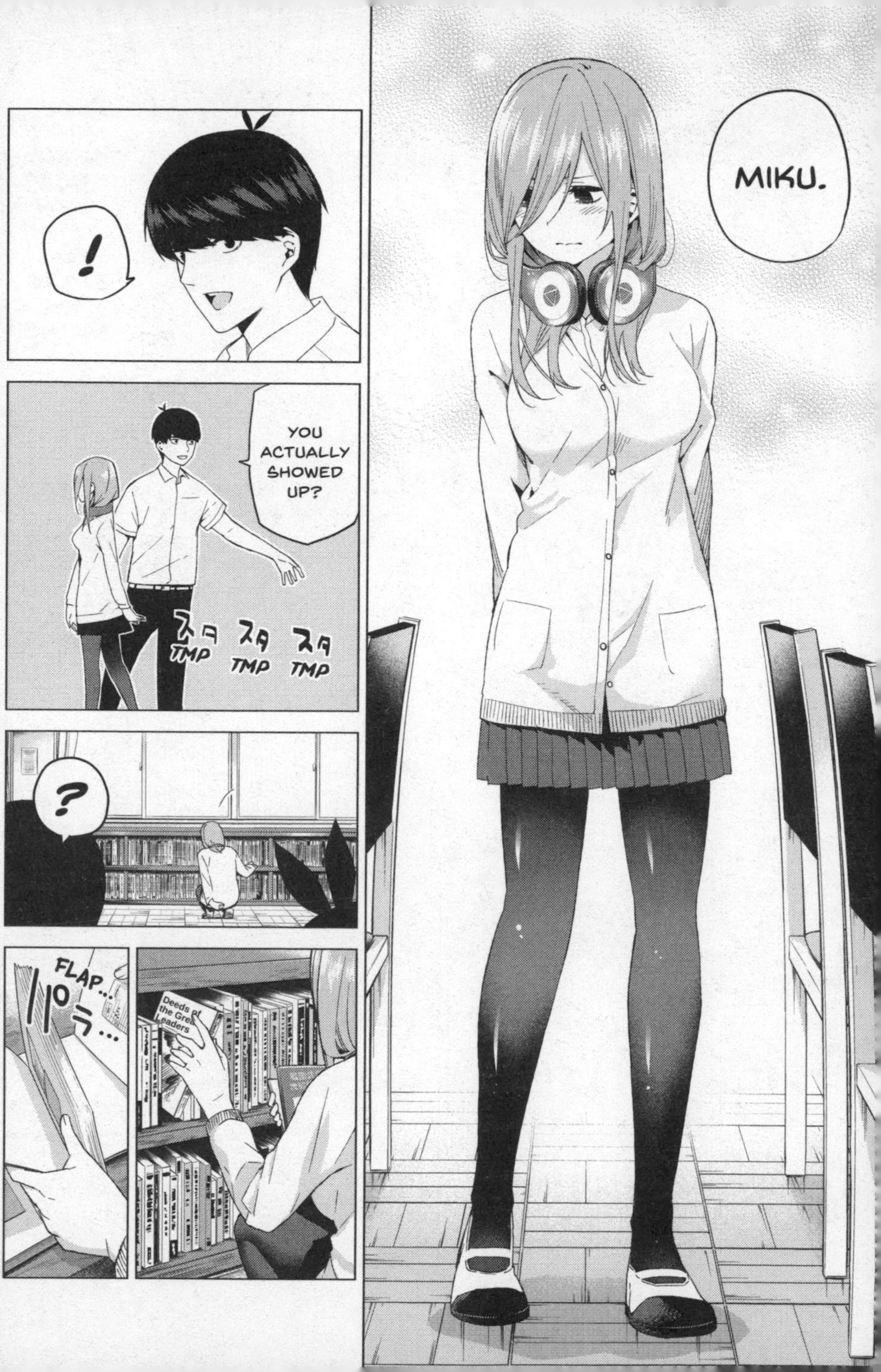
MIKU.
!
YOU ACTUALLY SHOWED UP?
スタ TMP
スタ TMP
スタ TMP
?
Deeds of the Gre Leaders
FLAP...
パラ...

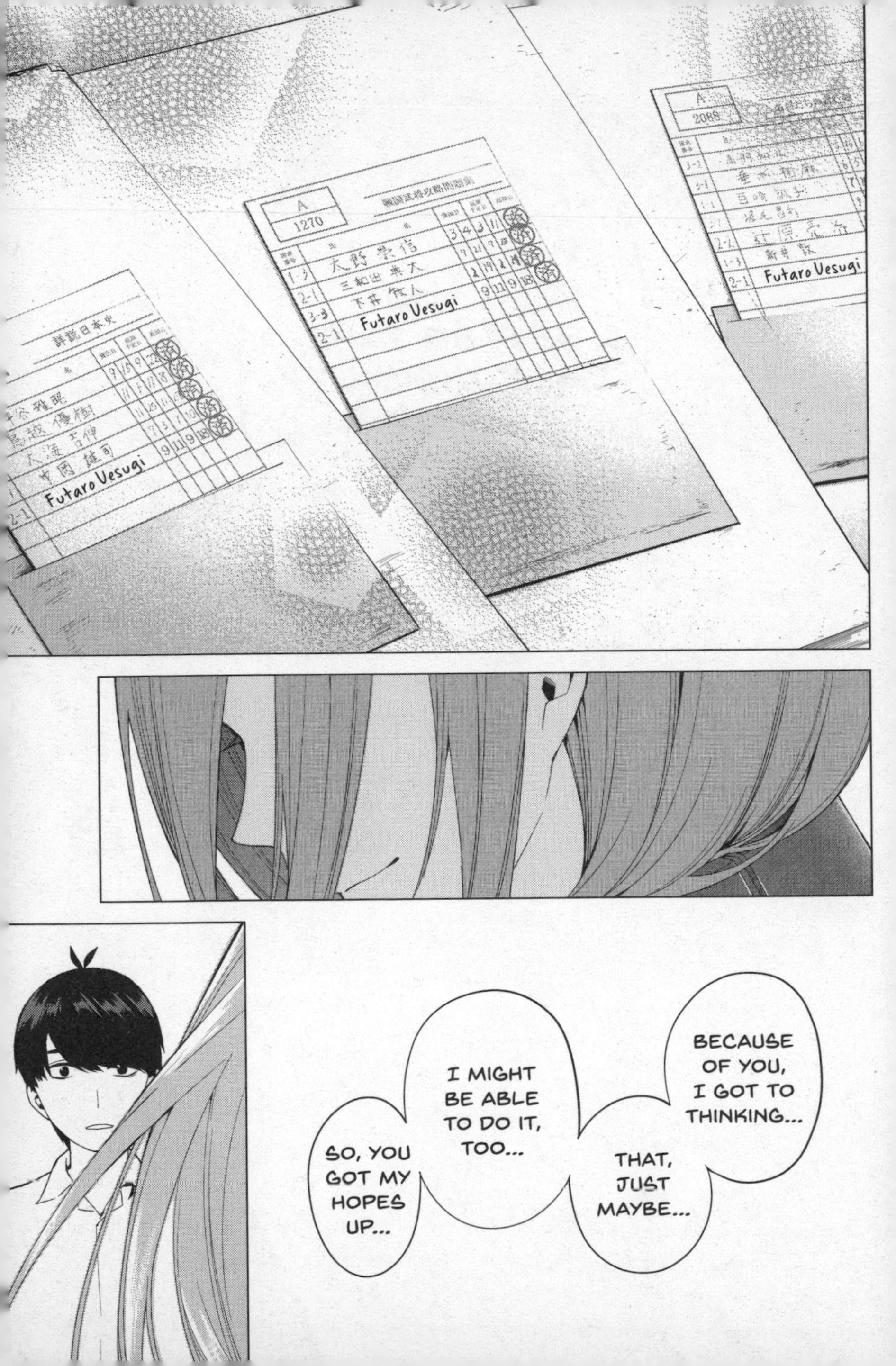
A
2089
Futaro Uesugi
A
1270
Futaro Uesugi
Futaro Uesugi
BECAUSE OF YOU, I GOT TO THINKING...
THAT, JUST MAYBE...
I MIGHT BE ABLE TO DO IT, TOO...
SO, YOU GOT MY HOPES UP...

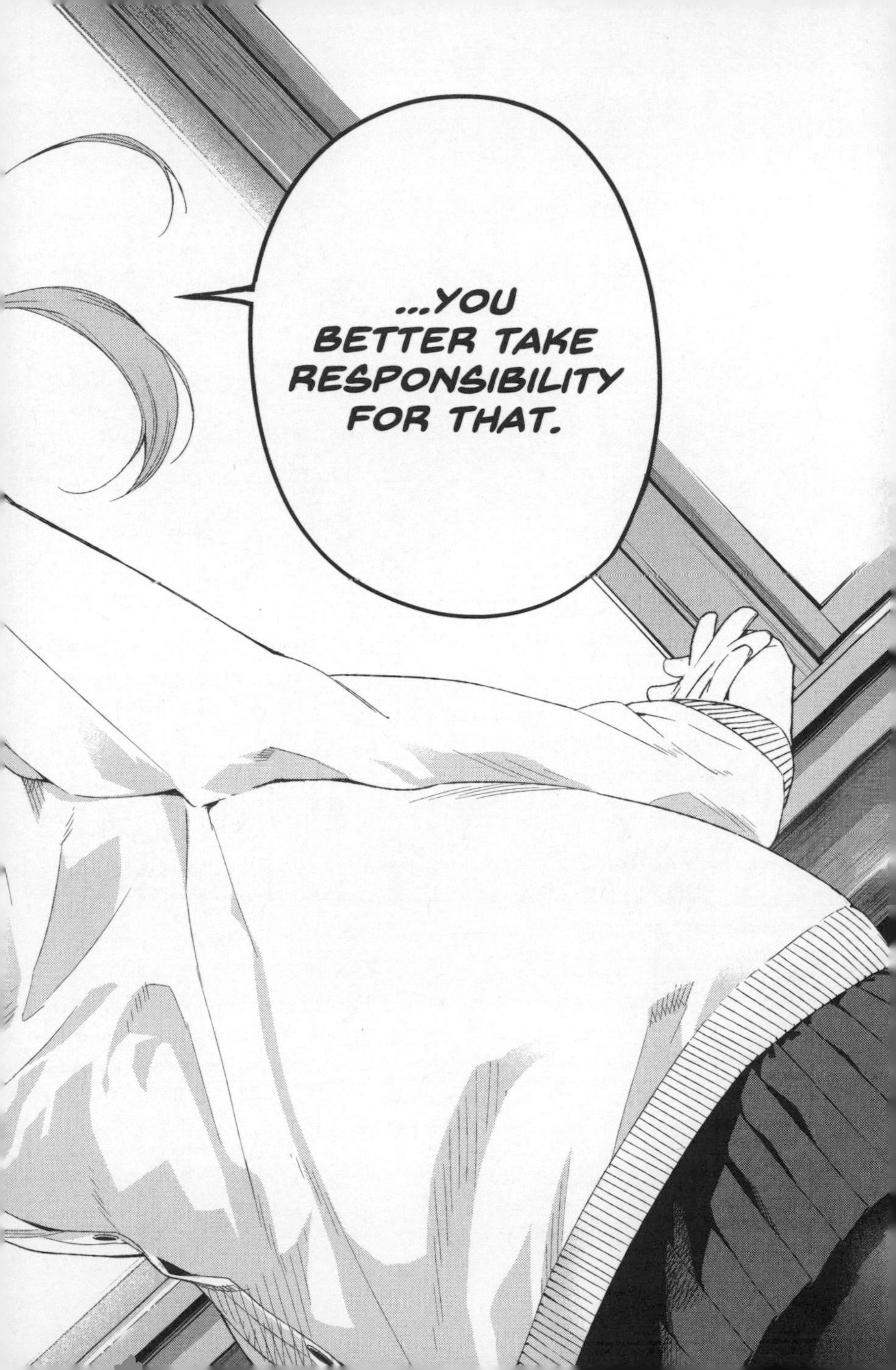
...YOU BETTER TAKE RESPONSIBILITY FOR THAT.

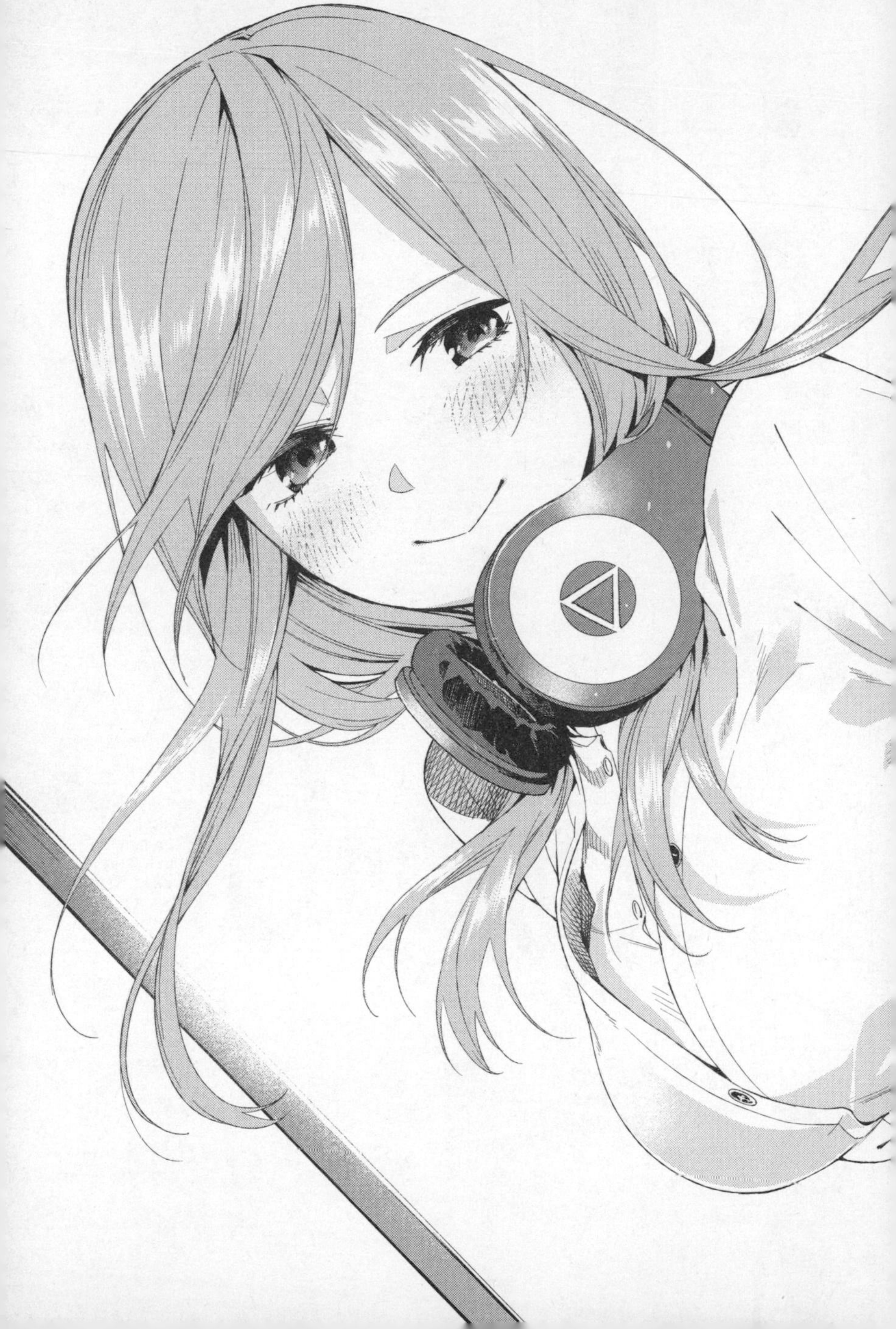

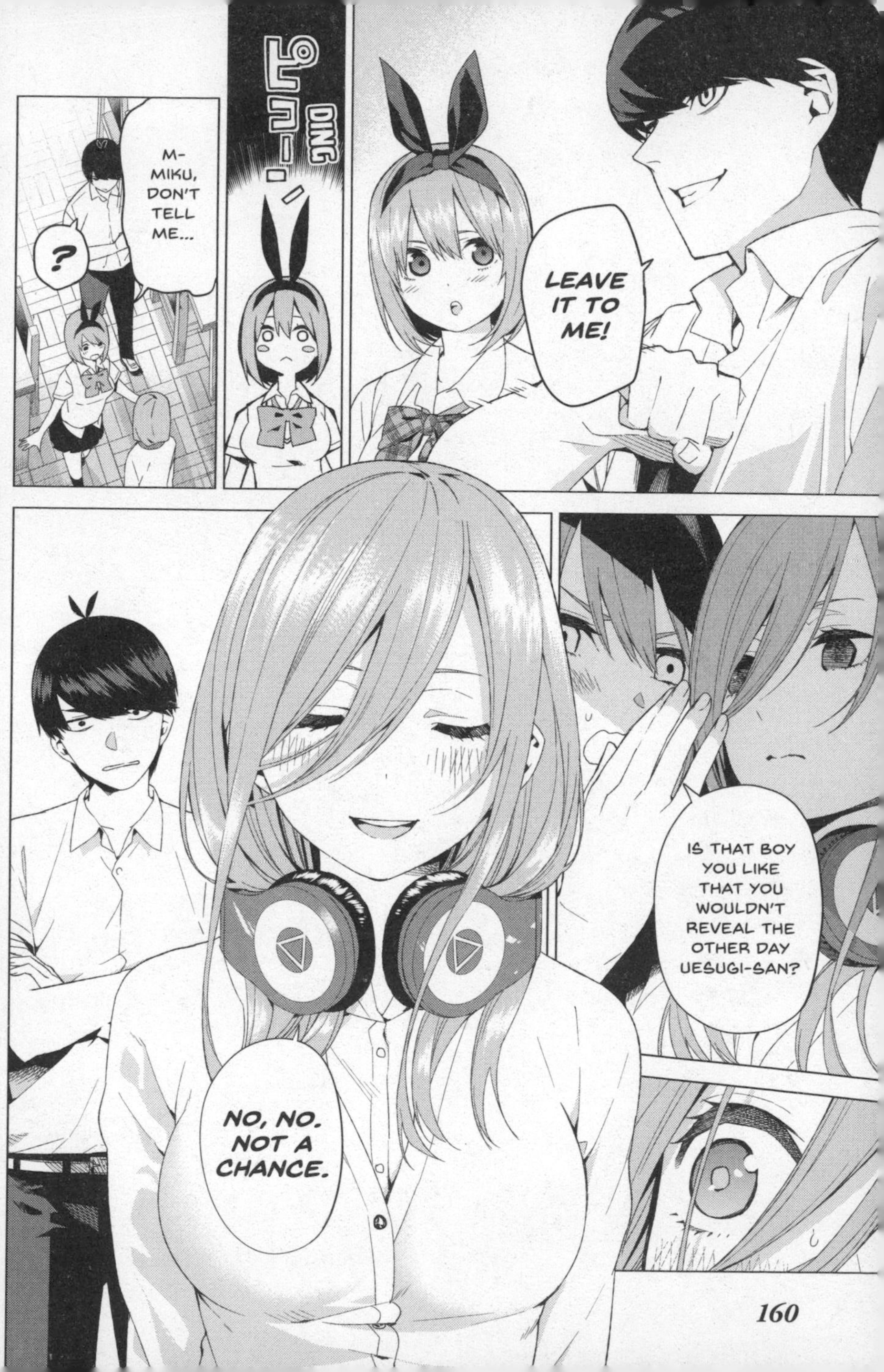
LEAVE IT TO ME!
ピコーン
DING
M-MIKU, DON'T TELL ME...
?
IS THAT BOY YOU LIKE THAT YOU WOULDN'T REVEAL THE OTHER DAY UESUGI-SAN?
NO, NO. NOT A CHANCE.

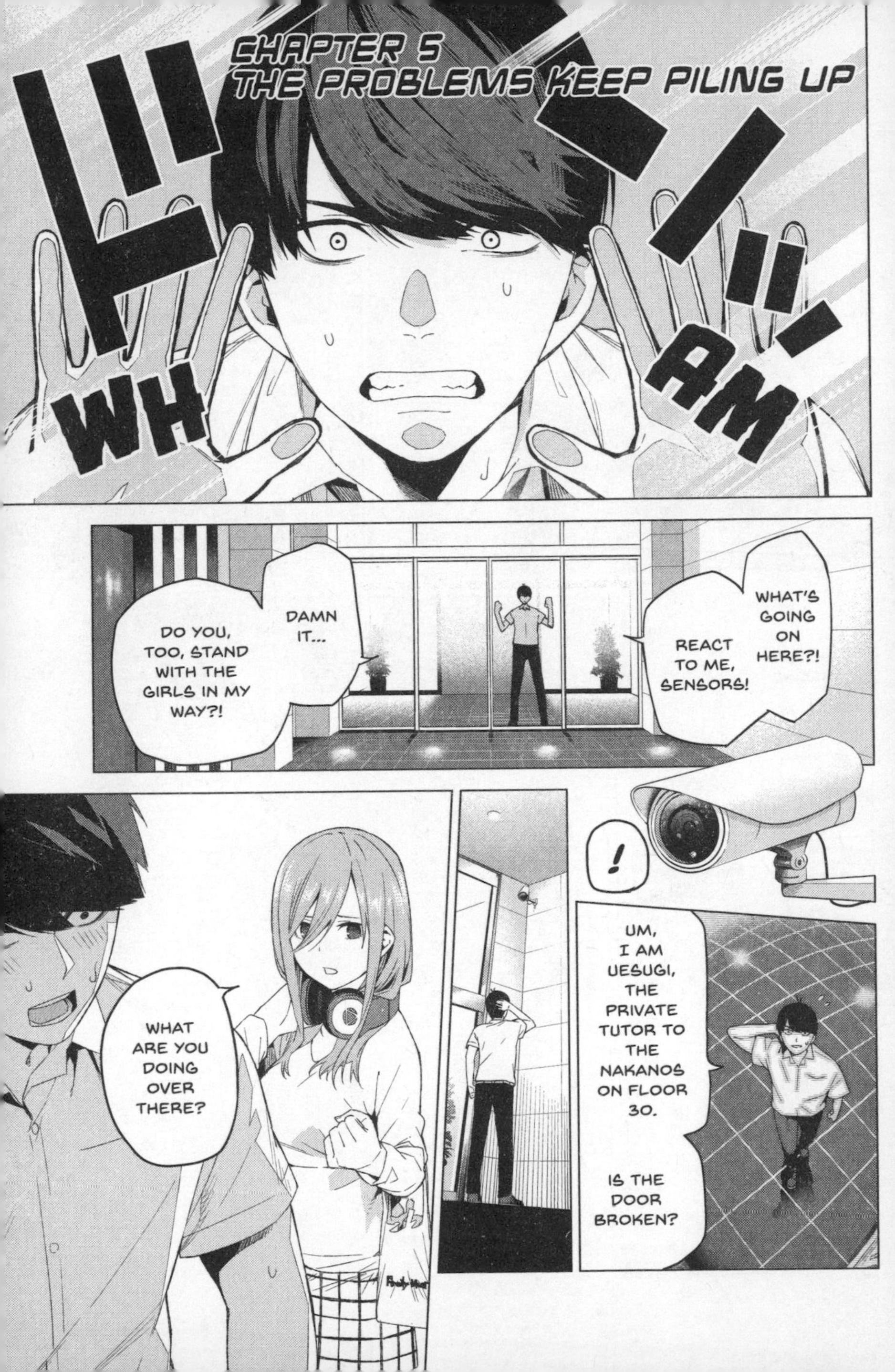
CHAPTER 5
THE PROBLEMS KEEP PILING UP
WH
AM
WHAT'S GOING ON HERE?!
REACT TO ME, SENSORS!
DAMN IT...
DO YOU, TOO, STAND WITH THE GIRLS IN MY WAY?!
!
UM, I AM UESUGI, THE PRIVATE TUTOR TO THE NAKANOS ON FLOOR 30.
IS THE DOOR BROKEN?
WHAT ARE YOU DOING OVER THERE?

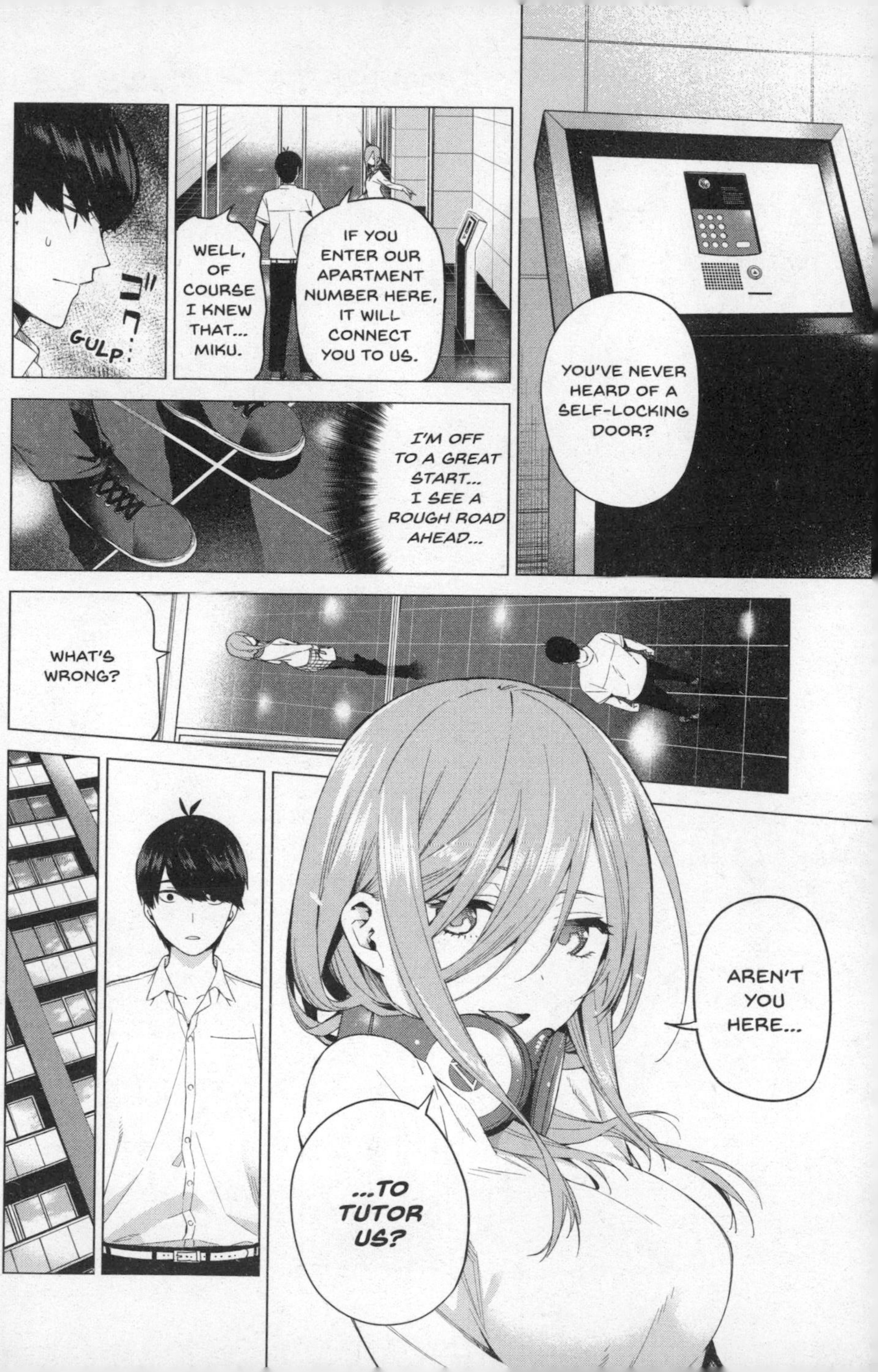
YOU'VE NEVER HEARD OF A SELF-LOCKING DOOR?
IF YOU ENTER OUR APARTMENT NUMBER HERE, IT WILL CONNECT YOU TO US.
WELL, OF COURSE I KNEW THAT... MIKU.
GULP
I'M OFF TO A GREAT START... I SEE A ROUGH ROAD AHEAD...
WHAT'S WRONG?
AREN'T YOU HERE...
...TO TUTOR US?

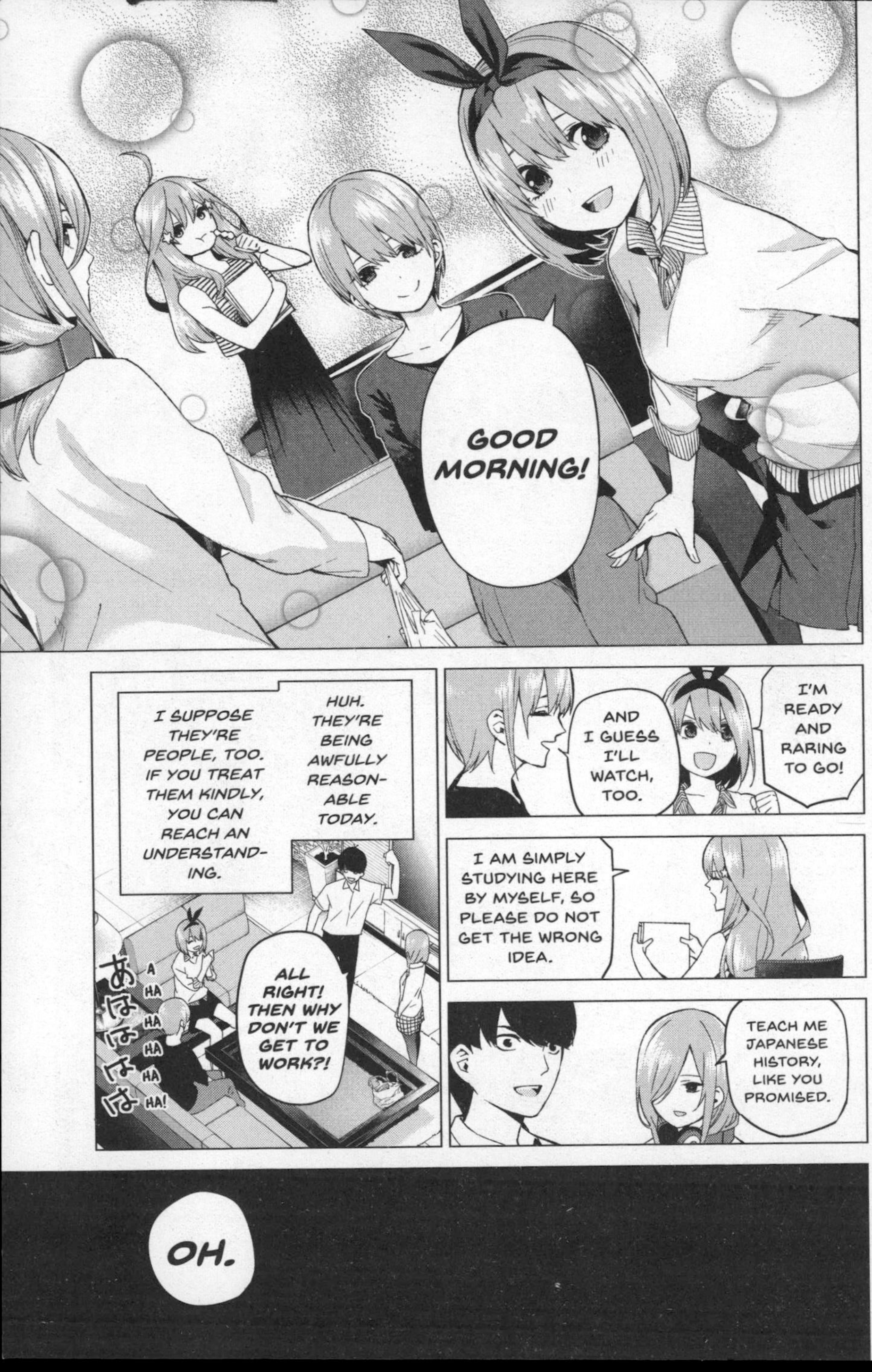
GOOD MORNING!
I'M READY AND RARING TO GO!
AND I GUESS I'LL WATCH, TOO.
I AM SIMPLY STUDYING HERE BY MYSELF, SO PLEASE DO NOT GET THE WRONG IDEA.
TEACH ME JAPANESE HISTORY, LIKE YOU PROMISED.
HUH. THEY'RE BEING AWFULLY REASONABLE TODAY.
I SUPPOSE THEY'RE PEOPLE, TOO. IF YOU TREAT THEM KINDLY, YOU CAN REACH AN UNDERSTANDING.
ALL RIGHT! THEN WHY DON'T WE GET TO WORK?!
あははは
A HA HA HA HA HA!
OH.

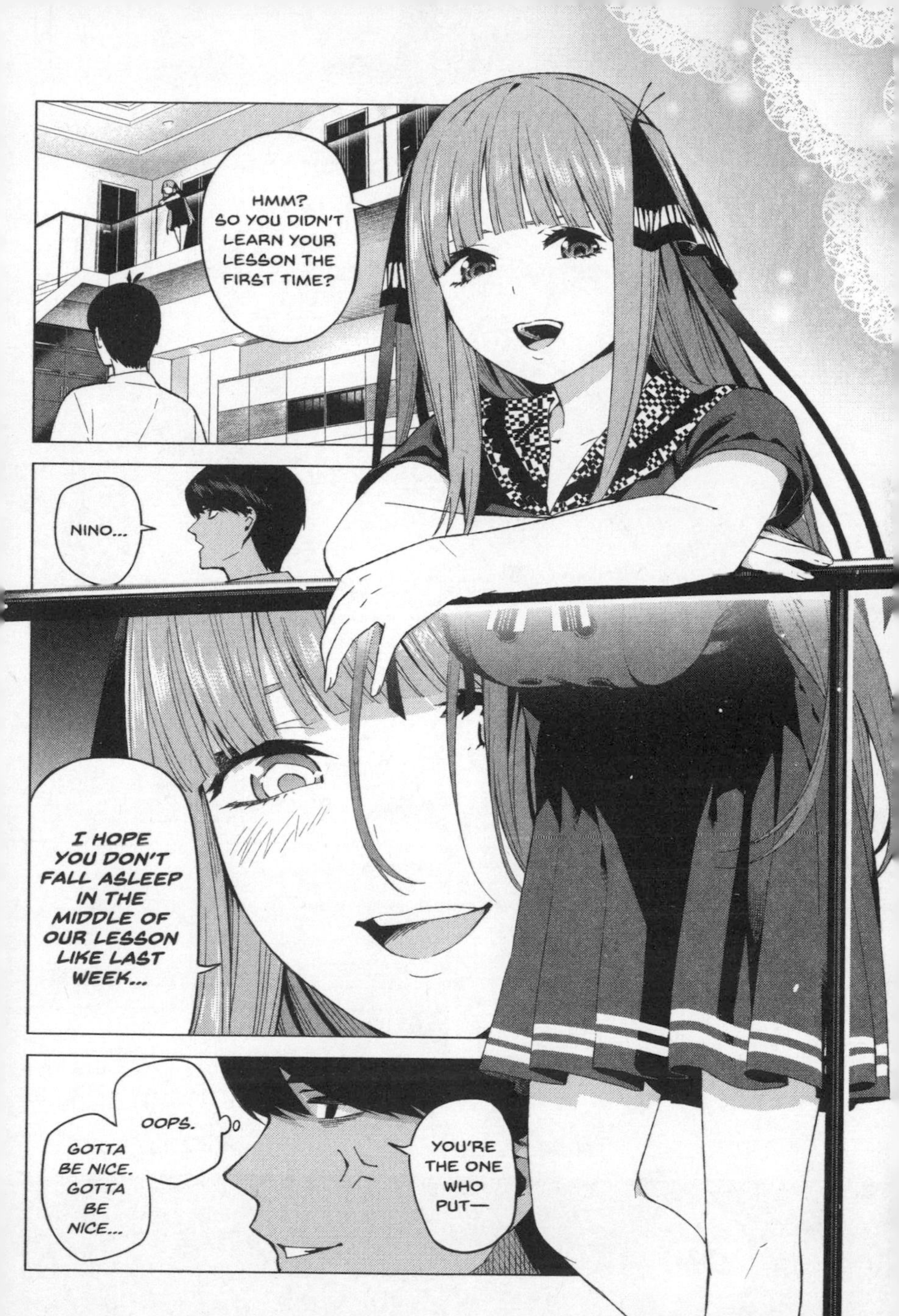
HMM? SO YOU DIDN'T LEARN YOUR LESSON THE FIRST TIME?
NINO...
I HOPE YOU DON'T FALL ASLEEP IN THE MIDDLE OF OUR LESSON LIKE LAST WEEK...
YOU'RE THE ONE WHO PUT—
OOPS.
GOTTA BE NICE. GOTTA BE NICE...

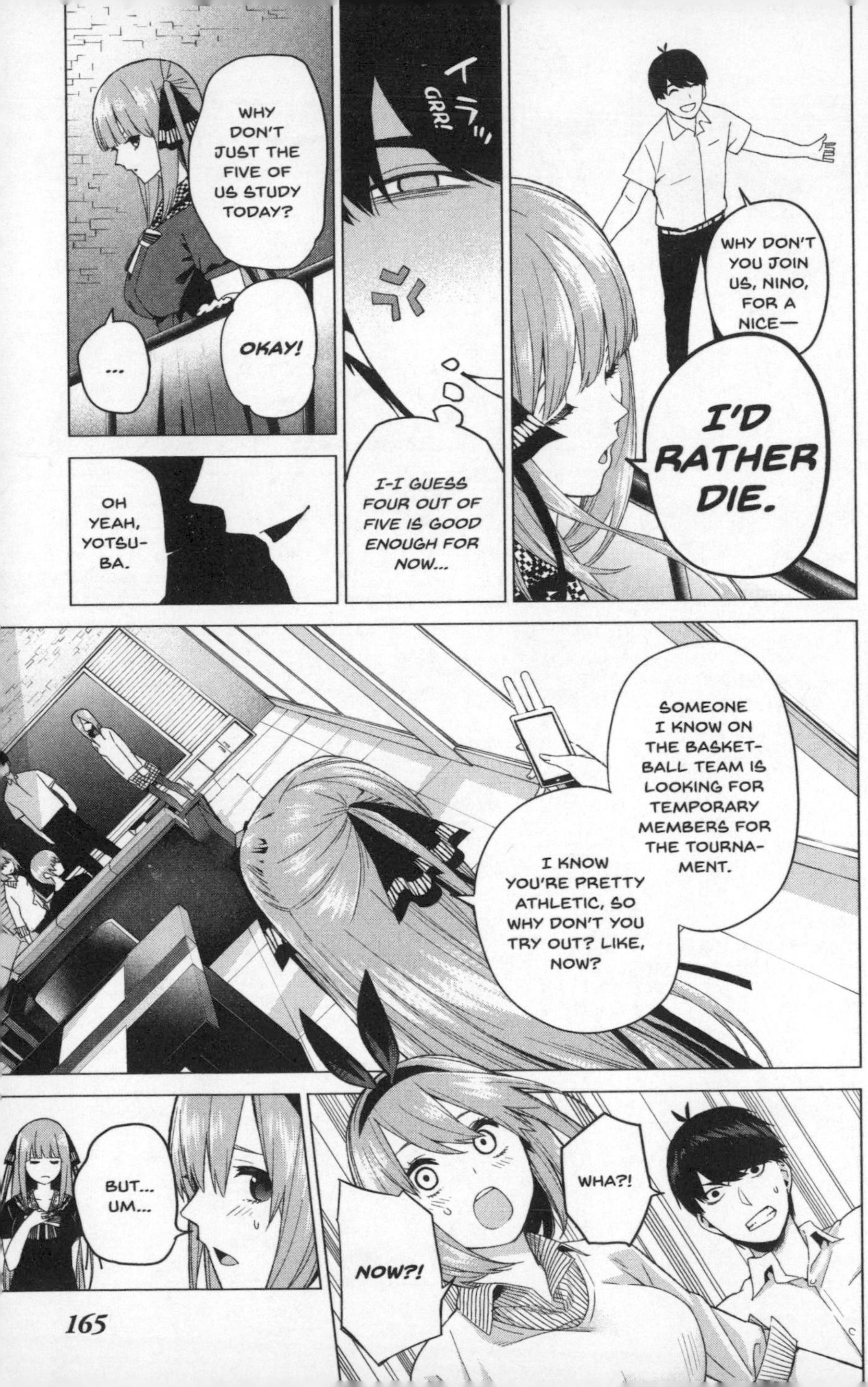
WHY DON'T YOU JOIN US, NINO, FOR A NICE—
I'D RATHER DIE.
GRR!
I-I GUESS FOUR OUT OF FIVE IS GOOD ENOUGH FOR NOW...
WHY DON'T JUST THE FIVE OF US STUDY TODAY?
OKAY!
...
OH YEAH, YOTSUBA.
SOMEONE I KNOW ON THE BASKET-BALL TEAM IS LOOKING FOR TEMPORARY MEMBERS FOR THE TOURNA-MENT.
I KNOW YOU'RE PRETTY ATHLETIC, SO WHY DON'T YOU TRY OUT? LIKE, NOW?
WHA?!
NOW?!
BUT... UM...

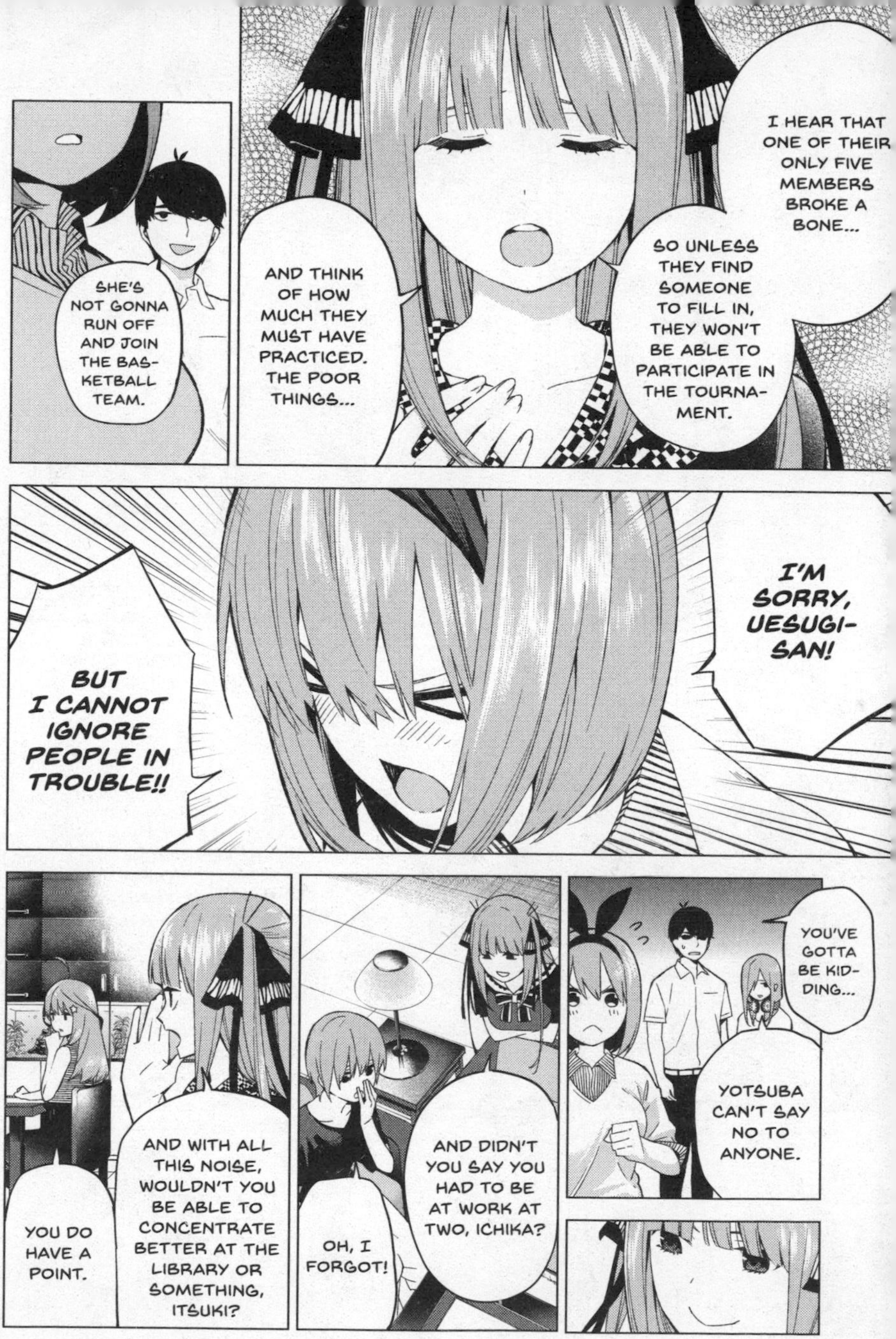
I HEAR THAT ONE OF THEIR ONLY FIVE MEMBERS BROKE A BONE...
SO UNLESS THEY FIND SOMEONE TO FILL IN, THEY WON'T BE ABLE TO PARTICIPATE IN THE TOURNA-MENT.
AND THINK OF HOW MUCH THEY MUST HAVE PRACTICED. THE POOR THINGS...
SHE'S NOT GONNA RUN OFF AND JOIN THE BAS-KETBALL TEAM.
I'M SORRY, UESUGI-SAN!
BUT I CANNOT IGNORE PEOPLE IN TROUBLE!!
YOU'VE GOTTA BE KID-DING...
YOTSUBA CAN'T SAY NO TO ANYONE.
AND DIDN'T YOU SAY YOU HAD TO BE AT WORK AT TWO, ICHIKA?
OH, I FORGOT!
AND WITH ALL THIS NOISE, WOULDN'T YOU BE ABLE TO CONCENTRATE BETTER AT THE LIBRARY OR SOMETHING, ITSUKI?
YOU DO HAVE A POINT.

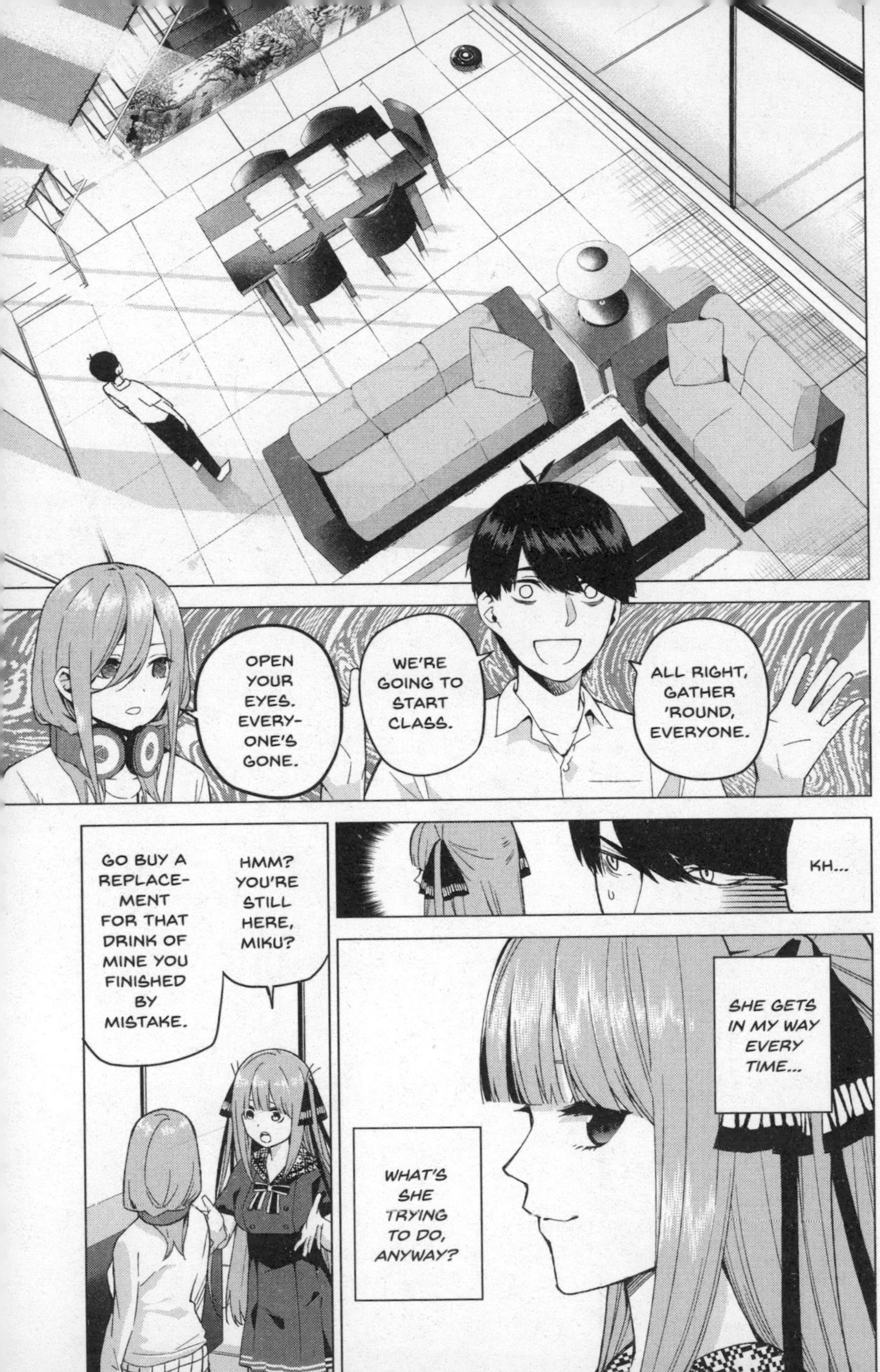
ALL RIGHT, GATHER 'ROUND, EVERYONE.
WE'RE GOING TO START CLASS.
OPEN YOUR EYES. EVERYONE'S GONE.
KH...
SHE GETS IN MY WAY EVERY TIME...
WHAT'S SHE TRYING TO DO, ANYWAY?
HMM? YOU'RE STILL HERE, MIKU?
GO BUY A REPLACEMENT FOR THAT DRINK OF MINE YOU FINISHED BY MISTAKE.

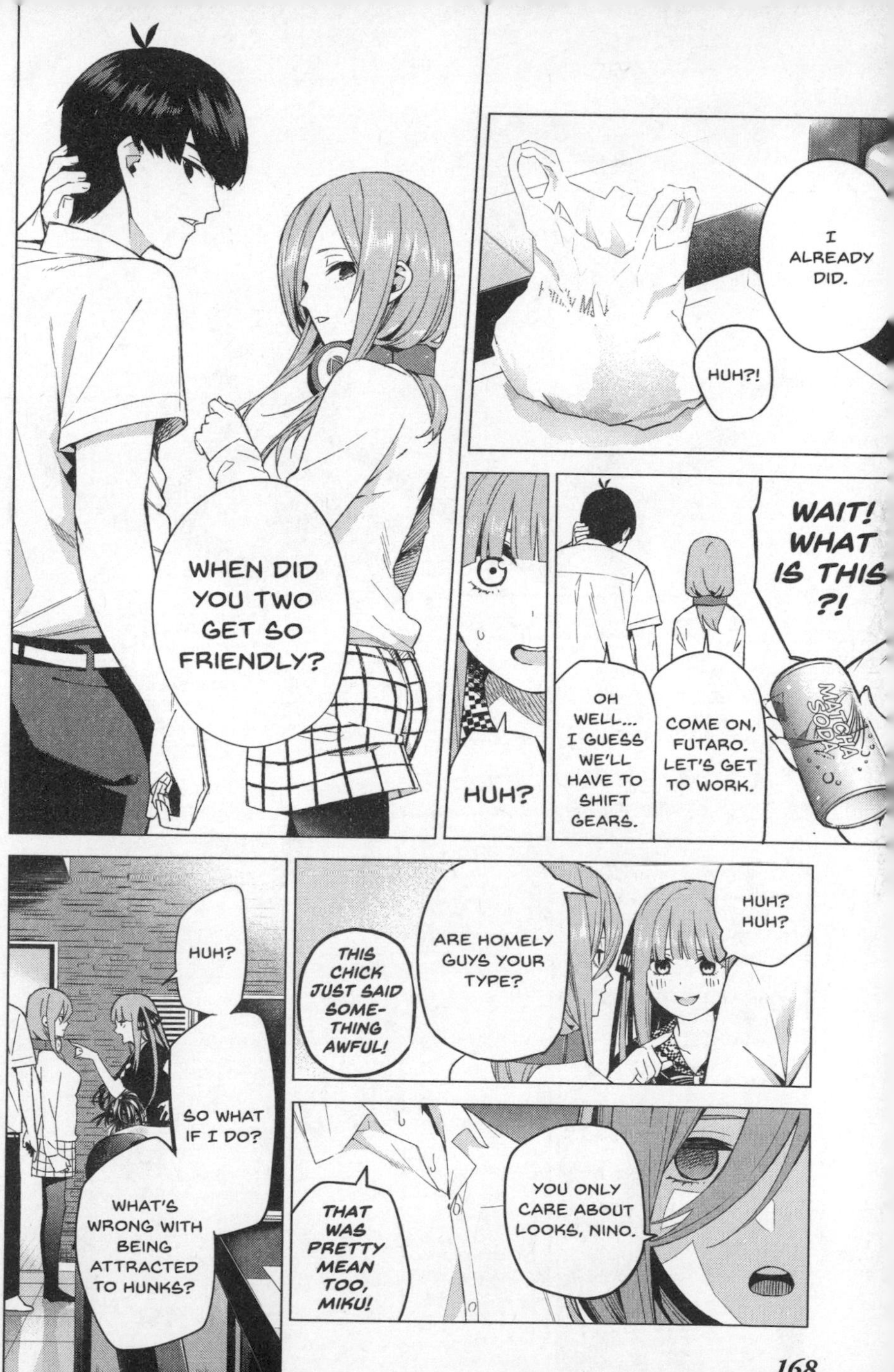
I ALREADY DID.
HUH?!
WAIT! WHAT IS THIS?!
MATCHA SODA
COME ON, FUTARO. LET'S GET TO WORK.
OH WELL... I GUESS WE'LL HAVE TO SHIFT GEARS.
HUH?
WHEN DID YOU TWO GET SO FRIENDLY?
HUH? HUH?
ARE HOMELY GUYS YOUR TYPE?
THIS CHICK JUST SAID SOME-THING AWFUL!
YOU ONLY CARE ABOUT LOOKS, NINO.
THAT WAS PRETTY MEAN TOO, MIKU!
HUH?
SO WHAT IF I DO?
WHAT'S WRONG WITH BEING ATTRACTED TO HUNKS?

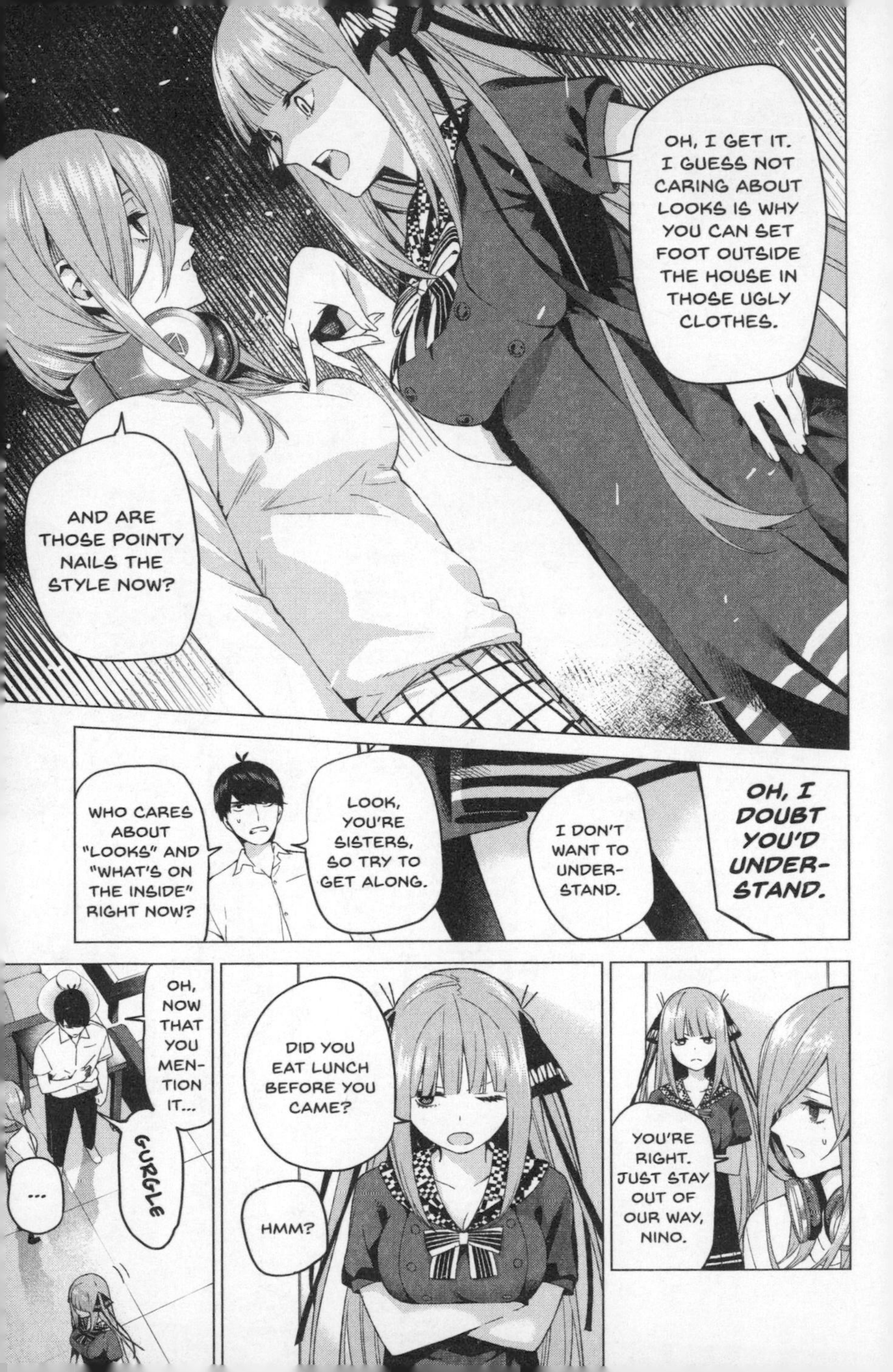
OH, I GET IT. I GUESS NOT CARING ABOUT LOOKS IS WHY YOU CAN SET FOOT OUTSIDE THE HOUSE IN THOSE UGLY CLOTHES.
AND ARE THOSE POINTY NAILS THE STYLE NOW?
OH, I DOUBT YOU'D UNDERSTAND.
I DON'T WANT TO UNDERSTAND.
LOOK, YOU'RE SISTERS, SO TRY TO GET ALONG.
WHO CARES ABOUT "LOOKS" AND "WHAT'S ON THE INSIDE" RIGHT NOW?
YOU'RE RIGHT. JUST STAY OUT OF OUR WAY, NINO.
DID YOU EAT LUNCH BEFORE YOU CAME?
HMM?
OH, NOW THAT YOU MENTION IT...
GURGLE
...

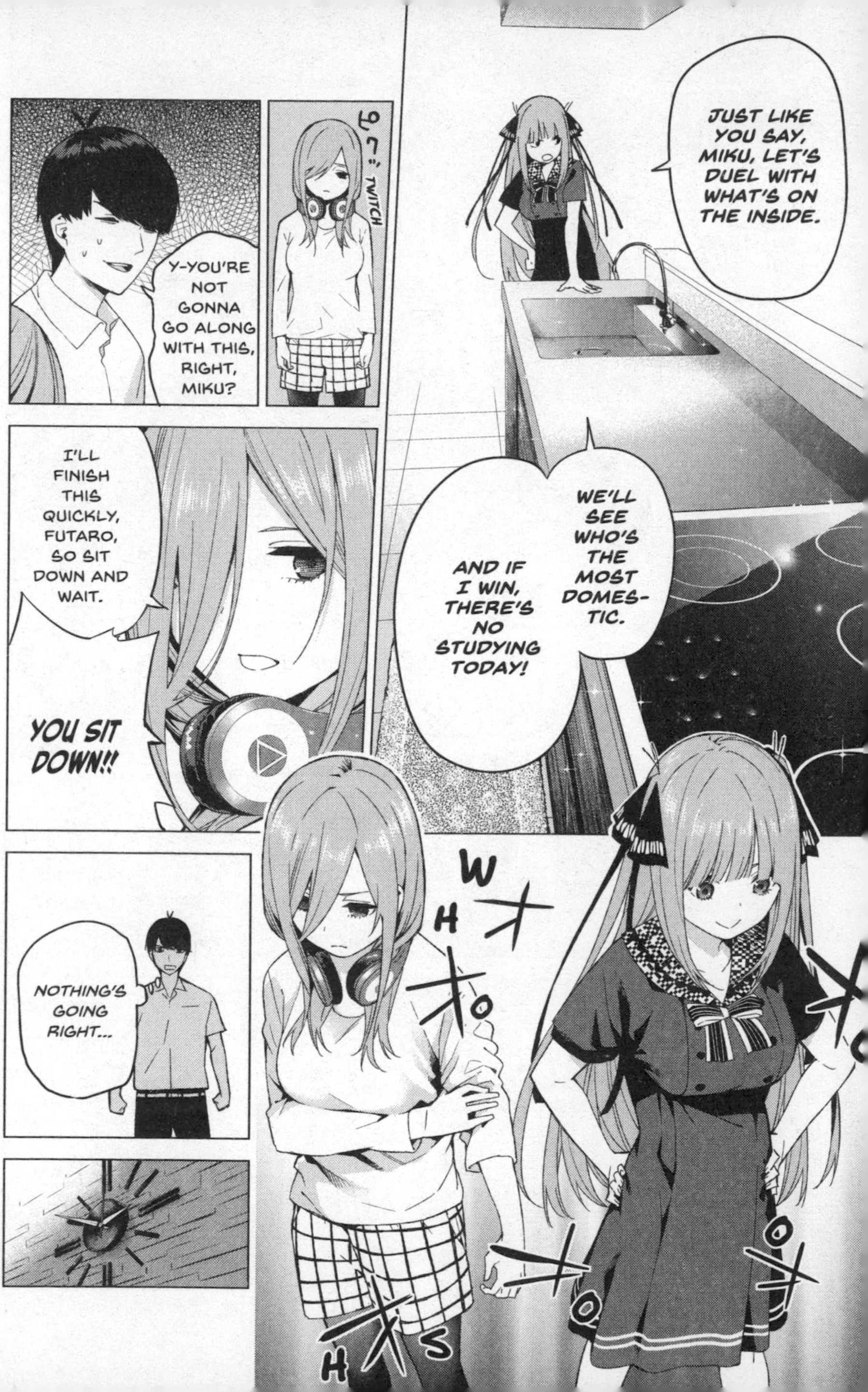
JUST LIKE YOU SAY, MIKU, LET'S DUEL WITH WHAT'S ON THE INSIDE.
WE'LL SEE WHO'S THE MOST DOMES-TIC.
AND IF I WIN, THERE'S NO STUDYING TODAY!
TWITCH
Y-YOU'RE NOT GONNA GO ALONG WITH THIS, RIGHT, MIKU?
I'LL FINISH THIS QUICKLY, FUTARO, SO SIT DOWN AND WAIT.
YOU SIT DOWN!!
WHOOSH
NOTHING'S GOING RIGHT...

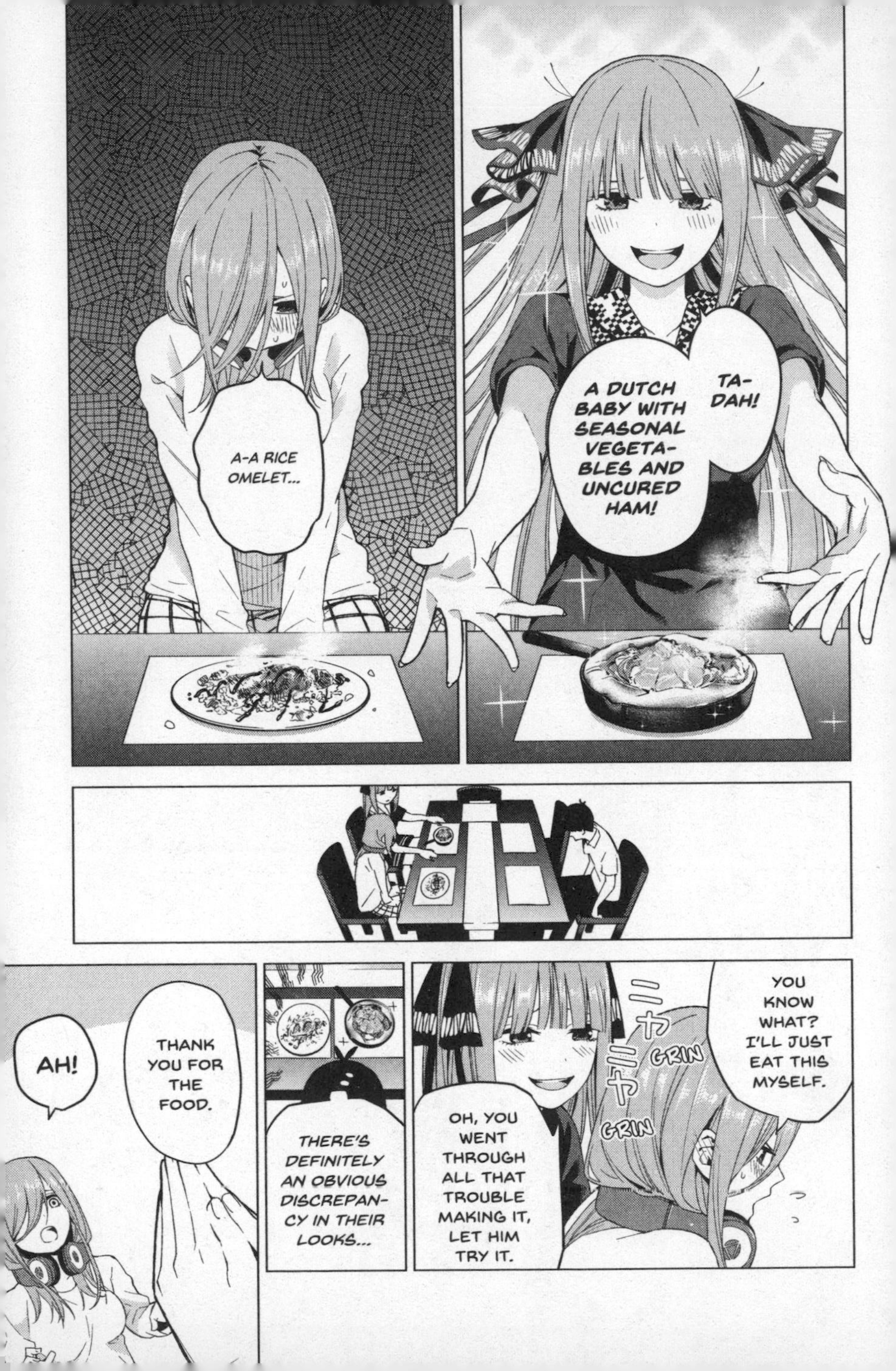
TA-DAH!
A DUTCH BABY WITH SEASONAL VEGETABLES AND UNCURED HAM!
A-A RICE OMELET...
YOU KNOW WHAT? I'LL JUST EAT THIS MYSELF.
ニヤ ニヤ
GRIN GRIN
OH, YOU WENT THROUGH ALL THAT TROUBLE MAKING IT, LET HIM TRY IT.
THERE'S DEFINITELY AN OBVIOUS DISCREPANCY IN THEIR LOOKS...
THANK YOU FOR THE FOOD.
AH!

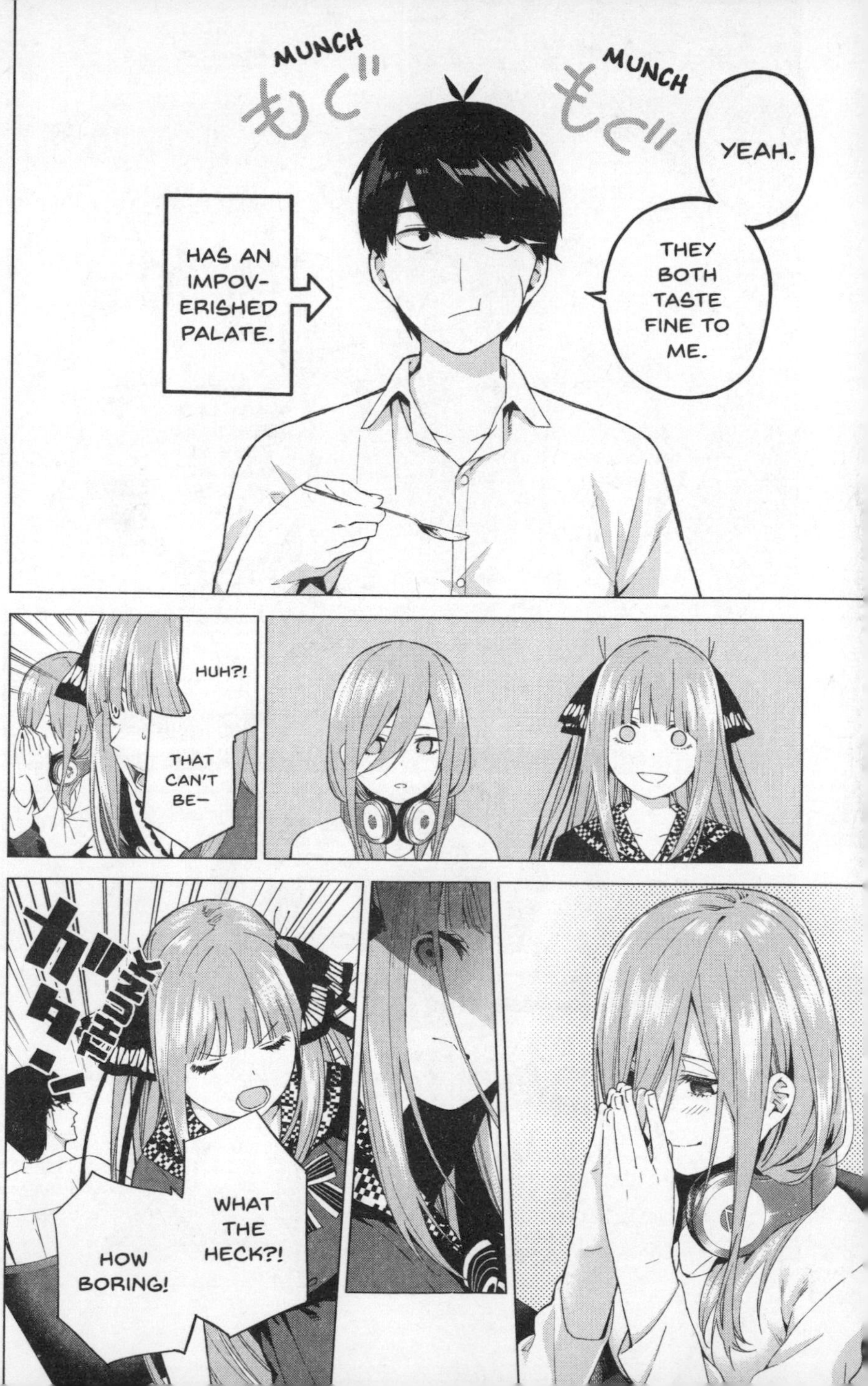
MUNCH
もぐ
YEAH.
THEY BOTH TASTE FINE TO ME.
MUNCH
もぐ
HAS AN IMPOV-ERISHED PALATE.
HUH?!
THAT CAN'T BE—
ガタッ
THUNK
WHAT THE HECK?!
HOW BORING!

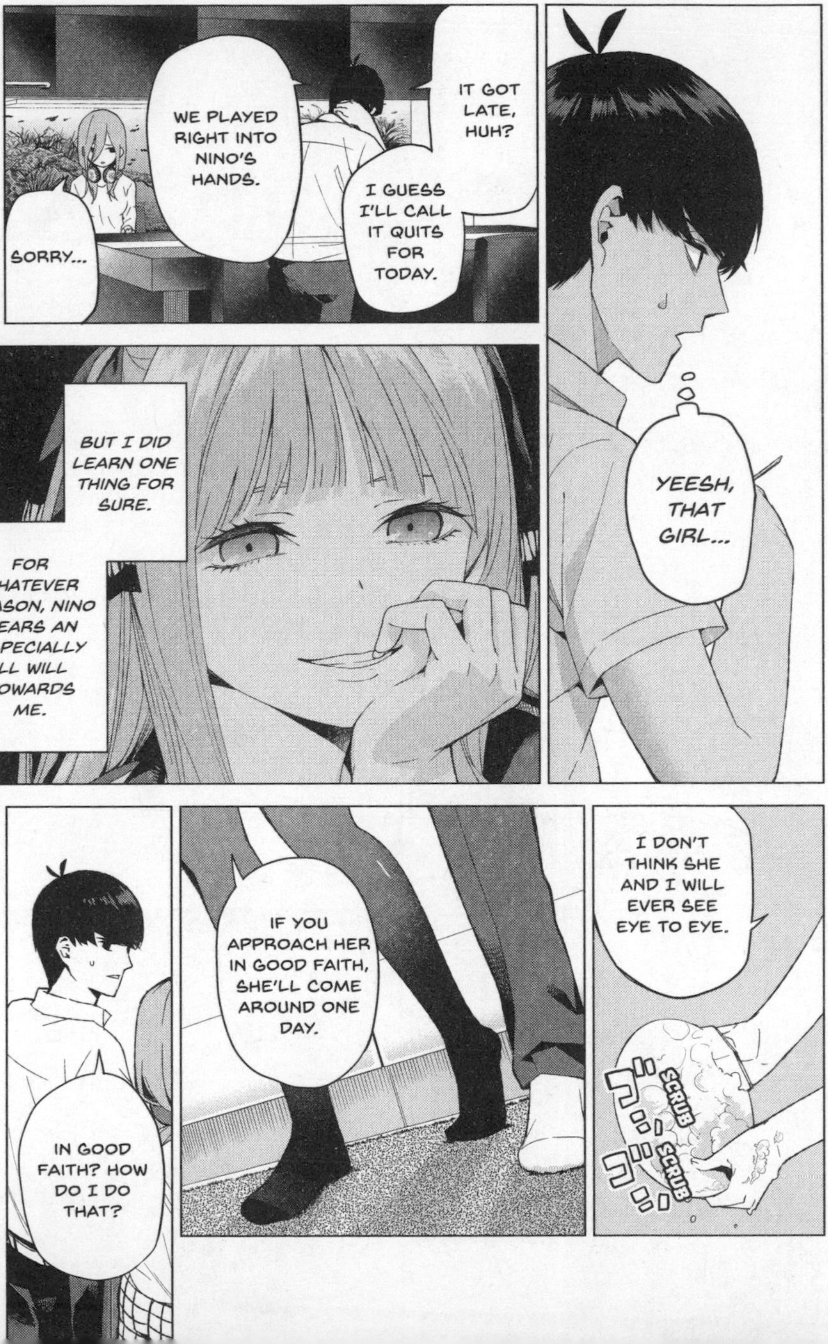
YEESH, THAT GIRL...
IT GOT LATE, HUH?
WE PLAYED RIGHT INTO NINO'S HANDS.
I GUESS I'LL CALL IT QUITS FOR TODAY.
SORRY...
BUT I DID LEARN ONE THING FOR SURE.
FOR WHATEVER REASON, NINO BEARS AN ESPECIALLY ILL WILL TOWARDS ME.
I DON'T THINK SHE AND I WILL EVER SEE EYE TO EYE.
SCRUB SCRUB
IF YOU APPROACH HER IN GOOD FAITH, SHE'LL COME AROUND ONE DAY.
IN GOOD FAITH? HOW DO I DO THAT?

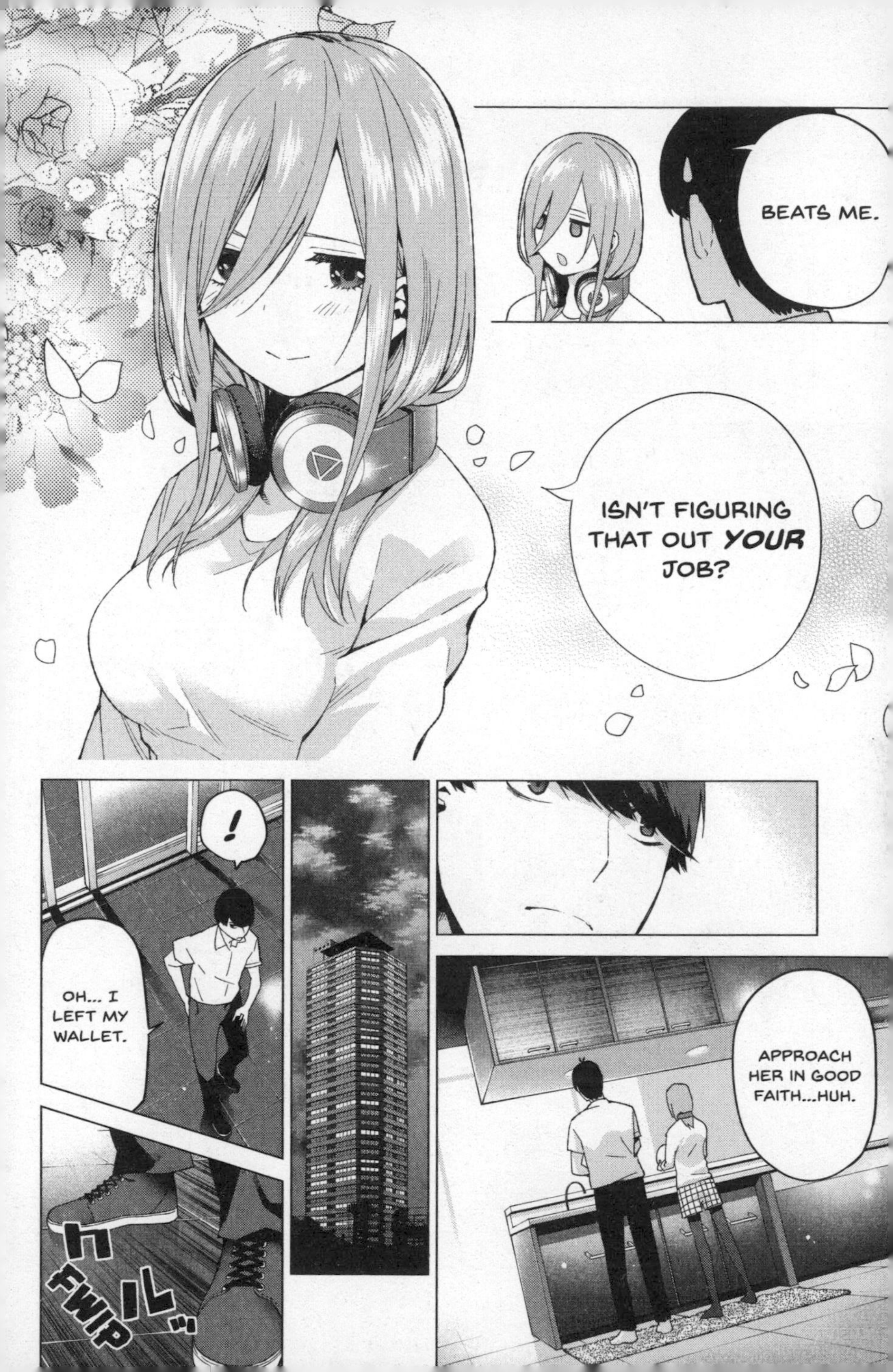
BEATS ME.
ISN'T FIGURING THAT OUT **YOUR** JOB?
APPROACH HER IN GOOD FAITH...HUH.
!
OH... I LEFT MY WALLET.
FWIP

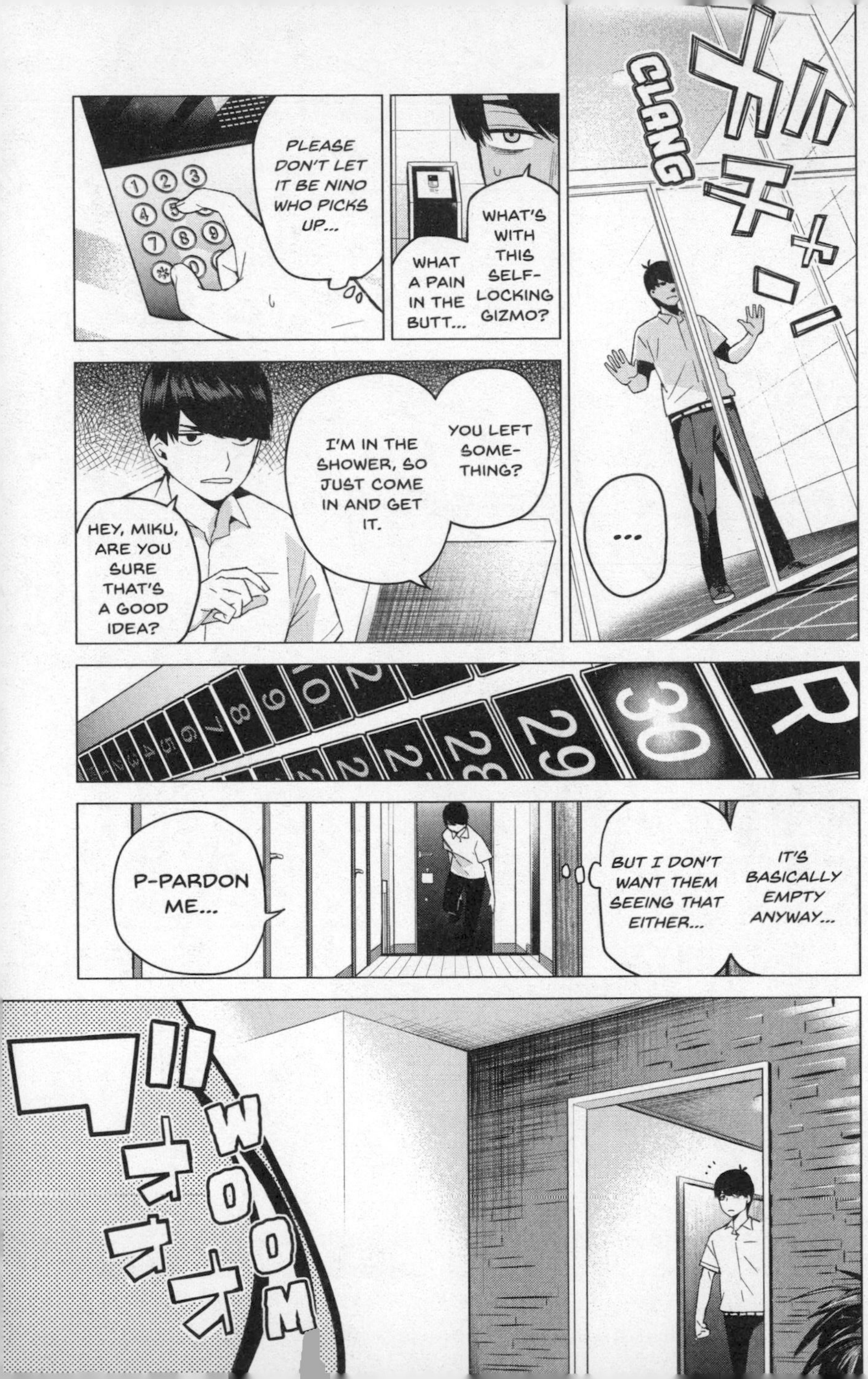
CLANG
...
WHAT'S WITH THIS SELF-LOCKING GIZMO?
WHAT A PAIN IN THE BUTT...
PLEASE DON'T LET IT BE NINO WHO PICKS UP...
YOU LEFT SOMETHING?
I'M IN THE SHOWER, SO JUST COME IN AND GET IT.
HEY, MIKU, ARE YOU SURE THAT'S A GOOD IDEA?
IT'S BASICALLY EMPTY ANYWAY...
BUT I DON'T WANT THEM SEEING THAT EITHER...
P-PARDON ME...
WOOM

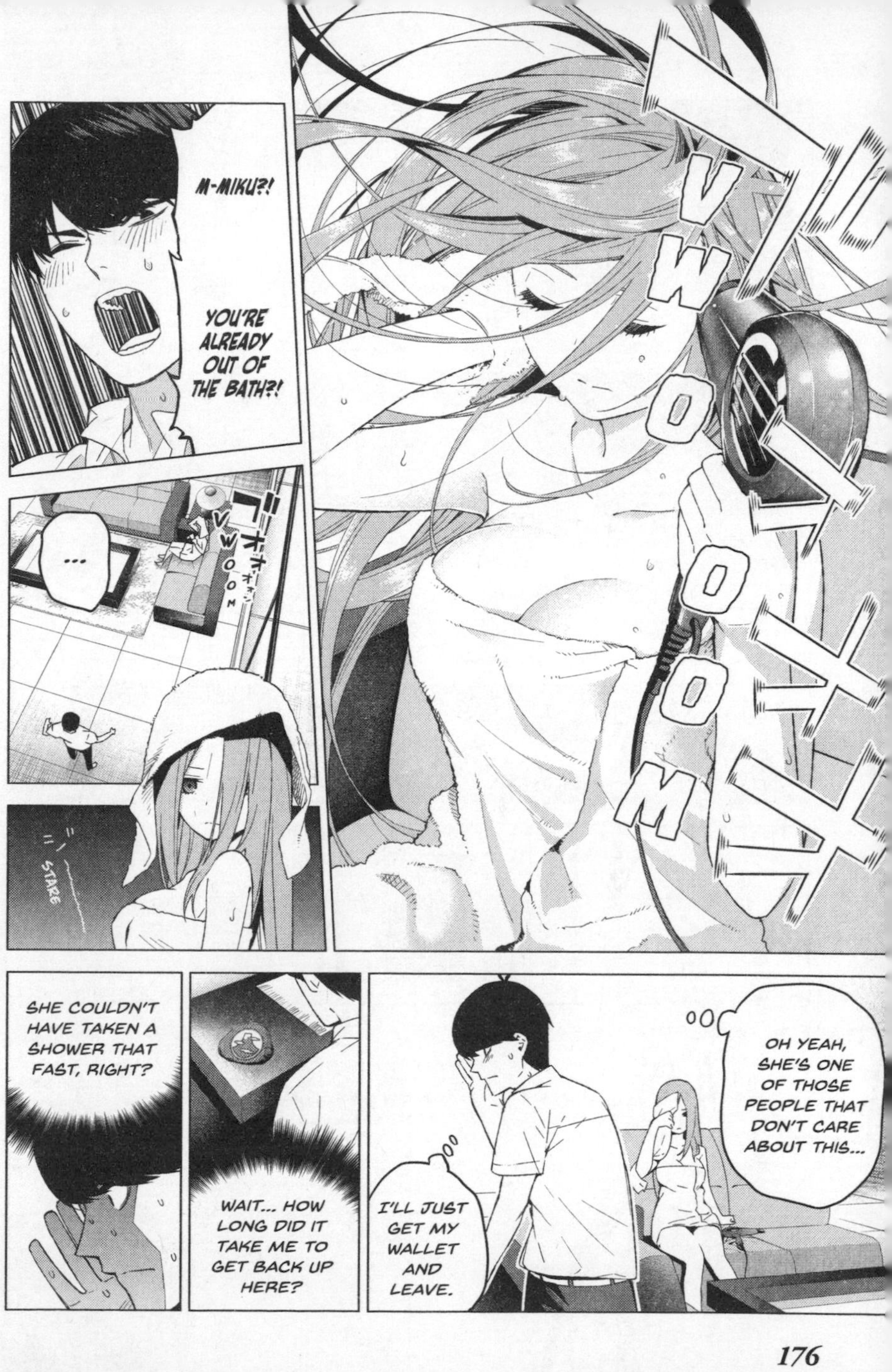
VWOOOM
M-MIKU?!
YOU'RE ALREADY OUT OF THE BATH?!
...
VWOOOM
STARE
OH YEAH, SHE'S ONE OF THOSE PEOPLE THAT DON'T CARE ABOUT THIS...
I'LL JUST GET MY WALLET AND LEAVE.
WAIT... HOW LONG DID IT TAKE ME TO GET BACK UP HERE?
SHE COULDN'T HAVE TAKEN A SHOWER THAT FAST, RIGHT?

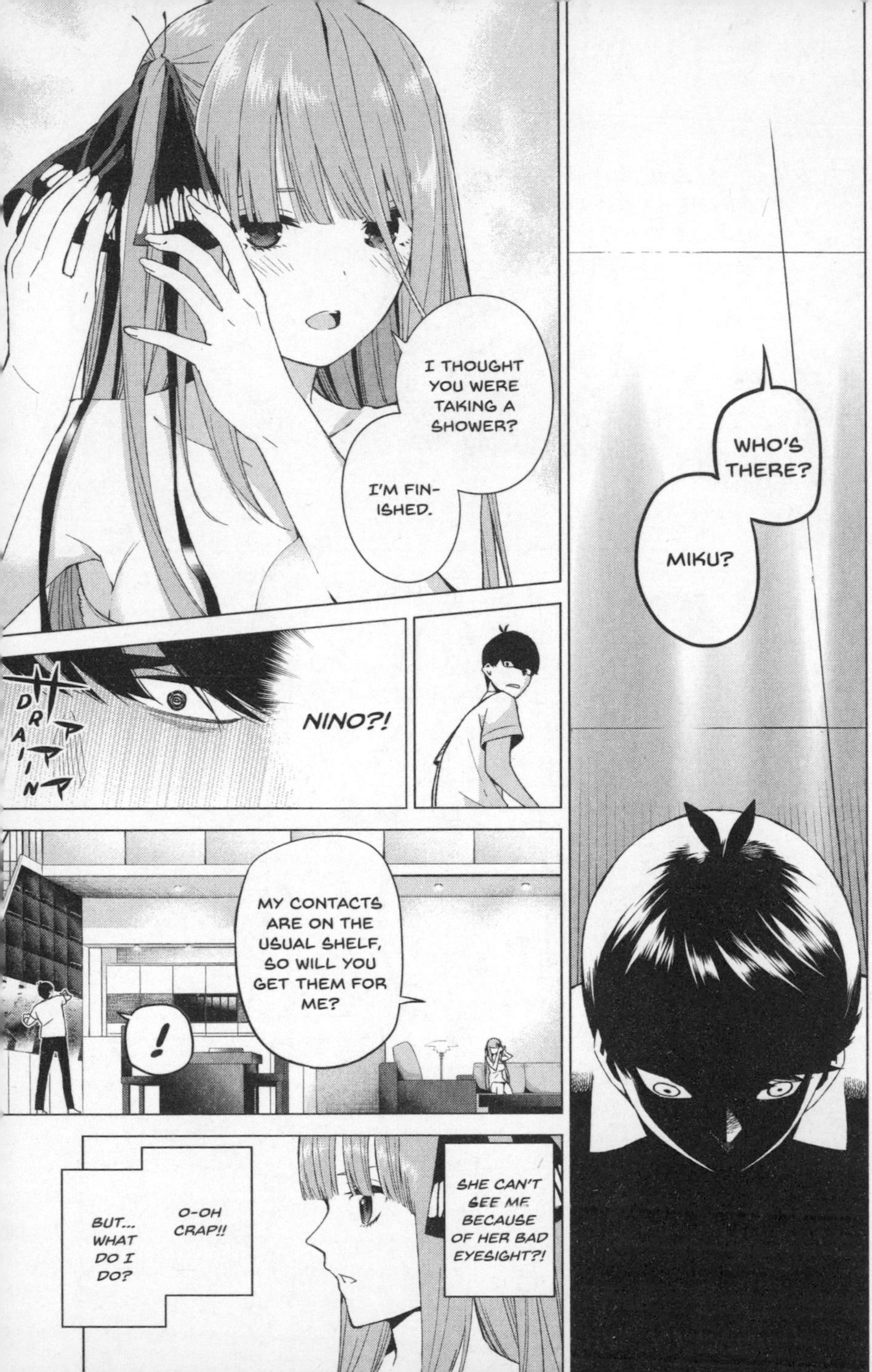
WHO'S THERE?
MIKU?
I THOUGHT YOU WERE TAKING A SHOWER?
I'M FIN-ISHED.
NINO?!
DRAIN
MY CONTACTS ARE ON THE USUAL SHELF, SO WILL YOU GET THEM FOR ME?
!
SHE CAN'T SEE ME BECAUSE OF HER BAD EYESIGHT?!
O-OH CRAP!!
BUT... WHAT DO I DO?

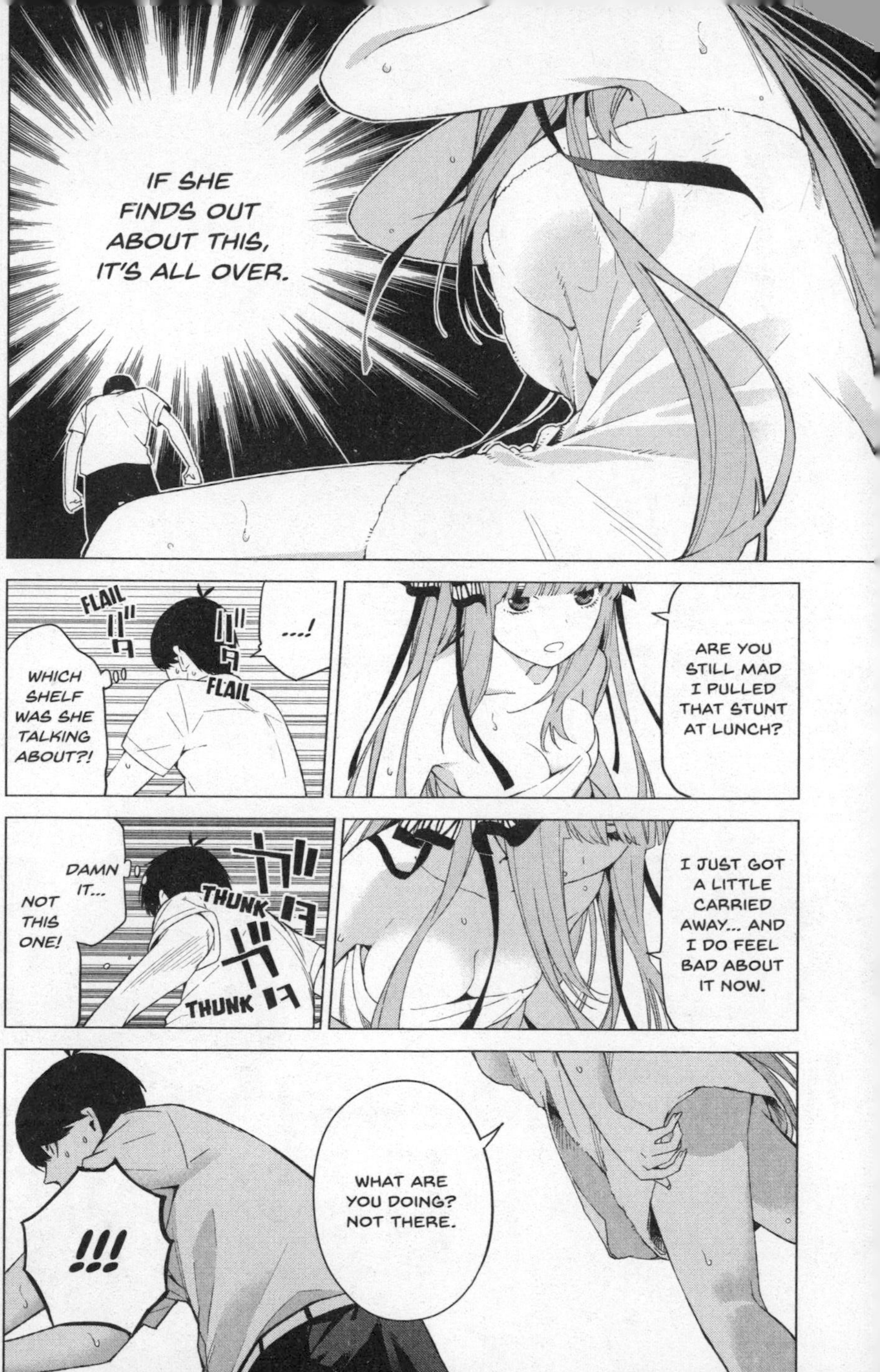
IF SHE FINDS OUT ABOUT THIS, IT'S ALL OVER.
ARE YOU STILL MAD I PULLED THAT STUNT AT LUNCH?
...!
FLAIL
FLAIL
WHICH SHELF WAS SHE TALKING ABOUT?!
I JUST GOT A LITTLE CARRIED AWAY... AND I DO FEEL BAD ABOUT IT NOW.
THUNK
THUNK
DAMN IT...
NOT THIS ONE!
WHAT ARE YOU DOING? NOT THERE.
!!!

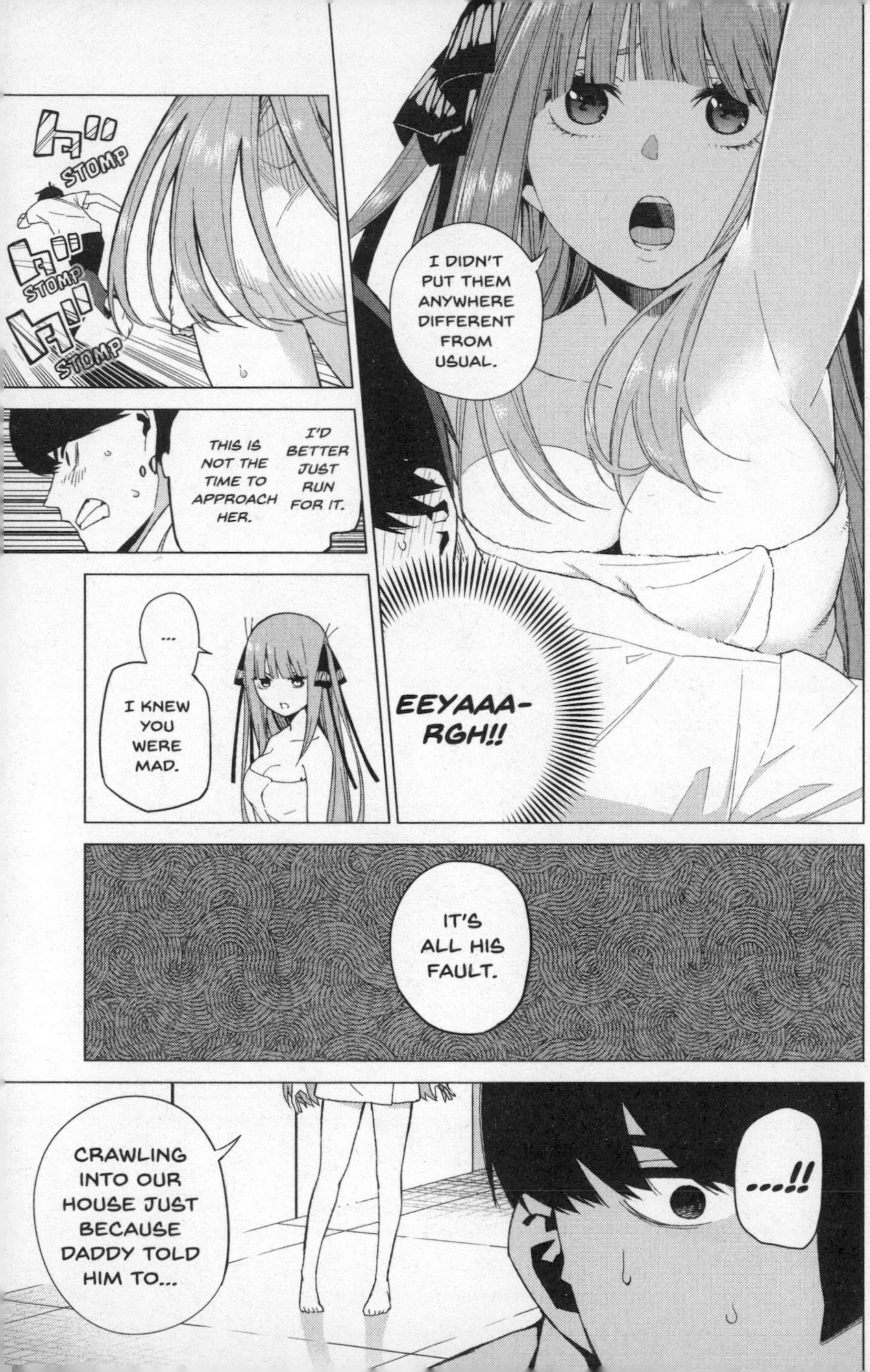
I DIDN'T PUT THEM ANYWHERE DIFFERENT FROM USUAL.
EEYAAA-RGH!!
STOMP
STOMP
STOMP
I'D BETTER JUST RUN FOR IT.
THIS IS NOT THE TIME TO APPROACH HER.
...
I KNEW YOU WERE MAD.
IT'S ALL HIS FAULT.
...!!
CRAWLING INTO OUR HOUSE JUST BECAUSE DADDY TOLD HIM TO...

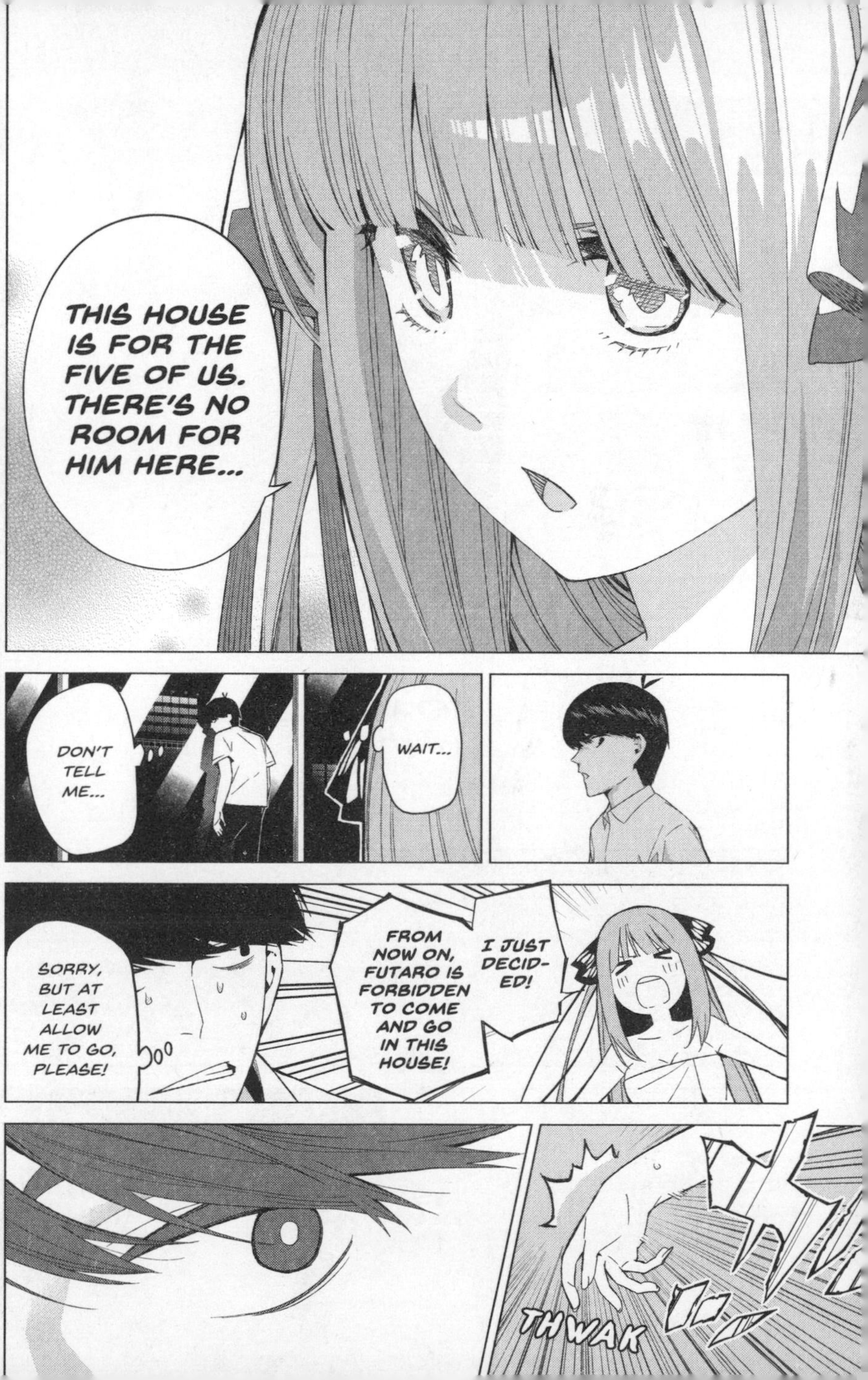
THIS HOUSE IS FOR THE FIVE OF US. THERE'S NO ROOM FOR HIM HERE...
WAIT...
DON'T TELL ME...
I JUST DECID-ED!
FROM NOW ON, FUTARO IS FORBIDDEN TO COME AND GO IN THIS HOUSE!
SORRY, BUT AT LEAST ALLOW ME TO GO, PLEASE!
THWAK

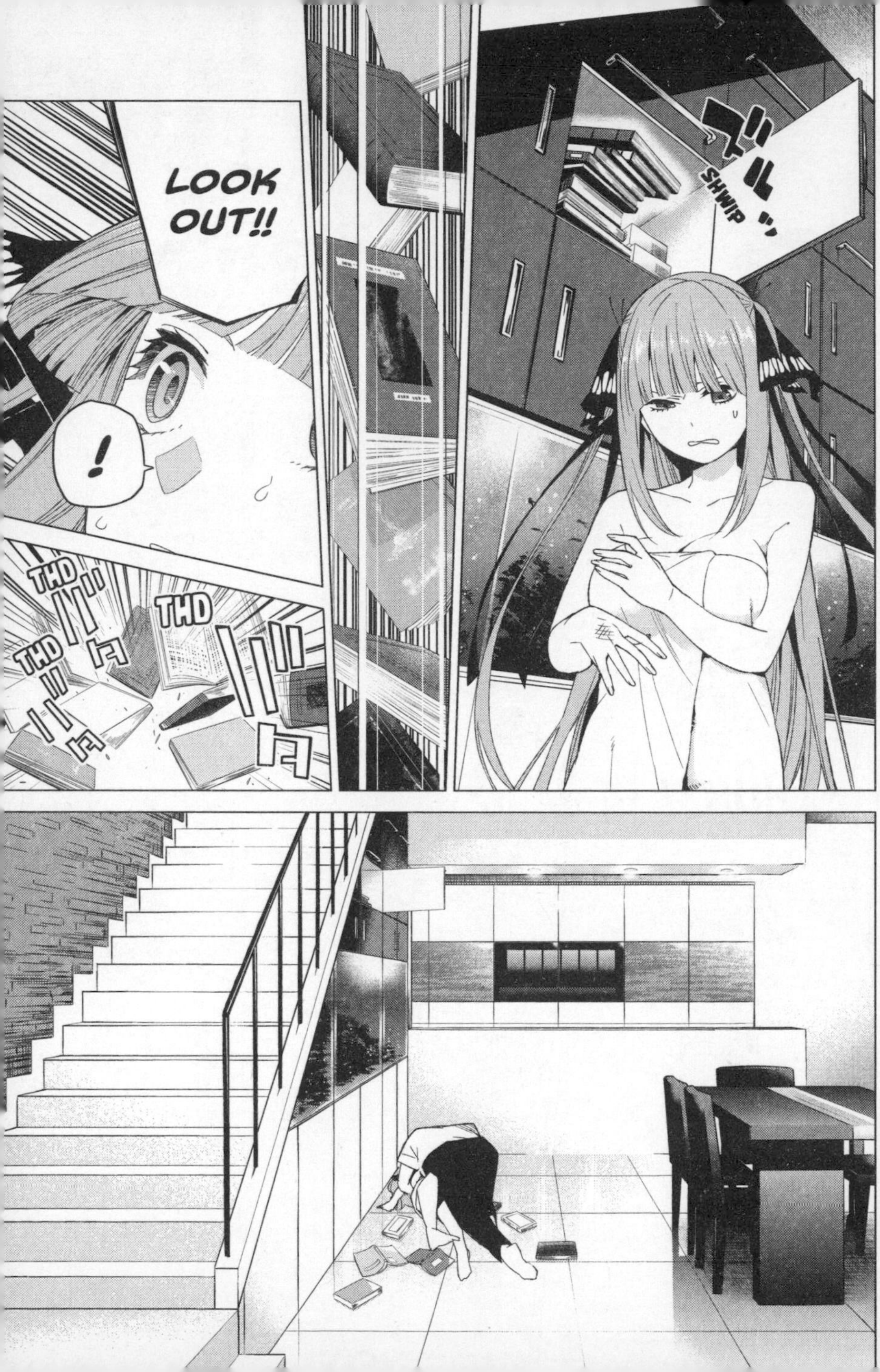
SHWIP
LOOK OUT!!
!
THD
THD
THD

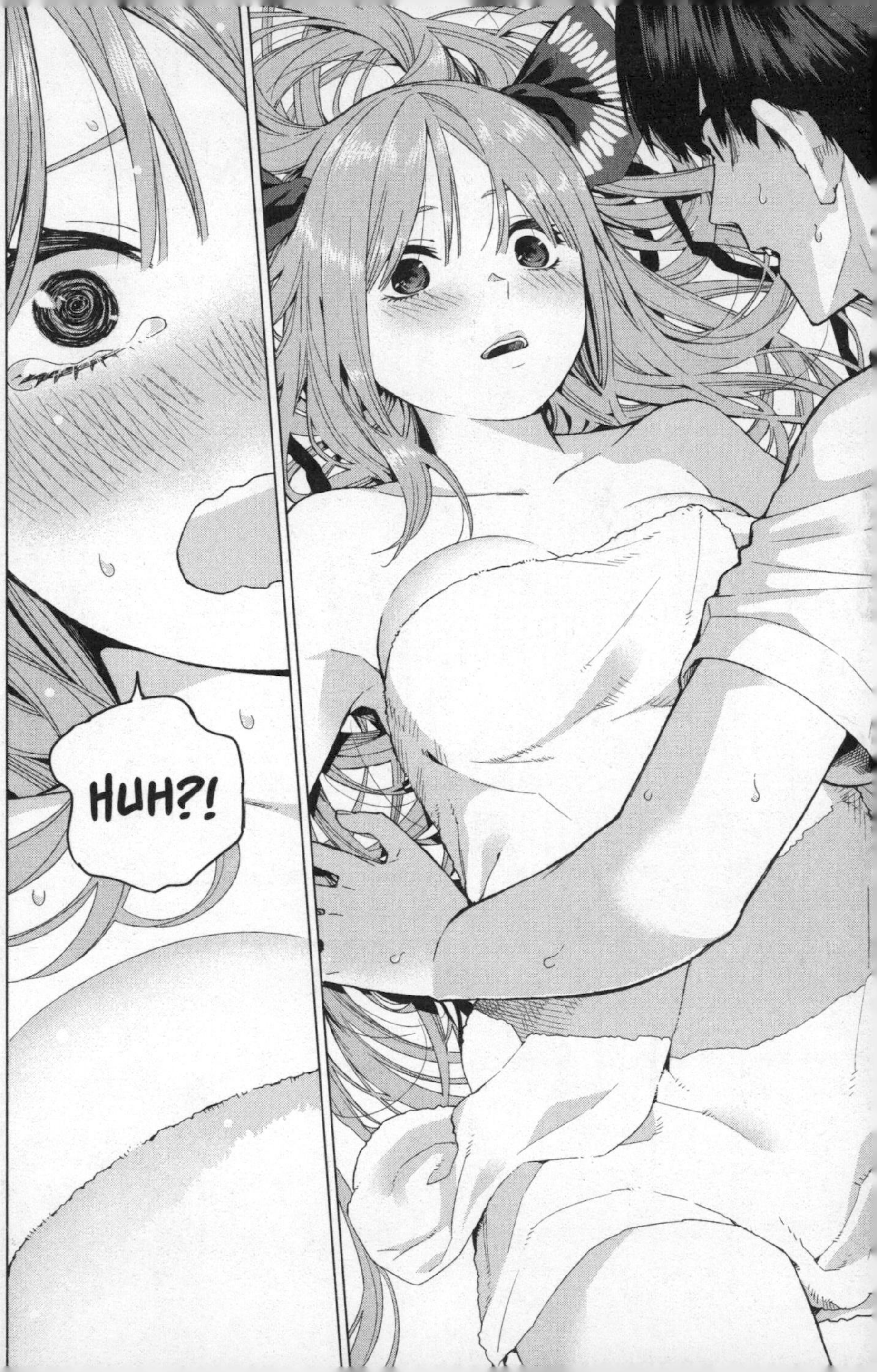
HUH?!

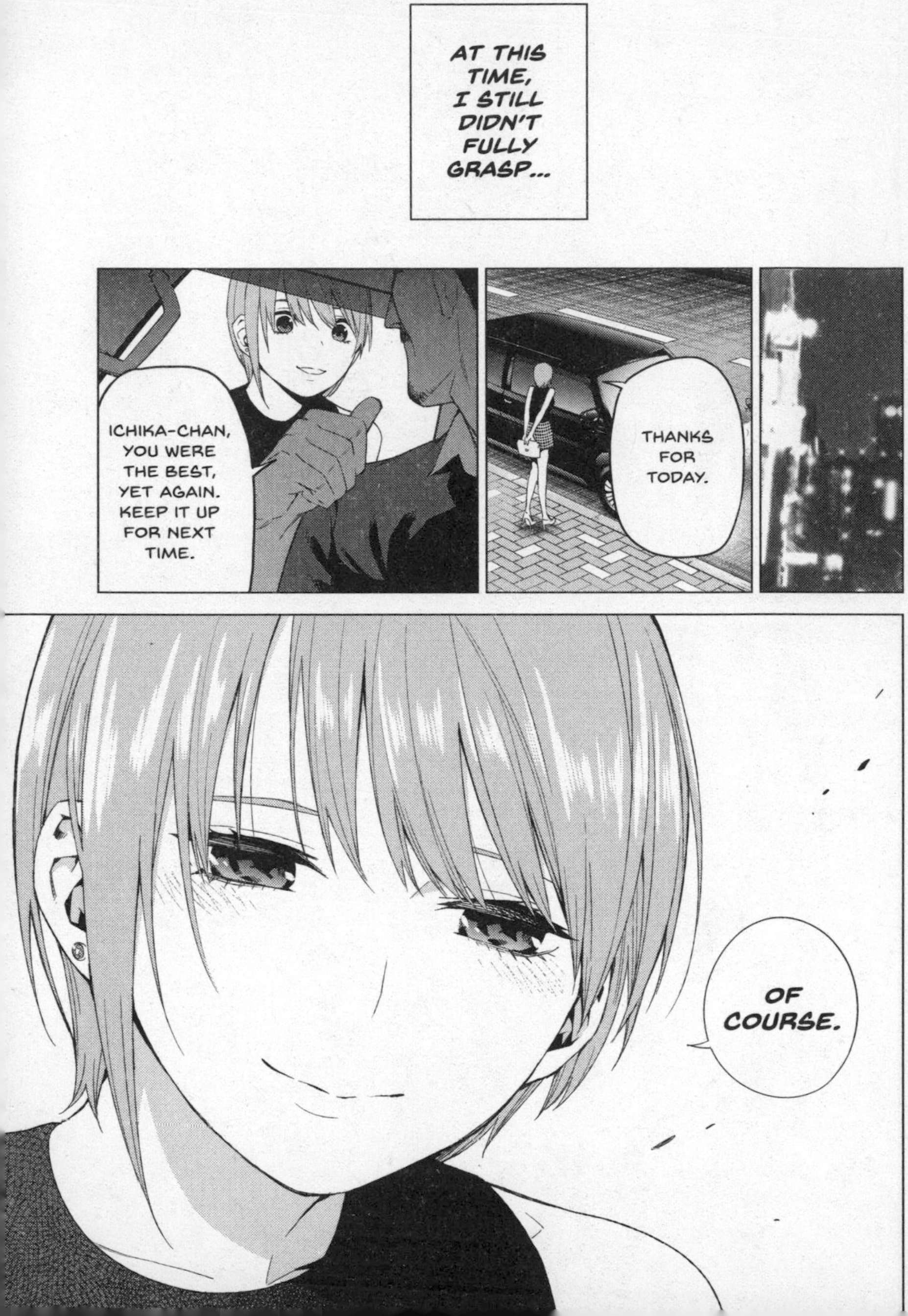
AT THIS TIME, I STILL DIDN'T FULLY GRASP...
THANKS FOR TODAY.
ICHIKA-CHAN, YOU WERE THE BEST, YET AGAIN. KEEP IT UP FOR NEXT TIME.
OF COURSE.

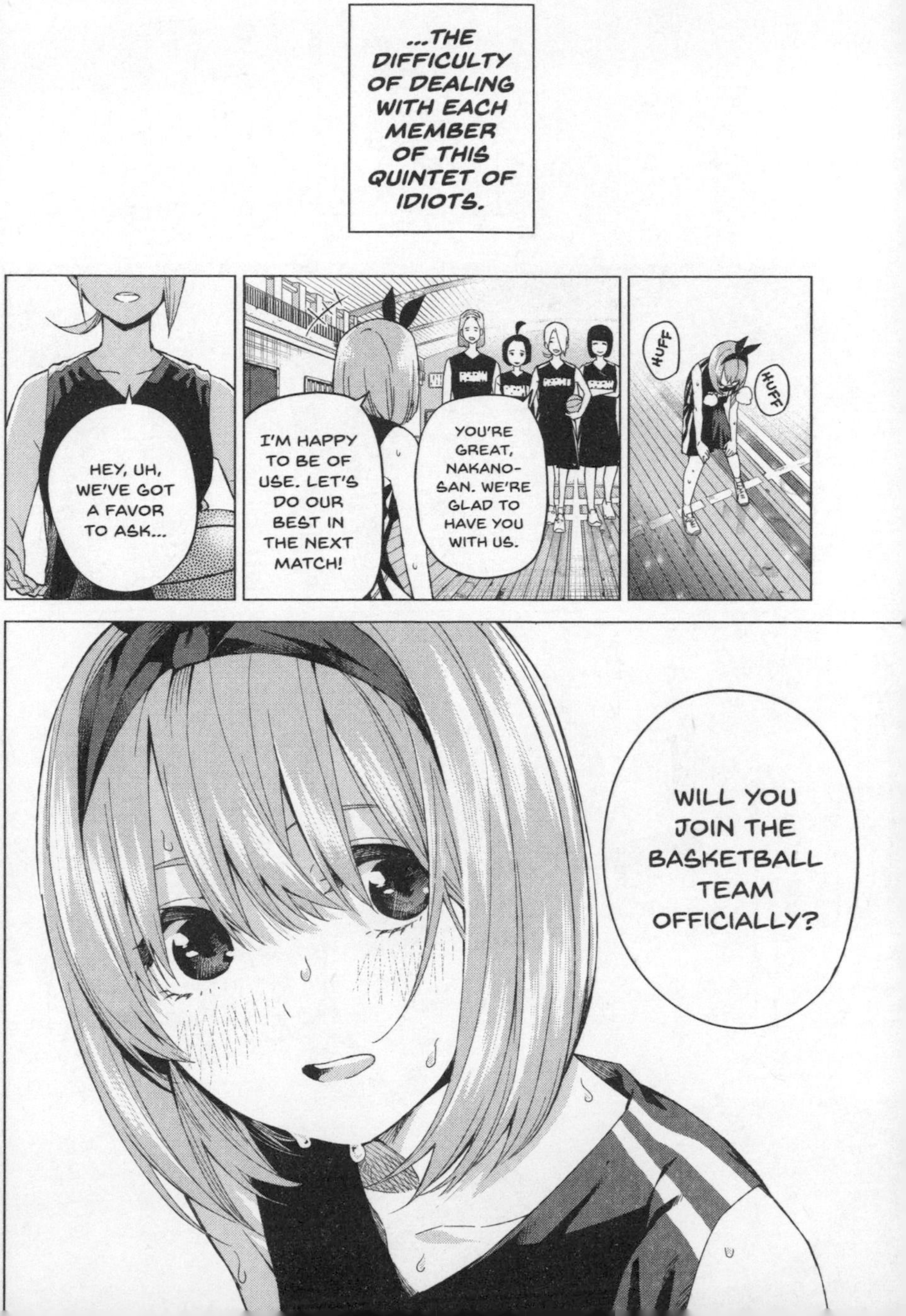
...THE DIFFICULTY OF DEALING WITH EACH MEMBER OF THIS QUINTET OF IDIOTS.
HUFF
HUFF
YOU'RE GREAT, NAKANO-SAN. WE'RE GLAD TO HAVE YOU WITH US.
I'M HAPPY TO BE OF USE. LET'S DO OUR BEST IN THE NEXT MATCH!
HEY, UH, WE'VE GOT A FAVOR TO ASK...
WILL YOU JOIN THE BASKETBALL TEAM OFFICIALLY?

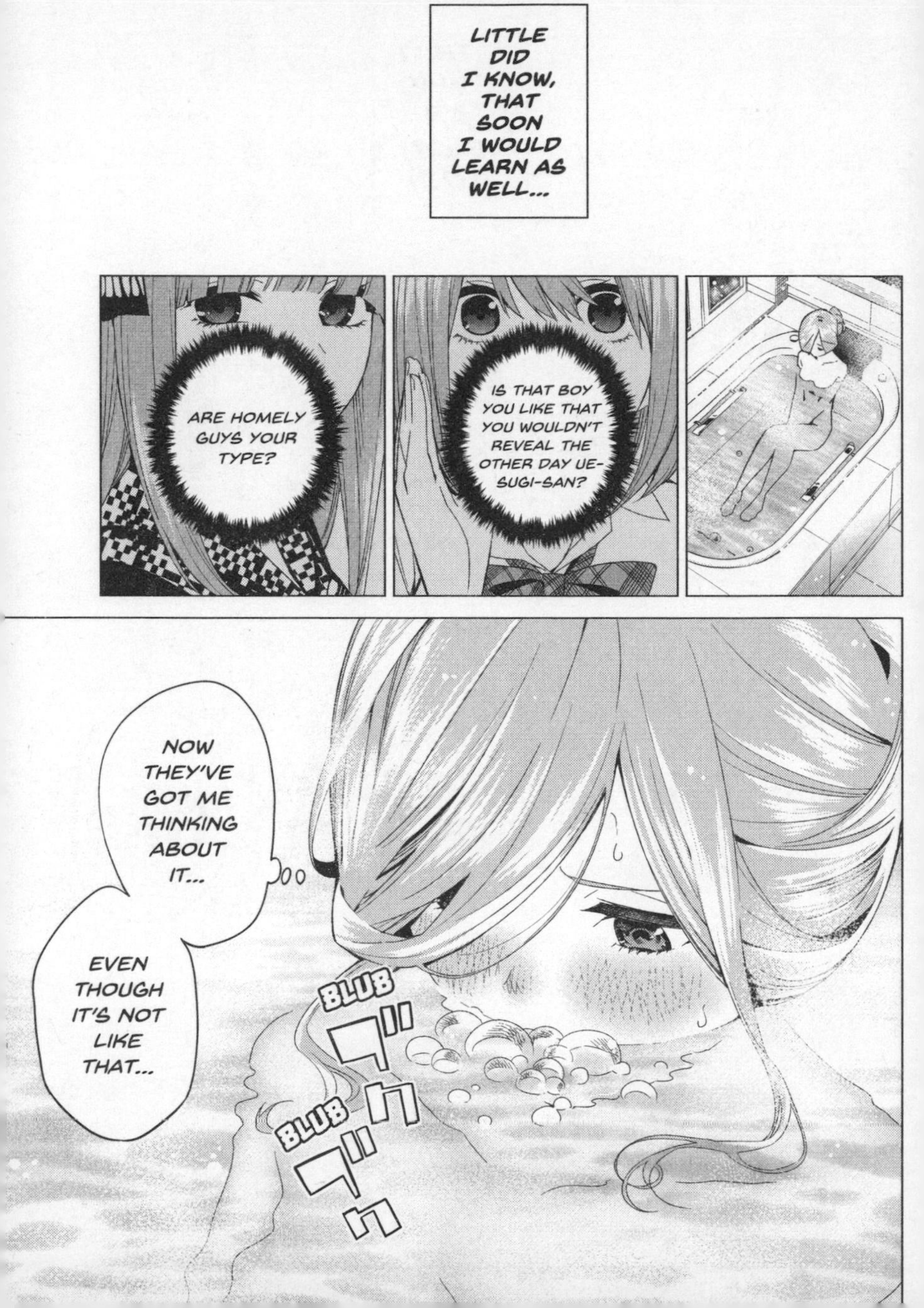
LITTLE DID I KNOW, THAT SOON I WOULD LEARN AS WELL...
IS THAT BOY YOU LIKE THAT YOU WOULDN'T REVEAL THE OTHER DAY UE-SUGI-SAN?
ARE HOMELY GUYS YOUR TYPE?
NOW THEY'VE GOT ME THINKING ABOUT IT...
EVEN THOUGH IT'S NOT LIKE THAT...
BLUB
BLUB

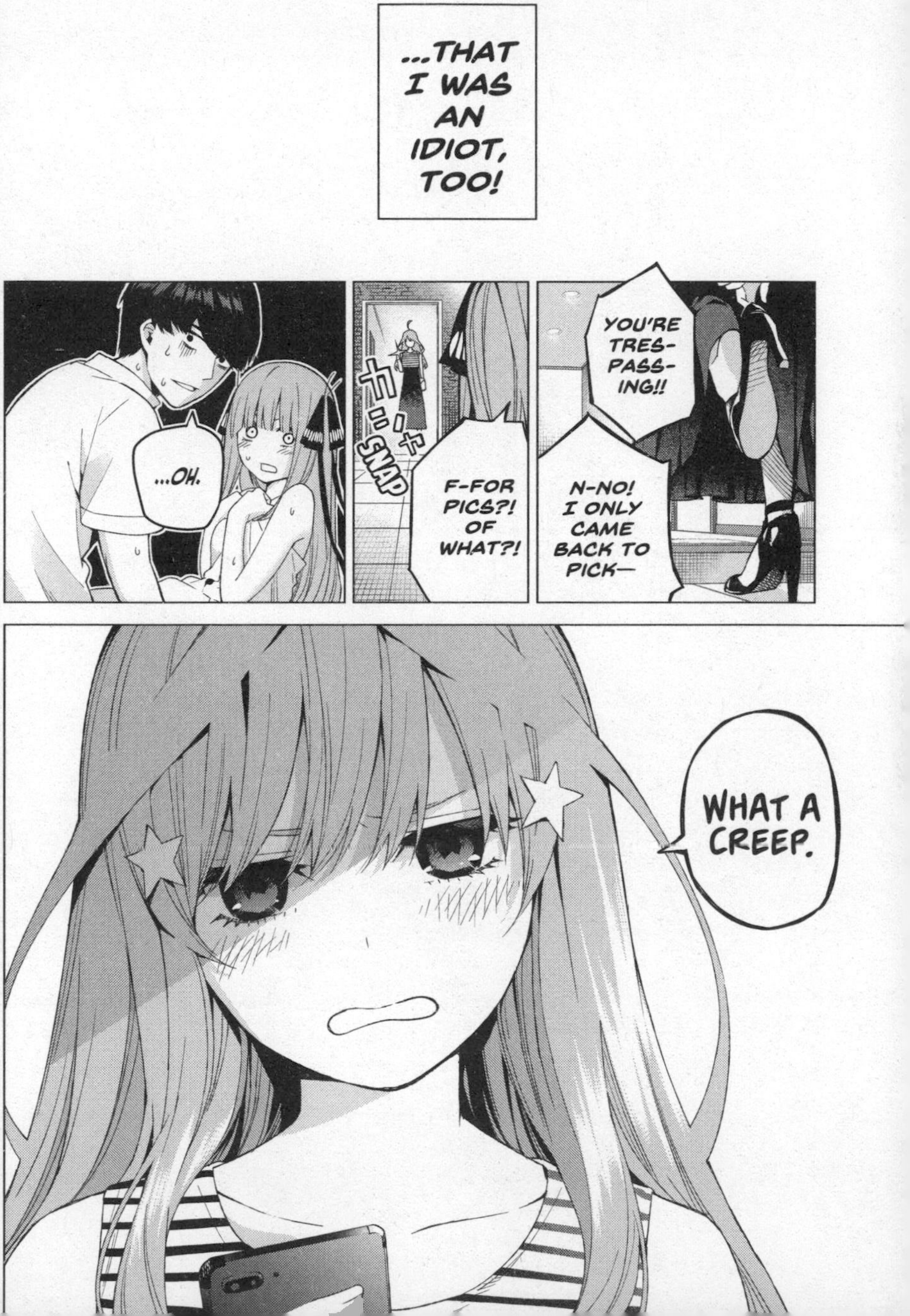
...THAT I WAS AN IDIOT, TOO!
YOU'RE TRES-PASS-ING!!
N-NO! I ONLY CAME BACK TO PICK—
SNAP
F-FOR PICS?! OF WHAT?!
...OH.
WHAT A CREEP.

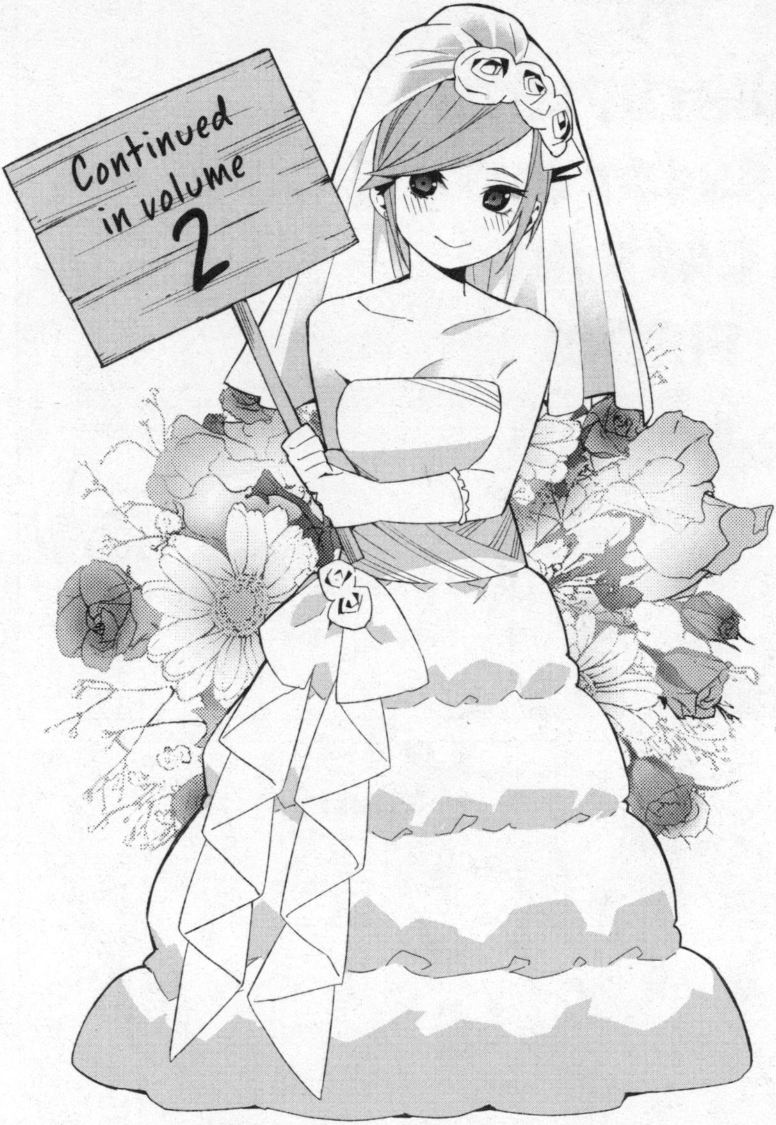
Continued in volume 2

Staff Ueno Hino Ogata

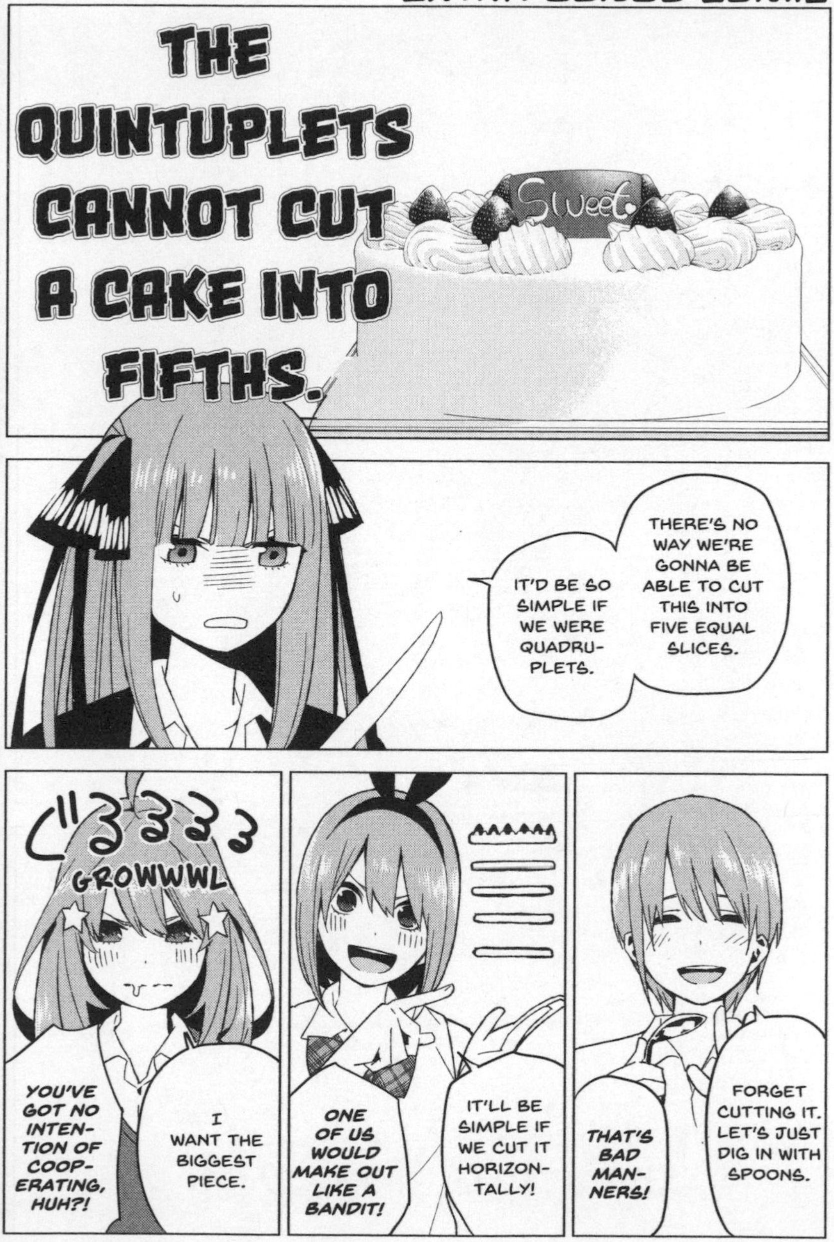
THE QUINTUPLETS CANNOT CUT A CAKE INTO FIFTHS.
Sweet
THERE'S NO WAY WE'RE GONNA BE ABLE TO CUT THIS INTO FIVE EQUAL SLICES.
IT'D BE SO SIMPLE IF WE WERE QUADRU-PLETS.
FORGET CUTTING IT. LET'S JUST DIG IN WITH SPOONS.
THAT'S BAD MAN-NERS!
IT'LL BE SIMPLE IF WE CUT IT HORIZON-TALLY!
ONE OF US WOULD MAKE OUT LIKE A BANDIT!
GROWWWL
I WANT THE BIGGEST PIECE.
YOU'VE GOT NO INTEN-TION OF COOP-ERATING, HUH?!

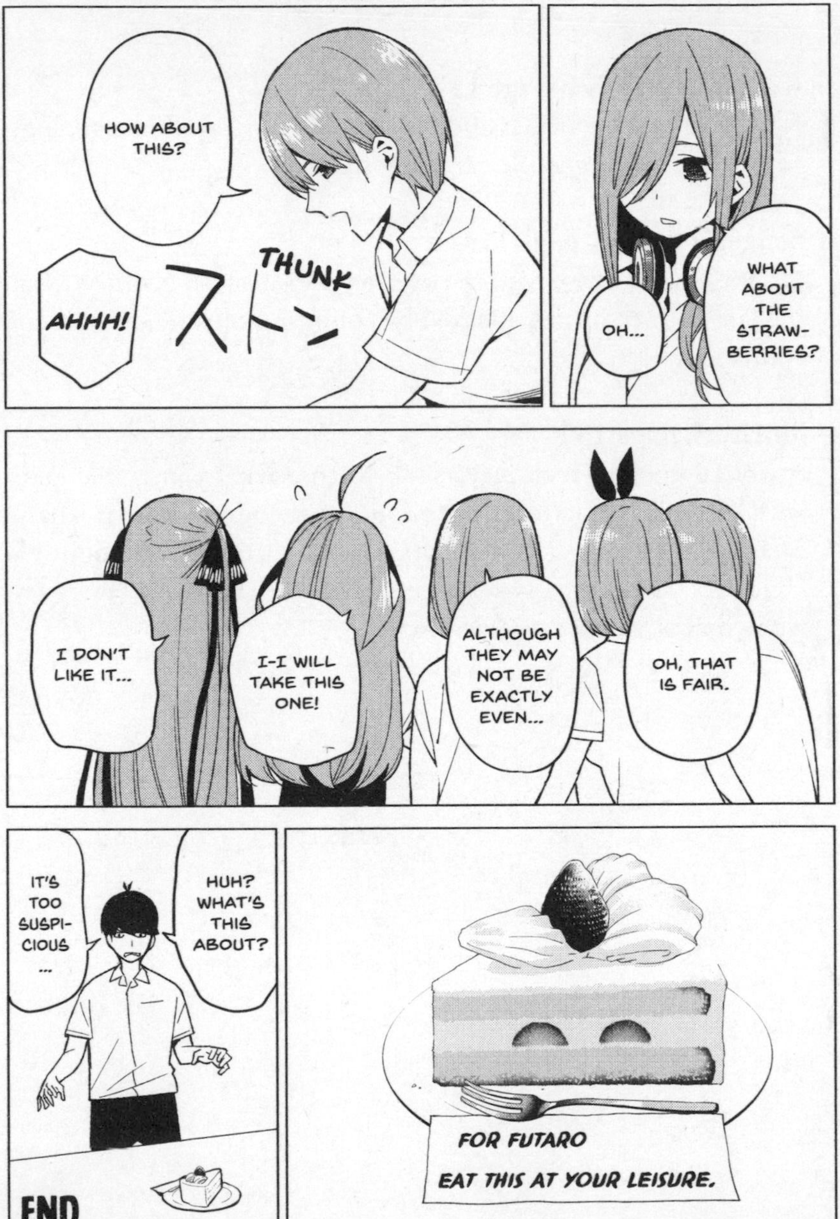
WHAT ABOUT THE STRAW-BERRIES?
OH...
HOW ABOUT THIS?
THUNK
ストーン
AHHH!
OH, THAT IS FAIR.
ALTHOUGH THEY MAY NOT BE EXACTLY EVEN...
I-I WILL TAKE THIS ONE!
I DON'T LIKE IT...
FOR FUTARO
EAT THIS AT YOUR LEISURE.
HUH? WHAT'S THIS ABOUT?
IT'S TOO SUSPI-CIOUS ...
END

Translation Notes

Kinjiro Ninomiya, page 13
An agricultural reformer and philosopher portrayed in statues as a young boy reading while carrying firewood.

Sengoku Period, page 119
A period of Japanese history covering the late 15th century through the late 16th centuries, marked by constant political and military conflict.

Shiritori, page 139
A word game in which players take turns saying words that end with the Japanese letter the previous word ended with. In Japanese, each letter is syllabic. When Futaro asks if "fu-" would count like "bu-," it's because the base letter for "fu" (ふ) becomes "bu" (ぶ) when diacritic dots are added to it.

THE
QUINTESSENTIAL QUINTUPLETS

A Kodansha Comics Trade Paperback Original.

Published in the United States by Kodansha Comics,
an imprint of Kodansha USA Publishing, LLC, New York.

Publication rights for this English edition arranged through Kodansha Ltd., Tokyo.

First published in Japan in 2017 by Kodansha Ltd., Tokyo,
as *Gotoubun no Hanayome* volume 1.

Cover Design: Saya Takai (RedRooster)

ISBN 978-1-63236-774-7

Printed in Mexico.

www.kodansha.us

9 8 7

Translation: Steven LeCroy
Lettering: Jan Lan Ivan Concepcion
Additional Layout: Belynda Ungurath
Editing: Haruko Hashimoto, Thalia Sutton
Editorial Assistance: YKS Services LLC/SKY Japan, INC.
Kodansha Comics Edition Cover Design: Phil Balsman